PROFILES IN COURAGE

Standing Against The Wyoming Wind

PROFILES IN COURAGE

Standing Against The Wyoming Wind

Rodger McDaniel

WordsWorth ✳ Cody, Wyoming

Copyright © 2022 by Rodger McDaniel
All rights reserved. No part of this book may be reproduced in any manner without written permission from the publisher.

ISBN 978-1-7334897-1-3
Library of Congress Control Number: 2022923096
First edition paperback

Cover photo: Dr. Phil Roberts
Photo taken in Goshen County, Wyoming. Used with permission.

Published by WordsWorth
Cody, Wyoming
www.wordsworthpublishing.com

In Memory of Fatback
and other allies of marginalized peoples.

The research and writing of this book were aided by a Lola Homsher grant from the Wyoming State Historical Society for which the author is grateful.

Some of the material in this book was previously published in other books by Rodger McDaniel including *Dying for Joe McCarthy's Sins: The Suicide of Wyoming Senator Lester Hunt, The Man in the Arena: The Life and Times of U.S. Senator Gale W. McGee,* and *Howard Zinn and Lois Mottonnen Fistfight in the Equality State.*

A Note Of Gratitude

This is the fifth book I have written. It was the most difficult and the most rewarding. It was made difficult by COVID-19 and the fact that I started writing it in January 2020, a month before the pandemic shuttered the American Heritage Center, every library I needed, and other research facilities. The reward came from both the breadth and variety of the compelling stories it allowed me to research and tell and those who helped along the way.

I am grateful to the Wyoming State Historical Society for awarding me a Lola Homsher Grant to help with the costs. The American Heritage Center at the University of Wyoming is an extraordinary resource for writers, and even through the pandemic, its staff members were of enormous courtesy in so many ways as I researched this book. I received great assistance from the staff at the University of Wyoming Coe Library and the Laramie County Library. Thanks go to Robin Everett and Suzi Taylor of the Wyoming State Archives for all their help.

Kathy Karpan opened her considerable Teno Roncalio personal archive. Yufna Soldier Wolf pointed me in helpful directions to research the history of the Wind River Indian Reservation. Phil White graciously shared his encyclopedic memory of the Black 14 tragedy. Pete and Al Simpson shared stories of their parents, Milward and Lorna. Jill Morrison and others at the Powder River Basin Resource Council and the staff of High Country News leaned over backwards to help dig up helpful information.

When I was unable to locate Susan Harlow's 1981 master's thesis on Tom Bell and the history of *High Country News*, Ms. Harlow, living in Vermont, kindly spent hours going through her files, found it, copied it, and sent it to me. Vickie Goodwin allowed me access to hundreds of letters, newspaper clippings, and other memorabilia helping me to tell the story of her incredible marriage to Larry "Sissy" Goodwin.

Kathie Lowry employed her skills as a ruthless proofreader to make the book better. Chesie Lee, the executive director of the Riverton Peace Mission, Keith Becker, Tom Bell's successor as executive director of the Wyoming Outdoor Council, Vickie Goodwin, and the family of Lynn Dickey took time to read and correct my factual mistakes. A special thanks to all the wonderful writers, many from Wyoming, whose books, essays, journals, and newspaper articles helped me get a better understanding of the lives of those whose stories are told. They are listed in the bibliography.

My wife Pat deserves a note of thanks for her support and encouragement and the hands-on help she gave me in proofreading and preparing the final draft as well as her research and finding interesting facts and photos to include so we could, together, hand it off to my accomplished publisher Renée Tafoya of WordsWorth Publishing in Cody, Wyoming.

Finally, I am grateful for all who honor the memory and life of each man or woman whose courage inspired this work by taking time to read these stories.

Table of Contents

10 *Chapter One*
Wyoming Winds and the Courage to Stand Against Them

18 *Chapter Two*
Jeran Artery

39 *Chapter Three*
Tom Bell

74 *Chapter Four*
The Black 14

101 *Chapter Five*
Lynn Dickey

126 *Chapter Six*
Sissy and Vickie Goodwin

154 *Chapter Seven*
Senator Joseph C. O'Mahoney

181 *Chapter Eight*
Congressman Teno Roncalio

216 *Chapter Nine*
The Simpsons

239 *Chapter Ten*
People of Wind River

289 *Chapter Eleven*
People of Heart Mountain

323 *Chapter Twelve*
Lester C. Hunt, Gale W. McGee, and Liz Cheney

Chapter 1

WYOMING WINDS AND THE COURAGE TO STAND AGAINST THEM

"A nation which has forgotten the quality of courage, which in the past has been brought to public life, is not as likely to insist upon or regard that quality in its chosen leaders today, and, in fact, we have forgotten."

from *"Profiles in Courage" by John F. Kennedy*

In the iconic opening chapter of *Centennial*, James Michener offers readers a lesson on geology. Among other things, he teaches that the Wyoming wind was a big player in the formation of the land. Before humans walked the earth, the Rocky Mountains were formed in part by the winds blowing incessantly across the Northern Plains. He chronicled how "high winds whip over the prairies, exhausting the land and everything that grows upon it."[1]

Even today, the winds here are said to be among the strongest in the nation.[2] As high air pressure across the mountains seeks lower pressure below, the wind gains speed and power. The wind pattern is most often from west to east. Where the wind blows strongest, damage to the few buildings that dot the prairie is not uncommon. Depending on the stature of the victim, it's been known to blow some folks off their feet.

Wyoming is also known for its political winds. They too blow hard, whipping across the land, exhausting everything and everyone attempting to stand against them. They form the social, economic, academic, and political landscape just as prehistoric winds formed the mountains and the plains. From wherever you stand, they usually blow hardest from the right and are frequently strong enough to blow people who venture from the beaten path off their feet. As often as not, those who stand against the Wyoming wind are racial, religious, and other ethnic or cultural minorities or their allies and advocates.

It was July 10, 1890, when Wyoming celebrated its acceptance into the Union of the United States. The *Cheyenne Daily Sun* reported a parade included "our colored brothers" and the "Girl Guards," which the newspaper concluded gave the feeling of "warm and patriotic devotion to the state in which all men and women are free and equal by the terms of the magna charta (sic)."[3] Governor Francis E. Warren believed that becoming the first to grant women the right to vote "was consistent with progress in other forms, all of which would move Wyoming along the pathway from its isolated frontier condition to a civilized end."[4] Judge M. C. Brown spoke that day of a state "ordained by the people of Wyoming [where] each citizen of the state should enjoy the same rights guaranteed to every other citizen, whether high or low, black or white, male or female."[5]

Alas, it was not to be. One hundred ten years later, at the end of the 20th century, a panel of esteemed Wyoming historians evaluated the news stories of the preceding 100 years. The panel included Dr. Phil Roberts, Mike Massie, Dr. David Kathka, Bob Righter, Mark Junge, John Albanese, Don Hodgson, Patty Myers, Dr. Michael Cassity, Loren Jost, and Roy Jordan. By any measure these women and men are well qualified to make thoughtful judgments about the state's history.[6]

Looking back over the one hundred years from 1900 to 2000, they evaluated thousands of stories chronicling Wyoming's history, rendering a judgment about which were the top ten narratives of the century. Their conclusions call into question the basis for referring to Wyoming as "The Equality State." Some will be less surprised than others to learn that three of the top ten stories this panel identified dealt with the unjust treatment Wyoming dealt out to homosexuals, women, and racial minorities including Native Americans.

Panelist Roy Jordan, a Northwest Community College academic, said, "There's been no conviction or commitment to women's rights throughout our whole history." Ranked fourth on the list was Wyoming's "mistreatment of minorities." The panel cited the Heart Mountain Relocation Center, the Black 14 incident at the University of Wyoming, and the murder of Matthew Shepard. The seventh ranked narrative centered on the "mistreatment of Indians."

That those stories were among the top ten for the entirety of 20th century Wyoming is *prima facie* evidence of the direction from which the predominate Wyoming winds blow and the courage it takes to stand against those winds.

How were the stories told in the coming pages chosen? Courage is in the eye of the beholder, or in this case, the mind of the author. Another writer of a book with this title may have chosen different people. The ones I've chosen spring from my personal convictions. I have considered each person in the context of the political and cultural forces to which they responded in an evaluation of the courage each displayed. Nora Ephron, the writer who won an Academy Award for her screenplay for the movie *Silkwood*, said it well. "All storytelling is a Rorschach." After seeing the human struggle from a variety of angles in my careers holding political office, practicing law, working in child protection and poverty programs, administering mental health and substance abuse services, and preaching progressive Christianity, this book is my Rorschach, grounded in a sense that all honest history should include discourse on the way in which the most vulnerable among us have been treated while honoring those who courageously stood with them.

Having said that, I borrow a disclaimer used by John F. Kennedy in the introduction to his *Profiles in Courage*, where he acknowledged, "I am not a professional historian" and "all errors of fact and judgment are exclusively my own." Neither am I a professional historian. I am what Isadora Helfgott, chair of the University of Wyoming's Department of History and American

Studies, once called a "citizen historian," and, therefore, all errors of fact and judgment are exclusively my own. *Mea culpa.*

After this opening chapter's introduction, Jeran Artery is the subject of the second chapter. He grew up gay and closeted in Wheatland where his uncle preached fire and brimstone sermons condemning homosexuals to hell's fire. When he emerged, Jeran confronted the forces of bigotry and led the campaign to achieve marriage equality for the LGBTQ community.

Tom Bell's extraordinary story is told in chapter three. A kid who grew up on a Fremont County ranch became a World War II hero and later, with a sixth sense about his relationship with the air, water, land, and animals, became the Godfather of the Wyoming environmental movement. Chapter four is the story of the "Black 14," a sensational clash between racism and courage.

Lynn Dickey is the subject of the fifth chapter. Called by a contemporary "Joan of Arc on a steel stallion," Lynn, though confined to a wheelchair and suffering lifelong pain, was an activist for social justice, taking on causes that placed her perilously out of the mainstream.

The lives of "Sissy" and Vickie Goodwin are the subject of the sixth chapter. Sissy was a crossdresser who decided it was unfair to him and the rest of us to hide who he was. Vickie was his wife and the one who backed him in that determination while having her own life fully engaged in Wyoming politics. The seventh chapter tells of Senator Joseph C. O'Mahoney who gave up his dream of becoming a U.S. Supreme Court justice because he refused to back down on his principles.

Chapter eight is the story of Congressman Teno Roncalio. Full disclosure. I was a member of Teno's staff for eight years. In many ways, Teno was a "father figure" in my life. He gave me a gift when I graduated from law school. Bob Woodward's 1979 book, *The Brethren: Inside the Supreme Court.* Teno inscribed it, "To Rodger…my 'son,' and soon to be my 'brother.'" So, yes. I might be prejudiced but let his story speak for itself. Those who knew Teno even fleetingly, would not hesitate to use the word "courageous" as one of many traits they would attribute to him.

Chapter nine is about the Simpsons; Milward, Alan, and Pete. Wyoming Governor Milward Simpson risked his governorship to stand for his deeply held moral belief that it was wrong for the state to put a human being to death. It's also about his sons Peter and Alan whose lives reflected the integrity each inherited from their father. The tenth chapter is the history of how the Eastern Shoshone and Northern Arapaho Nations of the Wind River Indian Reservation withstood the winds of genocide. The eleventh is the story the of the survivors of Heart Mountain, one of the greatest acts of injustice in American history.

The final chapter heralds the courage of three Wyoming politicians who stood against some of the strongest political winds in the history of this nation. It tells the story of Senator Lester Hunt's deadly confrontation with McCarthyism, Senator Gale McGee's successful battle with the John Birch Society, and Congressman Liz Cheney's heroism in the face of Donald Trump's determination to destroy the Republic.

Thomas Campbell believed the hero "is one who knows when to surrender and what to surrender to."[7] Campbell defined the experience.

> "The call to adventure signifies that destiny has summoned the hero and transferred his (sic) spiritual center of gravity from within the pale of this society to a zone unknown. This fateful region of both treasure and danger may be variously represented as a distant land, a forest, a kingdom underground, beneath the waves or above the sky, a secret island, lofty mountaintop, or a profound dream state, but it is always a place of strangely polymorphous beings, unimaginable torments, superhuman deeds, and impossible delights."[8]

The 19th-century anthropologist Edward Burnett Tylor was the first to identify the hero's journey in literature. Many of the great adventure stories throughout history follow the basic formula. This is true from the Biblical story of David and Goliath to *Star Wars* today. Think of it as having three parts. The first is the *call to adventure*, where the hero-to-be is stimulated to act in some bold way, usually to meet a daunting task, say, fighting Goliath or the Empire. The second is the *ordeal*, in which the hero is brutally tested and must beat long odds, such as vanquishing a giant in battle or blowing up the Death Star. The third is *victory*, where the hero wins against long odds and returns triumphant.

∽

It was 1955 when John F. Kennedy wrote *Profiles in Courage*. He said then, "Today the challenge of political courage looms larger than ever before. For our everyday life is becoming so saturated with the tremendous power of mass communications that any unpopular or unorthodox course arouses a storm of protest."[9]

If he'd been allowed to live a naturally long life, JFK would still not likely have been around long enough to witness the extraordinary power of mass communications available today to punish a wayward politician. Between a 24/7 cable news cycle, the Internet, and all forms of social media, the punishment can be an immediate and brutal deterrent. Neither an attack nor a response need be factual. We live in a post-factual world unlike anything Kennedy could have imagined. "We were—and are—living in an age of international mass manufacturing of disprovable lies with planetary reach and consequences that are certainly not always foreseeable."[10] As a result political courage becomes less likely, thus, more worthy of celebration.

Kennedy's *Profiles in Courage* honored people whose courage played out on a large national stage. Arguably, exhibiting courage is more difficult on the smaller stage of rural-state politics. Courage has not often been honored on the relatively few occasions it has been exhibited in what some Wyoming politicians refer to as a "small town with long streets."

Indeed, the names of many of those whose stories are told here are unknown to most of the people of Wyoming. Some have been lost to memory, others to history. Readers with a working knowledge of Wyoming history will undoubtedly offer anecdotes about the times each failed to measure up to the standards of courage, when these people withered under fire and chose an easier way out. But is it not true that even the most courageous among us are, at times, faint-hearted if not cowardly? Just like a baseball player will find himself in the Hall of Fame if he hits the ball only three times in ten attempts, so it is with politicians who can be deemed courageous even if there are times when they weren't. The darkness of that reality does not overcome the bright light created by those moments of stout-hearted resoluteness.

This book is about the flashes of courage these women and men exhibited when it mattered most. This book is written to resurrect those moments and to restore the meaning of courage as an honored attribute in Wyoming politics. There has never been another time in the state's history when the winds blew stronger against those who would otherwise act courageously than we witness today. It follows that there has never been a time when recognizing political courage was more important.

Endnotes

1. Michener, *Centennial*, 43
2. "Windiest States in America," December 27, 2019, https://stacker.com/stories/3809/windiest-states-america, accessed October 1, 2021, article uses data compiled be the "Global Wind Atlas" to reach this conclusion, https://globalwindatlas.info
3. "Wyoming Celebrates it Admission into the Union," *Cheyenne Daily Sun*, July 24, 1890, 1
4. Nicholas, *Becoming Western*, 88-89
5. Id., 89
6. "Historians label unequal treatment of women as Wyoming's top story of the 20th century," *Wyoming History News*, Published by Members of the Wyoming State Historical Society, Vol. 47, No. 1 (February 2000)
7. *The Hero's Journey*, Edited by Phil Cousineau, New World Library, Novato, California (1990), 12
8. Id., 1
9. Kennedy, *Profiles in Courage*, 38
10. Xavier Pickett, "What's Faith Got to Do with Political Theory/Theology" June 25, 2022, https://politicaltheology.com/whats-faith-got-to-do-with-it-reflections-on-george-shulmans-political-theology/ accessed June 28, 2022

Chapter 2

JERAN ARTERY

How much do you love the strange and the stranger? Hey, Caveman, do you see only danger when you peer into the night? Are you afraid of the country that exists outside your cave? Hey, Caveman, when are you going to evolve? Are you still afraid of the way the earth revolves around the sun and not the other way around? Are you terrified of the ever-shifting ground?

Sherman Alexie 2017

"the function of freedom is to free somebody else"[1]

The plaintiffs in the landmark lawsuit that brought about marriage equality in Wyoming were getting married. It was February 7, 2015, four months after Federal District Court Judge Scott Skavdahl decided the Constitution protected the right to marry the one you love. Ivan Williams and Chuck Killion stood together at the front of the sanctuary of Highlands Presbyterian Church in Cheyenne. They finished taking their vows. As the preacher's voice reached a crescendo, heading for the denouement, he looked out across a bigger-than-Easter-size crowd in the packed sanctuary to find the face of Jeran Artery. Making eye contact at that moment would be a way of sharing the joy of the day with one who had risked so much to allow this wedding to happen, to allow these men to marry the one they loved. In some ways, the day was as much a celebration of his courage as it was a celebration of the nuptials of the couple at the altar. Jeran was seated, unassumingly near the back, with the man he had recently married, Mike Bleakley. They and scores of others had come to witness this special marriage.

The preacher noticed tears running down their smiling faces as he announced, "With the authority granted me by this church and," lifting his voice, the preacher continued, "AND by the laws of the State of Wyoming, I hereby declare you happily married."

The preacher said he had never officiated a more joy-filled wedding in his pastoral career. Jeran's interactions with church and clergy had not always been such joyous occasions.

A few years earlier, as the Wyoming legislature debated a bill to outlaw marriages between two people who, although they loved one another, were of the same sex, the self-proclaimed lobbyist for the Catholic Diocese of Wyoming cornered Jeran in the corridor of the State Capitol. Richard Wall said he was concerned about Jeran Artery's soul. He told Jeran about Exodus International. It was a Christian ministry promoting conversion therapy as a way of "curing" homosexuality. This was two years before the organization shut itself down and apologized for its attacks on gays.[2] At the time it closed, Exodus International announced its new goals, 180 degrees from its former objectives. "Our goals are to reduce fear, and come alongside churches to become safe, welcoming and mutually transforming communities."

But, in 2011, adherents like Wall were still telling people like Jeran that Exodus International could save them from being condemned by God to burn in Hell for all of eternity. Jeran assured Wall that he was happy with who he was.

Jeran Artery hadn't always been that comfortable with who he was. Blame it on those pews. When you have to sit in them every Sunday and take whatever comes from the pulpit, it has an impact on a young mind. Jeran can't remember a time when he didn't know he was gay. But he does remember sitting in those pews of the First Christian Church in Wheatland, Wyoming. Jeran recalls it was his great uncle, the Reverend Andy Gudahl, the brother of Jeran's grandfather Don, who was preaching fire and brimstone anti-gay sermons, telling him and the others that homosexuality was an abomination.

The sermons echoed throughout most churches in those days. "It says right here in God's word, and I quote from the Book of Leviticus, 'If a man lies with a male as with a woman, both of them have committed an abomination; they shall be put to death, their blood is upon them.'"³ In those days, it was not considered bigoted or hateful when Rev. Gudahl and his colleagues in the ministry assured the flock that homosexuals who did not repent would be, as Richard Wall warned Jeran three decades later, "condemned by God to burn in Hell for all of eternity."

Years later, when Jeran became the chief advocate for LGBTQ rights, his adversaries would accuse him of not knowing the Bible. Little did they know how well he knew Scripture, especially the verses used to "clobber" gays. They were seared into his mind from the days he sat in those pews

Young Jeran listened to Uncle Andy's sermons and internalized them. If God believes you are unworthy, you must be. If your own uncle thought you were doomed, you must be. Jeran sat in church daydreaming about the best way an unworthy, doomed kid could die. Maybe an airplane crash, he contemplated. If you knew the plane was going down, you'd have time to repent before it hit the ground. Your soul could be saved.

Jeran Artery was born in Wheatland in 1971. He arrived as an economic boom was underway in the small town. The county recorded its largest population increase in history in the 1970s. The county added nearly 10% to its numbers, almost double the second greatest increase, which happened between 1910 and 1920. Back then, Jeran's great-grandfather Leonard was homesteading the farm near Slater. Jeran grew up learning how to work that farm, a fifth generation to do so.

His father was a "man's man." A farmer, hunter, athlete. He owned hundreds of guns. There were mounted animal heads everywhere. His father once appeared on ESPN guiding University of Wyoming and Dallas Cowboy football star Jay Novachek on a hunting trip. One thing Jeran remembers about his father is how often he used the word "faggot."

In those days, there were two people who knew Jeran was gay. He and his mother. "Mom knew," Jeran remembered, "but said nothing." She was his supporter, a protector providing cover. One Halloween, Jeran wanted to dress up like a girl. Mom allowed him to do that after school until it came time for Dad to come home. Mom monitored his behavior to make sure others didn't notice. "If I became too flamboyant, Mom would look that look at me and say, 'JERAN!' That was a signal to dial it down."

Other signals were as clear. He knew that he "needed to fix the gay," in him or risk "getting the shit beat out of me" by the other boys. He dated girls and did what the boys did. He played sports though he hated every minute of it. Jeran wanted to act. Acting was an acceptable outlet. And he was good at it, winning the lead in most of the high school plays. Jeran performed at a high enough level and achieved good enough grades across the board that he received a full-ride academic scholarship from the University of Wyoming. But he wanted out of Wyoming. He had set his sights higher.

Instead of Laramie, he headed for Los Angeles to attend the American Academy of Dramatic Arts, the oldest acting school in the English-speaking world. The renowned institution boasts alumnae like Lauren Bacall, John Cassavetes, Robert Redford, Don Rickles, and Paul Rudd, who was a student there when Jeran attended the school.

Still in the closet, but not far enough to avoid detection, a faculty member called him out, telling Jeran, "If you can embrace who you are, you'll be a successful actor." Jeran wasn't ready. Remaining in the closet may have saved his life. It was the midst of the AIDS crisis. In the years Jeran was in Los Angeles, Ryan White became a household name after being diagnosed with AIDS at age 13. He was forced into a well-publicized legal battle to stay in school when authorities feared he would pass the virus to fellow students. His story was a vehicle for public education about AIDS. He died of an AIDS-related illness in 1990. The following year, Los Angeles Laker basketball star Magic Johnson was diagnosed HIV positive and Freddy, lead singer and songwriter of the band Queen, died of AIDS-related illness. During the years Jeran studied acting in LA, the disease was fast on its way to becoming the leading cause of death for all Americans ages 25-44 years old. Remaining closeted and abstinent may have been how Jeran avoided an illness befalling thousands of gay men in Los Angeles and elsewhere.

After two years at the Academy, Jeran realized he wasn't the actor he hoped to become. He packed his bags and returned to Wyoming to attend the University in Laramie, this time without a scholarship. During the first week of classes, he walked into the Student Union and saw a note on the bulletin board announcing a meeting of gay students. He went to a pay phone and dialed the number, hands shaking as he did. Someone answered. He heard a voice ask for his name. Jeran quickly hung up.

During the summers, Jeran returned to Wheatland where he worked part time at a popular restaurant named Vimbo's. It was a mainstay in the small town, the place he and his family gathered for lunch every Sunday after one of Uncle Andy's sermons. It was where he met Maya. Jeran believed one way to persuade others he was not gay was to marry a woman. In 1993, he and Maya entered what some mental health professionals call "a Lavender marriage," which is a marriage designed to cover up one's sexual orientation. Jeran became a stepfather to Maya's children, Holly and Anthony. The couple soon gave birth to their daughter, Elizabeth.

As those things go, it wasn't long before Maya realized Jeran was not heterosexual. The arguments between them became more troublesome as they began to center on Jeran's sexual orientation. Maya blamed their marital discord on his homosexuality and demanded Jeran come out to their friends and families. But, in 1998, the gruesome murder of a gay student persuaded Jeran and thousands of other gay men to remain in the closet.

On a cold October night in Laramie, Matthew Shepard, a student at the University of Wyoming, was savagely beaten by two men he met that evening at a bar. Aaron McKinney and Russell Henderson targeted Matthew while he enjoyed a drink at the Fireside Lounge. Police believe that "once Henderson and McKinney learned that Matt was gay, whether because he told them or because they simply guessed, they devised a plan to rob him."[4] It was near midnight on October 6, 1998, when they coaxed Matthew into McKinney's pickup truck, pretending they were also gay. After driving to a secluded place outside of Laramie, McKinney announced, "Guess what?

We're not gay, and you're getting jacked."[5]

What followed was a merciless 45-minute beating that left Matthew fighting for his life. Alone, hanging on a snow fence at the edge of the Medicine Bow National Forest, sometime in the cold night a doe deer came and lay near Matthew. It was if "some power stepped in," Matt's mother Judy later wrote, "to, as much as possible, set things right."[6] Five days after the beating, while millions around the world watched and prayed and waited, Matthew Shepard died, becoming an icon for the gay rights movement worldwide.

The graphic descriptions of Matthew's injuries were ubiquitous. While his murder stirred LGBTQ activists to seek reforms, the horror of seeing one of their own stalked, targeted, and brutally murdered because he was gay had a ripple effect throughout the gay community. Many gay men on the verge of coming out on October 6, 1998, changed their mind on October 12th. The risk was perceived now to be too great. What happened to Matthew, it now seemed clear, could well happen to any other non-heterosexual person.[7] Jeran said he then understood "why so many young gays kill themselves." He would remain closeted for more than another painful decade.

By 2009, it was clear that the world was changing. Ellen DeGeneres came out and kept her job as the host of a popular TV show. "Will and Grace," featured a gay character and with high ratings was among TV fan favorites. Attitudes toward gays and lesbians became significantly less negative. A year later, a poll supported by the National Science Foundation, demonstrated that most Americans had reversed their earlier disdain for homosexuals. By then a plurality supported same-sex marriage. "The change toward acceptance of homosexuality began in the late 1980s after years of remaining relatively constant. In 1973, 70 percent of people felt same-sex relations are 'always wrong,' and in 1987, 75 percent held that view. By 2000, however, that number dropped to 54 percent and by 2010 was down to 43.5 percent."[8]

In 2009 the family celebrated Grandma Artery's 80th birthday. Not the best day for a "coming out" party. On the other hand, with the exception of his father who was hunting in Mexico, most of the family would be in town for the festivities. It was an opportunity to let everyone know at one time, rather than spreading the news out over several days through multiple painful encounters.

Following the birthday party at the Wheatland Country Club, brother Brad and most of the cousins gathered for an "after-party" at his father's lodge. By then, Grandma Corky had gone home, tired by the festivities. Jeran had an announcement to make. The room quieted. He told them he could no longer live a lie. The folks in that room took it well, hugging Jeran, sharing tears, and providing support. There were other visits to be made before the word circulated through the small community. The next stop was Grandma Corky, Jeran's father's mother. Known for her beehive hairdo and athleticism, she was never "particularly religious." In her younger years, she won a national archery championship, earning her a tickertape parade in New York City. She was an accomplished bowler with trophies "from floor to ceiling."

As Jeran came out to her, she got a puzzled look on her face. "But," she said, "you look like such a big, burly guy." Yet, she evidenced not an air of anything but acceptance.

Then on to Grandma Gudahl's home. Jeran knew this would be the toughest moment. As he anticipated, it did not go well. She believed what her brother-in-law Andy preached. She had been told from the pulpit for decades that homosexuals were an abomination. Now she had to choose between a grandson and the Bible. The scripture, she believed, did not make an exception for grandchildren, regardless of how much you love them. She began sobbing quietly and said, "It's best if you just go now." Their relationship was never the same.

Relieved that his life was no longer a secret, Jeran still wanted to avoid the small-town gossip and judgment. He moved to Cheyenne. He was an agent for New York Life insurance and his business grew robustly. He looked for ways to get involved in the community and make like-minded friends. Someone told him about "Rendezvous." It was a week-long camping experience for the LGBTQ community. He didn't own a tent or a sleeping bag, so he borrowed them and went camping with a couple hundred other gay people.

Jeran found the experience exhilarating. To be among welcoming and affirming people with good hearts and open minds was exciting. It felt safe and enlivening. He was no longer alone or lonely in his sexuality. "This was upscale camping. Not hot dogs cooked over a campfire. This was rosemary shrimp skewers and fancy meals."

There he met Cheyenne attorney, Joe Corrigan. Joe introduced himself as the chair of the board of Wyoming Equality. Joe explained that the organization supported LGBTQ rights and invited Jeran to attend their next meeting. A couple of weeks after attending that first WE meeting and joining the organization's board, Joe called. He wanted Jeran to go to a legislative hearing and testify against legislation that would nullify same-sex marriages that had been entered into in states where they were legally recognized.

For the first 108 years of lawmaking in Wyoming, marrying the person you loved regardless of gender had never been an issue. From 1869 when the first territorial legislature granted suffrage to women until 1977, the domestic relations statutes didn't prohibit same-sex marriage. That year the legislature undertook a complete revision of those statutes. No one was debating marriage equality in those days. It was not an issue. Nonetheless, when the Senate bill arrived in the House Judiciary Committee, a massive amendment was attached. Among the changes was wording providing henceforth that "marriage is a civil contract between a male and a female."[9] Nonetheless, the "full faith and credit" clause of the constitution required Wyoming to recognize marriages entered legally under the laws of other states. The Wyoming legislature was now considering whether to ignore that provision.

By the time Jeran became head of Wyoming Equality, the Wyoming legislature had been on an increasingly conservative trajectory ever since the courts ordered it divided into single-member districts.[10] Thereafter, instead of electing legislators at-large within county lines, the majority party of the state legislature was tasked every decade, following the federal census, with drawing lines allowing for the election of a single lawmaker within a district. Cultural issues like abortion and gay rights found prominent places on the legislative agenda they had not been given before because the new rules made it easier for single-issue candidates to win a seat.

Thus, not only was Republican control of the legislature institutionalized, but the legislature veered farther to the right with each subsequent election. In the decade before the federal court ruling the 30-member state senate had an average of 18.5 Republican members each session. In the decade following, the average number of Republican senators jumped to 23. In the following five elections, 2012-2020, the average reached 26.5, leaving only 3.5 senate seats for Democrats. In the 60-member house, the average number of GOP representatives went from 40 (1972-1990) to 44.5 (1992-2010).[11] The 2010 election produced a senate controlled by the GOP 26-4 and a House with a 51-9 Republican super majority. Those numbers alone don't capture how much more conservative the legislature had become. It's what awaited Jeran in his initial foray into lobbying.

As Jeran entered Wyoming politics for the first time as an advocate for gay rights, it was not unlike the time Daniel was tossed into the lion's den. In 2011, House Bill 74 was introduced. If enacted, it would no longer matter that your same-sex marriage was lawfully entered elsewhere. You would not be considered married if you came to Wyoming. The bill was sponsored by a large group of powerful Republican legislators including Representative Ed Buchanan, the Speaker of the House, and Tom Lubnau, the House Majority Leader, who would, a session later, become Speaker.

At the outset of the 2011 legislative session, Wyoming Equality members were warned it would be a dangerous time for the LGBTQ community. The organization's newsletter *United Voice*, explained, "The Wyoming legislature shifted far to the right in the last election. WE has fewer friends in the legislature."[12] This was the political environment Jeran was asked to enter as a defender of gay rights. Jeran had no legislative experience. No political experience. Now he was asked to stand in front of a confrontational group of lawmakers who believed his lifestyle offensive and defend the rights of people of the same sex to marry one another. Jeran went. He told them he was a 5th generation Wyomingite who believed their bill did not represent Wyoming values. It was then that Jeran learned how deeply the "hate for gays" was ingrained in Wyoming's political leaders and conservative advocacy groups.

A lobbyist for "Wyoming Family Values," Lynn Hutchings, told Jeran she was "worried you are going to destroy your colon." She was elected to the state house in the next election. Later, after being elected to the state senate, when a group of high school students lobbied her on a bill to ban workplace discrimination against the LGBTQ community, she, according to the students, said, "If my sexual orientation was to have sex with all of the men in there and I had sex with all of the women in there and then they brought their children and I had sex with all of them and then brought their dogs in and I had sex with them, should I be protected for my sexual orientation?"

A now defunct conservative organization known as WyWatch, recognized as "one of the most conservative organizations in 21st century Wyoming,"[13] was represented. Its lobbyist, Becky Vandeburghe, joined Hutchings. The two told legislators that homosexuals were dangerous, that they died of cancer and AIDS at a young age, and that they were recruiting "our children" to their "sinful lifestyle."

As Jeran sat in that legislative committee hearing, enduring an onslaught of such remarks from conservative lobbyists and lawmakers, he recalled the Wheatland days of his youth, days he sat in those pews. He remembered "the people [who] try to force their views on everyone else. People who say being gay is a sin and homosexuals will spend eternity in hell. People who say being gay is a choice. People who pass judgment on everyone else that looks, acts, or believes differently than they do. They constantly lecture on how everyone else should be living their lives and even lobby lawmakers to pass laws that would impose their beliefs on to all of society."

Ironically, the committee met on Martin Luther King's birthday to approve the bill defining gays and lesbians out of marriage by a vote of 7-2. "Opponents said the approval of the legislation was a disappointing tribute for Martin Luther King Jr. and Wyoming Equality Day.[14] HB74 passed the full House a few days later by a 32-27 vote. It was then sent to the state senate for consideration.

During the debate, Senator Cale Case, a marriage equality proponent, sponsored an amendment requiring billboards to be posted "along all major highways and in all airports," reading, "Warning: your marriage or civil union may be void or voidable in Wyoming. Proceed with extreme caution." The "tongue-in-cheek" amendment failed, but the point was made.

During the debate, a group of demonstrators gathered in front of the Capitol Building where they shredded their own marriage licenses arguing that, under the bill, a marriage license was becoming a "tool of discrimination."

The bill passed the Senate 16-14, but with amendments. The House refused to concur with the Senate's changes. A Joint Conference Committee met and tried to resolve the differences between the two houses, but in the end the Senate voted 16-14 not to accept that committee's changes. The bill therefore died by a slim two-vote margin.[15] Wyoming Equality succeeded in garnering enough votes in the House that same year to block a constitutional amendment banning same-sex marriage although it had passed the state senate.

Jeran was energized. The fight over HB74 "put Wyoming Equality on the map."[16] National LGBTQ rights organizations began calling, offering help and seeking advice. They had something to offer Jeran and they could learn from him what is like to be a gay activist in a small state as opposed to serving in a populated, urban environment. In October 2011, Jeran became WE chair. He was also elected as a delegate to the 2012 Democratic National Convention, in recognition of his influence among the LGBTQ community. Coming back from being part of nominating America's first Black president to a second term, Jeran was further emboldened. He immediately established the goal of achieving marriage equality "by the end of the 2013 legislative session."[17]

His first foray into politics was a master's level education in political science and human behavior. If only these legislators had more information, he thought, they would reject the hate. If education didn't work, they would have to elect new lawmakers. He wrote a column in the WE newsletter the following month. "The majority of state legislators don't understand 'sexual orientation' and 'gender identification' and they don't want to understand it," Jeran editorialized. He urged members to "to provide them with this information" while recruiting candidates to replace them in the coming election.[18]

In 2012, Jeran and Mike Bleakley announced their engagement. They wanted a Wyoming wedding attended by friends and family. But they began planning for a smaller ceremony in Hawaii because the prospects for achieving marriage equality in Wyoming any time soon seemed dim. The 2012 Wyoming election saw WE supporters defeated and produced more anti-gay legislators. Jeran wrote, "I fear that we will once again be battling some very ugly anti-gay legislation in 2013. Passage of civil unions may be more of a battle than we had originally hoped for." Still, Jeran was upbeat. "I will not rest," he said, "until I can marry the man that I love."[19]

Wyoming Equality, led by Jeran, and accompanied by LGBTQ allies took the offense during the next legislative session. Jeran said he was tired of fighting on defense and arranged to have the legislature consider bills establishing same-sex marriage by defining it as a "civil contract between two natural persons." That proposal was defeated narrowly. Another bill created "domestic partnerships," an idea favored by Governor Matt Mead. Nonetheless, it went down on a 24-35 House vote. A third same-sex marriage bill was defeated by House members during that session 17-41.

Boldness begets boldness. Courage begets courage. Under Jeran's leadership, WE created a new, aggressive presence in the public arena. They established Gay-Straight Student Alliances in high schools and at the University of Wyoming. PFLAG chapters (a support and advocacy voice for the parents of LGBTQ children) sprang up around the state. Soon people around Wyoming and throughout the country were clamoring to join Jeran and Wyoming Equality in this battle.

In 2013, the Gill Foundation came calling. Founded a decade earlier by Ted Gill, a software entrepreneur and philanthropist, the Gill Foundation is one of the nation's leading funders of efforts to secure full equality for lesbian, gay, bisexual, transgender, and queer (LGBTQ) people. It had invested millions in the fight for equality nationwide and was now willing to invest in Wyoming. Gill began by training this neophyte political advocate on how to best convey the message.

Next, Freedom to Marry, a national organization committed singularly to the goal of achieving marriage equality in every state, invited Jeran to spend a week at their headquarters in New York City. There he learned how to "crack the code." Using what they learned from polling and focus groups, which demonstrated a quickly increasing number of Americans warming to the idea of "the freedom to marry," he learned how to talk about the issue in a way that spoke to grassroots supporters and those leaning toward their position.

The Human Rights Campaign came to assist in coalition building. Soon, groups of allies appeared across Wyoming in the most unlikely places. Clergy organized to support marriage equality. Lawyers and public officials as well as business organizations came on board. Jeran organized town-hall meetings in Rock Springs, Jackson, Casper, Laramie, and Cheyenne. Hundreds of voters attended, eager to learn how they could help.

Ahead of the 2013 legislative session, a well-known and talented public relations expert was hired to help muster Republican support. Liz Brimmer was one of the most respected political advocates in Wyoming.

Conservatives not inclined to listen to Jeran or Wyoming Equality would listen to Liz. An unlikely coalition was recruited. The Wyoming Mining and Petroleum Associations, the Wyoming Business Alliance and the Wyoming AFL-CIO, together with the Wyoming Chamber of Commerce, Wyoming Lodging and Restaurant Association, the Wyoming Education Association and the Wyoming Association of Churches signed on.[20] Brimmer then lined up a group of GOP lawmakers to introduce a bill prohibiting discrimination based on sexual orientation.

Senate File 115 was sponsored by seven of the most influential Republicans in the state senate. Even so, opponents and proponents alike were shocked when it passed the Senate on a 24-6 vote.[21]

Suddenly it was the anti-LGBTQ organizations fighting a defensive battle. They proposed amending the bill to eliminate legal protections for transgender citizens. Those who had fought such legislation "tooth and nail" were now willing to support a bill that gave gays and lesbians legal protection, but not transgender citizens. Liz Brimmer told the coalition they should accept the compromise. It was the only way to get the bill passed. There was a heated debate among people sharing a common goal, i.e., to end legal discrimination against gays and lesbians, transgender, bisexual, and other non-binary friends. On one side were the practical politicians like Brimmer. On the other side were those like State Representative Cathy Connolly, the only openly lesbian member of the legislature. She had endured years of rhetorical abuse and not-so-veiled threats from those who opposed LGBTQ rights. She was unwilling to "sell out" transgender people. Likewise with Jeran.

Before taking the reins at WE, he had never met a transgender person. Now he had worked with them, side by side, to fight for LGBTQ rights and he wasn't willing to leave the T's behind. By now he knew the abuse and violence with which they were subjected. As gays and lesbians gained more acceptance in the community, transgender people were increasingly the target of hate. He and Representative Connolly decided that the slogan "freedom means freedom for all" was not just a slogan, but creedal. It would be better to have no bill than one that left transgender friends behind. And that was what they got.

The House voted 26-33 to kill the bill. Liz Brimmer, after all her work, was crushed. Jeran, on the other hand considered the confrontation to have been a success. The movement had been true to its values and that victory was sufficient unto itself.

Despite the defeat, which was predictable, Jeran felt the momentum had shifted. For the first time the LGBTQ community had an eloquent, well-informed, high-profile leader willing to take bold positions in public fights. At the same time, Jeran was fast coming to the conclusion that marriage equality could not be achieved in the legislature. In his relatively brief political career, he had discovered to his chagrin that legislators were not bound by truth, nor by law. He listened helplessly while opponents persuade colleagues with false statistics and wildly unsupported claims. He heard their disdain for a provision in the Wyoming Constitution that guaranteed equal rights. Article 1, Section 3, seemed clear to him but not most of the legislature.

> *Equal political rights. Since equality in the enjoyment of natural and civil rights is only made sure through political equality, the laws of this state affecting the political rights and privileges of its citizens shall be without distinction of race, color, sex, or any circumstance or condition whatsoever other than individual incompetency, or unworthiness duly ascertained by a court of competent jurisdiction.*

The last five words of that section of the state Constitution caught Jeran's attention. "A court of competent jurisdiction." Rights could be protected, the Constitution promised, by a "court of competent jurisdiction." Though he was not an attorney, he knew that courts were fundamentally different from legislatures, judges were fundamentally different from legislators. Judges were bound by rules that didn't apply to legislators. Legislators speaking on the floor and those who testify in committee hearings can lie about material facts with impunity. They distort the truth and represent opinion as fact when, if lawyers said the same things in a court room, they would lose their license to practice law. Witnesses at a legislative hearing are free to say whatever they want while those who lie on the witness stand in a court room are charged with perjury and face jail sentences.

Unlike the political process tolerated in the legislature, the courts have a rules-based process that assures, for the most part, that the information on which they make decisions is truthful. The courts employ an adversarial process with rules assuring false claims are called out. In short, unlike the state legislature, the state courts are bound tightly by truth and the rule of law.

Jeran thought, "Why should we continue this 'gladiator-like fight' in the state Capitol? Why should we continue to listen to the hate and watch legislators ignore the lies? Why not walk a few blocks down the street and invite the courts to rule on the Constitutionality of Wyoming denying the right to marriage based on sexual orientation?"

The March 2014 edition of WE's newsletter, *United Voice*, made the historic announcement. "Wyoming Equality and Four Couples Sue the State."

The filing of the lawsuit followed months of strategic planning. Jeran and WE worked quietly with the National Center for Lesbian Rights. The Center's coordinator turned out to be an old Wheatland High School classmate of Jeran's, Dorothy Fernandez. Together they recruited plaintiffs, meeting with each, briefing them of what they knew would be a brutal road ahead. Each was fully informed of the tactics they could expect to face from the anti-marriage-equality groups. Jeran had faced them for the last several years and wanted each of the potential plaintiffs to be prepared for the brutal onslaught.

It was not without Jeran's forethought and keen sense of messaging that the caption on the complaint filed in the state district court in Laramie County read "Courage v. Wyoming." Wyoming Equality joined Cora Courage and Wyoma "Nonie" Proffit of Evanston, Carl Oleson and Rob Johnston of Casper, Anne Guzzo and Bonnie Robinson of Laramie, and Ivan Williams and Chuck Killion of Cheyenne in agreeing to be named as plaintiffs. The defendants included Wyoming Governor Matt Mead and Debbye Balcaen Lathrop, the Laramie County Clerk, whose office had a legal responsibility to issue marriage licenses under state law.

The opening allegation in the complaint reminded readers that "Wyoming's state motto is Equal Rights."[22] The complaint explained that plaintiffs Courage and Proffit were married in Iowa, while Oleson and Johnston were married in Canada. Those jurisdictions allowed for same-sex marriage. "However, in their home state of Wyoming, they are treated as legal strangers to their spouses."[23]

The complaint explained that plaintiffs Guzzo and Robinson, Williams and Killion were unmarried but "wish to publicly declare their love and commitment before their family, friends, and community; to join their lives together and enter into a legally binding commitment to one another; and to share in the protections and security that marriage provides."[24]

The compliant detailed more than a dozen significant rights available under state law to heterosexual couples that were denied to same-sex couples.[25] As a result, these men and women were denied protections under the Wyoming and U.S. Constitutions. The 105-paragraph, 21-page document asked the court to declare prohibitions on same-sex marriage illegal. Before the state court could act, the 10th Circuit Court of Appeals ruled in a Utah case:

> *"The Fourteenth Amendment (of the U.S. Constitution) protects the fundamental right to marry, establish a family, raise children, and enjoy the full protection of a state's marital laws. A state may not deny the issuance of a marriage license for two persons, or refuse to recognize their marriage, based solely on the sex of the persons in the marriage union."*[26]

When the United States Supreme Court refused to set aside the 10th Circuit decision, it became the law of the land in all 10th Circuit states, including Wyoming. The following day, October 7, 2014, the plaintiffs in the state court case filed suit to have the ruling in *Kitchen v. Herbert* recognized by the Federal District Court for the District of Wyoming. A hearing was held before Federal District Court Judge Scott Skavdahl in Casper. With Judy and Dennis Shepherd, parents of Matthew Shepherd, seated in the front row, lawyers argued their case. Ten days later Judge Skavdahl issued his historic decision.

In a 16-page ruling, the judge found that any interest the State of Wyoming may have in upholding a state statute prohibiting same-sex marriage "is overridden by the public's interest in protecting fundamental rights."[27] Marriage equality had become the law in Wyoming. Within a few months, the United States Supreme Court ruled 5-4 that it was the law of the land and prohibited any state from enforcing laws to the contrary.[28]

Celebrating the victory, dozens of same-sex couples around the state were married within the first month after the court issued it's ruling.

Press conference outside the federal courthouse in Caper after Judge Scott W. Skavdahl ruled in favor of marriage equality on October 17, 2014. Jeran is the second person to the left of Plaintiffs' counsel Tom Stoever who is speaking to the press. Dennis Shepard, back row, second from left; Judy Shepard, far right between plaintiffs Chuck Killion (top right) and Robert Johnson. Photo taken by Matthew Baker is used with his permission.

Two months hence, on December 13, Mike and Jeran were wed in that small ceremony on the beach in Hawaii, which had been planned much earlier when the possible didn't seem so. They returned to Wyoming and hosted a standing-room-only reception for all their friends.

***

All these years later, with public opinion polls showing vast majorities of Wyoming people supporting marriage equality, it is difficult to comprehend the courage it took to lead the way in an earlier time. Opinion didn't change on its own or in a vacuum. The opinion polls of today reflect the evolution of thinking brought about by the courage that it took to act a decade earlier. The polls were much different then. The opposition was much more energized and vitriolic. The opposition included many of the most powerful politicians in Wyoming. Much of the opposition was religiously based. Churches throughout the state and the influential Catholic Diocese used the pulpit to generate disdain for marriage equality. It was politically correct and politically advantageous to join the anti-LGBTQ crusade. Candidates won elections decrying "the gay agenda."

Maybe it was "those pews," the space he filled while being told that people like him would "burn in hell." Maybe it was those hard, wooden pews at the little church back in Wheatland that made Jeran so uncomfortable that he knew something in him had to change if anything outside of him was going to change. Maybe it was simply the idea of love. The dream that we can marry the person we love is a simple, yet existential force. If we can't marry the person we love, how can we live? The Wyoming Equality slogan summed it up. "Freedom Means Freedom for Everyone."

In his book *Servant Leadership*," Robert Greenleaf writes, "Not much happens without a dream. And for something to happen, there must be a great dream. Behind every great achievement is a dreamer of great dreams."[29] For Jeran Artery, it was the simple dream that one day he could marry the man he loved.

Endnotes

1. Toni Morrison, Barnard College commencement speech (1979)
2. Payne, CNN, https://www.cnn.com/2013/06/20/us/exodus-international-shutdown/index.html, July 8, 2013, accessed March 21, 2021
3. Revised Standard Version of the Bible, 20: 13
4. Shepard, *The Meaning of Matthew*, 144-145
5. Shepard, *The Meaning of Matthew*, 146
6. Shepard, *The Meaning of Matthew*, 162
7. Noelle, Monique, "The ripple effect of a sexual orientation hate crime: The psychological impact of the murder of Matthew Shepard on non-heterosexual people." (2000). Masters Theses 1911 - February 2014. 2354. Retrieved from https://scholarworks.umass.edu/cgi/viewcontent.cgi?article=3490&context=theses, January 4, 2021
8. https://www.norc.org/NewsEventsPublications/PressReleases/Pages/american-acceptance-of-homosexuality-gss-report.aspx. Retrieved January 4, 2021
9. *Wyoming Digest of Senate Journal, 44th State Legislature (1977)*, 106-114
10. *Gore v. Karpan*, 775 F. Supp 1445 (1991), https://law.justia.com/cases/federal/district-courts/FSupp/775/1430/1555228/
11. https://sos.wyo.gov/Services/docs/LegComposition.pdf, accessed September 1, 2021
12. "United Voice," January 2011, Papers of Wyoming Equality, American Heritage Center, University of Wyoming, box 1
13. "Watch Leaves Wyoming without even saying goodbye," *Jackson Hole News and Guide*, October 19, 2016, https://www.jhnewsandguide.com/jackson_hole_daily/state_and_regional/wyofile/wywatch-leaves-wyoming-without-even-saying-goodbye/article_5fa6e20f-a330-5517-b7de-99e0ef77be0b.html, accessed August 29, 2021. NOTE: The chair of the WyWatch board of directors, Frank Eathorne, later became the chair of the Wyoming Republican Party.
14. "Definition of marriage bill passes first hurdle in House" *Wyoming Tribune-Eagle*, January 18, 2011, A-3
15. Digest, 2011 Wyoming Legislature, https://www.wyoleg.gov/Legislation/2011/HB0074, accessed August 30, 2021
16. Author's interview with Jeran Artery, June 19, 2020
17. Wyoming Equality Papers, AHC, box 1, 4
18. "United Voice," *Wyoming Equality Newsletter*, February 2011, 1,6
19. "United Voice," *Wyoming Equality Newsletter*, November 2021, Wyoming Equality Papers, AHC, box 1, 4
20. The Wyoming Catholic Diocese opposed the bill
21. https://www.wyoleg.gov/Legislation/2015/SF0115, accessed August 31, 2021
22. *Courage, et al. v. State of Wyoming, et al.*, https://www.clearinghouse.net/chDocs/public/PB-WY-0001-0001.pdf, accessed September 9, 2021
23. Id., Paragraph 8
24. Id., Paragraph 11
25. Id., Paragraph 45

26 *Kitchen v. Herbert*, 755 F. 3d 1193, 1199 (10th Cir. 2014), cert. denied, 2014 WL 3841263 (October 6, 2014)
27 https://www.scribd.com/document/243372518/2-14-cv-00200-44-Wyoming-Injunction-Temporary-Stay, accessed September 9, 2021
28 *Obergefell v. Hodges*, 576 U.S. 644 (2015)
29 Greenleaf, *Servant Leadership*, 30

Chapter 3

TOM BELL

"a one-man conservation movement"

In the Spring of 2013, my first book, *Dying for Joe McCarthy's Sins: The Suicide of Wyoming Senator Lester Hunt*, was published. I drove to Lander for a book-promotion event. The day before, Marjane Ambler, a close friend of Tom Bell, called. Tom wanted me to stop by his home for a visit. I hadn't seen Tom for years. To say I was pleased by the invitation is an understatement. It was as though the Dalai Lama had summoned me to the mountaintop.

By now, Tom had lost his wife and his health was failing. An eye patch covered a near-fatal World War II wound. He told me he suffered from Meniere's Syndrome and how the affliction affected his balance. Tom wore a hearing aid in both ears and spoke of his reconciliation with chronic dizzy spells. But he was fully engaged and as witty as ever. He motioned me to sit with him at a table stacked high with letters, books, magazines, journals, and newspaper clippings. Tom spoke of his college-days friendship with Senator Hunt's son Buddy as we talked politics. Together we lamented the lack of political will to address climate change and reminisced about long ago days when, once upon a time, Wyoming had a governor and a congressional delegation fighting for clean air and water and wilderness. It didn't seem so long ago listening to Tom's anecdotes, reliving the monumental battles. Within three years, Tom would leave us, but at that moment, and every moment Tom was in the arena for more than six decades, he was a bright, shining light that led the way for thousands who were advocating for a better planet.

Tom Bell gave an eye and nearly his life for his country. His friend and Wyoming writer Geoff O'Gara once wrote that "Bell's efforts on behalf of Wyoming cost him his ranch, many of his friends, and very nearly, his sanity."[1] He dedicated his life to our grandchildren's future. Tom Bell's life is the history of Wyoming's environmentalism. "This is a man who had dedicated his whole life to the environment, his country, and the people of Wyoming. History will prove that Tom Bell is one of Wyoming's great Heroes."[2]

***

It wasn't where he thought he'd be at 18, but it was the first spring after December 7, 1941, and most young men his age were not where any of them thought they'd be in those days following that day, the one President Franklin Delano Roosevelt said would live in infamy.

Thomas Alton Bell was born on April 12, 1924, in a town that no longer exists. Winton, Wyoming started its life as a coal mining town in 1917. It's where his father and grandfather mined coal. You can find its skeletal remains 14 miles north of Rock Springs. A Union Pacific authorized history of the company's mining operations includes a chapter ironically titled, "Winton, the Town That Will Live on For Years."[3] Less than a decade after the book was published, Winton dried up and blew away. But the company town, where Union Pacific owned everything from the miners' small shacks to the grocery store with overpriced goods on the shelves was Tom Bell's first impression of the morality of mining companies.

The Bells moved to Fremont County where Tom grew up on a small ranch outside of Lander. There was no running water, no electricity, and no money for basic life needs. When his grandfather was sick with prostate cancer, they couldn't afford a doctor to drive from town to treat him. Tom, a 10-year-old, listened as his grandfather begged his daughter, Tom's mother, "to get a gun" and kill him. "My mother's soft voice was hardly audible, but I could hear her say, 'Oh Dad, you know I can't do that.' 'But Hilda, it's so awful.' And then, after a little interval, it was quiet, so quiet that I knew my grandfather was dead. I could hear the low sobbing of my mother."[4]

They survived the Great Depression living hand to mouth and mostly off the bounty of the land. They never had more than a few animals; cows, pigs, horses, and sheep. Before sunrise on those cold Wyoming winter mornings, young Tom milked the cows while icicles formed on his fingers as the view of Red Butte appeared through the door of the barn. The sun coming up warmed his soul. The ranch was where he developed a love affair with the land. There he met the coyotes, skunks, deer, pronghorn, geese, and other wildlife he would spend a lifetime protecting.

Tom told friends years later, "As a boy, I knew where every sage hen nest was, when they fed, when they went to water. I've always loved the land."[5]

He attended a one-room rural school until enrolling at Fremont County Vocational High School where he was elected student body president. After graduating from high school in May 1941, he went to Alaska and spent the summer exploring its great isolation. He returned in time to enroll at the University of Wyoming. Before the end of his first semester, the Japanese attacked Pearl Harbor and before the end of his freshman year, he enlisted in the Army Air Force (AAF).[6] While awaiting orders to report for basic training, Tom heard they needed laborers at a new government facility up the road between Powell and Cody. He was hired to inventory building materials as they were unloaded at the rail dock for constructing the barracks of the Heart Mountain Relocation Camp.[7] Soon his orders came and by February 1944, he had finished basic training and bombardier school and was a commissioned officer, flying dangerous combat missions, guiding the paths of bombs to destroy Nazi targets across Europe. Eight long months later, he was medically discharged and by January 1945, 20-year-old Tom Bell was back on the campus in Laramie.

Tom wanted to be a fighter pilot but "washed out" after months of pre-flight, primary flying school, and basic flying. He was 19 years old and crushed but chose the next best thing. He volunteered for bombardier school, determined to be "one of the best." Months of training included formation and night flying and bombing practice. Tom led his class in "day bombing for accuracy and was one of the tops in night bombing."[8]

Lieutenant Tom Bell was assigned to the 742nd Squadron of the 455th Bomb Group and sent to Cerignola, Italy, near the spur of the Italian boot. By the time Tom arrived, the city had been laid to waste. "There were few standing houses," Tom observed as he walked through the ruins. There were children wandering aimlessly through the streets, nearly naked, dressed in rags. He stopped to speak to an Italian war widow sitting under a makeshift lean-to. Seeing he was an American soldier, she was blunt about her anger with both sides of a war that had been visited upon her and her community. Tom looked at the beautiful hand-made tablecloth laid across a few old, broken boards. Whether he bought it to ease his homesickness or out of a sense of altruism or guilt we'll never know.[9]

He most certainly crossed paths with South Dakotan Lt. George McGovern, a future United States Senator and Democratic Party nominee whom Tom, a Republican, supported for president in a contest against Richard Nixon in 1972. McGovern was stationed at San Giovanni Field at the same time as Tom and flew for the 741st Squadron.[10]

It took extraordinary confidence to fly combat missions. John Steinbeck helped the AAF create a propaganda campaign to tout their brave recruits. He presented them as "relics of the past and harbingers of a new future."[11] Brave they were. "Twice as many air officers died in battle than in all the rest of the Army, despite the ground force's larger size."[12]

Tom climbed into the bombardier's seat on May 10, 1944, two years to the day since he enlisted. He had flown 30 previous missions, 20 of them through heavy enemy fire. He'd been through enough to be able to say, "I wasn't scared stiff, just scared."[13] Many of the toughest assignments entailed flying over Balkan countries to destroy German rail lines, the Nazi's lifeline for supplies of oil and other raw materials. Those lines were among the most guarded sites, meaning destroying the rail lines also meant dodging rocket fire "thicker than hail," which is what Tom and his fellow airmen encountered on a bombing run over Steyr, Austria a month earlier. Many of his colleagues did not survive that day. Tom wrote in his log simply, "Helluva day."[14] It was his 11th mission and one for which the 742nd was awarded a Presidential Unit Citation. Tom turned 20 four days later. A month later, he flew his final mission.

At 5 feet 7 inches tall and 125 pounds, Tom Bell had an easier time than most squeezing himself into a small seat in the cramped compartment of the B-24, behind the gunner. As he hunched over the bombsight, the navigator kicked down the retractable seat near Tom and reviewed his charts and maps. He circled an aircraft factory, a target of such importance that 300 B-24s and B-17s took part in the raid. The pre-mission briefing warned the men they would encounter exceptionally heavy resistance.

Once the rest of the crew climbed through the bomb bay doors and took their places, Tom could see the feet of the pilot and co-pilots at eye level through the narrow bulkhead separating him from them. For such large planes loaded with bombs and full of gasoline, the danger began with take-off. On May 10th as every time before, the pilot lined his B-24 up to taxi down the runway. The other bombing groups were parallel. All took off, side-by-side. The plane vibrated. The engine noise was deafening. It seemed to Tom every time like the plane would not lift off the runway but each time it did. After liftoff, the planes moved quickly into formation, a squadron box with two three-plane echelons, a seventh plane flying slightly behind to intercept German fighters if they attacked, and they always did. Once all reached 25,000 feet they headed for the target.

Arriving at the Initial Point (IP) over Bucharest, they made a 90-degree turn, tightened the formation, and put each plane in a position to make as sure as possible that all the bombs would fall on target. After crossing the IP, Lt. Bell and the bombardiers on every other plane took control of their planes. Now, the big bombers were wing-to-wing and the flak from German guns was as unrelenting as a mid-summer hailstorm on the Red

Desert. It appeared in vivid colors of red, white, and blue as the deadly shells flashed around his plane. "I couldn't help but note the irony," he told a film maker seven decades later.

Suddenly an explosion knocked the young airman to the floor. "The right side of my face was pulverized by shattered plexiglass and small bits of metal." As blood poured from a socket that a few moments ago housed his right eye, the crew's navigator gave Tom a shot of morphine. Tom saw angels watching over him.[15] The cabin was not pressurized, which meant the plane filled with air so cold that crew members suffered frostbite. The air that night was a blessing as it froze the streaming blood, saving Tom's life. Then Tom checked the control panel, concerned about whether in the turmoil following his injury, he had dropped all the bombs aboard. All had been dropped over the target. His plane headed back to the base. Tom would never have to face German flak again.

Of the 300 planes taking part in the attack, 28 did not return. The 280 crewmen aboard were killed or captured. The official after-action report for Tom's 742nd Squadron was less bleak. "10 May 1944. 9 aircraft with 36 officers and 54 enlisted men participated in the bombing of Bucharest, Romania. The mission was successful; all aircraft returned; one officer was wounded in action."[16]

Tom was moved to a hospital in Bari, Italy to recover from his wounds, gradually regaining sight in his left eye. There he made friends with Japanese American soldiers from the heroic 442nd Regimental Combat Team. It was an all-Japanese American combat unit, the most decorated for its size and length of service in the history of the U.S. military. Its 18,000 soldiers were awarded over 4,000 Purple Hearts, 4,000 Bronze Stars, 560 Silver Stars, 21 Medals of Honor, and seven Presidential Unit Citations. "While working at the Heart Mountain Camp, I had not given much thought to the injustices we were doing to our fellow Americans," Tom later admitted. "During my stay in the hospital, I had time to think, and I realized those relocation camps violated my concepts of citizenship and patriotism."[17] It was during this time Tom developed the sense of social justice that defined much of the rest of his life.

Back home, the local newspaper reported, "Tommy Bell, son of Mr. and

Mrs. Lafe Bell, formerly of Lander and now living in Laramie, lost one eye and had the other badly damaged when a flak burst caught his plane on its 32nd mission and 21st over Germany." Not yet old enough to vote or buy a beer, he was awarded a Silver Star for bravery under fire, and a Purple Heart. He also received a medical discharge. Tom's career in the Army Air Force was over, but a new career as an environmental warrior was about to begin.

Tom Bell at his ranch in Fremont County.
Photo used with permission of *High Country News*

Tom was back in Wyoming to enjoy Thanksgiving with his family. He spent time in the solitude of the Red Desert healing mind, body, and soul. By January, the resilient young man was ready to resume his life. He re-enrolled at the University of Wyoming. The numbers of returning veterans gave birth to demanding increases in student enrollment at the school and every other university and college in the country. When Tom returned to the campus, enrollment was on its way to tripling by the end of the war. There were a myriad challenges in meeting the immediate needs of so many students. UW's 1946 Yearbook cleverly described the faculty as "haunted by the expanding future and maltreated by the shifting present." Housing students was as big a challenge as teaching them. The Laramie Chamber of Commerce donated fifty trailer houses, adding capacity to the new dormitories built expeditiously by the school. "Even a water tower behind Dray's Cottage where Washakie Center is now located was remodeled and occupied."[18]

Tom was an active student, starting the rodeo club and pledging a fraternity (Sigma Nu). He was elected to the student senate and joined the veteran's club and the Iron Skull, a group promoting the University's traditions. He was elected student body president in his senior year and received a Bachelor of Science degree in 1947. At UW, he met Muriel "Tommie" Wilcox, whom he married in 1947. During the summer, he worked for the U.S. Department of Agriculture as an "unskilled laborer" for $5 a day.[19]

After graduation, it seemed more doors were closing than opening. He wanted to continue to grad school and was initially accepted. Then Tom and Tommie learned they were expecting their first child "and such an unforeseen event involves too many economic difficulties for me to try to continue."[20] He wanted to go to work for the Wyoming Game and Fish Department, but they weren't hiring. He bought a small house and a few acres in Sheridan County and took a job driving a truck. "It wasn't long before I found this to be disappointing and not to my liking."[21] In the meantime, he took a job teaching math and science to junior high students in Lander. Eventually Tom was able to go back to UW where he earned a master's degree in Zoology in 1957.

Tom had an inkling that neither legislators nor policymakers grasped the economic value of wild animals and wild places. Researching his master's thesis was an opportunity to quantify that value. Entitled, *A Study of the Economic Value of Wyoming Wildlife Resources*, Tom's thesis demonstrated that while the livestock industry contributed approximately 24 million dollars to the state's economy annually and farming offered another $19.5 million, hunting and fishing revenue was "no less than $23,350,000." Tom also pointed to the nearly 128 million dollars spent each year by tourists. "It is not inconceivable to presume that many tourists visit the state to see and enjoy our wildlife."[22] Tom Bell argued it was in Wyoming's self-interest to protect the land and the wildlife.

In the spring of 1957, the Wyoming Game and Fish Department offered Tom a job as a "Game Bird Biologist." It wasn't the position he wanted but it paid $380 a month and Tom had long hoped to work for the Department. He'd soon find that he, more than some, took seriously the idea that conservation decisions should be based on science, not politics.

> *"I have never lost my love and respect for science. Scientific evidence, obtained and analyzed by trained men and women, will always prevail over the darkness of ignorance, paranoia, political correctness, and unfounded rumors and allegations. The truth will always win out."*[23]

But in 1958, a new governor was elected. New Game and Fish Commissioners were appointed. One of them was "a dentist from Sheridan who had driven halfway across the state to tell me how to manage pheasants." The rookie Commissioner heard that Magpies were raiding pheasant nests and he ordered Tom to kill them all. Tom knew the magpies occupied their own place in the ecological system and the problem could be managed without wiping out a species. Tom may have been armed with the scientific knowledge, but the dentist had the political power. He ordered Tom to comply with his request. "I looked him in the eye," Tom recalled 54 years later, "and politely told him, 'You can go to Hell, Doc.'"[24] Tom walked to his office and typed a letter of resignation.

Tom explained himself to the Game and Fish Commission. He said he'd wanted to work for the Department from the time he was a sophomore in high school. To do so, he had attained both a bachelor's degree and a master's degree in wildlife conservation. He knew the science. However, the agency's "guiding philosophy in Wyoming seems to be that no training is required for game and fish management." Later, Tom fact checked himself. Surveying every state surrounding Wyoming, he learned that except for Montana, they all required a minimum of four-year college degrees for game wardens. Montana required two years of college or equivalent experience. Wyoming required only a high school diploma.[25] In 1964, largely because of Tom Bell's badgering, Wyoming established a college degree as a minimum requirement.

Tom admitted the public didn't yet appreciate the need for trained game managers and told them, "I leave the department with great conviction that something should be done to change the public's attitude."[26] That was now Tom Bell's *raison d'être*.

It was only a few days after his resignation that Tom began a new career. The game bird biologist became a newspaper columnist. "High Country by Tom Bell" appeared for the first time in the *Wyoming State Journal* on December 17, 1959. Tom debuted his campaign to teach the public about the role of science in conservation. "There is a lack of reliable information," he advised readers. Tom warned them, "No matter what anyone might lead you to believe, we still don't know very much about our wildlife."

Along with his columns, his byline appeared on an occasional sports story about the local high school where he continued to teach as well. It was the opportunity to speak out about significant conservation issues that Tom most enjoyed. His columns also afforded Tom moments of personal reflection. Reading them half a century later, you get a sense of the deep philosophical reservoir that sustained the man through decades of harsh political battles. The fond memories of a child first experiencing the joy of "the light flashing from a rainbow's side in limpid waters" and "the hoot of an owl from dusky woods at eventide" were haunted by a growing fear that his grandchildren might be deprived of those "fulfilling experiences." Tom wrote, "I suppose it's these apprehensions which motivate my waking moments. I would have it no other way."[27]

Ahead of his time, Tom Bell articulated a view of conservation in words few others used until much later. He argued conservation was not simply an issue but should become a "way of life." He said, "You can't love game animals and hate predators; you can't conserve the water and waste the range; you can't build the forest and mine the farm." He saw the land as "all things on, over, and in the earth, teaching his readers to think of it as 'all one organism.'"[28]

In the spring of 1965, the Wyoming Wildlife Federation recruited Tom to be its president. The *Wyoming State Journal* made the announcement under a frontpage headline. "Tom Bell New President of Wildlife Group." The newspaper clipping is among Tom's papers at the American Heritage Center of the University of Wyoming. Tom's handwriting in the margin indicates the great significance the event held in his life. "This was the beginning of my career."

Throughout 1966 and 1967, Tom was determined to be taken seriously as a writer. "The good Lord and my creditor's willing, I hope to become a fulltime writer."[29] He repeatedly submitted manuscripts to national sportsmen and conservation magazines on topics ranging from sage grouse to fish rehabilitation and predator control. Editors repeatedly rejected them. He wrote his Aunt Lillian in December 1966 to tell her he needed "a job that will keep me going until I prove one way or another that I can do serious writing."[30]

Tom also revealed to Aunt Lillian "an idea in the back of my mind." It stemmed from the success he'd witnessed of the Colorado Open Space Coordinating Council. Founded in April of that year, it "was already a strong effective and well-organized group." Tom had begun the legal process for creating a non-profit and received the backing of the Wyoming Wildlife Federation and the Izaak Walton League. He was busy shopping the proposal to others including the League of Women Voters, the Wyoming Federated Garden Clubs, and a group of businesspeople.

> "Some of us here in the Rocky Mountain region have reason to believe that our open spaces, our mountain wilderness areas, our majestic natural scenery, and our other natural resources are a national

treasure. The battles to preserve them are here and it is we who live here that stand in the forefront of the battle ranks."

That idea in the back of Tom's head manifested itself in what is today the oldest independent conservation advocacy organization in Wyoming. The Wyoming Outdoor Coordinating Council was founded in March 1967. The most prominent name among those committing to the new organization was Mardy Murie. Already an icon among environmentalists, she was a national consultant for the Wilderness Society and an accomplished conservation writer who was also the widow of internationally renowned conservationist Olaus Murie. The group Tom assembled also included Dr. Oliver Scott, president of the Wyoming Audubon Society, Cheyenne businessman and Izaak Walton League activist Clayton Trosper, Ann Lindahl, state president of the League of Women Voters, prominent outfitter Les Shoemaker of Dubois, and Bruce Ward of Casper who would labor in that vineyard, side-by-side with Tom Bell for many years. Tom was named the organization's executive director.[31]

Tom's characteristic single-mindedness about employing good science in environmental decision-making and advocacy was central to the work of the Council as was the drive to aggressively defend Wyoming's cultural and outdoor resources. He continued to be a teacher and now his classroom was much larger. His new pupils were state legislators, the governor and the congressional delegation, state and federal land use agencies, community and business leaders, and the people of Wyoming. The curriculum was a growing body of scientific evidence that Wyoming's lifestyle was increasingly threatened by abuses of land, water, air, wildlife, and fishing resources. These were the infancy days of America's environmental consciousness and Tom Bell was its Godfather.

> *Oh, Beautiful for smoggy skies, insecticided grain,*
> *For strip-mined mountain's majesty above the asphalt plain.*
> *America, America, man sheds his waste on thee,*
> *And hides the pines with billboard signs, from sea to oily sea.*
> — George Carlin

"The birth of the modern Wyoming environmental movement occurred in Lander in the early 1970s as Tom Bell founded both *High Country News* and the Wyoming Outdoor Council. Bell's efforts were tremendous and provided the basis for much of the environmental legislation that now governs Wyoming." That was the judgment of one of Wyoming's astute political observers, Bill Sniffin of the *Wyoming State Journal*.[32] It would be unfair not to give some credit to Tom for spurring the development of another successful Wyoming environmental organization, the Powder River Basin Resource Council (PRBRC). It was Bell who first grasped the gathering threat to Wyoming land, air, and water and Wyoming's way of life. Tom had an old rancher friend who raised cattle on "ground zero" in Campbell County. Bell picked up the phone and called Bill Barlow. "Your way of life is threatened," Bell said bluntly. Barlow remembered, "I really didn't know what he was talking about."[33] He soon learned about massive coal and power plant development planned for this part of the state. Bell's warning led Barlow to organize the PRBRC.

If Tom Bell was the Godfather of the Wyoming environmental movement, the womb in which it developed was a growing national consciousness nurtured by a host of voices across the land.

"Say, the order of your time feels unjust and unsustainable, and yet massively entrenched," hypothesized science-fiction writer Kim Stanley Robinson in his book, *Ministries of the Future*, exploring a future of uncontrolled climate change.[34] Tom Bell may not have been the first to worry aloud about the phenomenon described by Robinson, but he was among them. Many of the country's early conservationists believed that if Americans "entrusted their government with the nation's resources, the government would provide future generations with the same or greater affluence as that enjoyed by the present generation."[35] Not many had vision sufficient to follow that blind trust to a logical conclusion, which is demonstrated by the 1964 compromise with the Sierra Club, "a necessary political evil," that allowed for the construction of the Glen Canyon Dam as part of the Colorado River drainage system.

Two generations later, climate change has resulted in the dam's water levels declining so significantly that there may soon be "no choice but to stop sending water through the turbines, killing power generation and depriving the grid of enough electricity annually to power about a quarter of a million Arizona homes. It would also drain between $100 million and $200 million annually from dam electricity sales, a chunk of which goes to fund endangered species recovery, salinity control, and water studies on the Colorado River."[36]

By the time Tom organized the Wyoming Outdoor Coordinating Council, some of the early environment sirens were angry about how much their voices had been ignored to the damage of the earth. Edward Abbey voiced their outrage in his 1968 *Desert Solitaire*.

> "Do not jump into your automobile next June and rush out to the Canyon country to see that which I have attempted to invoke in these pages. In the first place you can't see anything from a car; you've got to get out of the goddamned contraption and walk, better yet crawl on your hands and knees over the sandstone and through the thornbush and cactus. When traces of blood begin to mark your trail you'll see something, maybe. Probably not. In the second place, most of what I write about in this book is already gone or going under fast. This is not a travel guide but an elegy. A memorial. You're holding a tombstone in your hand. A bloody rock. Don't drop it on your foot. Throw it at something big and glassy. What do you have to lose?"[37]

Aldo Leopold, in whom Tom Bell found a soulmate, tried to teach the world of its interconnectedness. "A chesty bawl echoes from rimrock to rimrock, rolls down the mountain, and fades into the blackness of the night. It is a burst of wild, defiant sorrow and of contempt for all the adversities of the world." Leopold knew that sound and believed, "Only the mountain has lived long enough to listen objectively to the howl of a wolf." He vividly described what cinched his views about the interconnectedness of all things. It was, he remembered, the day he saw a wolf die. Back then Leopold self-described as "young and full of trigger-itch." His bullets were among those that killed a wolf that day. "We reached the old wolf in time to watch a fierce green dying in her eyes." Before that day, Leopold counted himself among outdoorsmen who believed "fewer wolves meant more deer; that no wolves would mean hunter's paradise." With the memory of that wolf's last breath stained in his memory, the conservationist wrote, "After seeing the green fire die, I sensed that neither wolf nor the mountain agreed with such a view."[38]

In 1960, before Congress passed the Wilderness Act of 1964, Wallace Stegner was one of the few who could see the preserved forests, rivers, deserts, and prairies as tangible resources, "mystical to the practical mind."[39]

In 1963, Sierra Club founder David Brower eulogized the Glen Canyon sacrifice. The dam built there was part of the Colorado River storage project the Sierra Club agreed not to oppose in a political compromise Brower came to regret. He accepted responsibility for the damage the Glen Canyon Dam did and implored environmentalists and others to see their complicity in ongoing threats from those "who have plans for the Colorado River whereby a natural menace becomes a natural resource."[40]

The year before, Rachel Carson grabbed the attention of an increasingly large audience. Her 1962 book, *Silent Spring*, is seen as "the single most important book in the birth of environmentalism," its enormous readership suggesting "environmentalism might become a movement with a broad constituency."[41] Carson wrote of the power of humans "to alter the nature of this world," demonstrated only recently, "within the moment in time represented by the present century."[42] She warned of the devastation wreaked by the "universal contamination of the environment" by nuclear testing and spraying pesticides and herbicides on crops and gardens.

> *"Along with the possibility of the extinction of mankind by nuclear war, the central problem of our age has therefore become the contamination of man's total environment."*

Tom Bell had been preaching similar sermons for years but finding the right pulpit in a conservative rural state, economically dependent on mining and agriculture, proved elusive. "Wyoming newspapers," Tom believed, "were almost single-mindedly dedicated to unquestioned growth and development."[43] Tom had his weekly column in the Lander newspaper. But it didn't reach beyond parts of Fremont County, leaving Tom wondering whether when that tree fell in the forest, had it made a sound. "If that was all Bell had ever written," Wyoming writer Geoff O'Gara suggested, "he might never have been known beyond the snug confines of the Wind River Valley."[44] Tom also wrote letters to the editors of newspapers around the state, but few were published; fewer yet as the term "environmentalist" began to be associated with loss of jobs and access to wild lands. He wrote letters to decision makers like the one he wrote the newly elected Governor of Wyoming, Stan Hathaway. A copy of the January 21, 1967, letter is among his papers. Across the top are the handwritten words of a frustrated Tom Bell. "My very first letter to Hathaway. It was not answered and never heeded."[45]

Then the Cuyahoga River caught fire. June 22, 1969. It was a stunning sight. A river so polluted that it was ablaze. The widely disseminated photographs were worth far more than the proverbial thousand words. Before that happened, Tom was aware of the power of the written word and now he desperately sought a place for his words and warnings to be published.

That was when Pat Hall, editor of *Camping News Weekly*, paid a visit to his friend Tom Bell. Pat Hall was an exceptional journalist and accomplished photographer. His newspaper was, he said, a means of helping campers, hunters, fishermen, and other outdoor enthusiasts "find special spots where the camping family can enjoy a certain amount of solitude."[46] The publication was struggling financially and looking for ways to increase circulation and sell more advertising. Hall invited Bell to use his newspaper as a vehicle to promote the work of the Wyoming Outdoor Council.[47]

Tom was visionary enough to recognize this could be the opportunity he'd been seeking. *Camping News Weekly* could be that "pulpit," he needed to widen the circulation of his thoughts while exposing a wider audience to WOC's views and educate and encourage the public to be involved in environmental causes. In May of 1969, Tommie Bell bought the first ever subscription to *Camping News Weekly*, a gift for her husband.[48] By August of 1969, Tom was the owner of the newspaper. He was excited enough about its potential to begin investing his own money to keep the publication alive.

"I continued to put more of my money into the paper," he recalled in an August 21, 1971, memorandum, "until I had a total of almost $30,000 invested. Others had invested cash or services in the amount of $14,600, and we had made bank loans in the amount of $9,500." Yet, by January 1970, there was not enough cash on hand to pay an editor. And so it was that the January 2, 1970, edition of *Camping News Weekly* lists Tom Bell as its editor.[49] He had invested too much of himself and his money to see it go under and beside that, "There was no one else to do it, so I took over as editor." His first editorial predicted there would be "tremendous change." He was speaking optimistically about what he saw was "the development of an ecological conscience in a growing percentage of decision makers," but could just as easily have been writing about the changes ahead in his own life.

A month later, *Camping News Weekly* became *High Country News*.[50]

"*High Country News* is a testament to Tom's vision," said Craig Thompson as he looked back over more than three decades of the newspaper's history. Thompson was a National Wildlife Federation board member who nominated Tom for NWF's Conservationist of the Year in 2002. While presenting the award, he said Tom "saw the need for a vehicle to expose and address the threats to this region 30 years ago. The paper has done more to make people understand and fight the threat to the health of the West than anything I can think of. It is Tom's tool for molding the activists of tomorrow."[51]

At first *High Country News* looked like a cross between *Camping News Weekly* and a publication advocating environmental causes. Before long it transitioned completely to the latter. In tandem with WOC, environmentalists now had a bullhorn. The two shied away from no controversy. Out for a hike one summer day, Bell happened upon a fence line on what he knew to be public land. He discovered Herman Werner, the influential rancher and president of the powerful Wyoming Stockgrowers Association, had built 69 miles of fencing cordoning off those public lands. He wrote scathing articles about Werner and his fences and demanded the Bureau of Land Management tear them down. At a hearing on the controversy, Werner strolled up to Tom and said threateningly, "I don't like what you've been writing about me, young man." Tom didn't blink. Looking the large man in the eye, he said, "I didn't build those damned fences, Herman."[52]

On another occasion while flying in a small plane over the Red Desert, Tom looked below and saw a bulldozer tearing up ground along what he knew to be the historic Oregon Trail. He saw they were clearing land for a phone line. When the plane landed at Lester C. Hunt Field in Lander, Tom made his way to a phone booth. Somehow, he was able to obtain the home phone number for the president of American Telephone and Telegraph. It was a Sunday afternoon when Tom dialed his number. In no uncertain terms, Tom demanded the bulldozer be halted. And it was. Tom's characteristic persistence worked.[53]

Tom and WOC also waded bravely into the swamp of grazing fees, challenging state and federal agencies for setting the fees lower than market. Ranchers are a disproportionately small segment of the population but have always had a disproportionately large influence on Wyoming politics. A University of Wyoming law school professor wrote about it in a book provocatively entitled *The Western Range Revisited: Removing Livestock from Public Lands to Conserve Native Biodiversity.*

Debra Donahue expressed her opinion that a "fundamental reason for the western range problem," is the "influence in politics and western society of stockmen."[54] As if bent on proving her point, the powerful President of the Wyoming State Senate, Jim Twiford, promptly introduced a bill to close the UW law school in retaliation for one of its professors expressing an opinion. Senator Twiford argued, "We've got some unlicensed, unbridled folks over there that ought to be smarter than to be biting the hand that's feeding them."[55]

Influential stock growers were not accustomed to being openly challenged by anyone. Tom Bell was unaccustomed to remaining silent. At a 1973 hearing on grazing fees, he followed a number of ranchers who stood at the podium before him and angrily opposed increasing fees. "Coolly and without emotion, Bell stands among the hostile gathering. 'I think the fees ought to be raised,' he says evenly." Tom said, "They may hate me, but they also respect me."[56] He didn't have much evidence to prove the latter.

WOC and *HCN* also took on the mining industry, advocating for higher severance taxes. They challenged the timber industry when they opposed clearcutting of forests. The list of those with whom they were willing to butt heads continued to grow when they demanded more wilderness lands and the protection of the Red Desert.

Tom Bell and other Wyoming environmentalists joined concerned people around the country in responding to Wisconsin's U.S. Senator Gaylord Nelson's call for nationwide teach-ins by celebrating the first Earth Day on April 22, 1970. *High Country News* marked the occasion by shining a light on near-secret plans to build massive pipelines to divert water from the Green River to the Platte River Basin. The newspaper exposed the project and informed its readers that plans included the construction of large reservoirs that would "drown expensive private ranch properties" and "many miles of superlative, blue ribbon trout fishing streams and irreplaceable big game winter range."

Bell disclosed the fact that the plan was completed at "an almost secret meeting." Governor Stan Hathaway and State Engineer Floyd Bishop attended along with "other ranking state officials" and "a select, handpicked group, supposedly sympathetic to the plan."[57]

Readers of the dramatic Earth Day 1970 exposé were given three takeaway messages. First, they learned for the first time of a proposal that had significant environmental impact, though it was in an advanced stage with no public input. That highlighted the second takeaway. The National Environmental Protection Act and its provisions requiring Environmental Impact Statements was not yet law and Wyoming had few environmental protection laws. There were no land use planning statutes, no requirements for public input on a project with significant environmental implications, and no environmental protection agency. The only existing state agencies were there to promote development.

The third message was subliminal. As Tom wrote that day, "None of this ever reached the state press. The public is unaware of the political by-play." That had to change. This was the beginning of a new day when policymakers learned they would have to answer for their backroom antics. Politicians who were astute enough to read between the lines understood it just got a lot harder to do the public's business behind closed doors because of *High*

Country News and the Wyoming Outdoor Council. This was the underpinning of a long-standing, bitter conflict between Bell and Hathaway.

While there were reasons to be optimistic about the newspaper's growing role in environmental affairs, the financial wolf was always lurking near the door. With hindsight, the first sign of impending doom came when Tom announced, "The time has come when my wife and I must commence the move from our little ranch back to town." Reading his March 19, 1971, column you can sense Tom was trying to put the best face possible on what must have been an anguished decision. In September, he disclosed why he sold his beloved ranch. It was to keep *High Country News* afloat. In a memorandum to "Concerned Individuals," Tom said there were "many reasons. The most compelling was that we had mortgaged it to put money into the paper. The note was coming due and although we could have renewed the note for another four years, we felt it was best not to do so."[58] By then he had already sold his "small herd of registered shorthorns" and the only continuing source of income was a small disability pension from his war injury. However, Tom was about to be handed an opportunity to demonstrate the critical role the newspaper could play in keeping the public informed and animated.

On May Day 1971, a couple of high school students were hiking in Jackson Canyon, a rugged area on the west end of Casper Mountain. It was known as a roosting spot for eagles wintering along the North Platte River. They stumbled upon a gruesome sight, the carcasses of eleven Bald Eagles and five Golden Eagles along with another "that was partially paralyzed and near death." The search expanded and on May 11, another Bald Eagle was discovered dead four miles east of the initial discovery.[59]

State Representative John F. Turner, then a PhD candidate for a degree in ecology at the University of Michigan, was an expert on eagles. Turner took care of the paralyzed eagle and nursed it gradually back to good health. But Turner was alarmed. He said that among these birds that mate for life, there were less than 200 mated pairs believed to be living in just six states. They were a severely endangered species and some of the dead eagles may well have been among the dozen mated pairs roosting in Wyoming.

By the end of May the tragedy worsened considerably. As the search continued, the carcasses of 23 more Bald and Golden Eagles were discovered, thought to have been poisoned. It was suspected 35 more had been shot. Once again Tom Bell crossed paths and swords with Herman Werner.

Werner's son-in-law was Van Irvine, a rancher James Michener once called "an authentic westerner, one who has been involved in most of the situations cattlemen face."[60] Van Irvine grew up hating eagles. As a youngster in the 1930s, he'd rope Golden Eagles when he found them in vulnerable positions where they could not quickly take flight, such as in the bottom of a deep ravine. Back then, Irvine would drag them to higher ground and release them. By the time he was in his mid-20s, he began shooting the birds "whenever possible."[61] Irvine called the eagle killings a "habit" he'd learned from his father-in-law, Herman Werner. They saw the birds as a threat to livestock and, therefore, their livelihood on the Diamond Ring Ranch.

A few years later, Irvine was approached by the owner of the Bolton Ranch between Saratoga and Rawlins along the North Platte River. It was for sale. He wasn't much interested. "Too many eagles and coyotes I suspected."[62] But his father-in-law was "enthralled" with the ranch. After the property was deeded to him, Werner and his son-in-law flew over the ranch "and we saw coyotes in packs and eagles by the score."[63]

Werner built some fencing and put several thousand lambs on the land. Irvine never learned to like the ranch. Werner did. His son-in-law said Werner "kept bringing in sheep and feeding the coyotes."[64] According to Irvine, his top ranch hand came one day and told him they had only one lamb left. "Herman, like any red-blooded American entrepreneur, tried to do something about it. He purchased a helicopter, hired a pilot and a gunner, secured a pick-up load of ammunition, and went to work."[65]

It wasn't long after that those high school hikers stumbled upon that grisly find. There wasn't much of a mystery about who did this. Herman Werner was proud of his accomplishment. During a Natrona County Woolgrowers Association dinner the previous November he displayed a photograph "of a pile of dead eagles 6 or 8 feet high and 10 or 12 feet in diameter." Van Irvine said, "The shit hit the fan a few days later."[66] The photo vanished. Sometime later a man showed up unannounced at the offices of the Department of the Interior in Washington. "I'm the man you're looking for," he said. It was James Vogan, the pilot of the helicopter used in the shootings.[67]

Wyoming Senator Gale W. McGee, who didn't get along with Werner much better than did Bell, ordered a Senate investigation. Hearings were held in June and December of 1971 before McGee's Subcommittee on Agriculture, Environmental, and Consumer Protection of the Appropriations Committee. Receiving a grant of immunity, Vogan testified, admitting he flew the helicopter while others, to use Vogel's term, "sluiced" the birds from the aircraft. The term refers to the unsportsmanlike practice of shooting a sitting bird.[68] He acknowledged witnessing the shooting deaths of "over 500 eagles" and knew of others. He claimed he had personally never shot a bird from a helicopter. "This does not say that I have not taken a shot at an eagle from the ground, because I have. But I missed."[69]

Testimony further disclosed 222 coyotes, 6 elk, 5 bobcats, a bear and several deer and antelope were also killed in the operations.[70] Vogan told the Committee of Herman Werner's involvement. Werner, he said, paid $25 per eagle and $50 for a coyote, fox, or bobcat. Later Vogan told the press that at least 770 eagles had been shot. John Turner worried this slaughter "could push the eagle to the horizon of oblivion."[71]

In addition to the shootings, other birds had been poisoned. Placed in the carcasses of antelope, thallium sulphate caused the deaths of eagles feeding on the dead animals. A witness at the December hearing said he knew of sheep men who would "drive across grazing areas tossing it out left and right."[72] Natrona County Attorney John Burke said carcasses of seven antelope found on the Diamond Ring ranch were baited with enough thallium sulfates to kill all the animals in the state.[73]

In early July, the frontpage headline of *High Country News* announced, "Eagles' Death Are Vindicated."[74] A few weeks later the *HCN* headline flipped. "Eagles' Deaths NOT Vindicated."[75] The first story reported that four persons had been charged, including Van Irvine, who had succeeded his father-in-law to the presidency of the Wyoming Stockgrowers Association. The Interior Department's Assistant Secretary for Fish and Wildlife refused to file more serious charges. Thus, the defendants were charged with a total of 114 misdemeanor state game violations. The story appearing with the second headline reported Van Irvine pleaded nolo contendere (no contest) to the 29 charges filed against him on the condition that the charges against the other three men be dismissed. He was fined the minimum amount on all charges, $675 plus $4 court costs and given no jail time.[76] John Turner called it "token justice."

Accusations against Werner were more serious, but it first appeared he would not be charged at all. Even though serious federal crimes were implicated, the U.S. Attorney in Wyoming "balked" at prosecuting Werner. Richard V. Thomas figured no Wyoming jury would ever convict him, so why bother.[77] Nathaniel Reed, the newly confirmed Assistant Secretary of the Interior for Fish and Wildlife and Parks under President Richard Nixon, refused to allow Werner to walk away. He appealed to U.S. Attorney General Elliott Richardson. Werner was charged. However, he would never be convicted.

Herman Werner's trial was set to begin on October 29, 1973. He died on August 8, after the truck he was driving inexplicably veered into the path of an oncoming truck outside of Rawlins.[78]

A subtext to the drama was the deepening disdain Tom Bell had for Governor Hathaway and, in equal measure, Hathaway for Bell. WOC petitioned the Governor to conduct "a comprehensive investigation of the whole matter of the use of poisonous substances." Hathaway replied by taking a shot at WOC, blaming their lobbyists for ignoring his bill to address the subject, saying WOC was too focused on killing his Green River water diversion project. Bell fired back. Hathaway's pesticide bill, Tom said, was "riddled with special interest amendments" and that was what brought about its defeat.

In the midst of the eagle controversy, the Governor told the 1971 Wyoming Stockgrowers convention, "I like eagles, but…" and then qualified that by telling them ranchers did not get enough credit for how they "nurtured wildlife through the years." Hathaway demeaned "the radical conservationists" as "either newcomers or drugstore cowboys." Bell responded. He called the Governor "an anachronism in a world suddenly attuned to environmental matters, a dinosaur who doesn't know his time has come."[79]

This feud would get worse before it got better.

In March of 1973, the *Denver Post* called *High Country News* "the strongest environmental voice in the Rocky Mountain empire." Achieving that status did not ward off the financial wolves. In that same month, Tom decided it was time to throw in the towel. "I write this with a great deal of regret and dismay," his March 2nd *HCN* editorial began. "*High Country News* will cease publication with the March 30 issue." Tom laid out all his cards. He'd sold his ranch and put $30,000 of his own money into the paper. He had a $7,500 outstanding bank note. In the last two years he'd been paid only $910.97 for his fulltime work. The small staff had been barely paid anything, some worked as volunteers.[80] In his desperation, he asked himself, "Why the hell am I doing this? I'm losing friends, I'm going broke, we're watching the best of Wyoming and the West disappear and no one sems to care."[81]

Part of the problem was Bell's principled stance against selling ads in the paper. "Frankly," he wrote in an *HCN* October 27, 1972, editorial, "I would rather struggle and starve than be compromised." The other issue was too few subscribers. When Tom took over *Camping News Weekly*, it had a subscriber base of 3,000. Because they signed up primarily for camping news and not environmental advocacy, in the first year after it became *High Country News*, only 1,771 continued to be willing to pay the $5 subscription cost. By the time Tom announced it would cease publication, there were still only 2,400 subscribers.[82]

Nonetheless, Tom worked hard to create a relationship with his readers, what he called "a bond between people from across a far-flung land." He said, "The warmth that flows through us is an expression of the feeling many people have for the Good Earth that sustains us all."[83] Many of those with whom the paper established that bond were aghast at the idea its voice would be silenced. Louise Dunlop of the Environmental Policy Center in Washington, DC, called it, "the most vital citizen voice on environmental issues."[84] Others decided to put their money into saving *HCN*. Checks began pouring in from around the country. They were postmarked Santa Fe, Worthington, Ohio, New York City, a $100 check from a state legislator in Montana, ten dollars from a couple in Powell, Wyoming, the Audubon Society sent $200, and before long Bell had received $7,500 in cash and pledges for another eight thousand dollars. By July, Tom had received $29,467.75 in cash and was now more than able to pay off the bank loan. *High Country News* would live on.

As 1973 gave way to 1974, Tom flirted with the idea of running against Stan Hathaway for Governor. There were rumors the incumbent might seek an unprecedented third term. Tom bought a new suit for his announcement as he started sending out feelers to close friends and planning his campaign.[85] Don Fausett, an old friend from Laramie, urged Tom to run. "There is no one in the state of Wyoming who is better qualified than you to be our governor."[86] Another friend urged Tom "to look at it as a realist, not an idealist." A political campaign, he warned, would "run a real risk of destroying your effectiveness" and ruin his reputation as the most renowned environmentalist in the state. [87]

A contest between Hathaway, who considered Tom Bell a "radical distorter and malcontent," and Bell, who said the Governor had "a facility for duping the people" would have been a barn burner.[88] Alas, it was not to be. Hathaway opted not to run again. As he finished his second term and prepared to leave the governorship, Hathaway was asked what he planned to do first when he became a private citizen. "I'm gonna go to Lander and punch Tom Bell in the nose," he is rumored to have said. Hathaway's top staffer, Jack Speight, said he didn't hear Stan say that, "but I'd be surprised if he didn't. Tom Bell was such a pain in our backside in those days."[89]

Noteworthy is that Wyoming's voters selected Democrat Ed Herschler over Dick Jones, the pro-development Republican nominee, signaling they preferred a governor more attuned to a growing concern about the impact of mining on the air, water, and land. Tom Bell was arguably responsible for that new attitude.

There may have been another, more likely reason Bell declined to run. The stress of keeping *HCN* afloat had taken its toll on him. Tom was on the verge of a nervous breakdown. He had been an effective voice for the cause but using that voice had cost him many of his friends. He had saved the newspaper from financial collapse, but it had cost him his ranch, and at 50 years of age, he was unable to assure his family a financially secure future. Despite having created an effective environmental advocacy organization and saving *High Country News*, Tom's innate sense of pessimism got the best of him. He was "discouraged and dismayed" with "an economic and political system wedded to ever more growth and consumption." Tom foresaw a day when that system would crash.[90] But he feared he might crash first. "No one, not even my wife," Tom later admitted, "knew how close I came to going over the brink in those months of 1974."[91]

Tom had not so much reached a fork in the road as he'd found himself on the edge of a cliff. "It was either continue and destroy myself or turn completely away and seek solace and recovery. I chose the latter and went to Oregon for nine years."[92]

In the context of the chaos of his life in those days, he also discovered his religious roots, walking to the front of a Lander church and announcing publicly he was "giving my life to Christ." Tom became a born-again Christian.[93] Now he was burdened by the thought that he was "too inextricably tied to *HCN*, Wyoming, and the hometown area of Lander" and needed to break those connections to dedicate his life as he felt called to do.[94]

In June 1974 Tom submitted his resignation to a stunned WOC board. "The reactions were startled disbelief, deep regret at such a loss, and appreciation for all he has done for this state and the environmental movement."[95] Bell then turned *HCN* over to Bruce Hamilton and his spouse, Joan Nice. Finally, Tom informed his readers that, "Through the last several years, I have felt my spiritual batteries slowly being drained." It was time for a change. He said he was "afraid for my family," which with Alan, David, and Jim out on their own, consisted of his wife and the three young children he and Tommie had adopted, Vic, Rachel, and Chris. Tom wanted to return to the land. He felt a self-sufficient lifestyle was best for his family where they could grow their own food and live frugally.[96] He and Tommie acquired 40 acres in Oregon, near the Idaho border. "It will be good to work with dirt under my fingernails, although I will miss the printer's ink." The *Denver Post* waved goodbye. "So, Monday, the Wind River Mountains towering above them, Tom and Muriel Bell and their three youngsters will head down the Oregon Trail."[97] Getting an early start the morning of August 12, Tom loaded his belongings and his family in his pickup and left the only home he'd ever known.

Halfway, Oregon was a small town in Baker County, named because its post office is midway between Pine and Cornucopia. Only a couple of hundred souls lived there. The Bell's farm was just outside of town. They lived in a small trailer house with no running water and bathed in a creek that ran across the farmland. A small garden and a few chickens fed the family. He also returned to the classroom, teaching science to high school kids. Most of all, Tom got his wish for plenty of dirt under his fingernails.

As Tom and his family drove out of Lander, the *Wyoming State Journal* hoped the break was simply a timeout. "Certainly, he deserves to put down his sword for a while. And he'll enjoy these years in Oregon tilling the soil and writing those long-delayed articles. But when he's finished growing his crops and his ire is stirred up again by what he sees is happening back here, we hope he'll return. Wyoming needs him."[98]

It wasn't long before Tom's ire was stirred. The following April, word about Hathaway came to Halfway. President Gerald Ford had nominated Tom's nemesis to be Secretary of the Interior. Bell promptly sat down and wrote the President to object. "I lived through eight years of Hathaway's governorship and find little to commend him for the post he now seeks."[99] Over the objections of nearly every environmental organization in the country, Hathaway's nomination was, nonetheless, confirmed by the Senate.

Beset with a host of personal problems and suffering from clinical depression, Hathaway was hospitalized after a nervous breakdown and was forced to resign after having served as Interior Secretary for little more than one month. Years later, Tom looked back on his life and saw the parallel with Hathaway's, remembering how close he had come to just such a fate during roughly the same period. Bell told Bruce Hamilton many years later, "I guess neither one of us was good for the other."[100]

Sometime in 1983, Tom and Tommie began to think about heading home to Lander. While they were contemplating their move, the board of the High Country Foundation, overseeing *HCN* operations, was debating their own move. The new leadership concluded it would be best for the paper's future to move its headquarters from Lander to Paonia, Colorado. After two days of agonizing debate and deliberation, the board was deadlocked. Then, Wyoming State Representative Lynn Dickey (see chapter 5), a board member, decided the move would be best for *HCN*, changed her vote, and the motion passed.[101]

Tom thought it was the "irony of ironies" that as he was driving "a U-Haul with all my possessions back into Lander, a pickup loaded with all the history, the artifacts, and the records of *High Country News* was headed south out of Lander to Paonia."[102] Despite his disappointment, Tom knew it was for the best, and took solace in believing, "My dream would live on." Indeed, it did. *High Country News* is flourishing as it maintains a reputation as a sure-footed source of environmental truth and advocacy just as Tom Bell intended when it all started more than half a century ago. What was true in 1981 when Susan J. Harlow wrote a master's thesis about *High Country News* and its evolution, is just as true today.

> "Tom Bell's legacy still remains in the basic pro-environmental philosophy, its concern for the west, the informal tone, and the goal of providing people with the information they need to make informed decisions on issues critical to the West."[103]

Reflected in the new leadership at *High Country News* and the Wyoming Outdoor Council was both Tom Bell's successful mentorship and his new status as the patron saint of Wyoming's environmental movement. His constructive pessimism not only led him to create the movement but also inspired a form of discipleship among many of the best and brightest thinkers, organizers, and doers in the state. His time in Oregon gave them occasion to develop into leaders in their own right. Writing about Tom in 1987, not long after his return from Oregon, Geoff O'Gara found him "clearly pleased that many of the things he envisioned have come to pass, though a little embarrassed when homage is paid him."[104] His humility was on display when he spoke to a WOC gathering celebrating the organization's 20th anniversary on September 12, 1987. "I was only one of many people in 1967 who saw strength in numbers," Tom said. Recounting the environmental threats seen "by a number of us," Bell said in his self-effacing manner, "It didn't take much of a catalyst to set the process in motion."[105] Those around him who witnessed the many sacrifices Tom had made over many years knew better.

When Tom was named "Outstanding Alumnus" of UW's College of Arts and Sciences, Mac Blewer of the Wyoming Outdoor Council remembered the catalyst who made it all possible. "He was totally alone when he started out there." Blewer recounted Bell's sacrifices and the hardships he endured to create the movement, adding, "History will prove Tom Bell is one of Wyoming's great heroes."[106] Presenting Tom the National Wildlife Federation "Conservationist of the Year" award in 2002, NWF president Mark Van Putten summed it up. "He has waged dozens of successful battles to protect the wonders of Wyoming, the Northern Rockies, and the Northern Great Plains, inspiring and empowering others to follow in his footsteps."[107]

With the disclaimer that "I don't want to leave anybody out inadvertently," Bart Koehler, WOC's third executive director, provided a list of those whom Tom Bell had mentored into leadership in his remarks for the organization's 40th birthday. "Mary Black, Les and Alice Shoemaker, Art Fawcett, Martha Christensen, Bill Barlow, Dick Randall, Ed and Rosemary Schunk, Hank Phibbs and Leslie Peterson, Laney Hicks, Ron Beiswenger, Coleen Cabot, Dennis Knight, Mac Blewer, Marjane Ambler, Lorna Wilkes, Lynn Dickey, Wildman John Perry Barlow," also, adding as he spoke, Mardy Murie, Keith Becker, John Turner, Jack Pugh, Joyce and Mike Evans, and Bruce Hamilton and Joan Nice.

There are a lot of other names that could be included. However, the author of this book will not attempt to add to that list out of the same fear Bart felt, that "I don't want to leave anybody out inadvertently." Suffice it to say there are many more flowers in the garden Tom Bell planted and nourished.

Among the heirs of Tom's endeavors, the importance of his work was celebrated. Paul Larimer called him "the canary in the coal mine" and taught his own young son that Tom was a legend who "rode around Wyoming on the back of a Pronghorn, hell bent on saving the West." Activist Todd Guenther said, "He was the first person I knew who actually spit nails." Bart Koehler called Tom "the Paul Revere of Wyoming." Keith Becker, who followed Tom and preceded Koehler as executive director at WOC, proclaimed, "No one could threaten him. He was absolutely fearless and confrontational. He acted as though he had nothing to lose." Becker said, "Most of us mellow with age, but not Tom. He didn't know how to back up, and God bless him for it."

Writer M.J. Clark said, "We in Lander just think of him as Tom Bell, but people around the nation think of him as TOM BELL."

Tom wore his "emeritus" status very well to the end of his days. Forever the tireless advocate, he counseled governors and senators about ongoing environmental challenges, while encouraging a long string of new leaders to pick up his mantle. He had grown comfortable with the fact that, as he said shortly before he died on August 30, 2016, "I have as many friends as enemies." Tom proudly referred to himself as "a maverick and a gadfly."

With his wife gone and his own health deteriorating, Tom wrote a thank you letter to the *High Country News* board and staff, expressing alarm at the failure of the world to deal with what he saw as the coming apocalypse of climate change, which he recognized earlier than most was to be "the biggest and most complex scientific and political challenge the world has ever faced."[108]

> *"I feel vindicated in all my dreams and beliefs and writings. However, my vindication is a bitter pill. All I have stood for and worked so hard to achieve now seems to be a fruitless effort. A changing societal and political culture, a lack of political will, and a great loss of moral integrity in just the last 30 years has led us to where we are. It is now no consolation in the old baseball metaphor, 'Nature always bats last.'"*[109]

Among Tom Bell's last wishes was to have his ashes given to the wind in the place he'd gone to heal his body and spirit upon returning from the war. It was a typically windy day at Oregon Buttes in the Red Desert when John Monczynski walked to a steep cliff carrying the urn. At that moment, as if to post as an honor guard, a large Golden Eagle swooped down, landed on a rock jutting from the cliff nearby, watching as Tom's ashes were released into a suddenly gentle breeze.[110]

Endnotes

1. Kerry Brophy, "Bell adds UW honor to awards trove," unidentified publication, Bell papers, box 1, folder: "Tom's Papers," AHC
2. Id.
3. *History of the Union Pacific Coal Mines*, 154
4. Letter from Tom to Katrina Vanden Heuvel, editor, *The Nation*, May 15, 2012, Bell papers, box 3, folder: "Family Correspondence," AHC
5. Quote attributed to *Denver Post*, March 18, 1973, Bell papers, box 1, folder "Tom's Papers," AHC
6. The Army Air Force was the predecessor of the U.S. Air Force. The former was created in 1941, the latter took its place in 1947. The Army Air Force controlled all Army aviation throughout WWII
7. Letter from Tom to Karen Roles, March 7, 2011, Bell papers, box 9, folder "1950-2014," AHC
8. Letter to "Ryan" from Tom Bell, March 10, 1996, Bell papers, box 1, folder "Armed Services," AHC
9. "An Italian tablecloth/bedspread," Tom's notes, Undated, Bell's papers, box 12, folder: "455th Bomb Group," AHC
10. Ambrose, *The Wild Blue*, 124
11. Ambrose, Id., 108
12. Ambrose, supra., 100
13. "Local Veteran Interviewed for Documentary, *Lander Journal*, February 9, 2005, A-8
14. Tom's notes, Bell papers, box 1, folder "Armed Services," AHC
15. Lillian Schrock, "Wyoming Conservationist Tom Bell Dies in Lander," https://trib.com/news/state-and-regional/famed-wyoming-conservationist-tom-bell-dies-in-lander/article_bc98a3e5-bef7-5d92-b9ca-4e36485b8397.html#tncms-source=login, accessed April 28, 2022
16. 742nd Bombardment Squadro Historical Records,June 1944, box 12, folder :"Bill Beck," AHC
17. Letter from Tom to Karen Roles, March 7, 2011, Bell papers, box 9, folder "1950-2014," AHC
18. Hardy, *Wyoming University*, 146
19. Letter to Tom from the USDA, June 21, 1945, Bell papers, box 1, folder "War Department Correspondence," AHC
20. Letter from Tom to Dr. Reed W. Fautin, April 19, 1950, Bell papers, folder: "Correspondence," AHC
21. Letter from Tom to Charles Hanscum, August 15, 1951, Box 2, folder "Correspondence," AHC
22. Letter from Tom to State Representative A.J. Hardendorf, January 30, 1957, Bell papers, box 2, folder "Correspondence, AHC
23. Tom's notes, undated, box 1, folder: "Personal," AHC
24. Bell, "The Last Great Defining Moment," April 2012, Bell papers, box 2, folder: "Correspondence," AHC
25. "High Country by Tom Bell, *Wyoming State Journal*, January 17, 1964, 3
26. Letter from Tom to R.W. Pratt and James F. Powers, November 17, 1959, Bell papers,

box 1, folder: "Correspondence," AHC
27. Paul Larmer, "High Country News Founder, Tom Bell, passes," September 30, 2016, includes reprint of a 1970 "High Country by Tom Bell" column, https://www.hcn.org/issues/48.16/tom-bell-High-Country-News-founder-passes, accessed May 1, 2022
28. "High Country by Tom Bell," *Wyoming State Journal*, February 25, 1960, 3
29. Column, "High Country," *Wyoming State Journal*, June 16, 1966, 4
30. Letter from Tom to Aunt Lillian, December 11, 1966, Bell papers, box 2, folder: "Family Correspondence," AHC
31. "Organized Wyoming Outdoor Co-ordinating Council, *Wyoming State Journal*, March 9, 1967, 1
32. Bill Sniffin, "A Front Row Seat," *Wyoming State Journal*, December 21, 1981, A-2
33. "Powder River council rides herd on coal," *High Country News*, November 21, 1975, 12
34. Robinson, *Ministries for the Future*, 124
35. Stoll, U.S. *Environmentalism Since 1945*, 10
36. "Powell's looming power problem," *High Country News*, April 11, 2022, https://www.hcn.org/articles/south-water-powells-looming-power-problem, accessed May 12, 2022
37. Abbey, *Desert Solitaire*, xii, 51-52, 54-57
38. Leopold, *A Sand County Almanac*, 129-133, 203-205
39. Stegner, *The Sound of Mountain Water*, 145-155
40. Brower, Foreword in Eliot Porter's *The Place No One Knew: Glen Canyon on the Colorado*, Sierra Club Books (1963), 7-9
41. Stoll, U.S. *Environmentalism Since 1945*, 76
42. Carson, *Silent Spring*, 5
43. Memorandum September 20, 1971, Bell papers, box9, folder: "1946-2014," AHC
44. Geoff O'Gara, "Saga of a High Country Newsman," *Sierra*, March/April 1987, 72
45. Letter from Tom to Governor Hathaway, January 21, 1967, Bell papers, box 9, folder: "1946-2014," AHC
46. Pat Hall, Editorial, *Camping News Weekly*, May 2, 1969, 2
47. Bell, "Memorandum," August 21, 1971, Bell papers, box 9, folder "1946-2014," AHC
48. Harlow, "High Country News: Survival and Change," 6
49. *Camping News Weekly*, January 2, 1970, 2
50. *High Country News*, February 6, 1970
51. National Wildlife Federation news release, March 5, 2002, Bell papers, box 1, "Tom's Papers," AHC
52. Charlie Meyers, "Tom Bell: Defender of Environment," *Denver Post*, March 18, 1973, 57
53. Todd Guenther, Wyoming Outdoor Council panel, Conservation Cafeteria, December 11, 2011, https://www.youtube.com/watch?v=MtzHeNHsqWQ, accessed April 19, 2022
54. Donahue, The Western Range Revisited, 67
55. Katharine Collins, "A prof takes on the sacred cow," *High Country News*, February 28, 2000, https://www.hcn.org/issues/173/5582, accessed May 19, 2022
56. Charlie Meyers, "Tom Bell: Defender of Environment," *Denver Post*, March 18,

1973, 57
57 "Wyoming's Environmental Problems Are Not Unique," *High Country News*, April 22, 1970, 1
58 Memorandum, "To: Concerned Individuals," September 20, 1971, Bell papers, box 9, folder "1946-2014," AHC
59 Tom Ball, "Wyoming Eagles Die Mysteriously," *High Country News*, May 14, 1971, 1
60 Van Irvine, *Anybody Can be Slow*, book jacket.
61 Letter, Van Irvine to L.J. Hunter, August 20, 1992, 1, copy provided to the author by Hunter.
62 Letter, Van Irvine to L.J. Hunter, 6.
63 Letter, Van Irvine to L.J. Hunter, 6.
64 Irvine, *Anybody Can be Slow*, 298.
65 Letter, Van Irvine to L.J. Hunter, 7.
66 Letter from Van Irvine to L.J. Hunter, 7
67 Dennis Drabelle, *Unfair Game*, undated, http://archive.audubonmagazine.org/archives/archives0801.html, accessed September 18, 2015, no longer accessible.
68 "Sluicing the Eagles," *TIME*, August 16, 1971, http://www.time.com/printout/08816877209.html, accessed September 9, 2015, no longer accessible.
69 "Sluicing the Eagles," 153.
70 Holzinger, *The Eagle Killings*.
71 "Sheepmen vs. Eagles-Slaughter in the Sky," *LIFE*, August 20, 1971, 35.
72 "Predator Control and Related Problems," Senate Hearings, 4.
73 Holzinger, *The Eagle Killings*.
74 "Eagle's Deaths Are Vindicated," *High Country News*, June 25, 1971, 1
75 "Eagles' Deaths NOT Vindicated," *High Country News*, July 23, 1971, 1
76 Holzinger, *The Eagle Killings*.
77 Drabelle, *Unfair Game*.
78 Irvine, *Anybody Can Be Slow*, 301.
79 Tom Bell, "High Country," *High Country News*, June 25, 1971, 2
80 Tom Bell, "High Country," *High Country News*, March 2, 1973, 3
81 Todd Wilkinson, "Ahead of Their Time," essay entitled "Tom Bell: Of Ink and the Patron Saint," 59
82 Harlow, *High Country News: Survival and Change*, 38
83 Tom Bell, "High Country," *High Country News*, March 30, 1973, 3
84 Jeff Stansbury and Edward Flateau, *Los Angeles Times Syndicate*, News Release, April 4, 1973, Bell papers, box 1, folder "Clippings," AHC
85 Bruce Hamilton, Wyoming Outdoor Council panel, Conservation Cafeteria, December 11, 2011, https://www.youtube.com/watch?v=MtzHeNHsqWQ , accessed April 19, 2022
86 Letter from Fausett to Bell, February 18, 1974, Bell papers, box 1, folder "Personal," AHC
87 Handwritten letter (signature indecipherable), from Gaviota, California, March 15, 1974, Bell papers, box 1, folder "Tom's papers," AHC
88 Hathaway quote from Stansbury and Flattau, supra. Bell quote from *High Country News*, June 25, 1971, 3
89 Author's telephone interview with Speight, July 13, 2022

90 "Tom Bell Leaving Lander," *Wyoming State Journal*, July 8, 1974, 2
91 Letter from Tom Bell to Bruce Hamilton and Joan Nice, July 12, 2005, Bell papers, box 3, folder: "Hamilton, Bruce and Joan, AHC
92 Speech to Western State College, Gunnison, Colorado, November 7, 2007, Bell papers, box 2, folder: "Correspondence," AHC
93 "Profile: Lander's Tom Bell: Wyoming's Green Pioneer," *WyoFile*, September 6, 2010, https://wyofile.com/profile-wyomings-tom-bell/ accessed May 25, 2022
94 Harlow, *High Country News: Survival and Change*, 20
95 Minutes, Wyoming Outdoor Council meeting, June 15, 1974, Bell papers, box 1, folder "Tom's Papers," AHC
96 Harlow, *High Country News: Survival and Change*, 20
97 "Lander Losing Scrappy Publisher Tom Bell," *Denver Post* article placed in the Congressional Record by Wyoming Congressman Teno Roncalio, August 20, 1974, E5599
98 "Come back, Tom," *Wyoming State Journal*, August 8, 1974, 4
99 Letter from Tom to Gerald Ford, May 2, 1975, Bell papers, box 1, folder: "Correspondence, AHC
100 Letter from Tom to Bruce Hamilton and Joan Nice, July 12, 2005, Bell papers, box 3, folder: "Hamilton, Bruce and Joan," AHC
101 "Lynn Dickey's Legacy, *High Country News*, June 5, 2000, https://www.hcn.org/issues/180/5836, accessed May 26, 2022
102 Speech to Western State College, Gunnison, Colorado, November 7, 2007, Bell papers, box 2, folder: "Correspondence," AHC
103 Harlow, *High Country News: Survival and Change*, 61
104 Geoff O'Gara, "Saga of a High Country Newsman," *Sierra*, March/April 1987, 77
105 "Talk given at the 20th anniversary meeting of the Wyoming Outdoor Council, September 12, 1987, Lander," Bell papers, folder: "Statements," AHC
106 Kerry Brophy, "Bell adds UW honor to awards trove," *Casper Star Tribune*, June 4, 2003, A-1, A-8
107 M.J. Clark, "Tom Bell named Conservationist of the Year," Bell papers, folder: "MJ Clark Piece," AHC
108 "Talk delivered to *Lighthawk*, Jackson, WY, June 22, 2002, Bell papers, box 12, folder: "Statements," AHC
109 Letter from Tom to "Board and Staff, High Country News, March 5, 2010, Bell papers, box 1, folder: "Tom's Papers," AHC
110 John Monczynski, Wyoming Outdoor Council panel, Conservation Cafeteria, December 11, 2011, https://www.youtube.com/watch?v=MtzHeNHsqWQ , accessed April 19, 2022

Chapter 4

THE BLACK 14

"black armbands, black hearts, and black stains"

"From my observation of almost half a century in Wyoming, I have never known of any prejudice against any race in the state of Wyoming."

Those words were spoken by U.S. Federal District Court Judge Ewing T. Kerr, on the record, during the civil rights case brought by the Black 14.[1]

Judge Kerr was known to sleep through the testimony of witnesses during trials in his courtroom. He'd have told you he wasn't asleep, just resting his eyes. His assertion above is evidence he was either asleep or resting his conscience through significant parts of Wyoming history since he arrived to practice law in 1927. Had he been awake during the decades before he ruled against the 14 African American student-athletes who were dismissed from the Cowboy football team in violation of their civil rights, Judge Kerr would have witnessed what happened at Heart Mountain during World War II. He'd have known that after Harriett Elizabeth Byrd graduated from high school, she wanted to attend the University of Wyoming but was informed that Blacks could not live in on-campus housing. Her father worked for the railroad and a rail pass his daughter could use was one of his benefits. Elizabeth used it to travel east where she attended predominately black West Virginia State College.[2] When she returned with a college degree, she ran headlong into another race barrier. Elizabeth was unable to receive a teaching certificate for many years after completing her college education because the State Superintendent of Public Instruction believed white parents didn't want Blacks teaching their children.[3]

During the time this federal judge claimed to have never seen "prejudice against any race in Wyoming," an aware person would have known of the lynching of Black men in Wyoming and witnessed the Ku Klux Klan crusading in the state. He or she would have seen signs in the windows of restaurants and other businesses limiting customers to those with white skin. "No Indians, No Mexicans, No Negroes," they read.[4] Had the jurist not been "resting his eyes," he'd have known that in 1957, the Committee on Human Rights for the Western States informed Wyoming's Governor Milward Simpson that, "Places of public accommodation in Cheyenne and Laramie, Wyoming discourage and refuse service to Negroes."[5]

Judge Kerr was awake long enough to attend a Cheyenne Quarterback Club dinner honoring Coach Lloyd Eaton while the Black 14 case against the Coach was pending in his court, ignoring any ethical considerations attached to taking part in such an event.[6] A week later, the Judge signed an order denying the players a temporary restraining order which sought to restore them to the team roster. In so doing, Kerr ignored *Tinker v. Des Moines Ind. School District*, the decision of the U.S. Supreme Court in a case involving students who were suspended from school for wearing black arm bands to protest the war in Vietnam. In a 7-2 decision, the Supreme Court held that neither students nor teachers "shed their constitutional rights to freedom of speech or expression at the schoolhouse gate."[7]

It seemed logical to conclude that those rights were not shed in the school's locker room or on the school's football field, and certainly not shed when the Black 14 came to the coach's office to talk about exercising their First Amendment rights, which is what happened in Wyoming just a few months after *Tinker*. Two years after *Tinker* Judge Kerr issued a decision that ignored the Supreme Court and the evidence that the players never asked Eaton if they could wear armbands. He relied on a freshly baked rationale never before used to justify the players dismissal when the University initially announced their removal from the team because they had violated a coach's rule.

Kerr ruled that the 14 players could lawfully be kicked off the team because, if the University had permitted "wearing black armbands in protest-demonstration to certain claimed religious beliefs of the Mormon Church and Brigham Young University" UW "would be in violation of the mandate requiring complete neutrality relating to religion and non-religion and in violation of the principle of separation of church and state." The 10th Circuit Court of Appeals upheld Kerr and the legal jousting ended but the episode remains a stain on the state and its only university to this very day.

With the possible exception of the Johnson County War, few, if any, subjects pertaining to Wyoming history have been written about more than the Black 14. One's opinion of the incident, then and now, is largely determined by the lens through which it is viewed. It's more than a little subjective to try to decide who the heroes were in this tragedy. It has become even more complicated in the post-George Floyd era. An attempt to view what happened on the University of Wyoming's campus half a century ago through eyes that witnessed the execution of Mr. Floyd require looking beyond the 14 young men at the center of the 1969 controversy. Those football players are heroes for simply surviving the tumultuousness of their experience. They demonstrated extraordinary courage during one of the most troubling episodes in Wyoming history. Yet, it would not be unfair to see them as having inadvertently stepped off a cliff, falling into a raging whitewater river, taken downstream uncontrollably and eventually washing up alive. Surviving that experience could well be seen as heroic as could the experience of those who voluntarily jumped into that river to liberate these 14 young men from their predicament.

The title of this book presupposes that courage can be attached to conduct which stands against the prevailing wind. In October 1969, the prevailing wind was stirred up by a governor, a university president, a popular head football coach, an attorney general, and a federal judge. The wind was strengthened by the state's conservatism represented by the telegrams, letters, petitions, and phone calls that largely supported the people on that list who used their political, economic, and academic power to harm the lives of the athletes. Indeed, in the first month after the players were expelled from the team, more than 13,000 such communications were received, all but 200 in support of the decision to rid the team of the Black 14. That did not include "one petition of 9,200 signatures" and "numerous smaller petitions and letters" sent directly to Coach Lloyd Eaton.[8] Anyone standing against a wind that ferocious must be deemed courageous regardless of one's opinion on the matter of the decision to kick the players off the 1969 UW football team.

The story of the Black 14 begins, not with Coach Lloyd Eaton's impulsively blusterous and arguably illegal decision to expel these men from the team, but with the murder of Abel in Genesis, the 4th chapter of the first book of the Bible. In 1859, Brigham Young explained its connection with Mormon doctrine which, until 1978, banned Black men from the priesthood.

> "Cain slew his brother. Cain might have been killed, and that would have put a termination to that line of human beings. This was not to be, and the Lord put a mark upon him, which is the flat nose and black skin. Trace mankind down to after the flood, and then another curse is pronounced upon the same race—that they should be the 'servant of servants;' and they will be, until that curse is removed."[9]

Young's reference is to a post-flood story in Genesis 9. Noah, back on dry ground, imbibes the fruit of his vineyard. It was his post-traumatic stress disorder. Who would not have started drinking heavily after witnessing what Noah had, the divine destruction of all life on the planet except that isolated in his makeshift boat? He becomes drunk and passes out naked on the floor of his tent. Ham sees "his father's nakedness." Ham is therefore called "the father of Canaan," and receives the "Curse of Ham," which is set forth in verses 24-27.

> "When Noah awoke from his wine and knew what his youngest son had done to him, he said, "Cursed be Canaan; lowest of slaves shall he be to his brothers." He also said, "Blessed by the Lord my God be Shem; and let Canaan be his slave. May God make space for Japheth, and let him live in the tents of Shem; and let Canaan be his slave."

Central to understanding this proclamation is the Mormon belief that there was a war in Heaven before humans came to earth. The forces of Jesus versus the forces of Satan. Joseph Fielding Smith, the 10th Mormon President said:

> "There were no neutrals in the war in heaven. **All took sides either with Christ or with Satan.** Every man had his agency there, and men receive rewards here based upon their actions there, just as they will receive rewards hereafter or deeds done in the body. The Negro, evidently, is receiving the reward he merits." (Emphasis in original).

It was this same Mormon president who also said:

> "Millions of souls have come into this world cursed with a black skin and have been denied the privilege of Priesthood and the fulness of the blessings of the Gospel. These are the descendants of Cain. Moreover, they have been made to feel their inferiority and have been separated from the rest of mankind from the beginning."[10]

Brigham Young, for whom BYU was namesake, was highly critical of the abolition movement. He said it was "calculated to lay waste the fair states of the South and let loose upon the world a community who might, peradventure, overrun our society and violate the most sacred principles of human society, chastity, and virtue." Another mid-19th century Mormon leader, Orson Hyde, called Africans the accursed linage of Canaan."[11]

Given the level of scriptural abuse underpinning this vitriol, one might be inclined to understand why these 14 student-athletes felt compelled to object to the policy of the Church of Latter-day Saints that forbade Black members from being a part of the priesthood, which was considered by Mormons to be a necessary prerequisite to "achieve exaltation or godhood in the highest degree of glory known as the celestial kingdom."¹²

On October 18, 1969, during the Black awakening of the Civil Rights movement, Brigham Young University, UW's arch-rival and a private school owned by the Church of Jesus Christ of Latter-day Saints, was scheduled to come to Laramie to play a football game.

Marcus Aurelius once said, "Our life is what our thoughts make it." Ralph Waldo Emerson said, "Man is what he thinks." More direct, what we believe determines how we react. If University of Wyoming President William Carlson, Coach Lloyd Eaton, and Wyoming's Governor Stan Hathaway believed that the quest for civil rights was about restoring the dignity of which racism deprived people of color, the tragedy of the Black 14 incident would have been avoided. But each believed something else about the turmoil of the 1960s. In these days before the advent of critical race theory and George Floyd, few spoke words like "white supremacy," but in hindsight they could have known it when they saw it.

Just weeks before the Black 14 tragedy stained UW, the school's history department offered a series of six lectures on Black studies and the Black experience in America. The programs conducted in March of 1969, were designed to educate the University community because, as UW English professor Robert Hemenway said at the time, "There has been little understanding and the Black experience is unique."¹³ The interest of others on campus was so great that the lecture series was moved to a larger auditorium though neither Hathaway, nor Carlson or Eaton took time to attend.

White Americans like those three were products of an education system that allowed students to receive high school diplomas and college degrees without learning anything about Reconstruction, Jim Crow, or how the 14th Amendment paved the way to the U.S. becoming the mass incarceration capital of the world. If the governor, UW's president, or the football team's head coach had taken time to attend that series of lectures, they would have learned what young Black students were reading and to whom they were listening in those days of awakening. They might have earned a glimpse of what it was that motivated those 14 ballplayers beyond winning a national championship.

They'd have heard the words Malcolm X employed to articulate the struggle of Blacks in America as could only one who had dropped out of America's public school system and studied what was not taught there. They'd have known how deeply Stokely Carmichael and Charles V. Hamilton's book "Black Power" moved discontented young African Americans or how effectively James Baldwin described the intersectionality between Blacks and other marginalized peoples such as those among the LGBTQ community. They would have understood how Martin Luther King Jr. gave the Black community a way to understand the connection between their lives and the immorality of the war in Vietnam.

By choosing not to attend the lecture series UW's leadership intentionally avoided a critical opportunity to learn that which could have helped them avoid the Black 14 tragedy. How little the University and state of Wyoming leadership understood the Black experience would soon be unveiled on a national platform.

The year before, Richard Nixon defeated Hubert Humphrey for the presidency. Nixon won nationally by less than one percent, but his "law and order" campaign with a "Southern strategy" appealing to white voters was rewarded in Wyoming with a 55%-35% landslide. That same year, Dr. Carlson attended a conference sponsored by the Western Interstate Commission on Higher Education. It was not long after Martin Luther King and Bobby Kennedy's assassinations. 1968 was also a year of nearly non-stop civil rights demonstrations and riots and antiwar demonstrations. The conference was held only a few days before the police riots at the Democratic National Convention in Chicago. With that backdrop, Carlson was drawn to a two-hour seminar at the conference on "the problem of student unrest and disruptive protests." On returning to Laramie, a shaken UW president promptly wrote the Governor to inform him of his takeaways. "The Communist influence in the revolutionary and disruptive activities throughout the country was discussed." Carlson told the Governor that "Maosito" Communists as well and "Trotskyites" and the American Communist Party were the underlying cause of campus unrest "probably through an infiltration process."[14]

Governor Hathaway told Carlson the conference presenters confirmed what "I have suspected for a longtime, that there was a direct Communist influence upon the campuses where most of the trouble occurred." The Governor expressed confidence in Carlson. "With your leadership, I am confident we are not going to have similar problems at the University of Wyoming."[15]

It wasn't the first time University of Wyoming officials saw the ominous shadow of Communists lurking on the campus. In October 1947, the president of the University board of trustees, Milward Simpson, and trustee Harold Del Monte were part of an audience of a meeting of the National Association of University Governing Boards at the University of Michigan. They were enthralled by a presentation entitled "The Little Red Schoolhouse is Redder Than You Think." The speaker warned university trustees from around the country that their school libraries and textbooks were being used to advance the cause of Communism. The message was delivered in the context of the early days of the anti-Communism demagoguery spewed by Wisconsin Senator Joe McCarthy.

Simpson and Del Monte hurried back to Laramie and implored their fellow trustees to do something about this threat. With no sense of the furor they were about to unleash on the campus and around the country, the trustees nonchalantly adopted a resolution requiring UW president Duke Humphrey to appoint a committee to "read and examine textbooks in use at the University of Wyoming" to determine whether the books are "subversive or un-American."[16]

The criticism was immediate, withering, and arrived in Laramie from far and near. Historian Arthur Schlesinger called the investigation "crude," saying it was ordered by a group of "ill-informed trustees.[17] The *St. Louis Post Dispatch* called the trustees' decision "an insult to the good sense and patriotism of the faculty" and "an affront to the intelligence" of the student body.[18] The political tornado created by the trustees tore through the campus in Laramie. Faculty and students alike complained vociferously.

An untenured history professor stepped into the middle of the fray, leading faculty opposition to the textbook review. Dr. Gale W. McGee, who would later serve three terms representing Wyoming in the United States Senate, openly criticized the trustees and the university president, calling the investigation "a gratuitous insult to faculty who seemed viewed by the board as incompetent to select and interpret their own course reading material."[19] His outspokenness gave permission to enemies on the board to begin a fishing expedition for evidence that Dr. McGee himself may be a Communist. One board member hired students to monitor McGee's history classes and report back on whether he was teaching subversive material. It all came to naught when the students reported that they liked his classes and heard nothing of a subversive nature.[20]

Eventually, the board found a dignified way out of the mess they created. They saved face by appointing a small group of faculty members to review some books and report back. After reviewing 64 textbooks, the committee reported they could find nothing subversive or un-American. "That's fine," said trustee Tracy McCraken. "Now the people of Wyoming will know that even though subversive teaching may be practiced at other schools, there is none of it in Wyoming."[21]

Thus, the Communist bogeyman departed the campus, and like an autoimmune disorder, awaited another opportune moment to infect the university.

The times, they were a-changing, and the political leadership in Cheyenne and decision makers at the University of Wyoming failed to keep up with the change. Most relevant were changing attitudes among once subservient athletes. This was the era when Mary Beth and John Tinker were suspended from that Iowa high school for wearing black armbands to protest the Vietnam war and fought it all the way to the U.S. Supreme

Court.[22] It was when Muhammad Ali sacrificed his heavy weight championship belt to take a stand against the war in Vietnam. Olympian Tommy Smith asserted Black power and risked his career by raising a defiant, black-gloved fist as he stood on the medal platform at the 1968 Mexico City Olympics. Baseball's super-star centerfielder Curt Flood was suing Major League Baseball to be freed from control the club owners exercised over players. "A well-paid slave," he said, "is nonetheless a slave."[23] Across the nation, bright, young, black college student athletes took notice.

No matter how much the Governor, the University president, and the head football coach wished it otherwise, Wyoming was not immune. Like smoke from a faraway forest fire, the whiff of political turmoil elsewhere across the nation filled the skies over the University of Wyoming in the fall of 1969. The school's newspaper, the *Branding Iron*, had a new editor. Phil White, a law student, instituted a weekly column defining racism. "Racism is" appeared in each edition. "Racism is," explained the September 19 issue, "when you have to admit that blacks should have their freedom but say they are getting too pushy." Plans for participation in the national Vietnam Moratorium were highlighted on the front page of the same issue of the *BI*. "Students, faculty and townspeople" were invited to organize "a vigil at the Vietnam War Memorial near Old Main, teach-ins, a peace march, and possibly a door-to-door campaign to hand out leaflets opposing the war."[24]

Plans for UW protests against the war again were front page headlines the following week. Al Wiederspahn, who would be elected later to the Wyoming state legislature and serve in both the house and the senate from 1979-1989, was then a member of the UW student senate. Wiederspahn introduced a resolution endorsing the moratorium.[25] An indication that politics was heating up on the campus came when the Episcopal chaplain at UW "revealed to the *BI* his resignation from the Wyoming Air Guard as a result of an ultimatum issued because of his support of the peace march last May 8." George Quarterman said he'd been asked "by the commander of the UW Army ROTC to talk to leaders of the peace march" to persuade them to "call it off."[26] The day before the moratorium, UW's football coaching staff called the players together and issued a warning. Participating in any anti-war protest was a violation of team rules.[27] That week's "Racism is" column taunted war backers. "Racism is," it said, "serving in Vietnam and wondering who the real enemy is."

Branding Iron editor Phil White created a stir on campus when he printed a photograph on the frontpage of the October 3rd paper. *BI* photographer Don Rich captured an image of a license plate on a car parked near the Coe Library and the UW Law School. Attached to the car's license plate was a picture of a very pregnant Pickaninny. "I went all the way with LBJ," was inscribed next to the caricature of the young black child. In the caption, White said the photo was "tangible evidence that racism may exist even in Wyoming."

Such was the political environment at the University of Wyoming on the day 14 Black players arrived at Coach Eaton's office to talk to him about protesting Mormon church policies during the BYU game.

Lloyd Eaton was named head coach of the Cowboy football team in 1962. He replaced the popular Bob Devaney who left UW mid-contract to coach the Nebraska Cornhuskers. Eaton had been the team's defensive coach under Devaney.[28] Unhappy that Devaney had fled Laramie without completing his contract, the board of trustees felt that because he married a Wyoming girl, Eaton might stay around longer.

In his first three seasons, Eaton's teams struggled to records of 6-4, 6-2-2, and another 6-4 season before turning things around in 1966. Between 1966 and 1968, the Cowboys won three consecutive Western Athletic Conference championships. In 1966, they won nine games and lost only one, before defeating Florida State in the Sun Bowl on Christmas Eve. The 1967 Cowboys went undefeated in the regular season. In those days there were four major bowl games, all on New Year's Day. An invitation to play in any of them was highly coveted. The Cowboys were invited to play in one of the four, the Sugar Bowl, because they enjoyed the longest winning streak in college football. There, a 13-0 Cowboy lead at halftime gave way to a heartbreaking 20-13 loss. The following year the Cowboys finished 7-3, outscoring their opponents 242-118. Eaton, his team, and the fans looked forward to 1969 with great anticipation. It began with four conference wins. The Cowboys beat Arizona 23-7; then Air Force 27-25, followed by a 39-3 trouncing of rival Colorado State University. It was Lloyd Eaton's 100th career win.

The following Saturday was unusually cold for an October afternoon in Laramie. It was twenty degrees above zero with snow on the ground when the University of Texas at El Paso (UTEP) took a first quarter lead against the 16th highest rated team in the country. When receiver John Griffin caught a touchdown pass, the Cowboys took a lead they would not relinquish in coasting to a 37-9 victory. John Griffin caught six passes in that game, earning post game accolades from Coach Eaton.[29] Neither Griffin nor his coach had any way of knowing this would be the last game in a Cowboy uniform for him and 13 of his teammates. The Cougars of Brigham Young were on the schedule for the following Saturday, October 18.

The morning before that game came only a few days after 600 people marched in a Laramie demonstration against the war in Vietnam. In that atmosphere, the 14 arrived at Coach Eaton's office at 9:30. They were wearing black armbands, the sight of which incensed Eaton. Within minutes they were no longer members of the 12th highest rates team in the nation, and the UW football program began a precipitous decline that lasted for years.

One of the now former Cowboys in the room, Jerry Berry, described the brief encounter. "As soon as we went into the office, Eaton said he would save us a lot of words. He told us we had made our bid and from now on, we were off the team."[30] In his history book *Wyoming in Mid-Century: Prejudice, Protest, and the Black 14*, Phil White wrote, "The black players claimed that during his outburst after booting them off the team, Eaton had told them that, 'I am the only father some of you ever had.'"[31] Williams remembered, "He came in, sneered at us and yelled that we were off the squad. He said our very presence defied him. He said he has had 'some good Negro boys.' Just like that."[32] Tony McGee quoted Eaton as saying "we could go to Grambling State or Morgan State. We could go back to colored relief. If anyone said anything, he told us to shut up."[33]

Phil White was walking through the Student Union late Friday morn-

University of Wyoming football team, 1969. Photo courtesy of Wyoming State Archives.

ing when a fellow student hollered, "Hey Phil, Coach Eaton just kicked all the Black players off the football team." White had been told earlier in the week that campus Blacks planned a protest during the BYU football game but what he just heard didn't register. White couldn't believe Eaton would boot the team's leading receiver John Griffin; the team's leader in kickoff returns, Ron Hill; rushing leader and team tri-captain, Joe Williams; starting offensive lineman Mel Hamilton; starting fullback Tony Gibson, starting strong safety Jerome Berry, and defensive end Anthony McGee along with the others who had contributed significantly to the team's success. Only one was a senior. Among the 14 were four offensive and three defensive starters, plus three key reserves. The Cowboys were looking to the future with these young stars and now they were gone.

Phil asked himself, "What kind of a coach decimates his own team of young athletes he had specifically recruited to make the Cowboys the national powerhouse it had become?" To Phil White it made no sense. He learned the 14 players were meeting with UW President Bill Carlson at noon. He headed for Old Main to report on the historic meeting thinking it was there that a compromise would be reached.

The long mahogany conference table was covered with boxes of pizza ordered in by Carlson to appease the players while they waited for Coach Eaton to come speak with them in the presence of the school's president. Carlson kept assuring the 14, "We're working on it." Eaton refused his boss's invitation. It was UW Athletic Director Glenn "Red" Jacoby who came through the door. The players were in shock, some more angry and aggressive than others. It didn't help when Jacoby insisted on cluelessly referring to the men as "you boys."[34]

Phil White watched and listened, taking notes as a reporter. As one who loved the University and the state, he kept telling himself that "someone will correct this." After all Joe Williams told Carlson and Jacoby that despite rumors already circulating, the 14 never told Eaton they would refuse to play unless permitted to wear the armbands. Williams assured them "we were going to play the game no matter what and we hadn't even decided to ask to wear black armbands on the field."[35] A few days later, Dr. Carlson backed Williams's version of events during a hastily called meeting of the UW faculty. "When the 14 came to his office wearing black armbands, they told Eaton," Carlson admitted, "they were not demonstrating, but were seeking a meeting with Coach Eaton to determine the extent to which they might be permitted to participate in a demonstration against BYU."[36]

White thought to himself, surely cooler heads will prevail. The University won't allow the Coach to destroy this team and the school's image with it. But no one stepped up to correct the situation. Cooler heads, if there were any, did not prevail then or later that night when the Governor and the board of trustees gathered in Laramie despite the snowstorm that engulfed the state. Although he refused to join the meeting in Carlson's conference room, the president told the players Eaton would be invited to attend the trustee's meeting to explain his conduct. It was an invitation the Coach initially declined but was eventually forced to accept. Each Friday night before gameday, the Coach treated the team to a movie. UW trustee chairman C.E "Jerry" Hollon went to the theater to find Eaton. He asked the manger to go into the dark theater to summon Eaton. Eaton arrogantly blew him off. Hollon dispatched the manager again, this time with a stern message. Eaton appeared and reluctantly agreed to join the trustees for a discussion.[37]

Governor Stan Hathaway huddled with Carlson, Eaton, Jacoby, and the trustees through the cold night from 8:00 PM until 3:15 the next morning when UW's public information officer Vern Shelton released a press statement saying the Governor and the trustees had decided to uphold Eaton's decision. The 14 "will not play today's game or any during the balance of the season." They had, Shelton announced, effectively been convicted of "violating a football coaching rule." The news release bolstered the decision with the words of Athletic Director Red Jacoby. "An open defiance of a coaching staff regulation cannot be tolerated."[38]

That "coaching staff regulation" unconstitutionally prohibited student-athletes from participating in any protests. Within a few days, someone on the University's legal staff read the U.S. Supreme Court's decision in *Tinker v. Des Moines Ind. School District*, where it was determined the Constitution protected the wearing of black armbands by students as a form of free speech. Thus, a week after the dismissal of the 14, Eaton was forced to modify his "coaching staff regulation" to prohibit such protests only while participating in team activities. Though the dismissed players had not violated the revised rule, Eaton would not budge on his decision to send them packing.

Years later, Carlson remembered the fateful meeting. He said that if the purpose of the meeting was to find a compromise, it was an unattainable goal from the beginning. Coach Eaton was in the driver's seat and was never going to compromise. "There was no give and no leverage," the UW President recalled. He said the University's contract with Eaton put the Coach "completely in charge of team discipline and rules to be followed." In essence, the purportedly most powerful person on campus was not as powerful as a football coach. The UW president admitted, "The administration was effectively precluded from questioning any rules the Coach might lay down."[39] Additionally, Carlson, who earlier committed to the Governor he would not tolerate campus unrest, said he knew Wyoming. It was "a law-and-order state and there was little tolerance for student protests."

Every power structure in the state came down in favor of Coach Eaton and against these 14 young men. The Governor, the president of the state's only university, its powerful board of trustees, the leadership of the legislature, nearly every newspaper editor, and the influential local Cowboy booster organizations. That was the wind the players sowed, the whirlwind they reaped, when they dared to talk to their coach about their concerns in a time when a civil rights movement empowered young Blacks to speak all across the land. But those who wielded power to marginalize the legitimate aspirations of these football players would find that they too had sowed the wind and would reap their own whirlwind.

The UW president foresaw what was coming when he acknowledged he was "very concerned that this would cause a real problem in the future." Indeed, it did. Carlson didn't have to wait long. As it had been in the wake of the school's textbook purge of the 1940s, this decision created a storm on the campus, throughout the state, and across the country. Worried about violence, armed guards were posted around Carlson's home for two weeks, with security concerns forcing him and his family to move into a local hotel for safety.[40] As the all-white Cowboy team took the field the day after the dismissal of the 14, the wind was blowing, snow was falling, and a Confederate flag was flying in the stands while fans chanted loudly, "We love Eaton." Protesters gathered at the gates, with mostly pro-Eaton signs and chants. "We Love Coach Eaton." Don Riddle, the western states coordinator of segregationist George Wallace's presidential campaign, took advantage of the prevailing winds, standing at the gate handing out pro-Eaton bumper stickers.[41]

Pat Putnam, a *Sports Illustrated* writer, came to Laramie to cover what quickly became national news. He reported Laramie Police Chief Vern Breazeale found it necessary for him personally to be on hand to keep the situation under control. The Chief told the national magazine's writer that the Black 14 were "good kids," not like players he said a former UW coach brought to Laramie. That coach, according to the Chief, recruited "ex-convicts to play. Real hoodlums. Always drunk. Always in trouble." Chief

Breazeale assured the writer he and his police force knew how to "keep the peace." "We used to club them over the head until the blood ran down the sides of their mouth."[42]

Fortunately, there was no need for clubs that day. No blood ran down anyone's face. The crowd was loud but civil though the rumors caused worries across the campus. The Black Student Alliance threatened picket lines to block fan entrance to War Memorial Stadium. Attorney Bill Waterman, who represented the dismissed players said he'd been told that "2,000 Black Panthers" were headed to Laramie. Governor Hathaway was mulling calling out the National Guard. When rumors circulated that ten busloads of protesters were en route from Denver, the Governor quietly dispatched Guardsmen to stand by in Laramie.[43]

It got crazier. When a few faculty members said they would resign if the 14 were not reinstated, the Casper Touchdown Club sarcastically raised money to pay their moving expenses. A state legislator threatened the University. "If Eaton backed down, there would be trouble with the University budget."[44] Other Western Athletic Conference schools, Putnam reported, "demanded Wyoming be dropped from their schedule."

Pro-Eaton bumper stickers were seen adorning the cars of many Wyoming folks. The editor of the *Wyoming State Tribune* opined that Eaton "could run for any office subject to the voters and be elected hands down."[45] Even the Wyoming Association of Insurance Agents found it useful to offer their opportunistic support for Eaton's decision. "No one is more aware of the importance of rules and regulations and law and order than the insurance industry," their news release read. They saw it as part of the nation's racial conflict, connecting the Black 14 to the "complete disregard of law and order and subsequent destruction of portions of America's largest cities."[46] The editor for the *Casper Star Tribune* assured his readers not to worry about the loss of these 14 players. "There are a good many athletes from all parts of the country who would be glad to earn their letters at the Cowboy school."[47]

T.A. "Doc" Larson, who later became a state legislator, was head of UW's history department. He recounted how the controversy ripped at the University's seams. A few hours after the Trustees voted to embrace Eaton's decision, the Student Senate voted 17-1 to "express shock at the callous, insensitive treatment afforded 14 black athletes who acted on a matter of conscience with restraint, with moderation and with responsibility." The Faculty Senate sided with the players, urging their immediate reinstatement. The Alumni Association came out in support of Coach Eaton, while the faculty of the College of Arts and Sciences "voted overwhelmingly to censure the coach," as nearly every member of the faculty and staff of the College of Agriculture signed a petition supporting Eaton and the trustees.[48]

Within a few days of the players' dismissal, most of the UW track team quit in protest, including a white runner, Greg Santos, who left at the end of the semester but returned by 1971. He told United Press International, "In Wyoming people say they aren't prejudiced when they are and they have closed minds when it comes to racial issues."[49]

An article published much later in the *Denver Post* recounted that "In the aftermath, nearly every white player refused to speak to their former Black teammates. Receiver Ron Hill, one of the 14 and Griffin's roommate, got in a fistfight with a white player behind a sorority house. Players saw locals riding through campus with shotguns hanging off the back of their pick-ups."[50]

Later, Bill Carlson would make an unsubstantiated claim. "We were also told by a reliable source that a number of black players were threatened by the Black Panthers," quickly adding, "Can I prove that? No."[51] The lack of proof stopped no one from circulating rumors about militant Blacks coming to town. Meanwhile, *Branding Iron* editorials urged reinstatement of the players, questioning the wisdom of using an authoritarian rule as the basis for removing them from the team. After several Laramie businesses canceled advertising in the *Branding Iron* and a few *BI* staffers left believing the campus newspaper was biased in favor of the 14, editor White responded. "Apparently, we turn away from the seemingly all-embracing words of the First Amendment with the simple, nauseating statement that 'it is a matter of discipline.' Nazi Germany was a matter of discipline."[52] *BI* editor Phil White covered his own resignation in the same issue.

> "White said he was bowing to the wishes of most UW students who apparently do not want to read anything about racism or the

Vietnam War or the urban crisis or drugs or prison abuses or politics. Admittedly, they are rather unpleasant subjects. Maybe if the BI doesn't mention them, they will go away. I hope so. After all, we don't have any problems here in Wyoming and we don't want any."[53]

With White's departure, a group of UW students began publishing a mimeographed daily called *Revelations*. In its October 27 edition, the students proclaimed, "It is sad that the 'Equality State' is about to become known as the 'denial of rights state.'"

The contest gradually shifted to the football field, where Wyoming beat BYU on October 18. After that game, James Flinchum, the editor of the *Wyoming State Tribune* wrote, "We applaud the coaches' and trustees' stand and say this. If it becomes a matter of whether Wyoming ever wins another football game or not or surrenders principle, then we waive all claims to the former and insist that rules being rules, they must be enforced." The sports editor of the *Casper Star Tribune* celebrated the first win after the 14 players were dispatched. He assured his readers that the "racial and disciplinary controversy" was "not enough to slow the drive to a fourth consecutive Western Athletic Conference football title."[54] As if to confirm that prediction, the Cowboys beat San Jose the following week. Ironically, San Jose players wore armbands during the game to show support for UW's Black 14. They issued a statement saying, "Our team has had the experience of attempting to reconcile individual conscience and the desire to play football. The plight of the black athlete who is a member of a team which has scheduled to play Brigham Young University is understandable, we believe."[55]

It was Coach Eaton's last homefield victory.

The contest then shifted to Judge Ewing T. Kerr's federal courtroom in Cheyenne where the civil rights case the Black 14 filed against Eaton and the University languished for a year. As the 14 football players and their lawyers walked into the courtroom, Judge Kerr asked the players to take a seat in the jury box. There was barely enough room. After the hearing during which the Judge announced his decision, Attorney General James Barrett told Kerr, "Every time I looked over to the jury box, I could see what was going to happen to Wyoming's football team."[56]

Kerr, after sleeping on it until long after the 1969 season ended, ruled against the players without conducting a trial. He found it was the players who had violated the First Amendment, when, representing a state school, they sought to protest the "religious beliefs" of the Mormon church,[57] even though the record demonstrated the University dismissed them for only one reason, i.e., they violated Coach Lloyd Eaton's unconstitutional rule against participating in any demonstration.

An appeal was taken to the 10th Circuit Court of Appeals whose judges reversed Kerr's decision on May 14, 1971. Kerr was ordered to hold a trial, which he did and the man who said, "From my observation of almost half a century in Wyoming, I have never known of any prejudice against any race in the state of Wyoming," ruled for the state again on Oct. 18, 1971, the second anniversary of the players' dismissal from the Cowboy football team. The appeals court eventually affirmed him. There were no further appeals.[58]

With ample time for the necessary hindsight to guide his rethinking of the Black 14, William Carlson later said, "The aftermath of all this was felt for years. The faculty and administration relationships were hurt. The student and administration interactions were suspect. The citizens and the university relations were tarnished." But hindsight didn't enable the old UW president from gaining any insight. He was never able to comprehend the legitimate aspirations of the African American students. Instead, he said, "Mostly the people of Wyoming would do anything for a winning football team and they felt terribly cheated that the team was damaged."[59] As he looked back on the stakes and the mistakes of the ugly episode that defined his presidency, Carlson didn't admit it was the worst decision he ever made. He reserved that honor for allowing the Cowboy Joe Club to be organized on campus. Without explaining his reasoning, Carlson wrote in his memoirs this "was one of the biggest mistakes I made while President of the University of Wyoming."[60]

For his part, Lloyd Eaton told the Cheyenne Quarterback Club, "I've never been happier to see a season come to an end than I was in 1969."⁶¹ After going 1 and 9 the next year, Eaton's time at UW was over. In the decade following the Black 14 debacle, the Cowboys had only one winning season under four different head coaches. War Memorial Stadium rarely saw half of its 25,000 seats filled. During that drought, the 1976 team was the only one invited to a bowl game. With an 8-4 record, they played in the Fiesta Bowl, losing to Oklahoma 41-7.

On June 9, 1978, a Salt Lake City, Utah newspaper, the *Deseret News*, reported LDS leaders had received a revelation from God. Thereafter, "every faithful, worthy man in the church may receive the holy priesthood."⁶² An Associated Press story datelined Salt Lake City said the change came after many hours of "supplicating the Lord for divine guidance." According to the article, this was "the most significant change in church doctrine since polygamy was discontinued in 1890." It took several centuries and countless damaged lives but, by God, the curse of Ham had finally been lifted, at least among the Mormons.

In May of 1982, a reporter tracked down Lloyd Eaton, now divorced and living in a cabin in Idaho. He said he regretted nothing about the incident and would do the same thing again if the opportunity presented itself.⁶³

Fifty years later the University of Wyoming issued a formal apology to the 14. There was a reunion. Most of the players returned to Laramie. A memorial was dedicated. A halftime show honored them. A letter of apology signed by the University President read:

> "To have your collegiate careers derailed as both students and athletes is a tragedy. Please accept this sincere apology from the University of Wyoming for the unfair way you were treated and for the hardships that treatment created for you. We want to welcome you home as valued members of this institution, and hope you accept our old Wyoming saying, 'Once a Cowboy, always a Cowboy.'"

Those who attended the weekend festivities were invited to the football team's pregame breakfast. The current football coach, Craig Bohl, told his players, "These guys got their jerseys taken away from them, so we're going to give them back to them."[64] On Thanksgiving Day 2021, members of the Black 14 partnered with the Church of Latter-day Saints to donate 40,000 pounds of food to Laramie area charities to feed the hungry.[65] John Griffin said, "We decided we need to give back. We need to turn a tragedy into philanthropy and that's what we've done."

Yet, the question remains. Could it happen again? Did anyone learn anything? Ask Colin Kaepernik. Civil rights activist and PhD sociologist Harry Edwards thinks he understands coaches like Eaton and the white hierarchy that blackballed Kaepernik for refusing to stand during the National Anthem as a protest against racial inequality.

> *"Part of the problem, Edwards explains, is that many NFL owners are wealthy, entitled and arrogant, and they essentially view their players as property, not human beings with rights guaranteed by the Constitution. And they're ignorant of history. They don't or won't understand the context of these actions, the long national narrative of racial injustice, and what the players are saying now: This land is not free. My people are not free. It's a carryover from 400 years of slavery and oppression. [NFL team] owners are acting like plantation owners, insisting that any act of 'rebellion' must be squelched."*[66]

The root of the problem then and now is the inability of powerful people like Hathaway, Carlson, and Eaton to comprehend and acknowledge what Critical Race theorist Anthony E. Cook, a Georgetown law professor, called, "the concrete experiences of the powerless and the oppressed."[67] Cook critiques Martin Luther King's philosophy as underpinned by an understanding of "the hegemony of repressive ideologies to deconstruct the limits they appear to set on the possibility of change."

He could have been talking about Lloyd Eaton and all his colleagues then in control of nearly every NCAA locker room. Those coaches never aspired to create what Dr. King called "the Beloved Community." They were authoritarian and feared the loss of any control would undermine them.

Furthermore, they aligned themselves with the power structures at the university and the politicians, businessmen, and boosters who disagree with most of the causes for which college student-athletes might be motivated to march or wear black arm bands, e.g., ending the war in Vietnam or righting racial injustices. Together they created a strong Wyoming wind. Standing against it, as did those 14 courageous students, Phil White, and a handful of others, is a profile in courage.

Epilogue

Where are the Black 14 today? Phil White, who, as historian, journalist, and lawyer, followed this story more thoroughly and longer than anyone else, is one of the heroes for the tenacity he demonstrated in making sure the truth was told. Phil came to love and respect these men and followed them in life and reported:

"Tony McGee became a dominant player in the NFL, starting in a Super Bowl for the Redskins. For many years McGee has hosted a sports television talk show in Washington D.C. Joe Williams also earned a Super Bowl ring with the Dallas Cowboys and then developed his own investment consulting business.

"Several of the Black 14 managed to obtain college degrees. Mel Hamilton graduated from UW and has had a long career as a public school teacher and administrator in Casper. Guillermo Hysaw, originally from Bakersfield, Calif., and Lionel Grimes from Alliance, Ohio, became employment diversity executives with Ford and Toyota.

"Tony Gibson retired in 2011 after working nearly 38 years as a lineman for a Massachusetts power company during which time he responded to mass outages in Puerto Rico, Canada, Florida, and several other states. Ted Williams has worked that long as a foreman at a specialized paint manufacturing company in Illinois. Ron Hill became a physical education teacher in Colorado. John Griffin has worked for the YMCA in Denver, for a hazardous waste abatement firm, and as a manager for Sports Authority in Denver. Ivie Moore has worked as a floor subcontractor in his native Arkansas.

"James Isaac died in San Bernardino, California in 1976; Don Meadows in 2009; Earl Lee in 2013. Lee had a distinguished career as a teacher, coach and principal in the Baltimore area. Isaac, an all-sports star for Hanna-Elk Mountain High School in Wyoming, played football and ran track for, and graduated from, Dakota Wesleyan University in South Dakota. Don Meadows had a restaurant business in Denver.

"Jay Berry (Jerry Berry) became a sports anchor for television stations in Tulsa, Chicago, and Detroit and was named by Associated Press as the top sports broadcaster in Texas in 1977. In the records section of the 2013 University of Wyoming Cowboys' Football Media Guide, the name Jerome Berry appears with two other players who are tied for most interceptions returned for touchdowns in a season, and with three others for most returns for touchdowns in a career.

"Berry's entire career at UW consisted of the first four games of the 1969 season. After his 88-yard return against Arizona he carried another interception 24 yards for a touchdown in the CSU game two weeks later."[68]

Endnotes

1. White, *Wyoming Mid-Century*, 247
2. White, *Wyoming Mid-Century*, 276
3. Guenther, *List of Good Negroes*
4. Id., 24-29
5. Letter, U.S. Representative Charles Diggs to Milward Simpson, October 10, 1957, box 161, Simpson Papers, AHC
6. "QB Club Ends Year by Honoring Cowboys," *Wyoming State Tribune*, November 25, 1969, 13
7. *Tinker v. Des Moines Ind. School District*, 393 U.S. 503 (1969)
8. Letter from Vern Shelton, Assistant to the UW President for Information, to Carlson, November 18, 1969, UW President's Office Records, box 303, folder 3, AHC
9. Brigham Young, *Journal of Discourses* (October 9, 1859), 7:290.
10. Joseph Fielding Smith, *The Way to Perfection* (Salt Lake City: Deseret Book, 1950), 101, for further reference, see https://www.mrm.org/priesthood-ban#_ftn15, accessed on October 24, 2021
11. Brodie, *The Man Who Knows My History*, 173-174
12. Id., https://www.mrm.org/priesthood-ban#_ftn15, accessed on October 24, 202
13. "Negro culture lectures begin," *Branding Iron*, February 28, 1969, 1
14. Letter from Carlson to Hathaway, August 27, 1968, UW President's Office Records, box 300, AHC
15. Letter from Hathaway to Carlson, September 5, 1968, UW President's Office Records, box 300, AHC
16. Minutes, University of Wyoming Trustees meeting, October 24-25, 1947, http://uwyo.edu/trustees/board-meeting-archives/1940-1949-minutes/1947-board-of-trustees-meeting.html, accessed October 30, 2021
17. Schlesinger, *Vital Center*, 205
18. "Sad Story from Wyoming," republication of *St. Louis Post Dispatch* editorial in *Laramie Republican Boomerang*, December 230, 1947, 4
19. Hardy, *Wyoming University*, 154
20. McDaniel, *The Man in the Arena*, 33 with accompanying footnotes, 308
21. "UW Faculty Committee Maintains Book Probe Hearing Still Needed," *Laramie Republican Boomerang*, January 21, 1948, 1
22. *Tinker v. Des Moines Ind. School District*, 393 U.S. 503 (1969)
23. Snyder, *A Well-Paid Slave*, 104
24. "Viet moratorium begins Oct. 15 to end the war," *Branding Iron*, vol. 77, no. 2, September 26, 1969, 1
25. "March, vigil set for Viet protest," *Branding Iron*, vol. 77, no. 3, October 3, 1969, 1
26. "Quarterman reveals resignation, Id., 1
27. "Remarks of the President of the University of Wyoming at a special meeting of the faculty senate, October 23, 1969, concerning the Black student incident," UW President's Office Records, box 437, folder 2, AHC, 2
28. White, *Wyoming Mid-Century*, 56, 57
29. "Eaton Happy with One-Two Quarterback Play Saturday," *Laramie Daily Boomerang*, October 12, 1969

30 Larson, *History of Wyoming*, 2nd Ed., 593
31 White, *Wyoming Mid-Century*, 197
32 Pat Putnam, "No defeats, loads of trouble," *Sports Illustrated*, November 3, 1969, 26
33 "Spirit of the Black 14," *Denver Post*, November 7, 2009, https://www.denverpost.com/2009/11/07/spirit-of-the-black-14/ accessed November 19, 2021
34 Recollections of Phil White from his book *Wyoming in Mid-Century*, 192-193, and authors' interview with White, November 18, 2021
35 Id., 193, note: footnote 253
36 "Remarks of the President of the University of Wyoming at a special meeting of the faculty senate, October 23, 1969, concerning the Black student incident," UW President's Office Records, box 437, folder 2, AHC, 3
37 Id., *Wyoming in Mid-Century*, 193, footnote 252
38 "Negro athletes out for failure to comply by athletic department rules, *Laramie Boomerang*, October 19, 1969, 1
39 Carlson, *Four Seasons in Wyoming*, 25-2, 1998, see University of Wyoming President's Office Records, Collection 510000, box 438, folder 6, AHC
40 Id., 25-6
41 White, *Wyoming in Mid-Century*, 196
42 Pat Putnam, "No defeats, loads of trouble," *Sports Illustrated*, November 3, 1969, 26
43 Carlson, *Four Seasons in Wyoming*, 25-4
44 Id.
45 "Wyoming would elect Eaton to any office," *Wyoming State Tribune*, October 26, 1969, 5
46 University of Wyoming President's Office Records, Collection 510000, box 438, folder 4, AHC
47 "Eaton Took the Logical Course," *Casper Star Tribune*, October 20, 1969, 4
48 Larson, *History of Wyoming*, 2nd Edition, 595-596
49 Id., 199
50 "Spirit of the Black 14," *Denver Post*, November 7, 2009, https://www.denverpost.com/2009/11/07/spirit-of-the-black-14/ accessed November 19, 2021
51 Carlson, *Four Seasons in Wyoming*, 25-3
52 "Editorial commentary," *Branding Iron*, October 23, 1969, 4
53 "Phil White resigns as BI editor," *Branding Iron*, October 23, 1969, 1
54 "Poke Express Rolls Toward 4th Crown," *Casper Star Tribune*, October 21, 1969, 8
55 White, *Wyoming in Mid-Century*, 200
56 Ewing T. Kerr, "Centennial Recollections," University of Wyoming College of Law, *Land and Water Law Review*, Vol. XXVI, No. 1 (1991), 10
57 Id., 10
58 *Williams v. Eaton*, 310 F.Supp. 1342 (D. Wyo. 1970), rev'd, 443 F.2d 422 (10th Cir. 1971), on remand, 333 F.Supp. 107 (D. Wyo. 1971), aff'd 468 F.2d 1079 (10th Cir. 1972).
59 Carlson, *Four Seasons in Wyoming*, 25-5
60 Id., 25-1
61 "QB Club ends year by honoring Cowboys," *Wyoming State Tribune*, November 25,

1969, 1
62. "Why the Mormon church finally let black men into the priesthood," *TIME Magazine*, June 9, 2015, https://time.com/3905811/mormon-priesthood-men-women-integration/ accessed November 18, 2021
63. Reilly, Rick, "Eaton Has No Regrets, Says He'd Do It Again," *Denver Post*, May 9, 1982, 6E
64. "Fifty years after the 'Black 14' were banished, Wyoming football reckons with the past," *Washington Post*, November 30, 2019, https://www.washingtonpost.com/national/fifty-years-after-the-black-14-were-banished-wyoming-football-reckons-with-the-past/2019/11/30/fb7e9286-e93d-11e9-9c6d-436a0df4f31d_story.html, accessed November 20, 2021
65. "Black 14, Mormon Church team up," *Wyoming Tribune-Eagle*, November 26, 2021, 1
66. "Sports Sociologist Harry Edwards on NFL 'Plantation Mentality," *California Magazine*, Cal Alumni Association, May 29, 2018, https://alumni.berkeley.edu/california-magazine/just-in/2018-05-29/sports-sociologist-harry-edwards-nfl-plantation-mentality accessed November 20, 2021
67. Crenshaw, et al, *Critical Race Theory*, 85
68. Phil White, "The Black 14: Race, Politics, Religion and Wyoming Football," November 8, 2014, https://www.wyohistory.org/encyclopedia/black-14-race-politics-religion-and-wyoming-football, accessed November 21, 2021

Chapter 5

LYNN ESTELLE DICKEY

"Joan of Arc on a steel stallion"

It was May 2000. Her life bookended by two highway accidents, Lynn Dickey lay near death in the Winchester Medical Center in Winchester, Virginia. The sad news spread across the country and around the world. So many well-wishers called the hospital it became necessary to install a second phone line at the nurse's station of the Intensive Care Unit. Lynn's sister, Ellen, fielded dozens of calls from family, friends, former and current colleagues, calls seeking updates on her condition and offering prayers. The Ambassador to Ireland and the Governor of Wyoming were among them. On the second day of Lynn's hospitalization, while studying her chart and gazing at her face for several minutes, her doctor asked no one in particular, "Who is this woman?"

Ironically, that is much the same question Lynn confronted after a 1966 car crash left her without the use of her legs and her mother, Imogene, a passenger, a quadriplegic. Years later, Lynn told a friend that until that horrifying accident, "I had no idea who I was."[1]

When the United States Senate debated the Americans with Disabilities Act, Senator Bob Dole explained to his colleagues why the legislation mattered. Dole told them there was "an ancient, almost subconscious assumption that people with disabilities are less than fully human and, therefore, not eligible for opportunities, services, and support systems which are available to other people as a matter of right."[2] Lynn Dickey was courageously unaware of any such ancient assumption. The Virginia doctor could not have imagined he was treating the most fully abled, disabled person he had likely ever encountered. Yes, she had spent more than three decades confined to a wheelchair but there was nothing confining about the way Lynn lived her life. Some came to know her as "Joan of Arc on a steel stallion."

―――

Lynn Dickey was born in Gillette, Wyoming, on the 4th of April 1949. The family moved to Buffalo a year later. Her father Willard was a Certified Public Accountant who was remembered by a family friend as "a quiet genius, solid, reliable," an accountant who "kept all the locals out of the poor house and out of the slammer."[3] That same family friend described Lynn's mother Imogene as an "in-your-face personality," admitting he "got more lectures from her than I did from my own mother." Her children remember her as "kind, independent," a strong person "whose political views were quite different from those of her children at that time."

Perhaps that explains the difficult mother-daughter relationship between Lynn and Imogene. Sister Ellen, ten years Lynn's junior, recalls her mother and sister were "both stubborn and passionate in their political convictions" and "polar opposites" on political matters. The dinner table was "highly charged with political conversations."

Several years into Lynn's political career, she and her mother agreed that if they were to maintain their personal relationship, which was very important to both, politics would have to be avoided. Imogene kept a scrapbook of all of Lynn's accomplishments and there were always discussions of a "what and where" nature, but they held fairly true to their agreement not to let politics come between them. During those years, Lynn served four terms as a Democrat representing Sheridan County in the state legislature while Imogene served as the co-chair of the Johnson County Republican Party.[4] Despite those differences, they were, for one another, "growth agents."[5]

Her sister Barbara described her as "curious about everything" from her earliest childhood. When she was a junior in high school, she tasted formaldehyde simply because "she wanted to know what it was like." It was why she ate chocolate-covered grasshoppers and ants. Lynn was very bright. It was obvious early. She memorized "The Night Before Christmas" at age two after overhearing her paternal grandmother Estelle help Lynn's older brother David learn it from memory.[6]

Sunday mornings in church were not optional. The whole family gathered to worship at the Congregational church. With her father an active Mason and her mother an Eastern Star, it was only natural that Lynn became the "honored queen" of her Job's Daughter's chapter. Lynn's curiosity about religion was fueled by that of her father who grew up a Christian Scientist, always welcoming living-room conversations with visiting LDS and Jehovah Witness missionaries. Lynn watched and listened as Willard exchanged ideas with them and others and developed an openness to the views of disparate thinkers.

Lynn was a listener who not only tolerated but encouraged different points of view, feeling that everyone had something to teach her. Ellen said, "She never judged others harshly just because their opinions or beliefs were different from her own."

The 7th of April, 1966, was a beautiful early Spring morning in Northeastern Wyoming. Not a cloud in the sky. Temperatures in the 40s, headed for the upper 50s. It was an exciting day for the Dickey family. Eldest son David was performing in an Easter concert the following day 400 miles away in Colorado Springs. All the Dickey children were going along with Imogene and a family friend. Ellen was 7, Paul 14, Barbara 15. Seventeen-year-old Lynn took the wheel.

An hour southeast of Buffalo on the two-lane highway leading to Imogene's hometown, Lynn was momentarily blinded by the sun. That caused her to miss a curve and the car left the road.[7] After overturning two or three times, it landed on Imogene and Lynn, who had not been wearing seatbelts and were thrown from the car. Barbara was able to get out of the car and saw her sister pinned underneath from the waist down. Lynn's eyes glazed over as though she was dead. She nearly was. The family friend, who was pinned in the car by the front seat, sustained injuries that required hospitalization. Barbara, Paul, and Ellen were not seriously hurt. It was immediately obvious that Imogene and Lynn had suffered life threatening injuries. Both had spinal cord damage and broken vertebrae. Imogene's neck was broken and she spent the remainder of her life a quadriplegic, Lynn a paraplegic.

After receiving preliminary care in Gillette, mother and daughter were rushed to the Casper hospital where doctors began a series of difficult surgeries on Lynn. She had suffered a severe cord spinal injury "with one-fourth of the cord remaining intact."[8] She also had a broken pelvis and back, a collapsed lung, broken ribs, and a scratched aorta leading quickly to an aneurism. Years later, as a state legislator wheeling her chair through the halls of the state capitol, she had a chance encounter with one of the doctors who treated her. He described his memories of how badly injured she was, telling her, "None of us thought you would live." Lynn spent months in the Casper hospital, undergoing countless surgeries and other painful treatment. She was placed in a rotating bed or "Stryker frame." A Stryker frame is made of metal bars and canvas and designed to allow spinal patients to be turned more easily.

Brother Paul and sister Barbara sat on a park bench across the street from Lynn's hospital room where they prayed while watching their sister praying in that apparatus. Eventually, Lynn was transferred to the Craig Rehabilitation Center in Colorado where she spent several more months. While hospitalized, she finished course work for her junior year in high school, sent to her by audio tape and paper assignments. It was not until the fall of 1966 that Lynn was able to return to school for her senior year.

These were the days before the Americans with Disabilities Act (ADA). Access for disabled persons was not on the mind of school architects or community planners. The Rehabilitation Act that prohibited discrimination against "otherwise qualified" handicapped people would not become law until after Lynn finished college. The ADA, with its requirements for ramps in public buildings, sidewalk and curb cuts, and handicapped parking places, was almost a quarter of a century into the future.

In 1966, there was no easy access to classrooms in the multi-story high school building in Buffalo or anywhere else in Wyoming. The burly boys from the Johnson County High School football team and brother Paul met Lynn each day after every class, carrying her and her wheelchair up and down the staircases. Lynn remained as active as ever, teaching piano lessons, singing with the school choir, and participating in Job's Daughters. She graduated on schedule with her class. No one ever heard Lynn complain then or later or ever about the pain she endured all the rest of her life.

Her sister Ellen recalled that in those days, after returning from months of a grueling hospital and rehab experience, Lynn was "hardcore happy." She resumed camping and canoeing. Her friend Margie Rea canoed with Lynn. Another friend carried Lynn through a barbed-wire fence so they could get the canoe to Goose Creek.[9] Lynn took a trip to Elitches Amusement Park in Denver and insisted on riding the mammoth roller coaster for which the park was famous. It resulted in her back surgery needing to be done again. But nothing would stop Lynn from living her life. She refused to be defined by the accident or limited by the wheelchair.

In an October 10, 2020, article published in the *Casper Star-Tribune*, Ellen Dillon describes their parents raising them to think. "Don't ever say, 'I can't do this,' until you've tried everything you can." Ellen said, "That mindset helped her a lot. She just ignored her disability; she didn't mourn the loss (of the use) of her legs." She excelled in her senior year of high school. A speech she wrote won first place in the Voice of Democracy competition.

She received a coveted invitation to join the National Honor Society and was named a National Merit Scholar.

There was never a question that Lynn would go on to college. The accident would not derail that goal, much less delay it. She set a course for her life and living in a wheelchair was not permitted to be a deterrent. She researched carefully and found a college that was enlightened on the matter of meeting the needs of disabled students. Unlike most schools and other public facilities of the time, the University of Illinois at Urbana didn't wait for the law to mandate handicap access. The school was among the first institutions of higher education to recognize that meeting the needs of students with disabilities was critical to their obtaining an education.

> *"The University of Illinois' pioneering Rehabilitation Program had its beginning during the 1947-48 school year and is now internationally famous. Under the direction of Timothy J. Nugent, the Rehabilitation Program has been instrumental in the initiation of similar programs on campuses across the nation."*[10]

It was, like the University of Wyoming, a land grant school, established in 1867, five years after President Abraham Lincoln signed the Morrill Act, giving federal land to states wishing to establish major state public universities. The school was initially known as "Illinois Industrial University," in response to a controversy over whether it should teach academics or solely industrial courses. It did both, under that name. In 1935, the name was changed to "the University of Illinois at Urbana Champaign" and, by the time Lynn Dickey enrolled it was known simply as "the University of Illinois."

Lynn wasn't on campus long before national movements toward diversity and broadened academic and political rights found their way to the campus.[11] It was a time of increasing opposition to the war in Vietnam. University of Illinois students took part in a National Day of Resistance in April 1968 and held a "Vietnam Commencement" ceremony honoring those who refused to be drafted into the U.S. Army. On the page just before the photos of the school's "University Queens," UI's 1968 yearbook, "The

Illio," said, "Students displayed signs protesting napalm manufacturing; draft cards were burned and students were arrested...the most prominent features were the protesters themselves, complete with sandals, beards, long hair, and signs."[12] The yearbook proudly featured a photograph of a student setting his draft card afire with a cigarette lighter. They protested Marine Corps recruiters on campus and African American students held anti-racism demonstrations and protested the police killings of Black Panther Party members in Chicago. On October 15, 1969, 9,000 people, many UI students, took part in the National Moratorium, marching from the University Union to West Side Park in Urbana.

The following year, the school created an Afro-American Studies Commission and its first women's studies courses while recognizing the "Gay Liberation Front." When the University said controversial civil rights attorney William Kunstler could not speak on the campus, days of demonstrations persuaded the school to change its mind. After the local National Guard Armory was firebombed, a Yippie Festival of Life was held in the same building.[13]

For the young woman from Buffalo, Wyoming, it was an awakening. She soaked it all in and participated in much of the political activity. There is nothing in her character that would lead one to think otherwise. Lynn was always engaged in the larger life around her. She joined Delta Sigma Omicron, a service organization for disabled students. Its role at UI was described this way. "To exercise our abilities to a maximum so as to minimize our disabilities, that we may live most and serve best."[14]

While in college, she took up archery, setting a world's record while competing at New York City *en route* to competing in Tel Aviv as a part of Team USA in 1968, where she won a bronze medal as a trainer for the U.S. basketball squad. In 1969, Lynn was invited to join the UI Gizz Kids and spent two weeks in Hawaii engaged in a variety of exhibitions of wheelchair sports including basketball, fencing, track and field events and archery.[15]

She had a deep sense of social justice so much so that before graduating in May of 1971, she applied to serve as a VISTA volunteer. VISTA, or Volunteers in Service to America, was an anti-poverty program created as part of President Lyndon Johnson's "War on Poverty" in the Economic Opportunity Act passed by Congress in 1964. VISTA offered volunteers an opportunity to serve in communities throughout the United States to provide educational programs and vocational training for people living in poverty.

It was when she applied to serve as a VISTA volunteer that a mandatory physical exam disclosed the car accident had left additional damage behind, promising it would cause even more if left untreated. Doctors found Lynn was suffering from an aortic aneurysm. During the 1966 accident, a broken rib scratched the aorta. It was not detected at the time but by now it produced a dangerous bulge in the wall of the aorta. Doctors scheduled emergency surgery to remedy this life-threatening situation. As a result of the blood transfusions, which accompanied the surgery, Lynn contracted Hepatitis C, a long-term condition limiting the ability of her liver to eliminate bodily toxins. Hers became progressively worse over the years and was especially burdensome during times of high stress, which Lynn experienced frequently in her work.

After graduating from UI, Lynn didn't return to Wyoming immediately, but spent a year living in a Kansas Mennonite colony near Wichita and teaching English in a public school in 1973 and 1974. Her students were adults preparing for the high school equivalency examination. A short visit home changed her life and Wyoming's.

In the early 1970s, Wyoming's way of life was under attack. Widespread, often irresponsible development of coal and gas threatened the livelihood of farmers, ranchers, outdoors enthusiasts and small communities. It was an existential challenge. It was time for Lynn to return to Wyoming.

In what can be called "theft through treaty," the Powder River Basin was stolen from the Oglala Lakota. To be honest, the Oglala stole it first. The Fort Laramie Treaty of 1868 awarded the land to the Crow Nation. Under the leadership of Chief Red Cloud, the Oglala defeated the Crows and believed they would live on those lands forever. And they might have if gold had not been discovered in the Black Hills. The gold rush was on, and the Indians were exiled.[16] By the 1970s, treaties confined the Oglala to the Pine Ridge Indian Reservation in South Dakota, where it became "one of the poorest tribes in the country."[17] Meanwhile, the colonization that started when the first white men came to the region continued in a new form. The wealth below the land from which the Native Americans had been driven in Northwest Wyoming was now manufacturing millionaires among mostly out-of-state corporations.

The Powder River Basin covers a large area of that part of Wyoming and Southeast Montana. It runs about 120 miles east to west and 200 miles north to south. Sixty million years ago coal began to form in that geologic basin as a result of the Hartville uplift to the south and the Black Hills uplift to the east. It was some five million years after the dinosaurs that once roamed that part of the planet were made extinct by "a large asteroid impact on what is now the north shore of the Yucatan Peninsula."[18] In what was then a subtropical climate, not unlike the Florida Everglades, the rotting corpses of plants were compressed. After thousands of years of erosion and uplift, flooded by rising sea water, laying under formations of sandstone and shale, buried under sand and mud, the result "reported to the future as coal," which was left near enough to the surface to be strip mined throughout the Powder River Basin.[19]

When coal is "strip mined," heavy equipment is used to remove what the miners call "the overburden." The ranchers call it "vegetation." Their cattle feed on it. Outdoor enthusiasts call it "wildlife habitat." They hunt on it with rifles and cameras. Typically, the surface of the land was owned by the rancher. The sub-surface was owned by someone else. Sometimes it was a private owner planning to make a fortune mining it. Sometimes it was the government who leased it to a mining company. In the beginning there were few, if any, laws regulating strip mining or requiring the miners to restore the land to its original conditions after the coal was removed.

Sometime in 1972, Tom Bell, the iconic Wyoming conservationist and editor of the *High Country News*, telephoned his old friend Bill Barlow, a Campbell County rancher. "Your way of life is threatened," said Bell to Barlow. Barlow recalled the conversation. "I really didn't know what he was talking about."[20] Barlow and his neighbors were about to learn the truth behind Tom Bell's warning. By the early 1970s, an energy-hungry world coveted that coal, causing it to become the defining political and economic issue of the times. In April of 1974, the *New York Times* described the mining impact on Gillette, saying the small Wyoming town on the edge of the Powder River Basin was "a raw jumble of rutted streets and sprawling junkyards, red mud and dust, dirty trucks and crowded bars, faded billboards and sagging utility lines, and block after block of house trailers squatting in the dust like a nest of grubs."

The *Times* quoted the Wyoming state geologist as expecting 760,000 acres of Northeast Wyoming farm and ranch land and wildlife habitat would "be torn up getting at the coal."[21] On October 18, 1974, the U.S. Department of the Interior released a long-awaited "Final Environmental Impact Statement on the Development of Coal Reserves in the Eastern Powder River Basin of Wyoming." They didn't have to read much beyond the page one summary of volume one before conservative farmers and ranchers and liberal environmentalists became alarmed in equal measure. The analysis said these projects would produce needed energy and significant tax revenues at a cost. The EIS warned that the eleven new coal strip mines coupled with the expansion of four existing mines and the construction of a new 113-mile railroad could irrevocably alter their way of life. The Interior Department summed up their findings saying these proposed projects would result in diminished air quality, the destruction of vegetation, and reduced water resources for agriculture, recreation, and wildlife.

The EIS cautioned that valuable archeological and paleontological treasures would be sacrificed, and wildlife habitat would be reduced. The report made apparent a heretofore unrecognized intersection of the interests of environmentalists and conservative ranchers and farmers, thus giving birth to the Powder River Basin Resources Council. Few were better prepared to bring those groups together than Lynn Dickey.

She was home on a brief vacation when she saw the "help wanted" ad. A citizen's conservation group calling itself "The Powder River Basin Resources Council" was looking for a director. Some 50 Northeast Wyoming ranchers met in Buffalo in 1973. They met to talk about coal development and what it might mean to their lives. They "came to believe that the industrialization forecasted for the basin could ruin agriculture."[22] When they hired Lynn Dickey to take the helm, the PRBRC came to life and was soon, with more than 460 members, able to honestly claim to be "the largest and most active conservation group in Wyoming."[23] All agreed Lynn's ability to listen empathetically and her low key approach to bringing a diverse group of people to the table was the reason for the success.

Lynn divided her time between organizing throughout the state and working the halls of the Wyoming state capitol and those of the U.S. Capitol. While lobbying successfully to override President Gerald Ford's veto of a federal strip-mining control act, she ran into access barriers apparent to anyone who ever stood at the bottom of the marble stairway leading to the entry doors of the historic Capitol building. Lynn was forced to sit patiently in her wheelchair until a good Samaritan offered to join others in doing what her old high school football team did, pick up her and her chair and carry them to the top of the stairs. On several occasions, one of the "Good Samaritans" was Senator Ted Kennedy who, with his own notoriously bad back to deal with, eventually arranged for the young lobbyist from Wyoming to use the Capitol's freight elevator.

Lynn's work required her to drive thousands of miles across Wyoming. Legislative committee meetings, conferences of all sorts, confabs with a few persons who needed persuading or many who needed motivation for the cause. Driving over the Big Horn Mountains late one wintry night, her car skidded off the road and landed in a steep embankment of fresh snow. Lynn was unable to get out of the car and the episode might have ended tragically but for her headlights barely penetrating the snow. The glimmering light was noticed by a couple driving across the mountains that night. They called for help and Lynn was rescued. She was, nonetheless, known to run roadblocks erected to stop drivers from traveling icy, dangerous roads. There were times she found the wheelchair opened doors. Lynn and passenger R.T. Cox stopped at the gate to Yellowstone National Park on a trip from Cody to Jackson Hole. The Park Ranger commented on Lynn's wheelchair in the backseat and waved her through the gate, saying, "There's no fee." Lynn turned to R.T. and said, "See, everyone should have a wheelchair."

By the end of her first year on the job, a former president of the council dubbed Lynn "Joan of Arc on a steel stallion." Under Lynn's tutelage, this group of ranchers, farmers and environmentalists found their public advocacy strength. They organized their own community, lobbied at the state and federal level, and filed formal protests against industrial facilities threatening their way of life. While she headed up the PRBRC, it became "a regular occurrence for government officials, media representatives, and members of other groups to solicit our opinions on relevant issues."[24] One afternoon as she and PRBRC researcher R.T. Cox were talking about an issue, a Park County state legislator walked through the door. It was Al Simpson. He was pondering a run for the U.S. Senate and wanted Lynn's advice. Cox said that was the sort of influence Lynn had amassed by then.

Governor Herschler wanted to name her "Handicapped Person of the Year." Lynn refused the honor believing there were others more deserving. Her knowledge of environmental issues caught Herschler's attention. In 1975, she accepted his appointment to the newly created Environmental Quality Council. Lynn's influence and capabilities worried the Wyoming Mining Association. Its executive director, Bill Budd, attacked the appointment. "This deliberate refusal to appoint anyone from the mining industry is bad enough," he cried, "but it is compounded several times over when the person who is appointed has stated publicly his (sic) bias against the mining industry." Lynn didn't shy away from the debate. She responded to Budd by reminding him of the purposes of the EQC under the statute that created it, i.e., to "preserve and enhance the air and water and to reclaim the land of Wyoming." Lynn said she hoped the Wyoming Mining Association shared those goals.[25] Her work on the Council, in the legislature, and with PRBRC earned special recognition from the U.S. Environmental Protection Agency in 1987.

In the coming few years, she relaxed by playing cards and praying with a small group of nuns in Dayton while doing the hard work of finding common ground between conservative ranchers and farmers and liberal environmentalists. At some point, Lynn converted from the Congregational roots of her family to Catholicism, having come to believe her deep concerns with social justice were well served in the Catholic Church. Lynn Dickey discovered her purpose in life at the intersection of public service and spiritual practices.

In 1976, she was appointed to the national board of directors of Common Cause, a national "watch dog" organization committed to holding public officials to high ethical standards. After Jimmy Carter was elected President in 1976, he appointed Lynn to the White House Environmental Policy Council. She was named that year as "Special Consultant" to the Congressional Office of Technology Assessment to assist in its study of the impact of a controversial proposal to use millions of gallons of water to move coal hundreds of miles through a pipeline. The following year, Governor Herschler tapped her to direct his Energy Conservation Department.

In 1979, Lynn purchased "The Book Shop" in Sheridan from a friend. It was a community hub for political dialogue. It also occasioned Lynn to take a personal stand against the lack of access for disabled persons. With no parking spaces reserved for handicapped people, Lynn was forced to find a spot as near as possible to the bookstore. She'd park, pull her chair from the back seat, unfold it, scoot her body from the car into the wheelchair and then find some kind person willing to help lift her over the curb onto the sidewalk. Moving her car every couple of hours to avoid parking tickets was out of the question. Parking tickets piled up. As a protest for the city's failure to address access issues, Lynn refused to pay them. It may have been her first foray into civil disobedience.

By 1982, she decided to enter politics. Lynn announced she would be a Democratic Party candidate for the Wyoming State House of Representatives. Few aspirants for the legislature have been as qualified. During her years at the helm of the PRBRC, she became familiar not only with the major issues confronting Sheridan County and the state, but also with the main players. Lynn knew them all. She worked with them all on a variety of projects. From the governor and the other four statewide elected officials to county commissioners, state legislators, the appointees running state and federal agencies, Lynn knew them, and they knew Lynn. So did the voters.

Lynn's campaign focused on education, childcare, and balancing the need for economic development with meeting human needs. A group of well-known Republicans endorsed this Democrat. They noted Lynn had been "instrumental in the passage of Wyoming's plant siting, clean air, reclamation, and severance tax laws." They called her "a practical idealist with a great love for this state."[26] In decidedly Republican Sheridan County, Lynn was elected in her first bid for office.

January 11, 1983 was a cold, blustery day with winds gusting to more than 40 miles an hour, with ice and snow on the ground. Lynn wheeled her chair out to the icy curb and after scraping snow from the windshield, slid into the driver's seat, folded her chair, tossed it into the back seat, and drove to the Capitol Building, joining her legislative colleagues for the opening ceremony of the Wyoming State Legislature.

At noon on the Constitutionally prescribed date, the assistant Secretary of State, Linda Mosley, called the role of the members of the 47th Wyoming State Legislature. "Here," said Lynn Dickey from her wheelchair behind a desk placed intentionally near the back of the House chamber to facilitate easier coming and going for the freshman. But coming and going wasn't

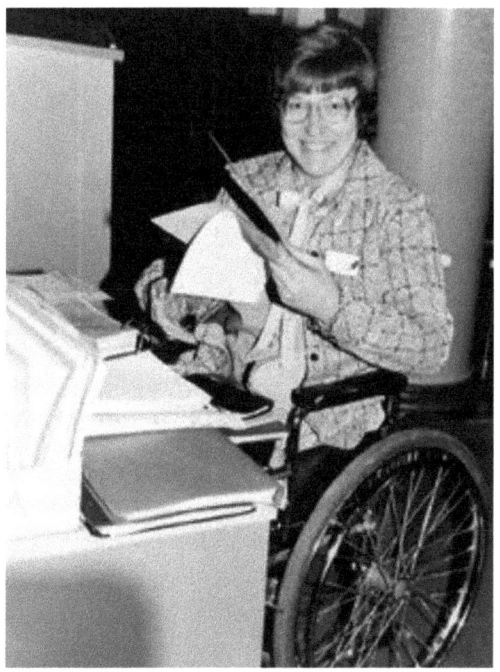

State Representative Lynn Dickey working at her desk in the House chambers. Photo from Dickey Family Collection. Used with permission

easy for her. The Americans with Disabilities Act was still years away and the builders of the old state Capitol building had not anticipated the need for being accessible to lawmakers or anyone else confined to a wheelchair.

The legislature meets for forty days in odd-numbered years and for twenty days in even-numbered years. It is grueling for all. They meet in the dead of winter. Outside it's usually cold and windy, often snow and ice on the ground. A legislator's day starts long before sunrise and doesn't end until night darkens the sky. Committee meetings can be called to order as early as 7 AM and end as late as committee's business demands. There are breakfast, lunch, and dinner meetings with constituents, state agency heads, and organizations representing dozens of causes that matter to the people you represent. Between meetings there are phone calls to return and letters to answer. Before going to bed at night, legislators must take time to prepare themselves for the next day's committee agenda and floor debate. There are reports to read, bills to study, research to conduct. Floor debates and committee meetings often stretch beyond dinner time and leave most members drained of energy.

If Lynn Dickey ever complained about the rigor of serving in the legislature, there are no known witnesses. Indeed, while her colleagues relaxed after the daily grind by attending lobbyist-sponsored cocktail parties and dinners, Lynn spent many of her evenings serving meals at the homeless shelter in Cheyenne and listening to the stories of the lives of the men and women who came there each day for a warm meal and a clean bed.

Though a first-termer, Lynn received the committee assignments she wanted in order to work on issues that mattered to her. She was assigned to the Education Committee and the Travel, Recreation, and Wildlife Committee. Her first bill to become law established the right of anyone who is "blind, visually, impaired, deaf or hearing impaired" to be accompanied into public facilities by a guide dog. As expected, she played an active role in debating a range of environmental issues.

By now, it was apparent to all who knew Lynn that she was a deeply spiritual person. At the invitation of the Republican Speaker of the House, she gave the opening prayer on January 26, 1985. "Lord God," she said, speaking to her colleagues as much as to the Divine:

> *"I am sure it is clear to you that everyone of us here is in need of your help. We all have personal bias, opinion and experience which sometimes stand in the way of looking at an issue from as broad a perspective as we should. Please help us to remember that the only job we have here is to be servants...servants to the public and to your will. We know that's our job and we need all the help we can get to perform it."*[27]

By 1988, the stress of serving in the state house was taking a toll on her health. By the end of each forty-day session, her Hepatitis C became symptomatic, and she suffered from both intensive migraines and the bowel problems which were ever present. The state Democratic Party was trying to persuade her to seek statewide office. But she felt increasingly in need of quiet time to herself. By now, Lynn regularly found refuge by gathering with a small group of nuns living together in nearby Dayton.

In 1983, five Benedictine Sisters were invited to Wyoming by the Catholic Bishop to establish a new community. They lived in Casper before moving to Big Horn and purchased land in Dayton 1989, where they started the San Benito Monastery. The nuns operated under the Rule of St. Benedict, "No one is to pursue what she judges better for herself, but rather what benefits another." Lynn took quickly to the joy of being in their presence.

They would play cards, pray, read scripture, talk, and work together many an afternoon. At times, Lynn stayed overnight with them. On March 21, 1987, Lynn joined the Benedictine Sisters by taking the vows of an oblate of St. Benedict. Oblates are lay people who choose to "integrate their prayer, work and family life with their Christian journey according to the principles established by St. Benedict some 1500 years ago."[28] The honor could only be bestowed after a candidate demonstrated the authenticity of her call during a 12-month period of guided study, regular meetings with a mentor, and discernment over whether the candidate is prepared for a life of service.[29]

The Benedictine Sisters of Perpetual Adoration were part of a contemplative order with three other communities in addition to Dayton. The primary house was in St. Louis and two others were located in Clyde, Missouri and Tulsa, Oklahoma. Beginning in 1988, Lynn visited the St. Louis and Clyde communities, sometimes staying several weeks or even months at a time, working in the library, making communion bread, or tending the garden. She found it a place that "overtakes me here, a place where I will truly receive God's word."[30] Service to the church had become central to her social conscience and the way she saw her purpose.

So, it was time meditating and praying with the Benedictine Sisters in Clyde, Missouri in the summer of 1988 when Lynn discerned whether she would remain in politics or take a different road. By June, the four-term incumbent who could have been a contender for the governorship or a seat in Congress, ruled out a political campaign for re-election to the legislature or for any statewide office.

"I actually think I'm done with electoral politics," she told the *Casper Star-Tribune*. She acknowledged having "fairly serious digestive and kidney problems which are the result of being paralyzed for so many years."[31] For someone who seldom accepted her limitations, she knew those health problems precluded anything as demanding as the immense amount of travel and other stresses that would accompany running for or serving in statewide office.

Her time of discernment at the Missouri monastery led her to believe she should devote herself to the bookstore she still owned and to voluntary activities in the community. She founded the Court Appointed Special Advocates (CASA) program in Sheridan County, was an active volunteer with Big Brothers and Big Sisters and was a founder of the local homeless shelter. But she was not done with public service. Mike Sullivan, who often said, "Lynn rules the Capitol building in her wheelchair," was entering the second year of his first term as Governor. He needed someone who knew the process and the issues, someone Republicans as well as Democratic members of the legislature admired. "She had a special talent," Sullivan observed. "She could work on a bipartisan basis. I think she was loved and respected by everyone she knew."[32] The Governor recruited Lynn to lobby the legislature for his agenda and to serve as his liaison with the Northern Arapaho and Eastern Shoshone Nations of the Wind River Indian Reservation. Neither job was stress free, nor was the position she accepted to serve on the state board of education for a six-year term.

Sullivan told Tribal leaders that he had selected Lynn because of her familiarity with the issues facing the Reservation and her ability to listen and communicate. "I have decided to hire Lynn Dickey, a former state legislator from Sheridan, and a person whom I respect highly to serve as my personal representative to the Shoshone and Arapaho Tribes," Sullivan notified the Joint Tribal Council."[33] Those who work with the Tribes know it takes a lengthy, determined effort to build relationships. In the beginning, Lynn experienced some difficulty in arranging meetings with those with whom she needed to talk. As long as anyone around her can remember, Lynn had crocheted. Scarfs for her sisters, sweaters for nieces and nephews. Socks for friends. She decided to knit her way into a relationship with the Tribal elders. She took her crochet supplies with her to the Reservation and sat in the waiting area of the Tribal government offices knitting. She was a "curiosity." It was a rather odd sight, this white woman sitting alone in a wheelchair in the lobby, crocheting. Soon they began to talk to her. Once they got to know her, they developed what became meaningful and productive relationships. By the Spring of 1992, Dickey reported, "I think they've kind of gotten used to me now."[34]

The year after leaving the state legislature, Lynn's courage in working to abolish the death penalty received national acknowledgment. Her bill abolishing state-sponsored executions was introduced while two inmates sat on death row. Representative Dickey told her colleagues:

> *"As long as there's a chance of human error, as long as there's a chance we could kill an innocent person, as long as there's a chance that a guilty person could repent, I feel the state is putting itself in a situation it just doesn't belong in, to kill someone."*[35]

Her bill received only 11 votes, which spoke to the courage it took to force fellow legislators to debate the controversial issue. For having done so, the American Civil Liberties Union awarded Lynn its annual "Justice William Brennan Award."

After leaving her job in Governor Sullivan's office, Lynn continued her political activism, lobbying against U.S. sanctions on the people of Iraq, telling Wyoming's U.S. Senator Mike Enzi that the sanctions had no "observable effect on (Saddam) Hussein" and "surely we could think of some other approach not quite so deadly to Iraq's innocent civilians."[36] She was willing to "speak truth to power" even if it meant confronting the popular Governor of her own Party and Air Force Military Police. After Governor Ed Herschler told Ronald Reagan's Secretary of Defense that he would support the MX Missile, a controversial weapons system, Lynn wrote him a scathing letter. She called him out for taking one position publicly and another privately in his correspondence with Secretary Caspar Weinberger. Telling the Governor how "extremely disappointed" she was, Lynn advised him there were "a hell of a lot of Democrats in Wyoming who aren't convinced the MX is a good idea."[37]

Lynn had earlier introduced a resolution in the State House to endorse an international nuclear freeze. She was an outspoken opponent of the MX and its deployment in Wyoming. Now she took her concerns to the streets, wheeling herself to the gates of Warren Air Force base alongside dozens of other protesters on June 7, 1987. The *Casper Star Tribune* saluted Dickey for "shaking a few cages," when she forced the State House to vote on a resolution opposing the MX in Wyoming. "What is important," the January 20, 1987editorial comment written by Erich Kirshner said, "is the nuclear issue was finally addressed by Wyoming's representatives in Cheyenne."

On Sept. 19, 2005, the 50 multiple-headed MX missiles deployed at Francis E. Warren Air Force Base in Cheyenne were dismantled and the parts trucked away, passing through the same gates where two decades earlier, then State Representative Lynn Dickey positioned herself at the gates of the military installation, protesting the placement of the controversial nuclear weapons in Wyoming.[38] Lynn was in the middle of the front line of more than a hundred protesters challenging Air Force officers who were ordering the group not to pass over a white line they had painted on the roadway. Lynn's wheelchair promptly crossed the line as an officer warned her and the others. "If you don't depart by going to the other side of the white line, we will have to apprehend you."[39] Lynn and the others were part of the "MX Faith and Resistance Retreat" of June 5-7, 1987. As "the largest act of non-violent disobedience ever to take place at F.E. Warren Air Force Base," they were there to civilly disobey such an order.[40] They were apprehended, photographed, and fingerprinted. Each was given a written order barring them from the base for two years.

The nuclear arms race of the 1980s, between the Soviet Union and the

U.S. was, Lynn argued, "a sign that we have lost touch with the values taught by the Gospel of Christ, and, in fact, by all the world's religions, values that place love of God and love of neighbor above all other values."[41] In addition to protesting sanctions against Iraq, she stood toe-to-toe in a public debate with Wyoming Congressman Dick Cheney in 1985.[42] She challenged the Republican supporter of the Contras to recognize the number of religious leaders who opposed U.S. intervention in the Central American country. Later she marched against U.S. aid to the contras in their counter-revolution against the Sandinistas of Nicaragua. Looking back on her political activism, Lynn acknowledged it followed her conversion to Catholicism and the deep spirituality that accompanied it.

> *"Before I began my instruction in the Catholic Church, I had not thought much about abortion or nuclear weapons or the death penalty. My growth as a Christian helped me to think about them."*[43]

In 1997, Lynn petitioned the Benedictine Sisters to become a nun. Her petition was rejected. Some of her siblings believed it was because the Sisters felt Lynn's place was in the world advocating for social justice rather than behind the walls of a convent. She was heartbroken but no less committed to a life of service. With that door closed, she decided to enroll in the Eastern Mennonite University in Harrisonburg, Virginia. In retrospect it seems her life had been a pathway to her decision to seek a graduate degree in Conflict Transformation. Her studies there gave her an academic sense of much of the work she had been doing since the 1966 car accident that left her bound to a wheelchair. At EMU, she took courses on understanding conflict and injustice, peacebuilding and justice practices, conflict transformation from an individual, interpersonal and community level, the dynamics of conflict and injustice, and experiencing the practice of peacebuilding.

When she enrolled, the faculty and admissions staff wondered what they could possibly offer a student whose entire professional life had integrated conflict resolution and social justice, whose life had converted the obstacles that beset her life into assets. They realized that while they might not be able to offer her much, she could offer them and her fellow students a great deal. Vernon E. Jantzi, the director of Eastern Mennonite University's Conflict Transformation Program, said Lynn was a "bridge" between "the grassroots, the middle and highest levels of power."[44]

One night in May 2000, Lynn suffered a heart attack while driving her car on a Virginia freeway. She suffered critical injuries and died a few days later in the hospital, much of her life bookended by two severe car accidents. On the night she died, Lynn's sister Ellen was at her bedside. She picked up Lynn's prayer book and noticed "Prayers for the Dead" in the index. She read the morning prayer and then the evening prayer to her unconscious sister. Lynn stopped breathing for a moment and then began again. Some of the sisters at Clyde were frequently on the phone seeking reports on Lynn's status. One spoke to Lynn as Ellen held the phone to her ear. Lynn breathed her last on May 21. A memorial service was held three days later at St. John the Baptist Catholic Church in Buffalo. Lynn's friend and partner in the Book Shop, Rev. Robert Miller, joined Deacon Joe Kristufek in officiating. To commemorate the extraordinary life of a woman who spent a lifetime trying to do justice, loving and exhibiting kindness, and walking humbly with her God, the words of Micah 6: 6-8 were read:

> *"With what shall I come before the Lord and bow myself before the God on High? Shall I come before Him with burnt offerings, with calves a year old? Will the Lord be pleased with thousands of rams, ten thousands of rivers of oil? Shall I give my firstborn for my transgression, the fruit of my body for the sin of my soul? He has showed you, O man, what is good; and what does the Lord require of you but to do justice, and to love kindness, and to walk humbly with your God?"*

At Lynn's request, the celebration of her life did not include a Mass because her family could not receive the Eucharist. Within a year and a half, her parents would also be gone; her father Willard dying of heart disease on September 1, 2001. Imogene died the following November 6, of complications from injuries suffered in the 1966 car accident, after becoming the longest living quadriplegic.

Ken and Sue Heuermann, longtime Sheridan friends, remember Lynn when they look upon two needlepoint pillows she gifted them. One reminds them of Lynn's awesome sense of humor, the other of her profound spirit. The first reads "Behold the hunter," the other, "Life is fragile. Handle with prayer."

Endnotes

1. Author's interview with John Jenkins, March 15, 2021
2. Senator Robert Dole, Congressional Record (1989), 19804
3. Id.
4. Imogene's Christmas Letter, 1990, Dickey family files
5. Author's interview with Ellen Dillon, February 13, 2021
6. Id.
7. "Dickeys reported progressing in Casper hospital," *Buffalo Bulletin*, April 14, 1966, 1
8. "Imogene Dickey's Condition somewhat improved this week," *Buffalo Bulletin*, April 21, 1966, 1
9. "Lynn Dickey overcame a life-altering car crash to 'own the capitol" *Casper Star-Tribune*, November 15, 2020, https://trib.com/news/state-and-regional/lynn-dickey-overcame-a-life-altering-car-crash-to-own-the-capitol/article_d96fe4ba-1ccd-5c73-acfa-50775380cf86.html, accessed September 9, 2021
10. "The Illio," 1968, https://archive.org/details/illio68univ/page/66/mode/2up, 72, accessed September 17, 2021
11. "Student Life at Illinois: 1960-1969," https://archives.library.illinois.edu/slc/research-education/timeline/1960-1969/ accessed September 13, 2021
12. "The Illio," 1968, https://archive.org/details/illio68univ/page/66/mode/2up, accessed September 17, 2021
13. "Student Life at Illinois: 1970-1979," https://archives.library.illinois.edu/slc/research-education/timeline/1970-1979/
14. "The Illio," 1968, https://archive.org/details/illio68univ/page/244/mode/2up, 246, accessed September 17, 2021
15. "Buffalo Girl Chosen to Spend Two Weeks in Hawaii," *Casper Star Tribune*, January 31, 1969, 11
16. Cozzens, *The Earth is Weeping*, 32-33
17. Treuer, *The Heartbeat of Wounded Knee*, 375
18. Knight, Jones, Reiners, Romme, *Mountains and Plains*, 13
19. McPhee, *Rising from the Plains*, 7. Note: Although the author is referring to lands along the Union Pacific in Southern Wyoming, the geological process mirrored the coal formations on the Powder River Basin.
20. "Powder River council rides herd on coal," *High Country News*, November 21, 1975, 12
21. James Sterba, "Town scarred by oil boom waits apprehensively for miners," *New York Times*, April 11, 1974, 33 and 36
22. Id., 12
23. Id., 12
24. "Lynn Dickey: PRBRC celebrates and remembers her life and work," *Powder River Breaks*, Vol. 28, No. 3 (May/June 2000, 1
25. "PRBRC coordinator fields charges," *Sheridan Press*, July 16, 1975, 1
26. Letter to "Dear fellow Republicans," October 26, 1982, from Dickey family personal collection

27 Opening Prayer, Wyoming House of Representatives, January 26, 1985, courtesy collection of Dickey family
28 https://www.glastonburyabbey.org/index.php/abbey/oblates/what-is-an-oblate/, accessed October 25, 2021
29 https://www.benedictinesisters.org/#
30 "Monastic life encourages availability to God," Lynn Dickey, *Catholic Register*, June 1991
31 "Dickey won't seek re-election to Wyoming House," *Casper Star-Tribune*,
32
33 Letter, Sullivan to the Joint Tribal Council, June 20, 1991, from the Dickey family's personal collection
34 "Reservation liaison makes progress improving ties," *Denver Post*, April 12, 1992, 20
35 "Dickey pushes bill to abolish death penalty," *Casper Star Tribune*
36 Letter, Dickey to Enzi, January 9, 1998, from Dickey family collection
37 Letter, Dickey to Herschler, undated, from Dickey family collection
38 "United States Retires MX Missile," *Arms Control Association Newsletter*, https://www.armscontrol.org/act/2005-10/united-states-retires-mx-missile, accessed September 30, 2021
39 "100 MX protesters detained for 'processing' at Warren," *Casper Star Tribune*, June 8, 1987,
40 "Respect for Each Other," *Wyoming Tribune*, Letter to the editor,
41 Id.
42 "Cheney gets debate on rebel aid package," *Casper Star Tribune*, April 21, 1985, A3
43 "Monastic life encourages availability to God," Lynn Dickey, *Catholic Register*, June 1991
44 "Lynn Dickey Memories," Vernon J. Jantzi, May 23, 2000, from the Dickey family's personal collection

Chapter 6

SISSY AND VICKIE GOODWIN

"determined to punish the very concept of the unknown"[1]

He was an Eagle Scout, a bucking bronc rider, and a Crew Chief aboard C-130 transport planes flying supplies to Thailand at the height of the Vietnam War. He was a highly skilled technician working at a coal-fired power plant for 30 years, a University of Wyoming graduate with a degree in mathematics and science who later taught at a community college. He was a political activist who served on the board of the American Civil Liberties Union and Veterans for Peace, drove trucks and school buses loaded with medical supplies through some of the most dangerous parts of Mexico and to Cuba, bucking the U.S. embargo, built water wells for people in Kenya, served as an international election observer in El Salvador, and helped build a university in Nicaragua.

He did these things and more because of who he was. And because of who he was, he had his teeth kicked in, suffered numerous physical and verbal assaults, was beaten viciously by complete strangers using their fists, was arrested three times, discharged from the Air Force despite a flawless record, and nearly lost that 30-year career in a powerplant. People threw the carcasses of dead animals on his porch and vandalized his property. He was publicly humiliated by a sitting member of the United States Senate and suffered emotionally as his wife and children were taunted and bullied by neighbors and strangers alike. All because of who he was.

Who was Sissy Goodwin? He liked to think of himself "as a guy who likes to wear women's clothing." And Vickie? She was a political activist and his wife of more than a half a century and likes to think of herself as a woman who "loves the person I have become because I was married to him."

When someone finds themselves suddenly facing the head winds of a political crisis, the gusts are usually unpleasantly strong. They come and go. There may be a sudden burst of buffeting winds followed by a lull. When someone's very existence is an afront to the dominant culture, the winds against which they must stand are not only withering but unremitting. That is especially true when the differences involve sexuality or gender. Gender bending, by its nature, brings on tornadic winds. After all, this is a state whose only university proclaims that "the world needs more cowboys." Without exception or choice, every car licensed in Wyoming is branded with a plate, front and rear, depicting a rugged cowboy riding atop a bucking horse. That is the standard for manliness. Alas, Wyoming is also where Matthew Shepard was brutally murdered more than two decades ago and is yet one of the four states refusing to enact a hate crimes law or anti-discrimination protections for its LGBTQ citizens.

Gender hegemony is assumed. Gender is required to be binary. The rules are enforced. Men are men. Women are women. The lines are black and white. Gender norms are not negotiable and cannot be challenged without severe consequences. Plural understandings of masculinity and femininity are not tolerated in the Equality State. Larry and Vickie lived in Wyoming long enough to know. They entered that arena eyes wide open. After standing against the Wyoming wind for most of his life, Sissy acknowledged "there's not too much diversity in Wyoming" and most people who "choose to live a different lifestyle are chased out of the community." He decided long ago "that is not fair to me; it's not fair to people like me; it's not even fair to people who live here." He decided he was not going to let the uber-conformists run him out of the state.

If you've ever laid in the grass on a summer day and looked to the infinite skies, you've undoubtedly seen a trail of white vapor across the blue expanse. It may be 30,000 or more feet away, so far that you cannot see the aircraft creating the vapor. But you know it's there and if you follow the vapor trail you know where the airplane is headed. A child's life is like that. If you watched Larry grow up, you might well have laid odds that he could become what the social scientists call "a transvestite," or a "cross dresser." The American Psychiatric Association defines transvestitism as "recurrent and persistent cross dressing by a heterosexual male." It estimates that 3 to 5 percent of all males engage in cross dressing. Sissy preferred the term "gender enhanced male."

> "I heard the term GEM. Uh, it's an acronym for 'gender enhanced male.' And I like that term. The term transvestite has gotten some negative connotation, kind of a nasty negative stereotype. So, I prefer gender enhanced male."[2]

Larry Goodwin's grandparents homesteaded 35 miles north of Douglas. Eventually they sold the land and moved to town. Larry was born in his grandparents' Douglas, Wyoming home on July 3, 1946. Life was hard. Memories were unpleasant. Among his most vivid childhood memories is the night his father, Fernando Desoto Matthews, was "barreling down a dark Wyoming road, when he screeches to a stop, reaches over my mom's lap, pops her door open and shoves her out, driving away with me and my sister screaming in terror in the back seat."[3]

After his mother, Doris Jean, divorced Larry's father, the young boy lived with his mother and sister at his grandparents for a time. When he was four or five years old, his mother married Larry's stepfather, James "Red" Goodwin." Not coincidentally, it was about this time that Larry began experimenting with cross dressing, wearing his younger sister's clothing. Larry was raised by what a friend called "a horror-movie mother and father."[4] Doris and Red were abusive drifters, a "hard drinking waitress and a hard drinking oil roughneck who imposed a cruel, nomadic existence" on Larry and his sister.[5] Beatings were as severe as they were frequent, fists and belts most often, once with a horsewhip. The emotional abuse was soul killing. A close friend observed:

> *An abused child doesn't know why he's being abused, doesn't know that not every kid isn't horse-whipped; or their moms dropped off in the country like an old dog. Some severely abused children manifest other roles—the class clown, the super good person, the troublemaker. All crutches. The abused child blames him or herself.*"[6]

Many years later, Larry co-authored a scholarly psychological study of the root causes of cross dressing with Dr. Robert Peterson, Ph. D. They surveyed one-hundred transvestites nationwide. Fifty-two responses were received. More than 80 percent reported severe physical and emotional childhood abuse. Most reported that wearing gender-bending clothing put them "at peace" and made them feel "safe" and that it had nothing to do with "sexual arousal."[7] Larry dealt with the violence by wearing his sister's clothing. "For me," he said years later, "it gave me a kind of pleasure and it was an escape from a hostile environment, it was my escape mechanism."[8]

Red Goodwin's family wouldn't have much to do with Red. His family didn't "like him," Larry recalled, "any more than other people." As a result of having no family connections and a violent disposition that often got him in trouble on the job, the family moved frequently, continually in search of work beginning when his mother and stepfather married and moved to Bremerton, Washington. After a short stay there, it was off to Montana and six months later, back to Wyoming. "I remember attending one school for just one day before having to move," Sissy said, adding that the family lived in countless Wyoming communities, some of which most Wyomingites have never heard. "Keyline, Edgerton, Midwest, Lynch, Shoshone, Lusk, Wildcat, Pasternak & Garfield, Oil Camp, Black Thunder, a lot of communities."[9] Many of these were nothing more than family-inappropriate, rugged camps owned by various oil companies where dank rooms, shacks, and tents were made available to oil field workers and their families at exorbitant rent. At times the family was homeless, living in a pick-up truck or an abandoned railroad car "down by the river." It was an isolated lifestyle conducive to abusing one's children without witnesses.

In particularly stressful times, Larry crawled through the train car widow, into a small lean-to that doubled as his bedroom. He put on sister Jean's panties and a dress.[10] He denies it was a choice, saying, "I certainly didn't choose to wear women's clothes. The easy way would have been to comply with societal norms." Many of the family's moves took them to rural settings. "One nice thing about the country is you can go out and put on a dress and no one would know."[11] But his family knew. While his sister seemed to understand, "If anything," Larry recalled, "my mother was more disgusted by me." She found opportunities like a family Thanksgiving Dinner to humiliate him by pulling his panties above his waistline while others watched and laughed. Years later as his mother was in a hospice bed near death, Larry visited out of duty. Her last words to her son were, "Don't come back, Larry, I don't want the staff to know you are my son."[12]

Most kids who survive such a troubled home life look back and remember that one person who gave them hope. For Larry, it was Roger Stratton. "That man took me under his wing and I'm confident I wouldn't be here if it wasn't for Roger." Larry often rode his horse over to the Stratton place where he was welcomed and affirmed. Roger secretly paid the costs for Larry to attend Boy Scout summer camps. Years later, Sissy visited Roger as he was on his deathbed. He had to clear his conscience. There was something he'd never told this man who had meant so much to him. "I need to tell you I wear girls' clothes," Larry admitted to his mentor. Roger smiled weakly and said, "I've known that since you were in the 6th grade." Sissy asked Roger, "How can I repay you?" "You just treat people the way I treated you."

At school, he feared being outed and so he complied with societal norms, making every attempt to appear "macho." He joined the rodeo team, Future Farmers of America, and the wrestling team. With the Vietnam War escalating as he graduated from high school Larry enlisted in the Air Force. He wanted to be a pilot but was barred for lack of a college education. Instead, he trained as an aircraft mechanic and was assigned to be a crew chief aboard C-130s flying supply routes between Guam and Thailand.

Laying on his cot in the barracks relaxing one afternoon where he was stationed in New Jersey, Larry turned on the radio. The announcer was talking about men who wear women's clothing. It was the first time he'd ever heard the term "transvestite." A caller proclaimed, "Oh, so this show is about sexual perversion."

> *"Well, of course, it caught my attention. Growing up, I didn't know what I was. 'Transvestite.' Even if I knew of the term, I would have had no idea what I was or if I was gay, homosexual. I was a basket case."*[13]

Sissy always said, "I served to protect your right to say or dress or look or act or have the religion you want." The Air Force didn't see it that way. One night, the First Sergeant saw Larry asleep in a "frilly blue nightie." The enraged NCO cried out, "Airman, what the hell is going on there?" Airman Goodwin was asked to agree to a dishonorable discharge as a homosexual. "I refused to sign because I wasn't and am not." After a three-day interrogation by the Office of Special Investigations, this airman with an exemplary record who had been recently named "Squadron Airman of the Month," received an honorable discharge and was sent home. Larry tried the rodeo circuit for a time and looked for other work. Hiding who he was had become a full-time job. It was then he decided that if he didn't "come out" he would commit suicide.

By then he was married to his high school sweetheart. He had not told her of his desire to wear women's clothing before they wed, "which was," he admitted, "a terrible thing to do to her." He put on a dress and told her. They soon divorced. Back in Casper, Larry found work with an airplane servicing company. One day, he wandered into the Pink Kitchen Restaurant west of Casper for lunch. Vickie Jones was his waitress. She remembered this guy from high school and how "he ran with kind of a lot of good-looking, nice-looking boys, I thought were pretty neat. And when he asked me out, I was just, wow, you know, this is pretty cool."[14] Gradually they fell in love. On one of their first dates, Larry treated her to a rodeo where he was one of the bareback riding contestants. Larry decided that with this woman, "I wasn't going to make that mistake twice." So, he told her he was a cross dresser. "I don't recall it was a crazy shock," Vickie said, "but I was surprised." She assumed he meant he would wear women's clothing "around the house and to bed." On Christmas Eve 1968, she married him anyway "during a pretty Christmas Eve morning ceremony." The wedding announcement in the *Casper Star Tribune* reported, "The bride, given in marriage by her father, wore a floor length gown with full skirt overlayed with lace."

They hadn't told Vickie's parents. There was some unhappiness when they learned. Vickie was encouraged to "leave him," but eventually, like anyone who took the time to get to know Larry, they became accepting.

Vickie graduated from Casper College with an Associate Degree in 1966. A year after they wed, she and Larry enrolled in classes at the University of Wyoming. In 1970, they moved to Cheyenne where Vickie served as a student teacher and Larry worked for the blood bank and attended airline mechanic classes at Cannon Aeronautical Center, where he was popular enough to be elected student body president.

During these years, Larry wasn't going out in public dressed in women's clothing. It was a secret known only to Larry and Vickie. By 1972 that changed, and Vickie was not pleased, nor was it easy for Larry. "The first time I went out in public, I put on a dress and went to a movie theater, and I was so nervous, I came home and ugh, got sick. I got physically ill because, uh, that's how much stress it caused me to, you know, to come out in public and wonder what would, would I be arrested, would I be beat up?"[15] It was equally hard on Vickie. "When I became more, I guess you might say, flamboyant, and started wearing dresses in public, she had some hard times with it."[16]

"We were both coming out," Larry recalled, "me as a crossdresser. Vickie as my wife."[17] For a long time, she refused to be seen in public with him. "I found myself challenged," Vickie recalled, "not so much by what he wore but by public reaction to what he wore. I cringed in public and hid behind dark glasses, I feared for his life. I wanted to protect him and, at the same time, protect myself."[18] It was then a complete stranger hollered at him angrily, "Sissy." It was meant as an insult, of course, but Larry embraced it and introduced himself as "Sissy" ever after. Like this woman, people he'd never seen before, to whom he had done nothing, were incensed enough by his very existence to spit out insults, profanity, curses, and slurs with no other provocation. "Faggot," "pervert," "queer," "pedophile." At times, the verbal outbursts were followed by unchecked violence.

Knowing how he was struggling with his self-image and having come to know him as a kind, thoughtful, loving husband, Vickie frequently insisted Sissy stand in front of a mirror and repeat, "I am a good person. I am a good person."

None of the violence Sissy endured would surprise behavioral scientists who study this sort of thing. The reactions to Sissy were textbook examples of what happens when someone bends gender or sexuality norms. In ancient Rome and Greece, the male body represented traits such as masculinity, bravery, courage, and any male whose appearance was different was subject to ridicule and worse. The "effeminate" male made the Apostle Paul's list of those doomed to hell (1st Corinthians 6:9, King James Version). The

Vickie and Sissy Goodwin. Photo courtesy of StoryCorps and NPR.

psychological underpinning that leads to violent reaction is what research on gender and sexuality has consistently discovered. "Heterosexuality as something essential, biologically determined and conditioned in the order of values and morals, constructed socially and historically by a network of meanings, which were naturalized, excluding other forms of experiencing sexuality."[19] A Brazilian study determined that of the members of the Lesbian, Gay, Bisexual, Transgender, and Transvestite community, the latter two groups were the "most affected by prejudice and discrimination," in addition to being what the study called "the main targets of violence on the streets." Seventy-five percent reported suffering violence, with neighbors and strangers accounting for 75% of the assaults.[20]

While neighbors and strangers most frequently dealt out the violence, transsexuals and transvestites are also on the receiving end of assaults by public officials, including law enforcement officers, which explains why Sissy never called the police when he was beaten, shoved, knocked to the ground, had his teeth kicked in, or when his home was vandalized.

During a business trip to Salt Lake City in April 2000, Sissy took a cab to Little America to find a gift for Vickie in the hotel gift shop. He browsed, wearing a tennis skirt. Someone complained about Sissy's attire. Salt Lake City police were called. The hotel manager claimed to have fielded a report that Sissy was lifting his skirt and showing his "pink underwear" to strangers. He was thrown to the ground. An officer put his knee in Sissy's back while he was handcuffed. He was arrested for disturbing the peace and taken to the Salt Lake County jail. His wallet and other personal property were taken from him, while other officers "laughed and whistled at him." After a few hours, they admitted they had no legal basis for holding him and Sissy was released, but not his wallet. He was now far from his hotel with no means of calling a cab. A young man who happened to be at the jail in a failed attempt to secure his father's release on a DUI arrest, witnessed Sissy's plight and offered to give him a ride to his hotel. Once there, he found that his room key was among the items the police had taken. He went to the front desk but was not permitted back into his room until he described in detail the property he had left there.

Sissy fought back legally. With evidence from Little America's security cameras proving he had done nothing to warrant the arrest, his claim was settled by an ACLU attorney for $1500, enough for a down payment on the new car he and Vickie needed. The settlement included a public apology. Little America admitted "Mr. Goodwin did not engage in any lewd or lascivious conduct at the time this incident occurred."[21]

Meanwhile back in Douglas, Sissy was standing on his property, watering the lawn while wearing a frilly blouse. A complete stranger walking by noticed Sissy. With no provocation but Sissy's appearance, he started heaping profanity on him. The stranger then attacked him physically, kicking Sissy in the kidneys and in the mouth, bashing out his two front teeth as his young son watched, screaming in terror.

Sissy brought his characteristic sense of humor to a retrospective on those ugly events. "Remember the neighbors we had? Sissy asked Vickie during an episode of Story Corp. "He came out with a knife one day and threatened to castrate me. I call those people fashion critics."[22]

The Goodwin home was a frequent target for vandals. Windows were broken with baseball bats, graffiti painted on the home. Carcasses of dead, dismembered animals were thrown on his porch, beer bottles broken in the driveway, their tires slashed. False "for sale" signs were planted in their front yard as a not too subtle message that some of the neighbors didn't want the Goodwin family living there. One morning Vickie walked out her front door to see their beloved Honey Locust tree severely vandalized. The loss of a tree is no small thing in arid Wyoming. She dedicated months to helping that tree survive and it did. Eventually the tree grew to two times the height of their house. Vickie brought her characteristic philosophical view when looking back. "It is proof," she said, "that anything can survive random acts of hate as long as it's loved."

On another occasion, Sissy was in the Salt Lake City airport. A group of young men walked out of a pizza parlor. When they saw Sissy, they reacted by calling him names. He asked them to lay off. They began punching him. One grabbed Sissy by the hair and threw him to the ground. Others kicked him in the face. Finally, one of the men stopped the beating, fearing his friends might kill Sissy. By then he had suffered a detached retina.[23] Sissy's vision in that eye was permanently damaged. He had already learned

Profiles in Courage

what happens when a cross dresser calls the Salt Lake City cops. He avoided that mistake this time. The airline kindly held his plane, giving Sissy time to clean some of the blood off his face and clothing before boarding.

While in the Kansas City airport, it happened again. Out of the blue, without the warning slurs that usually foreshadowed a physical attack, someone sucker punched Sissy, ripping his ear open. Once again, he just cleaned himself up and went on his way. Sissy never trusted the cops would help him if called and so he didn't. But others frequently called the cops, using them as a weapon against him.

He was arrested several times under trumped up charges that he was "disturbing the peace" or as Vickie called it, "dressing like a woman while male." Though Sissy violated no law, he apparently violated the sensibilities of some with the power to arrest him, embarrass him, and do harm. In Salt Lake City a security officer threw him down, and as Sissy hit the ground, he made a painful noise. He was sure that noise was the basis for a "disturbing the peace" charge that didn't hold up. On more than one occasion, policemen separated Sissy from his children, interrogating the kids on whether their dad had abused them or forced his son to wear female attire.

In Casper, he was Christmas shopping when a policeman appeared, threw him up against the car, handcuffed him and put him into the back seat of a squad car. Sissy challenged the cop. "I don't believe it's against the law for me to wear a dress." After taking Sissy to the police station and parading him in front of other taunting cops, they were unable to produce any statute under which the arrest was legal. The officer claimed the police chief, in the spirit of Christmas, had ordered Sissy released if he promised not to dress like a woman again. Sissy refused to be bullied. "Now they don't know what to do with me," Sissy recalled. "Long story short, we made an agreement that I wouldn't sue the city for false arrest if they wouldn't arrest me again." Later, Sissy and the arresting officer jointly taught diversity courses at Casper College.[24]

A sitting member of the United States Senate felt it was politically safe to join those who targeted Sissy. He was speaking to students in Greybull High School and Middle School in April of 2017. By then, Mike Enzi had been in the Senate for two decades. One of the students asked the Senator what he and his colleagues are doing "to improve the life of the LGBTQ community." Another inquired, "How do you plan to help Wyoming live up to its name as 'The Equality State?'" Senator Enzi replied:

> *"We always say that in Wyoming you can be just about anything you want to be, as long as you don't push it in somebody's face," the Senator went on. "I know a guy who wears a tutu and goes to bars on Friday night and is always surprised that he gets in fights. Well, he kind of asks for it. That's the way that he winds up with that kind of problem."*[25]

Vickie pointed out, "for the record," Sissy never wore a tutu, that is until after Senator Enzi weighed in. His unsettling remarks made the news across Wyoming and the nation. By then Sissy was teaching at Casper College. To protest Enzi's unfortunate choice of words, his entire class showed up the next day decked out in tutus and pink hair ribbons like the ones Sissy wore. "Tutu parties," were held in support of the man the Senator targeted. In Pinedale, Sheridan, Casper, Lander, Riverton, New York City, Washington, D.C. Wizened cowboys sat on bar stools alongside drugstore cowboys, students, construction workers and aging hippies in western shirts, jeans, boots, cowboy hats and "tutus with net and ribbon" all lifting toasts to Sissy. Bars throughout historic downtown Laramie offered free and discounted drinks to men wearing tutus.[26] Decked out in his best tutu, Sissy joined the celebration at the notoriously rough and tumble Buckhorn Bar in Laramie. "At one point," Vickie remembered, "we stood midway between where Matthew Shepard was picked up for his final ride and where Sissy was arrested 30 years before for being a man in a woman's dress."[27] Eventually the Senator phoned Sissy and offered his apology.

When they decided to move to another house in Douglas, Sissy had taken up golf and they found a home they loved on the golf course. Some were aghast when word spread that Sissy might become their new neighbor. They tried to intimidate the owner into not selling to Sissy and Vickie. When they listed their own home with multi-list, some realtors refused to show it, figuring that if it didn't sell, the Goodwins couldn't afford the new house. The owner of the house they wanted was an older woman. A proud member in the Republican party. She was a genuine "live and let live" conservative who didn't cotton up to others telling her how to live. She told the neighbors to mind their own business and called Vickie and Sissy with an offer to let them move into the house rent free until their house sold. Vickie and Sissy moved in. The three became close friends, so close that the neighbor was comfortable in critiquing Sissy's fashion choices. She could see Sissy's ability to match colors and styles was abysmal. She began making him beautiful matching blouses and skirts.

During these years, Sissy suffered a dose of "Scriptural Abuse" as well. That's what happens when religious fanatics come bearing a mouth full of scripture and heart full of hate. A local Baptist minister and his congregation made it their calling to "save" Sissy's soul. "Every time one of them would see me in town, they'd come out and hand me a card that read, 'We love you, but we hate your sin.'" They'd explain to Sissy how his soul was at risk because he was in violation of Biblical law found in the book of Deuteronomy, where, in Chapter 22, verse 5, it was written thousands of years ago, as one of the more than 600 Biblical laws applied to the ancient Jewish community, "A woman shall not wear a man's garment, nor shall a man put on a woman's cloak, for whoever does these things is an abomination to the LORD your God."

Hebrew Bible (i.e., the Old Testament) scholar Robert Alter explains that anthropologists understand the verse to represent "a general recoil of ancient Hebrew culture from the co-mingling of distinct, often binary categories – male and female, nurture and killing, seeds of different plants, wool from animals and linen from plants, conjugality and promiscuity."[28]

So it was that the zealots who were unable to break away from their limited, binary view of the world pummeled Sissy with either a Bible, their taunts, or their fists, raising the question, "What was it about Sissy's existence that caused people to become so enraged they would literally try to kill him?" As represented in the ancient religious texts, there is a primal notion deep in the human psyche that people must conform to the gender they were assigned at birth. If a person is biologically male but behaves in stereotypically feminine ways, sociologists call this gender nonconformity.

"Male and female God created them," says Genesis 5:2. Whichever sex you are dictates, for some, your appearance and behavior. Sissy's appearance as a male in clothing societally reserved for women was so jarring a threat for some that it triggered a visceral drive to destroy the threat.

Thus, Sissy was left to decide whether he would be the person they thought he should be, or the person God created him to be. As one psychologist who studied violence against gender nonconforming people put it, an "individual's gender expression is not responsible for eliciting the prejudice of others."[29] Nonetheless, their extreme forms of prejudice put the burden on Sissy to decide how to respond. He was determined that hate would not win.

"I am a good person," he repeated standing in front of the mirror. And he was.

Despite the turmoil and drama, Vickie and Sissy held a marriage together. There was never more than a fleeting thought to do otherwise. He knew who he was and was comfortable. She knew who she was and was comfortable. A son, Travis, was born in 1973, followed by daughter Kristi a year later. As they entered the public schools in Douglas, the children endured a great deal of bullying because of Sissy. But their parents gave them the kind of stability Sissy had been denied in his childhood. Same school and hometown from kindergarten through high school. Same friends. Although Travis experienced problems in the criminal justice system later in adulthood, his school record exhibited success. Travis earned academic honors as the "foreign language student of the year" and was a finalist for the National Honor Society. He also won three letters in varsity sports. Sissy described Travis as, "a popular, good looking intelligent young man." Daughter Kristi was equally successful, earning a degree in forensic science at Metro State University in Denver.

When Travis was 28, he telephoned his mother. There was a big secret needing to be shared. He was a transgender female. Despite his lifestyle or perhaps because of his own experiences, Sissy found the news unsettling. "To discover she's transgender, it's been a little difficult for me, but I love her, of course." Vickie listened to her husband and added words that could only come from someone who learned to love others for who they are. "She's gonna have some, I mean, it's a rough road. So, um, but she's our daughter and I love her the way she is."[30]

In 1974, Sissy began a thirty-year career working at the Dave Johnson Power Plant located near Glenrock, midway between Casper and Douglas. Vickie and Sissy spent a lot of time "soul searching" before applying. The job not only meant a pay cut of twenty-five cents an hour, but it also meant he'd be working with macho, blue-collar union workers. A male co-worker in frilly blouses and women's slacks would not be welcomed with open arms. Sissy had been working for Casper Air Service at a job with no benefits and an uncertain future. The job at Dave Johnson meant benefits and union protection, which a dozen years later proved critical. He decided he would tone down the dress and take the new job. Sissy started as a coal shoveler.

Initially, he dressed conventionally but gradually began wearing women's slacks and peasant blouses. Tolerated by his first plant manager, a new manager was less accepting. The harassment moved off the streets and into the workplace. When a group of 20 co-workers signed a petition in 1984 demanding Sissy be fired the new manager issued an order, "No more gender inappropriate clothing." Sissy attempted to comply, but his supervisors didn't stop there. They began looking for a reason to fire him. Despite a personnel file full of certificates of appreciation and recognition of his excellent work, small mistakes or misunderstandings now resulted in documentation placed in his personnel file. The manager was building a case that might pass the scrutiny of a union arbitration hearing. "They were obviously instigating paperwork to get rid of me."[31]

It took a heavy emotional toll. Sissy "became increasingly agitated and emotionally troubled." One day while at work, he reminded his co-workers about an incident in Douglas. An employee of another plant "had become unhinged and engaged in a violent rampage in the community which ended in the deaths of hostages and the suicide of the unfortunate individual." The comments raised concerns and caused management to place Sissy on disability leave for evaluation by Dr. Robert G. Peterson "due to managerial questions about his emotional stability."[32]

Earlier he had started training to become a Control Operator (CO). However, in 1986, management notified Sissy "he would not be allowed further training as a CO at this time due to described concerns related to his mode of attire."[33] The position would have meant a significant pay increase as well as additional responsibilities. On his behalf, the union filed a grievance. In January of 1989, the matter was the subject of an arbitration hearing. Sissy arrived at the hearing "in a blue blouse and trousers, which all agreed were similar to his usual workplace garb."[34]

Company witnesses said it was an embarrassment when outsiders toured the facility. Upon seeing Sissy, there were "nudges, remarks, or giggles from the visitors."[35] Co-workers told the arbitrator of Sissy's excellent work and called him "one of the superior AOs (assistant operators). Dr. Peterson testified about his treatment of Sissy and the steady improvement in his patient's mental condition. The hearing officer concluded the company had "arbitrarily denied the opportunity to complete training for the CO classification." The ruling noted, "The mere fact that the Grievant is an acknowledged transvestite is not grounds for concern." The decision relied heavily on Dr. Peterson's medical opinion.

> *"Aside from the oddity in dress, the majority of transvestites adopt normal behavior and lifestyles and are responsible, productive members of society. The unrefuted record reflects that Grievant is well within this category of individuals who have lived successful, normal, healthy lifestyles in relative peaceful coexistence with their transvestite behavior."*[36]

The company was ordered to allow Sissy to complete the training to become a Control Operator.

While the turmoil swirled around his job, Sissy decided to build an airplane. Did he know how to fly? No. But Vickie said he always wanted to be a pilot. He had an Airframe Powerplant License, which he earned when he was first in his class at Cannon Aeronautical School in Cheyenne in 1971. That meant Sissy was qualified to "inspect, perform, or supervise maintenance of aircraft." So it was that in March of 1981, Sissy armed himself with "one set of drawings consisting of 47 sheets, one step by step assembly and rigging manual, information on computing weight and balance with appropriate instructions on production flight test procedures and an illustrated parts catalogue."[37] For that and the rights to build a Pitts Model S-E1 airplane, Sissy paid Pitts Aerobatics of Afton, Wyoming $200. Buying the parts, however, required a second mortgage on their home.

It was a biplane with balsa wood wings and a used engine Sissy rebuilt. It took him a decade to complete the project, celebrated by painting it black and adding pink stripes. He named her "Classic Miss" and gave her the number N57LV (L for Larry, V for Vickie). Then it was time to learn to fly. He went to a flight school in Colorado, received his pilot's license, and took Vickie on a test flight. Vickie got airsick when the plane crossed a thermal uplift north of Rawlins.

Not long after that, Sissy decided that building the plane was sufficient unto itself. He came home one day and told Vickie that if he didn't sell it, he might just die in it. The plane now lives in Rock Hound, Texas.

Sissy took up bird watching, photography, and golf. During the 1980s, Sissy and Vickie were politically involved. Vickie chaired the Converse County Democratic Party and was the treasurer of the Wyoming Democratic Party. She also represented the state on the Democratic National Committee. In 1992, Vickie ran for the state house of representatives. Her opponent was a Republican incumbent and Converse County was heavily red. Even so, she turned it into a competitive race. Sissy was an alternate delegate to the 1980 Democratic National Convention committed to the renomination of President Jimmy Carter. In 1984, he was an organizer for Walter

Mondale's presidential campaign. He and Vickie were key party organizers in Converse County. Vickie was also the co-director of the Powder River Basin Resources Council, Wyoming's largest and most successful environmental advocacy organization. She was a popular substitute teacher. Still, people in Douglas couldn't figure out how to judge her. In her spare time, she made a few dollars selling Tupperware. Some said she'd do better if she wasn't married to Sissy. Others said she'd do better if she wasn't a Democrat.

In 1986, Sissy graduated from the University of Wyoming with a bachelor's degree in mathematics and science. Two years later, while visiting the Vietnam War Memorial Wall in Cody, Sissy noticed a name was missing. He was told that because his friend Jose Leo Lujan's name was not on the Memorial Wall in Washington, DC, they could not put it on the Wall in Cody. That didn't make sense to Sissy. He knew Lujan had been killed during combat in 1968. It took Sissy more than a year of phone calls and letters to the Department of Defense, but his sustained campaign paid off. On July 6, 1989, he wrote the Secretary of Defense, Richard Cheney, telling of the poor way in which Lujan had been treated by the military. When Leo died of injuries he suffered in Vietnam, "his body was sent (home) clad only in undergarments." Then his name was left off the Vietnam Memorial Wall. Sissy conducted a successful, one-person campaign to correct that. On August 22, 1989, the director of the National Capitol Region informed Wyoming Senator Alan Simpson that Lujan's name would be added no later than Armistice Day that year.

Sissy traveled to Washington to see Leo's name placed on the Wall. He called that event "the one thing that made the greatest emotional impact on me." Sissy said that moment caused him to understand "the horrible, human, spiritual, and economic impact of war."[38] As a veteran, Sissy felt compelled to speak out against the war in Iraq. As the head of Wyoming's chapter of Veterans for Peace (VFP), he said, "What President Bush is doing is substituting casualties for courage." He traveled the state to carry his antiwar message, speaking to gatherings in Casper, Cheyenne, and Laramie. As a veteran, he found his voice mattered on peace and justice work. He participated fully in VFP activities protesting wars and threats of war. Later he served on their national board of directors. He also took part in their international aid campaigns. But his activism went beyond talk.

Sissy studied Spanish in a four-week immersion language class in Antigua, Guatemala to prepare himself for a series of humanitarian aid trips to Mexico and Central America. Driving a school bus, Sissy led a caravan to Chiapas, Mexico, and Nicaragua after spending a year collecting prosthetics and other medical supplies.[39] Two years earlier, he had led a similar group to El Salvador driving a 12-ton box truck. "Seeing the destructive results of 12 years of war and the extreme poverty of the native peoples of El Salvador was startling." He called their courage "infectious." Sissy returned to Chiapas in December 1998, leading a Pastors for Peace Caravan bringing agricultural and medical supplies to families that had been devastated by Hurricane Mitch. A year earlier, the Chiapas village he visited had been attacked by Mexican military troops. A massacre of 45 men, women and children occurred. Sissy went, he said, not only to bring much needed aid but to show solidarity with those who were suffering.[40]

Vickie joined Sissy for a February-March trip to El Salvador where they toured a prosthetics shop where limbs were made for those who lost limbs during the civil war. In June 1997, Sissy was invited to return to El Salvador to serves as an election observer in that nation's national election. He represented Veterans for Peace as one of 100 international observes. In the fall of 2000, he participated in a Pastor's for Peace caravan to Cuba despite the U.S. embargo and the possibility of being charged with violating the "Trading with the Enemy Act," which carried a jail term of 10 years and a fine of $250,000.

As a male veteran in women's clothing, Sissy attracted special attention as he delivered medical supplies, solar panels, bicycles, and other items to Cuba. There he also attended the Second World Conference on Friendship and Solidarity. He listened to a speech by Fidel Castro and met Issa Salam Hamid of the External Relations Bureau of Iraq. Their conversation resulted in an invitation to that Middle Eastern nation. In March 2001, Vickie traveled to Iraq as part of a Veterans for Peace delegation to help build water treatment plants. Her husband felt strongly that the war was immoral and stood on a street corner in Douglas every Friday as the war in Iraq raged, protesting President George W. Bush's decision to go to war in Iraq and chronicling the numbers of U.S. soldiers dying weekly in that war. Next to him stood a cowboy with his own sign. "Support our troops, not the man in the dress," it read. It made Sissy smile.

In 2013, Sissy traveled to Nairobi, Kenya as a member of the University of Wyoming/Casper College Center Hillside Water Project Task Force. The delegation dug a well and trenches and laid 100 yards of pipe. "Thanks to the well, women and girls in the area are no longer required to regularly make the 20-mile roundtrip walk for water."[41] Sissy was awarded the "Veterans for Peace Service Medal" in February 1993 for his "selfless dedication to the principles for Veterans for Peace in pursuit of a more peaceful world for our children." The honor was presented to Sissy by Wyoming State Representative Bill Bensel.[42]

"Sissy" (left) protesting the war in Iraq as counter protester stands next to him on the streets of downtown Douglas, March 17, 2004. Photo used with permission of the *Douglas Budget*.

Profiles in Courage

There was another award Sissy received that he no longer wanted. Having suffered the slings and arrows of discrimination much of his life, he could no longer tolerate watching the Boy Scouts marginalize men and boys like him. He earned the Eagle Scout award on November 6, 1961, as member of Casper Boy Scout Troop No. 1. On August 30, 2000, he wrote to the Central Wyoming Council, Boy Scouts of America, telling them his Eagle Scout award "was an honor I have cherished throughout the years. However, developments within the scouting organization have caused me to seriously assess the Eagle award and what it represents." He called the intolerance advocated by the Boy Scouts of America a factor contributing to "violence against gay members of our country." Because BSA denied membership to gay men and boys, he said, "I am returning my Eagle Award." Fourteen years later the Boy Scouts changed their intolerant rule and allowed boys to join regardless oof sexual orientation.

By now, Sissy had retired from the power plant and taken a faculty position at Casper College. The college started a new "Electric Technology Program" and needed an instructor. Sissy knew he was qualified. The job required the instructor to teach students how to operate a power plant, something Sissy had been doing for thirty-three years. He got an interview. The interviewer was blunt. "There's an elephant in the room," he said, "and we need to talk about it." Sissy was just as blunt. "This is who I am," said the man in a dress sitting across from the person who would decide whether Sissy got the job. Sissy described his experience and qualifications, which fit the job perfectly. Then he added, "If the mode of dress is a precondition for employment, just let me know. No hard feelings. I understand and I'll go play golf."

At 61 years of age, he started a new career. He got the job because no other candidate was as qualified to teach students how to operate a power plant. Neither was any other candidate so qualified to teach men and women who might one day manage a plant and the human beings who work there to tolerate and accept diversity in their workforce. The college's decision to hire Sissy proved a success for the students as well as Sissy. It was August 6, 2007. The first day of his career as a teacher. "It's obvious," Sissy told his students as he walked to the front of the class wearing his characteristic frilly blouse, "I have a little different lifestyle. I'd be happy to talk to you about it but I'm not going to take up class time doing so. My door is always open. You'll find me open and honest." And they did. While some never understood, most became staunch defenders of this teacher, nominating him for a teacher of the year.

As a child, Sissy spent a summer in Washington State. In his memory, it was a wonderful time. As he neared retirement, he thought about it as he looked outside on Wyoming winter days. Sissy retired from Casper College in May of 2015. He and Vickie loaded up everything and headed for Washington. The *Los Angeles Times*, which had profiled Sissy in a 2013 article determined his departure from Wyoming was newsworthy.

> "After nearly seven decades in Wyoming, for much of that time facing heartbreak, discrimination and even physical violence, the cross-dresser has finally decided to leave the Cowboy State."[43]

Sissy told the reporter he'd miss his Wyoming friends and the state's open vistas "where the plains run like ocean waves, framed by mountains in the distance."

The move turned out not to be the happy experience his mind created of those days when he lived there as a child. From January through the end of March 2016, 61 inches of rain fell on their heads. Sissy missed the sun and he had misjudged how much his circle of friends back in Wyoming meant to him. Sissy became increasingly depressed. During a trip back to Douglas that spring to do some necessary work to help sell their old home, he called Vickie and told her he'd heard the Wyoming wind whistling as it does in that time of the year. The sound was comforting. After all, he had stood against it successfully his whole life. His psychiatrist asked him why he was staying in Washington when it caused him such despair. He answered by loading everything for a return trip to Douglas. They were welcomed back by a large group of old friends as they moved into the home they loved in April 2016.

Sissy and Vickie remembered their life together by telling the story to a National Public Radio audience on Story Corps. Sissy turned to his wife and said, "You didn't know you was marrying a fashion horse, did ya?" Vickie lovingly replied, "I didn't know that I was marrying someone who was going to take up two-thirds of the closet."

Sissy laughed. "I could have easily lived like my dad, become alcoholic. And I had tried suicide before I met you. But it's because of you I went to school and got my bachelor's degree. It was you makin' me look in the mirror and sayin', 'You're a good person.'" Then he asked her, "Where do you think we'll be in 20 years?" Vickie predicted, "Oh, probably walking along with our little canes, holding hands, you in your pretty dress and me in my jeans, being happy."[44]

Alas, it was not to be. In 2017, Vickie noticed Sissy had developed a tremor in his right hand causing it to "bounce up and down on the table or his knee." She suggested he talk to his doctor about it, but Sissy declined. The tremor didn't seem to limit him in any way. Within a year or so, Sissy exhibited noticeably greater fatigue and anxiety. As time went by, he had trouble coming up with words or understanding basic things. "He kept asking me if we were supposed to be somewhere." There were "questions about trips we hadn't taken, short-term memory loss, more pronounced tremors. He couldn't cut up his meat."

Sissy finally agreed to see a doctor. On February 5, 2020, an MRI disclosed a tumor on the right side of his brain. The doctor immediately scheduled brain surgery and told Sissy and Vickie he would pray for them. They went on a proverbial roller coaster ride for days as the medical team tried to understand what was going on in Sissy's head. Maybe it was cancer. Maybe not. Perhaps a stroke. During the night of February 15, while hospitalized, Sissy did suffer a stroke. Four days later, tissue samples showed Sissy suffering from Stage 4 brain cancer. Radiation and chemo were ruled out because they would not solve this problem and only create others. Vickie and Sissy agreed that comfort care was the best course. Within a few days. Sissy was transferred to hospice. Vickie explained to the nurse that her husband liked to wear women's nighties. The nurse said they already knew that about Sissy and had prepared one for him to wear.

On the morning of March 7, Natrona County State Representative Pat Sweeney came to visit. He brought along a resolution the Wyoming legislature passed in honor of Sissy, expressing gratitude for his life and legacy. As he lay near death, they read it to him.

> *"Joint Resolution acknowledging the life and legacy of a Wyoming original, Larry "Sissy" Goodwin. Whereas, Larry "Sissy" Goodwin was born in Douglas, Wyoming to a working class family; and whereas, "Sissy" became a rodeo cowboy and bull rider before joining the United States Air Force; and whereas, "Sissy" served honorably as an aircraft mechanic in the Vietnam War; and whereas, "Sissy" worked tirelessly to ensure the name of his fallen comrade, Army Communication Specialist Jose Leo Lujan, was added to the Vietnam War Memorial; and whereas, "Sissy" worked to establish and grow Veterans for Peace; and whereas, "Sissy" returned to his home state to marry his sweetheart and raise their two children; and whereas, "Sissy" worked for 33 years at the Dave Johnson Power Plant and taught Power Plant Technology at Casper College; and whereas, "Sissy" brought "gender independence" to the Equality State with his trademark ribbon skirts and hair-ribbons, despite being assaulted, arrested and abused; and whereas, "Sissy" returned this hate with love, generosity, and grace; NOW, THEREFORE, BE IT RESOLVED BY THE MEMBERS OF THE STATE OF WYOMING LEGISLATURE: That we express our gratitude for the life and legacy of Larry "Sissy" Goodwin."*

Sissy died that night, comfortable in his skin and in the silky soft nightie he wore as he went to sleep for eternity. The hospice nurse opened the window to allow his soul to fly free. He had completed his life, as he told himself so many times, as a good person.

As his life had earlier caught the attention of national news outlets, so did his death. *U.S. News and World Report* headlined an Associated Press report, "The Cowboy State's Sissy Goodwin: A Man with Global Impact."[45]

Epilogue

"In 2021, at least 37 transgender and gender non-conforming people were victims of fatal violence – more than the Human Rights Campaign has recorded in any other year. The grim milestone proves what we have long known: this violence is epidemic. Each one of the lives we lost was someone ripped from their family, their friends, and their community by an act of senseless violence, often driven by bigotry and transphobia and inflamed by the rhetoric of those who oppose our progress." ("2021 Human Rights Campaign Report: An Epidemic of Violence")

Larry "Sissy" Goodwin dedicated his life to the cause of confronting bigotry. He was, as his colleague Michael John Carley said, "determined to punish the very concept of the unknown." Sissy knew bigotry was unhealthy, not just for the targets but for the bigots themselves. He insisted on being who God created him to be in the hope that one day we will all be accepted for who God created us to be. In memoriam, Carley wrote an essay about Sissy after his death. It is entitled "The Toughest Boss I'll Ever Have."

> *"Sissy was the toughest boss I ever had, not because of his ability to replicate the staples of macho iconography. Any moron can do that so long as they're confident and willing. Sissy was the toughest because amidst all the cowardice around him, he was so determined to punish the very concept of the unknown, that to the very end, Sissy Goodwin mowed elderly neighbors' lawns and stopped for strangers stranded along the road. To the end he was a force for compassion, benevolence, for warmth, for respect, for affection, and for love in its highest."*[46]

The voice in the mirror looked back at Sissy and said, "Yes, you are a good man." And his wife Vickie? She stood against the Wyoming wind, side by side with her husband for 51 years. She once said that when she married Sissy, "I got the pick of the litter." Carley concluded his eulogy by quoting her. "I love the person I have become because of Sissy."

Endnotes

1. Michael John Carley, "The Toughest Boss I'll Ever have," *EP Magazine*, September 2020, 26
2. "51 Years Loving a Man Named Sissy," *Death, Sex, and Money*, WNYC Podcast, November 11, 2020 https://www.wnycstudios.org/podcasts/deathsexmoney/episodes/sissy-vickie-death-sex-money-2020?tab=summary, accessed December 24, 2021
3. Greg Hinton, "A Sissy in Wyoming," A Playwright's Reading for the Nicolaysen Art Museum Casper, Wyoming, October 24, 2021, first read by the playwright for the 2021 Kennedy Center American College Theatre Festival
4. Michael John Carley, "The Toughest Boss I'll Ever have," *EP Magazine*, September 2020, 23
5. Lloyd Grove, "A Man Named Sissy," *Washington Post*, August 21, 1997, C4
6. Hinton, *A Sissy in Wyoming*, supra, 20
7. Goodwin and Peterson, *Psychological Impact of Abuse as it Relates to Transvestitism*, Journal of Applied Rehabilitation Counseling, Vol. 21, Number 4, Winer 1990
8. Wyoming Diversity Project Interview with Sissy Goodwin, Casper College, April 28, 2008, 5
9. Id., 2
10. Id., 6
11. Id., 6
12. Hinton, *A Sissy in Wyoming*, supra., 15
13. Id., 6
14. *51 Years of Loving a Man named Sissy*, supra
15. Id.
16. Wyoming Diversity Project Interview, supra., 7
17. Hinton, *A Sissy in Wyoming*, 18
18. Vickie Goodwin, "From Cowboy to Crossdresser: How I Stayed Married to a Man in a Dress for 51 years," personal recollections, undated
19. Silva GWS, Souza EFL, Sena RCF, Moura IBL, Sobreira MVS, Miranda FAN. *Cases of violence involving transvestites and transsexuals in a northeastern Brazilian city*, Rev Gaúcha Enferm. 2016 jun;37(2):e56407. doi: http://dx.doi.org/10.1590/1983-1447.2016.02.56407, 2
20. Id., 4, 5
21. "Cross dresser, kicked out of hotel, settles dispute," *Associated Press*, August 1, 2001
22. NPR Morning Edition, https://storycorps.org/stories/sissy-and-vickie-goodwin-150403/ aired originally on April 3, 2015, accessed January 22, 2022
23. "51 Years Loving a Man Named Sissy," *Death, Sex, and Money*, WNYC Podcast, November 11, 2020 https://www.wnycstudios.org/podcasts/deathsexmoney/episodes/sissy-vickie-death-sex-money-2020?tab=summary, accessed December 28, 2021
24. Wyoming Diversity Project Interview, 10
25. "Sen. Mike Enzi: "A guy who wears a tutu to a bar 'kind of asks for it,"

Huffington Post, April 27, 2017, https://www.huffpost.com/entry/mike-enzi-tutu-bar_n_58ff9d28e4b091e8c710f23d
26 "Live and Let Tutu," *Laramie Boomerang*, April 28, 2017, 1
27 Recollections in Vickie Goodwin's personal files
28 Alter, The Hebrew Bible, "The Five Books of Moses," (2019), 619
29 Karen L. Blair, Ph. D., "What Precisely Do Transgender People Threaten?" *Psychology Today*, September 24, 2018, https://www.psychologytoday.com/us/blog/inclusive-insight/201809/what-precisely-do-transgender-people-threaten, accessed December 29, 2021
30 *51 Years of Loving a Man Named Sissy*, supra
31 Wyoming Diversity Project Interview, 4
32 "Award of Arbitrator," Case No. 77 300 0067 88, January 13, 1989, 7
33 Id., 5
34 Id., 6 fn
35 Id., 9
36 Id., 17
37 Contract between Larry "Sissy" Goodwin and Pitts Aerobatics, March 3, 1981, personal papers of Goodwin family
38 Id., 14
39 "Douglas' Good Samaritans help those in need in Central America," *Douglas Budget*, November 13, 1995, 1
40 "Douglas man brings relief to Mexican villagers," *Casper Star Tribune*, December 21, 1998
41 Casper College, "*Faculty and Staff Notes*, undated publication in personal files of Vickie Goodwin
42 "Goodwin to receive peace service medal, *Douglas Budget*, February 3, 1993, 1,
43 "Cross-dresser Sissy Goodwin decides to leave the Cowboy State, *Los Angeles Times*, April 4, 2015, https://www.latimes.com/nation/la-na-wyoming-cross-dresser-20150404-story.html, accessed January 22, 2022
44 National Public Radio, *Morning Edition*, https://storycorps.org/stories/sissy-and-vickie-goodwin-150403/ aired originally on April 3, 2015, accessed January 22, 2022
45 https://www.usnews.com/news/best-states/wyoming/articles/2020-03-21/the-cowboy-states-sissy-goodwin-a-man-with-global-impact?context=amp, March 22, 2020, accessed January 22, 2022
46 Michael John Carley, "The Toughest Boss I'll Ever have," *EP Magazine*, September 2020, 26

Chapter 7

U.S. SENATOR JOSEPH C. O'MAHONEY

*"nothing is more rewarded than loyalty,
nor more punished than disloyalty"*

If you stop people at random on any Wyoming street and ask them, "Who was Joseph C. O'Mahoney," not one in a thousand, if they are under 80 years of age, could tell you. Fewer yet could pronounce his name, though he served four terms as one of the most influential members of the United States Senate, was once nominated as Franklin Roosevelt's vice-president, and would have become only the second person from Wyoming to serve as a justice on the U.S. Supreme Court but for his principles.

He tried to solve the problem everyone had with pronouncing his last name with a rhyme. "You take the 'bahhh' of the lamb, the fruit of the bee and put them together for "O'mahhh'honey." It didn't always work. When the Senate Foreign Relations Committee held a hearing on President Jimmy Carter's nomination of former Wyoming Senator Gale W. McGee as Ambassador to the Organization of American States, Chairman John Sparkman of Alabama, then 78, who served with O'Mahoney, said he remembered his colleague used "a little jingle, but I don't remember what it was."[1]

Senator Sparkman did recall O'Mahoney's courageous role in the "bitterly fought" contest Franklin Delano Roosevelt waged to "pack the

Supreme Court." Senator O'Mahoney, Sparkman reminisced, "took a great hand in that." Indeed, he did.

◦◦◦

Joseph Christopher O'Mahoney was born in 1884 in Chelsea, Massachusetts. It was, fortuitously, an election day, the one on which Grover Cleveland became the first Democrat to win the White House in 28 years. Joseph was forever grateful they didn't name him "Grover." Chelsea was a small New England town, sitting on the ancestral lands of Naumkeag Nation, who had lived there for thousands of years when European colonists arrived in the 1600s. Chelsea Creek was the site of the second battle of the American Revolution.[2]

O'Mahoney's parents, Denis and Elizabeth, emigrated from County Cork Ireland in 1859. When the Civil War broke out, Denis, then 16 years old, enlisted in the Irish Brigade as a member of the 28th Massachusetts Volunteers, taking part in the Second Battle of Bull Run. He had the good fortune to not be among the one-quarter of the unit that died in combat. When he returned from the war, Denis opened a small business processing furs. He was a progressive who supported workers' rights. When he started his business, a 12-hour workday was the standard. Denis instituted a 10-hour workday for his employees.

Joseph was the second to the youngest of 11 children. Elizabeth raised the children, many of whom died in childhood. He recalls having "no childish desires that were not filled." Elizabeth died when Joseph was but nine years old, his father died a few years later while young Joseph was attending the Cambridge Latin School. The family disbanded with the older children going off on their own. He went to New York to live with his older brother Daniel after completing his studies at Cambridge, where he maintained excellent grades in Latin, French, and mathematics, finishing second in his class, while actively participating in sports and the debate team. He also dabbled in high school journalism. He wrote a newsletter for his classmates entitled, "A Letter from Our Correspondent in Washington," which was filled with the young man's opinions of what was happening in the nation's capital. He earned a few dollars writing editorials for the *Cambridge Democrat* during the week and delivering the paper door-to-door on Saturday. O'Mahoney attributed his interest in politics to his Irish heritage. "The Irish people," he told an oral history interviewer in 1958, "have always been interested in public life."

In 1904, the twenty-year-old enrolled in Columbia University, taking either the trolley car to the campus or riding the horsecar around the southern tip of Manhattan. He played basketball at Columbia while debating and writing for a daily student newspaper, the *Columbia Spectator*. Notable alums include R.W. Apple of the New York Times, several Pulitzer Prize winners, Langston Hughes, Jack Kerouac, and Herman Wouk. As he prepared for law school, O'Mahoney studied history, philosophy, anthropology, and economics. Still brandishing a keen interest in politics, he campaigned vigorously for William Randolph Hearst who was running for Mayor of New York as a Democrat.

Joseph was planning to complete his undergraduate work and enroll at the Columbia Law School, but his brother Frank developed tuberculosis and needed Joseph to provide care. The doctor suggested Frank's longevity would be enhanced by a geographical cure, which later proved helpful to Joe when it was discovered his lungs had also been scarred by the same ailment. It was one reason he left the east and remained in the Rocky Mountain West. It was also the reason he was ineligible to serve in the coming world war.[3] Before leaving for Boulder, Colorado, O'Mahoney voted for the Republican candidate for President, William Howard Taft, "because (Teddy) Roosevelt recommended him." It was, he said in a Columbia University oral interview in 1958, "the only time I ever voted Republican."

He and Frank arrived in Colorado knowing no one, with $15 in their pockets. Joseph quickly found a job, earning $15 a week as the editor Boulder's *Daily Herald*. His 1912 pro-Teddy Roosevelt editorials were so well received by local Republicans they asked him to run for the Colorado legislature. He declined. O'Mahoney worked for the *Daily Herald* until 1916. He found not only work, but also a spouse in Boulder. He married Agnes Veronica O'Leary in 1913 at her home in Massachusetts. The newlyweds returned to Boulder where Mrs. O'Mahoney enrolled in law school at the University of Colorado. Their lifetime partnership was sealed as Agnes attended classes during the day and helped Joseph edit the paper at night. She was a particularly capable person who, during World War II, was hired by the British Embassy to handle the correspondence between the U. S. and Britain

Earning insufficient wages at the *Herald*, O'Mahoney aspired to find a better-paying job. First, he accepted an offer to work for the Associated Press in Texas before seeing a help wanted ad seeking an editor for a small newspaper in Cheyenne, Wyoming. He went to work for the *State Leader*. As these things happen, the small newspaper was owned by John B. Kendrick.

By the time the two met, Kendrick was the Governor of Wyoming. He was born in 1857, in Cherokee County, Texas. Like O'Mahoney, he was orphaned early in life. His father, John Harvey Kendrick, a farmer, drowned trying to ford a river when Kendrick was three years old. Three years later, his mother, Anna Maye Kendrick, died "of fever." They didn't leave much of what was once a considerable estate to care for the children. It had been squandered providing financial support for the confederacy during the Civil War.[4] Kendrick was forced to leave school in the sixth grade. The future Wyoming governor and senator then signed on as a cowboy, moving cattle for five-month stints, from Texas through the Oklahoma Indian Territory, up through Dodge City, Kansas, and across the North Platte River into the grasslands of Wyoming.

His first Wyoming home was a ranch north of Cheyenne. He was later hired by out-of-state owners to manage a ranch on Old Woman Creek near Lusk. He frugally invested his paychecks in purchasing his own herd of cattle, though some say he rustled some of them. Either way, that was the start of what became the Kendrick Cattle Company, the foundation for his growing financial wealth and opening doors to significant political connections.

Kendrick's political career began in 1910, when he was elected to the state senate. It was the last year in which the Constitution allowed state legislators to choose U.S. Senators. The Democrats nominated John Kendrick; the Republicans chose Francis E. Warren.

> "Election of United States Senator: The hour of 11:20 o'clock A.M. having arrived, President Sage called the Senate to order and announced that this being the day and hour designated by the Joint Rules of the Senate and House of Representatives for the election of a United States Senator, to wit: the 28th day of January, 1913, President Sage declared that in pursuance with the Joint Rules, the special order for this hour was the election of a Senator in Congress for the State of Wyoming for the term of six years, beginning on the 4th day of March, A. D. 1913, in accordance with the Statutes in such case made and provided. By direction of President Sage, the roll call of the Senate was called by the Chief Clerk."⁵

Kendrick was defeated in the state senate 16-10-1. Although entitled to vote as a member of the senate, John Kendrick abstained. Warren's margin of victory in the house was much closer, 29-27. Kendrick cooled his heels until 1914. The rancher who, "spoke in a slow, halting manner" and "was willing to spend generous amounts of his considerable personal fortune in order to win," became Governor of Wyoming.⁶ Two years later, Kendrick and O'Mahoney met and established a friendship that would take them both to Washington, DC.

The *State Leader* was founded by Kendrick, in part, to offer a countervailing voice to balance, to some extent, the louder pro-Republican newspapers in the state. Working as Kendrick's trusted employee nurtured O'Mahoney's ambition to be politically active. He campaigned openly for Woodrow Wilson in the 1916 presidential contest.⁷ Years later, O'Mahoney told with great glee the story of how the *State Leader* became the first newspaper in America to report Wilson's victory over the Republican nominee, Charles Evans Hughes. As the votes were counted, there was a gathering consensus that Hughes would win. Many newspapers were put to bed that night after their editors wrote headlines to that effect, including the *Wyoming State Tribune*, the *Leader's* GOP competitor. These were the days before Steve Kornacki and his electronic board automatically collected and analyzed returns in real time. O'Mahoney stayed up all night analyzing returns, unable to accept the possibility that Wilson had lost.

> *"We went over (the election returns) carefully, and we found that Minnesota and California were out and that if Wilson carried either one of those states, he would be elected."*

Confident that the Democratic nominee would eventually carry California, O'Mahoney wrote the headline and "so we were the first morning newspaper…that went on the street with the announcement of Wilson's election."8

Naturally, he played a key role in organizing Kendrick's 1916 campaign for the senate. It was a tough race, pitting the incumbent Kendrick against Frank Mondell, a Republican who had already served 26 years representing Wyoming in the U.S. House of Representatives. Although he was the House Majority Leader and expected to become Speaker of the House, Mondell chose instead to run for the Senate. O'Mahoney taunted Mondell so vigorously during the campaign that he turned his attention away from his opponent to criticize his opponent's campaign manager, giving O'Mahoney "tremendous advertisement all over the state and people who never heard of me," O'Mahoney observed later that the voters "learned of my existence through that incident."

He was rewarded with an appointment to be the new senator's secretary, a position often referred to today as "chief of staff." Impressing Kendrick as "the most capable secretary I have ever had" solidified the young man's future political career.9 While in Washington, O'Mahoney worked days in Kendrick's office and attended classes at night, earning a law degree from Georgetown University. He graduated in 1920 together with fellow student Dennis Chavez, who went on to serve New Mexico for thirty-one years in Congress, the last twenty-eight overlapping O'Mahoney's senate career. Elected president of the senior class, O'Mahoney finished at the top while serving on the editorial board of the school's law journal. "He was the noblest Roman of them all," so said Georgetown's 1920 yearbook, *Ye*

Doomesday Booke. Where it was noted,

> "His sterling character, his prominence in student activities, and his all-round good fellowship have combined to make him one of the most popular and influential students in the law school."

Soon, O'Mahoney was back in Cheyenne where he hung a shingle and began practicing law. During one of his early trials, he examined a witness who told him of new mineral leases being issued for oil drilling in the Salt Creek field. Because of his work with Kendrick, O'Mahoney was deeply familiar with these things and told the man it was unlikely those leases would be granted since they were part of a Navy Reserve. The man told O'Mahoney that "there was an inside deal."[10] Joe, in turn, scrambled to Washington to meet with Senator Kendrick. He shared with him the rumors that Interior Secretary Albert Fall may be illegally leasing oil drilling rights for Naval reserves at Teapot Dome. At about the same time, Kendrick received a report from Wyoming Governor Leslie Miller, who became suspicious when he saw trucks with Sinclair Oil Company logos on the doors moving drilling equipment into the reserve.

Armed with the intelligence from both O'Mahoney and Miller, Senator Kendrick asked his former secretary to draft resolutions seeking a senate investigation. Thus, O'Mahoney played a key role in the discovery and investigation of the Teapot Dome scandal. Before it ended, Secretary Fall and oilman Harry Sinclair were in prison and "Teapot Dome" became synonymous with "scandal" until it was replaced by the term "Watergate" in the 1970s and the "January 6th Insurrection in 2021.

O'Mahoney remembered those years between 1920 and 1932, as "a disagreeable period." He lamented the course Republicans were charting for the country. He felt they were too single minded in representing the "big business classes." All the while, Joseph O'Mahoney made a name for himself in state and national Democratic Party circles. As he continued a successful law practice and served for a couple of years as Cheyenne's city attorney, O'Mahoney impressed party leaders with his political acumen. He was elected vice-chairman of the Wyoming Democratic Party from 1922-1930 and served on the Democratic National Committee. In 1925, O'Mahoney managed Nellie Tayloe Ross's campaign in a special election called to replace her husband who died in office. She became the first women in U.S. history to be elected governor.

He was a delegate to the 1932 Democratic National Convention that nominated Franklin Roosevelt for his first term as president. Roosevelt wanted the party to adopt a rather brief platform. O'Mahoney was appointed to the convention's platform committee to carry out FDR's wishes. He succeeded and caught the attention of FDR confidant James Farley. With Roosevelt's approval, Farley asked O'Mahoney to serve as vice-chair of the national campaign committee. After Roosevelt was elected president, Senator Kendrick made a yeoman's effort to have his young protégé appointed Secretary of the Interior.[11] Despite the Senator's sterling recommendation, O'Mahoney didn't get that job. Yet, because of O'Mahoney's loyalty, he was named a member of the new administration's "Little Cabinet" and appointed First Assistant Postmaster General.[12] Roosevelt dispatched Jim Farley to give the news to O'Mahoney. They met at the Biltmore Hotel in Washington. When informed of the appointment, O'Mahoney stared blankly at FDR's messenger. "Jim," he inquired, "who is the First Assistant Postmaster General now?" The question was met with silence. Farley didn't know. Finally, he said, "I get what you mean but I still want you to be the First Assistant Postmaster General."[13] It took more convincing for Agnes who was not enamored with the pay cut her husband would have to accept.

His service in this job didn't last long. Before 1933 ended, John Kendrick was dead of a cerebral hemorrhage. Senate Majority Leader Joe Robinson came to Wyoming for the funeral. He and O'Mahoney were destined to cross swords over FDR's court reform plan. That was in a distant future. For now, Robinson told the press that "although no one could fill Kendrick's shoes, he had been impressed with (O'Mahoney's) 'fitness and qualifications,'" adding reassuringly that "the White House thought highly of him."[14] Governor Leslie Miller got the message and appointed Joseph C. O'Mahoney as Wyoming's new senator. Before the end of his first term, he found himself in a serious political conflict with both the majority leader and the President. As the iconic Wyoming historian T.A. (Doc) Larson put it, "Rarely has a first-term senator made so much political hay by a single action."¹⁵

Opponents of Franklin Roosevelt's 1937 plan to reform the federal courts contemptuously dubbed it "court packing." Even today, as a radically conservative Supreme Court overturned Roe v. Wade and blurred the once clear line between church and state, the phrase "court packing" and the ignominious defeat of FDR's proposal of nearly nine decades ago, cast a long shadow. In contemporary times, as in the first years of the New Deal, an increasing number of voters have unfavorable opinions of the Supreme Court. Support declined precipitously from seven in ten in 2019 to little more half (54%) three years later.¹⁶ Then *Roe v. Wade* was overturned in June 2022. As this is written, 57% of Americans had an unfavorable view of the high Court.¹⁷ The fact that a solid majority of people no longer trust the Supreme Court is chilling. Yet, the memories of what politicians refer to as "FDR's court packing scheme" still precludes an honest debate over whether changes should be made in the form and function of the highest court in the land. To understand today's dilemma, one must understand Roosevelt's dilemma. Historian Burt Solomon wrote about the 1937 debacle and what led the president to undertake court reform, using words that resonate today.

> *"In a constitutional system of checks and balances, an extended reign of unpopularity will bring down the people's wrath, even on an unelected branch of government."*¹⁸

Nonetheless, when today's reformers dare propose change, they become weak-kneed at the mention of the loaded term "court packing." Such was the political post-traumatic-stress syndrome that took hold in the aftermath of the defeat of Roosevelt's proposal decades ago.

The hour arrived on that day in March of 1937. Straight up twelve o'clock noon. Chief Justice Charles Evans Hughes signaled the Court Crier. Although he'd performed this duty for twenty-three years, he recently experienced dreams, where instead of repeating his appointed script, he recited "Little Jack Horner" and so, this day he read verbatim from a written looseleaf notebook.[19] "The honorable Chief Justice and the associate justices of the Supreme Court of the United States." It was the jurists' signal. The Chief Justice entered the chambers first, followed by the eight associate justices, led by their longest serving colleague, Willis Van Devanter.

Justice Van Devanter is the only Wyoming citizen to ever serve on the high court. Joseph C. O'Mahoney had designs on becoming the second. Van Devanter, appointed by President William Howard Taft in 1910, was 79 years-old and President Roosevelt had, just that day, announced a proposal providing for the appointment of a new justice whenever a sitting justice celebrated his seventieth birthday. FDR's proposal was aimed at diluting the judicial power of Van Devanter and three of his conservative jurist brothers; Pierce Butler, James Clark McReynolds, and George Sutherland, a conservative bloc dubbed "The Four Horsemen."

Van Devanter is relatively unknown to Wyoming history. More wellknown is the event in which he played a leading role, a role rewarded with his appointment to the supreme court. One biographical sketch of the jurist called him a "brilliant lawyer," adding that he "made a name for himself in the 1890s as a loyal Republican and protector of the interests of the powerful."[20] Another was not so kind, saying that as an attorney, he worked "exclusively on behalf of the two biggest enterprises in Cheyenne; that of U.S. Senator Francis Warren and the once brazenly corrupt Union Pacific Railroad."[21] It was a reputation he earned representing Warren's interests in the invaders at the center of one of the most infamous events in Wyoming history, the Johnson County War. It was a war between "the cattle barons" and those the barons deemed "the cattle rustlers."

Perhaps the two best storytellers to preserve this piece of the state's history are an attorney who became a historian and a humorist who became a governor. John W. Davis and Jack R. Gage. Davis's 2010 book, "Wyoming Range War," found no evidence that the small ranchers the barons wished to kill were in fact "rustlers." It was more a conflict between big ranchers and small. In any event, an "invading force," assembled by the big cattlemen, who had "an implacable hatred of settlers," boarded a train in Cheyenne following a meeting of the Wyoming Stockgrowers Association and headed for Johnson County. Their plan was "to get to Buffalo as rapidly as possible, there to kill Sheriff Red Angus and his deputies and to kill all the county commissioners." Then they would install a government more to their liking.[22]

Gage said there were reasons to believe that a Cheyenne lawyer (Van Devanter) and a confidant of the barons, Francis E. Warren, "knew in advance all the plans for the invasion."[23]

The plan failed after the invaders murdered a couple of men and were surrounded by a large group of defenders. President Benjamin Harrison sent the cavalry to rescue them. They were charged and Willis Van Devanter became one of their defense attorneys. The defendants were acquitted. "Many years later, [Van Devanter] justified the acquittal of the cattlemen on the ground that nearly all of them were either leading citizens in Wyoming or from fine families."[24] Van Devanter inexplicably "destroyed many of his papers dealing with his years in Wyoming."[25]

When scrutinized, history demonstrates how often one thing inevitably leads to the next. In the aftermath of the Johnson County War, Willis Van Devanter garnered the loyalty of Francis E. Warren while earning that reputation as a "protector of the interests of the powerful," which led to the use of Warren's influence in obtaining Van Devanter's appointment to the U.S. Supreme Court. While here he was guided by his inclination to protect the interests of the powerful in the decisions he made as an associate justice. Those decisions, in which a majority of the Court joined with Van Devanter, threatened Franklin Roosevelt's New Deal and were the birth pangs preceding the nativity of the President's plan to reform the federal courts.

So, it was on that March day in 1937, as the nine justices took their seats, each was handed a copy of the President's message announcing his intention to reform the court. It was a direct attack on several of them.

> *"Whenever a judge or justice of any federal court has reached the age of seventy and does not avail himself of the opportunity to retire on a pension, a new member shall be appointed by the president then in office, with the approval, as required by the constitution, of the Senate of the United States."*[26]

Legal philosophy and not age was the real issue FDR targeted, although the ages of the nine justices sitting in 1937 was a good deal more advanced than at any other time in the nation's history apart from 1861.[27] A Harvard Law professor who clerked for Justice Louis Brandeis a few years earlier understood the genesis of the proposal. He'd seen it from the inside. Though "extraordinary and incredible," Paul Freund observed, the plan "can only be understood in the context of the Supreme Court's behavior up to 1937."[28]

The right of the courts to delegitimize laws enacted and signed into law by the other two branches of government is taken for granted today. That wasn't always so. The judiciary's right to exercise "judicial review" was not created by the drafters of the Constitution but, rather, by the court. It was 16 years after the Constitution was written that Chief Justice John Marshall wrote the majority opinion in *Marbury v. Madison*. There, in 1803, the Supreme Court gave itself and other federal courts the right to declare laws unconstitutional.

For decades, the courts were reluctant to use this extraordinary weapon. It was almost as though they were embarrassed by it. In the first 75 years after *Marbury*, the high court found only two laws unconstitutional. By 1934, judicial review had eradicated no more than 60 laws. However, in a five-month period of 1935, the Supreme Court declared four critical New Deal laws invalid. "This rate of mortality is without parallel in our history."[29] From the time Roosevelt was first elected in 1932 until the court reform proposal was released, the courts declared dozens of New Deal statutes to be contrary to their conservative interpretation of the Constitution.

Roosevelt and his congressional backers, including Senator O'Mahoney, relied on the Interstate Commerce Clause of the U.S. Constitution for the authority to implement a wide range of economic reforms to address the Depression's ills. The war between the two branches of government was triggered by what the President saw as "horse and buggy days" decisions imposing a narrowing view of the definition of "interstate commerce." In one decision a unanimous court held that chickens produced for interstate shipment and sale were not covered under the Interstate Commerce clause. Roosevelt saw the future under Supreme Court dictates as one where "the United States government has no control over any national economic problem."[30]

The decision emboldened New Deal opponents who filed, on average, five lawsuits per day against one New Deal law alone, the Agricultural Adjustment Act (AAA). "All hell broke loose" in 1935, when "more than 100 district court judges held acts of Congress unconstitutional; federal courts issued more than 1,600 injunctions blocking the enforcement of New Deal laws."[31] More ominously, awaiting the nine justices was a court docket giving them the opportunity to rule on cases involving not only the AAA, but also the Tennessee Valley Authority, and the Security and Exchange Commission among other statutes Congress had enacted as part of Roosevelt's effort to get the economy under control.

A President who had been elected to address the severe economic problems of the Great depression found that "rate of mortality" an unacceptable attack at a moment when he believed, "one-third of this nation is still ill-nourished, ill-clad, and ill-housed." Those words described Joe O'Mahoney's Wyoming as well.

> *"President Herbert Hoover's 1932 position that 'it is not the function of the government to relieve private institutions of their responsibilities to the public' was accepted in Wyoming longer than elsewhere in the country."*[32]

Senator O'Mahoney was a deeply committed New Dealer. Franklin

Roosevelt had easily carried Wyoming in 1932 (56%-40%) and by an even greater margin in 1936 (60%-37%). O'Mahoney, on a commitment to FDR's economic reforms, had won re-election in 1934 by a comparably comfortable margin (56%-42%). Additionally, the Wyoming lawmaker was part of FDR's inner circle, a trusted friend and political adviser. During the 1936 presidential campaign, O'Mahoney traveled with the President to the Western states, writing FDR's speeches.[33] Roosevelt confidant James Farley, with the President's encouragement, had brought O'Mahoney into the inner circle and provided him with an important national appointment that vaulted O'Mahoney into his senate seat upon John Kendrick's death. The prospect of being in the middle of a political battle where he might be seen as betraying such friendships at a crucial moment like this was not appealing. Wyoming historian Gene M. Gressley pointed out how deeply aware O'Mahoney was during his career, that "nothing is more rewarded than loyalty, nor more punished than disloyalty."[34]

More than anything, Joe O'Mahoney was acutely aware he was putting at risk his "strong desire for a Supreme Court seat." Gressley said, "Jim Farley, on at least two occasions, mentioned his former associate as a possible nominee."[35] Neither O'Mahoney nor Roosevelt could have known it at the time, but FDR would have nine opportunities to appoint O'Mahoney to the Supreme Court after the Wyoming senator decided how to vote on the court reform proposal. Despite his universally recognized qualifications for the job, it would have been unimaginable to expect FDR to consider appointing O'Mahoney if the Wyoming Senator joined forces to prevent that president from reforming the court. If he thought about it at all, O'Mahoney would have calculated that outcome into his decision. Beside those personal and political considerations, he recognized the need to reign in an out-of-control judiciary. O'Mahoney agreed with the Dean of the Wisconsin University law school who said, "Our national problems appear to have outrun our national capacity to deal with them."[36] The Wyoming lawmaker hoped he could help find a compromise.

The question of the appropriateness of one co-equal branch of government obliterating laws proposed by the executive and enacted by the legislative branch had long been debated. Two decades earlier a bill was introduced requiring the removal of any judge who attempted to void a federal law. Other legislative proposals sought to impose a super majority of justices, two-thirds or more, before declaring a law unconstitutional. O'Mahoney believed the defect could be remedied only by amending the Constitution. He proposed a Constitutional amendment requiring a unanimous 9-0 vote of the Supreme Court to overturn a congressional act while providing term limits on all federal judges and imposing the federal income tax on their salaries. (An earlier court decision had ruled separation of powers rendered judicial branch officials immune from the federal income tax.) It was a proposal O'Mahoney generated a year earlier when the Court invalidated the Agricultural Adjustment Act. Now it sounded more like a last-minute attempt to find a compromise with the President.

After learning of Roosevelt's plan, O'Mahoney sent a copy of his own court reform proposal to the President assuring him that "the liberal forces which rallied so strongly behind you last November would come to your aid now in procuring the ratification of such an amendment." Roosevelt was greatly annoyed by O'Mahoney's hesitancy to support his own proposal and responded immediately with a brief, tersely written letter, waving him off as a dreamer. "I am an optimist, as you know, but I think you are a worse optimist than I am."[37]

Unlike others who made rash statements in opposition to the Roosevelt court proposal, O'Mahoney was in no hurry to go public with his concerns. But, he recognized the plan had far-reaching negative consequences for his and the President's entire agenda. O'Mahoney considered FDR's age-based idea a subterfuge "which has fooled no one, and now threatened his entire liberal program."[38] While he had no appetite for dealing a political blow to his friend, the New Dealer was "convinced that the President can withstand a defeat, but the Democratic Party could scarcely withstand his victory on the issue."[39]

In March, the President gave a major speech on court reform while no fewer than 40 senators were already lined up to oppose the bill. O'Mahoney was not yet ready to join them publicly. He listened to Roosevelt, who was eloquent in his own defense. The President spoke of "thousands upon thousands of men and women laboring for long hours in factories for inadequate pay" and "thousands upon thousands of farmers wondering whether next year's prices will meet their mortgage interest." FDR took his appeal directly to the parents and grandparents of "thousands upon thousands of children who should be at school instead of working in mines and mills." Then came his most memorable Depression era line. "Here," he cried, "is one-third of a nation, ill-nourished, ill-clad, ill-housed."

A United Press International reporter said, "It was a dramatic climax to a speech which summoned support from agriculture and labor in the President's campaign for reorganization of the Supreme Court." Senator O'Mahoney allowed himself to be quoted. "It was the greatest speech he ever made," adding, "Maybe he has just begun to fight."[40]

O'Mahoney, "desperately desired an escape from the imbroglio."[41] He went back to work on a compromise, drafting a constitutional amendment based on what the court's decisions had called "a presumption of constitutionality." The lawyer in him reasoned that if four of the nine justices, a minority, "believe that a law is constitutional and so indicate by their votes, that action by itself raises the reasonable doubt which should protect the statute involved."[42] Accordingly, the O'Mahoney alternative required a two-thirds vote of the justices to overcome "the presumption of constitutionality."

O'Mahoney's approach was, in FDR's opinion, unrealistic. An amendment to the constitution required two-thirds of the state legislatures to approve. That process would take years and, worse, is subject to well-financed lobbying campaigns that supporters could not likely match. "Therefore, my good friends," FDR advised those considering that approach, "by the process of *reductio ad absurdum*, or any other better sounding name, you must join me in confining ourselves to the legislative means of saving the United States."[43]

Having made his best effort, Joe O'Mahoney could no longer avoid the moment he dreaded. There would be no compromise. FDR could not see any middle ground. The thing about being a senator is that you can't straddle a fence forever. One day your name will be called by the chief clerk of the senate, and you have to render your final judgment, out loud for all to hear. Aye or No. The time had come to decide. He would either have to set aside his deeply held convictions to stay in the good graces of the President he so admired or listen to his own counsel and oppose FDR's court reform proposal.

On April 8, O'Mahoney announced his decision to oppose the bill. His conscience, he admitted, would not permit him to support the President. One of the Senator's former law partners, Bard Farrell, was in the Cheyenne office of the United Mine Workers Union when his decision was announced on the radio. Farrell told the senator that the union members gathered around the radio, once among O'Mahoney's biggest allies, now "called you a dirty no-good S.O.B." and it was the "nicest name" he heard them call him that day.[44] There was similar dismay among FDR's inner circle. Democratic Party loyalist Charles Michelson, an FDR "ghost writer," said he believed O'Mahoney was "under deep obligation," if not to the President, then to Jim Farley. Unable to take "no" for an answer and figuring O'Mahoney was still salvageable, the White House dispatched Farley to make a last-minute attempt to flip the Wyoming Senator. Farley was stunned by O'Mahoney's blistering response. He bluntly called FDR's proposal "obnoxious, undemocratic, and an insult to the Senate."[45] Farley gave as good as he got, telling the senator "what he thought of him…that he never would have been known outside of Wyoming if it hadn't been for FDR's administration."[46]

If O'Mahoney was alert to ominous signs for his political relationship with the President, he needed look no farther than that reaction. Jim Farley felt especially betrayed by his protégé. "Well," he told a group meeting in the Oval Office, "when Senator O'Mahoney comes down here wanting help on a sugar bill, his conscience won't be bothering him then, will it?"[47] Farley publicly threatened reprisals against the Wyoming lawmaker and remained unforgiving for many years.[48]

Then came a mid-May announcement that allowed Supreme Court reformers to relax a little. One of "the Four Horsemen" decided he would spend his last years on his farm near Ellicott City, Maryland, rather than in Wyoming or on the bench. Justice Willis Van Devanter announced his retirement, effective June 2, 1937.[49] O'Mahoney was encouraged. He promptly wrote to his friend Rodney Guthrie, who later became a member of the Wyoming Supreme Court. "The resignation of Justice Van Devanter this morning will probably have a very beneficial effect."[50]

The four-vote conservative bloc, often joined by Justice Owen Roberts to form a majority, was fractured. "The era of constitutional laissez faire was over."[51] Although Justice Owens had already begun to break with the conservatives, the departure of the only Wyoming lawyer to ever serve on the high court was a moment of significance to the New Dealers. He might not get the opportunity to reform the Court, but Roosevelt could at least begin to reconstruct it. Soon, Justice McReynolds, another of the "Four Horsemen," accustomed to being in the majority, found himself writing 28 dissents in the court's 1937 term. Before Roosevelt was replaced by Harry Truman, names added to the membership of the court included lawyers like Hugo Black, Felix Frankfurter, William O. Douglas, Harlan Stone, and Robert H. Jackson, but not Joseph Christopher O'Mahoney.

Their nominations and senate confirmation lay unpredictable in an uncertain future. FDR still had to deal with the present need to mold a court more friendly to what he believed necessary to protect the nation from predatory capitalism. Van Devanter's move from Supreme Court Justice to Maryland farmer hadn't lessened the immediate urgency of court reform. Nor had it made the politics less messy. The President persisted.

Roosevelt had unwisely committed himself to appointing the Senate's Democratic leader, Joe Robinson of Arkansas, to the first vacancy on the Supreme Court. That vacancy arrived in the middle of this struggle and appointing the man leading the pro-Roosevelt charge on Capitol Hill would look like a political payoff while denying FDR the congressional general he needed to win this battle. The President decided to let the matter of a new appointee simmer. Roosevelt eventually filled the vacancy with Hugo Black.

On Monday, July 12, as the debate reached a crescendo, Robinson and O'Mahoney engaged one another in a fiery shouting match on the floor of the Senate. "On the edge of the pit, Robinson sat in his red leather swivel chair as Joseph C. O'Mahoney stood above him, jabbing his finger. Robinson's face turned crimson. He started to his feet several times, looking like he might take a swing at O'Mahoney. Finally, Robinson exploded with rage. He felt a stabbing pain in his chest." Within 36 hours he was dead but not before giving an interview in which Robinson talked about the future.

> "The time Is not very far in the future when this country will see an entirely new political alignment when men with forward-thinking ideas will be members of one party, let's hope it is the Democratic Party, and the men who are content to live in the past will band together in the other."[52]

There was one final "truth-is-stranger-than-fiction" moment in the drama. In June, the powerful Wyoming newspaper publisher Tracy McCraken, a member of the Democratic National Committee, who knew O'Mahoney better than anyone other than perhaps his wife Agnes, convinced himself and others that "the difference of opinion might be worked out," saying the Senator "would have to be given the opportunity to save face."[53] A meeting was arranged between O'Mahoney, Wyoming Governor Leslie A. Miller, and President Roosevelt. In the days before email and texting, McCraken's invitation to the White House meeting was sent by regular mail to the publisher's home address. McCraken's maid dutifully, or as McCraken later complained, "thoughtlessly," put it in a pile of accumulating mail. McCraken didn't see it until it was too late for any compromise.[54]

When it was all over and Roosevelt's bill was given its last rites, the chair of the Democratic Senate Campaign Committee, Senator Joseph Guffey of Pennsylvania, whose job it was to help Democratic Party incumbents get reelected, made it clear. Joe O'Mahoney was not on that list. In a radio address, Guffey named the Wyoming lawmaker as one of the "ingrates." He threatened "the next time O'Mahoney came up for election in Wyoming, he would have to 'go back to his home on the range.'"[55]

Nor was it over for the still-fuming President. There had to be one last act of revenge. In September 1937, Roosevelt scheduled a trip to Wyoming without inviting O'Mahoney, who caught wind of the plan. "It required little imagination on the part of O'Mahoney to realize that the President's western trip was aimed at administering some old-fashioned political medicine."[56] O'Mahoney was, however, a step ahead of the President. The

Senator Joseph C. O'Mahoney (Center) and two other unidentified Senators celebrate as they leave the Judiciary Committee meeting after the defeat of FDR's court reorganization bill in July 1937. Library of Congress, Prints & Photographs Division, photograph by Harris & Ewing.

Washington Daily News described what happened under a banner headline. "O'Mahoney Outsmarts F. D. R. and rides Presidential Special."[57] Roosevelt invited all of the Wyoming Democratic Party elite except O'Mahoney. "The snub did not come off as planned because the wiry Senator refused to be snubbed."[58] O'Mahoney and his wife drove hastily across country, an arduous trip in the days before interstate highways. They arrived in time to welcome the President when his train pulled up to the depot in Cheyenne. A surprised Roosevelt greeted the Senator. "Hello Joe. Glad to see you." The "take him to the woodhouse" speech FDR planned was never given.

Millions of Americans actively engaged in the national debate over the Roosevelt court reform proposal. Among O'Mahoney's massive collection of official papers archived by the University of Wyoming's American Heritage Center are four banker boxes of letters, telegrams, postcards, petitions, speeches, news reports, editorials, and other written communications from around the country. They came from Wyoming and every other state in the Union. They were written by plain old citizens, unions, trade and patriotic organizations, churches and religious organizations, civic clubs, law schools and lawyers, doctors, ranchers, farmers, housewives, butchers, bakers, and candlestick makers.

Many were reasoned and analytical. A few were angry and vitriolic. An off-the-cuff analysis would support an estimate than more than 80% of these communications supported O'Mahoney's position and opposed that of the President. Some were aware of how much Joe O'Mahoney had risked. "It matters little whether or not the position you have taken is the right one politically," wrote friend Joe Sullivan of Laramie. "Suffice it to say that your action is a brave one and should command the confidence of every thinking man and woman."[59]

An old friend, Joseph Tumulty, likened O'Mahoney's ordeal to "the Gethsemane through which you passed."[60] Historian Gene Gressley summed it up this way: "A stubborn President of Dutch aristocratic background had met an equally stubborn Senator of humble Irish origins." It was costly to both. The "stubborn President of Dutch aristocratic background" lost one of the most significant battles of his presidency. The "stubborn Senator of humble Irish origins" lost any chance he'd ever have of becoming a supreme court justice.

Gene Gressley said that for Senator O'Mahoney all the praise for his decision to buck a president he loved and supported felt more like "the last hurrah."[61] "Never again would FDR write him a letter referring to 'the fine loyalty with which you have always given me,' as he had near the end of the 1936 campaign."[62] That was no small loss to a man who so admired Franklin Delano Roosevelt and what he was doing to resurrect the nation in the wake of the Great Depression. Frank Coombs wrote a comprehensive 430-page biography of the Wyoming Senator as his PhD dissertation while at the University of Illinois in 1968. Coombs noted O'Mahoney's victory on the court-packing bill was, at the same time, the lawmaker's biggest defeat. "Most seriously," Coombs concluded, "it meant that the secret hope he had always harbored that he himself might someday be appointed to the high court, would never be realized."[63]

Even so, it was not to be O'Mahoney's last hurrah. He continued serving in the senate earning a reputation as a "trust buster" who effectively opposed the monopolistic practices of American and international corporations. O'Mahoney earned praise as the chair of the National Economic Committee and chaired the Senate Interior Committee while serving on the powerful Appropriations Committee. He was one of Roosevelt's staunchest backers in the buildup toward World War II.

A dozen years after the defeat of FDR's court reform bill, bygones were, at long last, bygones. Roosevelt was gone. Harry Truman was pondering whom to put on the Court. Jim Farley advised Truman the time for O'Mahoney's appointment was nigh. Truman agreed. O'Mahoney, the president acknowledged, "is one of the ablest men in the Senate."[64] The President, knowing the Republican Governor of Wyoming, Arthur G. Crane, would replace O'Mahoney with a Republican, eventually decided he needed O'Mahoney more in the Congress than on the bench.[65]

By the time he ran for re-election in 1952, he had risen to 7th in the all-important senate seniority system. Not long before this campaign, *LIFE* magazine recognized the Senator from Wyoming as "a tough man to debate because of the knowledge and preparation he put into his speeches." He was said to be especially knowledgeable on economic issues and the need to break up corporate monopolies. "In terms of senate influence," *LIFE* recognized O'Mahoney "stands near the top."[66] Nonetheless, two Republicans, Dwight Eisenhower, the popular GOP presidential nominee credited largely with having won the war in Europe, and Joe McCarthy, the Wisconsin Senator who manufactured the "Red Scare," combined to end O'Mahoney's bid for a fourth term, at least for the moment.

Governor Frank Barrett was the Wyoming Republican Party nominee for the senate. Spouting Red Scare demagoguery, McCarthy came to Wyoming in mid-October to campaign for Barrett. Four thousand people gathered on the grounds of a park outside of Riverton to hear McCarthy call O'Mahoney "a Commie-crat." It was deemed the largest crowd ever to attend a Wyoming political rally.

O'Mahoney had grown comfortable with landslide wins in his three previous campaigns; winning in 1934, 57%-43% over Wyoming congressman Vincent Carter; 59%-41% over Milward Simpson in 1940; and defeating Harry Henderson in 1946 by a 56%-44% margin. Just as FDR's coattails had once lifted O'Mahoney, Dwight Eisenhower's lifted Barrett in 1952. The Republican defeated O'Mahoney by a slender 52% to 48% margin.

It was not the last time McCarthy unleashed venom on the state's politics. In June of 1954, Wyoming Senator Lester Hunt took his own life after being victimized by a conspiracy to force him to resign from the Senate. Joe McCarthy and two other powerful GOP senators threatened to expose the June 1953 arrest of Hunt's son for soliciting a homosexual act. When he refused, they conducted a year-long orchestrated campaign that targeted Hunt and led to his suicide.

Upon Hunt's death, the Republican governor appointed a GOP party official to fill out Hunt's term. In November Joe O'Mahoney ran for Hunt's seat and was re-elected to another six-year term in the Senate. He suffered a stroke in the final year of his term. On August 29, 1960, Oregon Senator Wayne Morse pushed O'Mahoney's wheelchair onto the senate floor. Morse introduced their colleague as "the most capable and effective senator to protect the free enterprise system."

The loftiest political aspirations of our nation can seldom be realized without clashing with lofty personal aspirations. As we've seen too often, the latter frequently wins the day. What JFK quoted from the writings of columnist Walter Lippmann is sadly true.

> *"With exceptions so rare they are regarded as miracles of nature, successful democratic politicians are insecure and intimidated men. The decisive consideration is not whether a proposition is good, but whether it is popular."*[67]

Joseph C. O'Mahoney died on December 1, 1962. The *New York Times* published a lengthy two-column obituary. It didn't mention the "court packing" fight. It did remember that during his lengthy senate service, Joseph C. O'Mahoney was "an implacable foe of big business."[68] It was not his obituary but a speech he gave in the first year he served in the senate by which he might like to be remembered.

> *"All the pages of history tell the story of the progress of humanity toward freedom – freedom from the bondage of thought, freedom from the bondage of political power, freedom from economic bondage. Every major struggle that has been waged has been a struggle between those on the one hand those who sought to subjugate or exploit their fellows, and those, on the other, who resisted conquest and exploitation. Every step of progress achieved by mankind has been won through the efforts of those who fought for the liberation of the masses from the domination of self-constituted masters. The aspirations of the American people remain the same today as they were in the beginning."*[69]

From early in his career, O'Mahoney established, not only lofty aspirations, but also the guiding principles he set forth in that speech. When the moment came to choose between what he most wanted personally and what he believed the country most needed, he didn't hesitate to pursue the latter.

Endnotes

1. U.S. Senate Committee on Foreign Relations, Hearing, Nomination of Gale W. McGee to be Permanent Representative to the Organization of American States, March 17, 1977, 7
2. Much of the material in this section, not otherwise footnoted, comes from a series of oral interviews Senator O'Mahoney participated in with Dr. Donald Shaughnessy of the Oral History research Office of Columbia University in 1958. The manuscript may be found in the Joseph C. O'Mahoney Collection, Acc. No. 275, Box 78, Folder: "Biographical Information 1933-1958", American Heritage Center, University of Wyoming
3. Coombs, *Joseph Christopher O'Mahoney*, 12, 16
4. Cynde Georgen, "John Kendrick: Cowboy, Cattle King, Governor and U.S. Senator," Published November 8, 2014, https://www.wyohistory.org/encyclopedia/john-kendrick, accessed February 2, 2022
5. *Journal of the State Senate of the State of Wyoming*, January 28, 1913
6. Larson, *History of Wyoming*, Second Edition, Revised, University of Nebraska Press (1978), 388
7. "State should send men to Congress who will be for Wilson," *State Leader*, October 17, 1916, 1
8. Oral Interview, Columbia University, 45
9. Coombs, *Joseph Christopher O'Mahoney*, 14
10. Id., 42
11. Coombs, *Joseph Christopher O'Mahoney*, 66
12. "O'Mahoney, Moley and Tugwell in "Little Cabinet," *Columbia Alum News*, Vol. XXIV, No. 2, March 10, 1933, 16
13. Oral interview, Columbia University, 14
14. Coombs, *Joseph Christopher O'Mahoney*, 95
15. Larson, supra., 450
16. "Public's Views of Supreme Court Turned More Negative Before News of Breyer's Retirement," *Pew Research Center*, February 2, 2022, https://www.pewresearch.org/politics/2022/02/02/publics-views-of-supreme-court-turned-more-negative-before-news-of-breyers , accessed February 7, 2022
17. "Americans' approval of Supreme Court drops after abortion decision," *Reuters*, June 28, 2022, https://news.yahoo.com/americans-approval-supreme-court-drops-221844358.html, accessed June 30, 2022
18. Solomon, *FDR v. The Constitution*, 47
19. Solomon, Id., 21
20. Lori Van Pelt, "Willis Van Devanter, Cheyenne Lawyer and U.S. Supreme Court justice, February 14, 2015, https://www.wyohistory.org/encyclopedia/willis-van-devanter-cheyenne-lawyer-and-us-supreme-court-justice, accessed February 9, 2022
21. Knowlton, *Cattle Kingdom*, 267
22. Davis, *Wyoming Range War*, 134, 142
23. Gage, *The Johnson County War Ain't a Pack of Lies: The Rustlers Side*, 78
24. Van Pelt, Supra., citing Holsinger. M. Paul. "Willis Van Devanter: Wyoming Leader

1884-1897," *Annals of Wyoming*, 37 no. 2 1965, 171-206
25 Knowlton, *Cattle Kingdom*, 293
26 "The Case For and Against the Supreme Court," *American Bar Association*, (undated), Box 313, Folder: "Supreme Court 'Packing' Issue," O'Mahoney Papers, AHC
27 Charles Fairman, "The Retirement of Federal Judges," *Harvard Law Review*, Vol. LI, No. 3, (1938), 400
28 Lash, *Dealers and Dreamers: A New Look at the New Deal*, 295
29 Joseph L. Lewison, "Limiting Judicial Review by an Act of Congress," *California Law Review*, September 1935, 591
30 Jeff Sheshol, *Supreme Power*, 149
31 Id., 169
32 Larson, *History of Wyoming*, 2nd Edition, 443
33 Gene M. Gresley, "Joseph C. O'Mahoney, FDR, and the Supreme Court," *Pacific Historical Review*, Vol 40, No. 2 (1971), see footnote 8, 187
34 Id., 193
35 Id., 197
36 Sheshol, supra., 197
37 Letter FDR to O'Mahoney, February 20, 1937, Box 313, Folder: Supreme Court 'Packing' Issue #6," O'Mahoney Papers, AHC
38 Letter O'Mahoney to T.K. Cassidy, February 23, 1937, Box 313, Folder: Supreme Court 'Packing' Issue #6," O'Mahoney Papers, AHC
39 Letter O'Mahoney to Joseph P. Tumulty, May 5, 1937, Box 313, Folder: Supreme Court 'Packing' Issue #7," O'Mahoney Papers, AHC
40 "FDR blasts Supreme Court at victory dinner," March 5, 1937, *UPI Archives*., https://www.upi.com/Archives/1937/03/05/FDR-blasts-Supreme-Court-at-victory-dinner/3880131004048/ accessed February 10, 2022
41 Gressley, supra, 194
42 Letter O'Mahoney to John F. McNamee, March 26, 1937, Box 313, Folder: Supreme Court 'Packing' Issue #7," O'Mahoney Papers, AHC
43 Letter from FDR to C.R. Burlingham, February 23, 1937, M. Dawson File, Franklin Roosevelt Papers, Franklin D. Roosevelt Library, Hyde Park cited by Gressley, supra., 195
44 Coombs, *Joseph Christopher O"Mahoney*, 259
45 Charles Michelson, *The Ghost Talks*, 174, 175
46 Harold L. Ickes, *The Secret Diary of Harold L. Ickes*, 129
47 Solomon, *FDR v. The Constitution*, supra., 191
48 "Court Plan's Foes Echo 'No Compromise' on Vote's Eve," *New York Herald Tribune*, May 18, 1937, 1 (re: reprisals), and Ickes, "Secret Diary," 223 (re: unforgiving)
49 "Van Devanter Retires," *American Bar Association Journal*, Vol. 23, No. 6 (June 1937), 482
50 Letter "O'Mahoney to Rodney Guthrie, February 18, 1937, Box 313, Folder: Supreme Court 'Packing' Issue #7," O'Mahoney Papers, AHC
51 Russell W. Galloway, "The Supreme Court Since 1937," *Santa Clara Law Review*," Vol. 24, No. 3, January 1, 1984, 567
52 Shesol, supra., 487-488

53 Letter from Ralph M. Immel to James Roosevelt, June 9, 1937, Roosevelt Files, M. Dawson File, Franklin D. Roosevelt Library; cited in Gressley, supra., "Joseph C. O'Mahoney, FDR, and the Supreme Court, 200
54 Gressley, Id., 200
55 Coombs, *Joseph Christopher O'Mahoney*, 276
56 Gressley, Id., 183
57 "O'Mahoney Outsmarts F.D. and Rides Presidential Special," *Washington Daily News*, September 25, 1937, 17
58 Id.
59 Letter, Sullivan to O'Mahoney, May 7, 1937, O'Mahoney Papers, Box 313, Folder: "Supreme Court 'Packing' Issue #6, AHC
60 Letter Tumulty to O'Mahoney, May 7, 1937, O'Mahoney Papers, Box 313, Folder: "Supreme Court 'Packing' Issue #6, AHC
61 Gresley, supra., 202
62 Coombs, *Joseph Christopher O'Mahoney*, 283
63 Id.
64 Letter Truman to Farley, July 26, 1949, O'Mahoney Papers, Box 76, Folder: "Letters Regarding Supreme Court Appointment," AHC
65 At the time, state law did not require the Governor to appoint a person of the same party as the elected senator as is the case today.
66 *LIFE* Magazine, March 11, 1946, 99
67 Kennedy, *Profiles in Courage*, 23
68 "Joseph C. O'Mahoney, 78, Dies: Wyoming Senator for 25 Years," *New York Times*, December 2, 1962, 88
69 Coombs, *Joseph Christopher O'Mahoney*, 404

Chapter 8

TENO RONCALIO

"good public service is its own reward"

"Teno didn't just deliver the delegates – he delivered the whole New Frontier"

June 6, 1944. D-Day. As their LCI (Landing Craft Infantry) came to a near full stop, Platoon Leader Lt. Teno Roncalio hollered "Let's go," as he led his men into the roiling water and headed for the already blood-soaked beach. "They were walking into the face of a strong wind," said Roncalio's fellow platoon leader John Spalding. "The 'wind' consisted of bullets and fragments."[1]

After the Japanese attacked Pearl Harbor, Teno enlisted and was sent to officer's candidate school. Upon graduation he was assigned to the Big Red One. General Dwight Eisenhower called the unit "his own Praetorian Guard," a reference to the personal bodyguards protecting Roman Emperor Caesar Augustus. Less than two years after his father died and his mother was murdered, when grieving adult children need time to deal with the emotional impact that inevitably follows such a horror, he began a 35-month tour of duty, consumed with keeping himself and the men serving under him alive as they marched into some of the grisliest and grittiest combat of World War II. The previous July, he took part in the invasion of Sicily, first under the command of General George S. Patton and later General Omar Bradley. On D-Day, he was part of the 1st Division's landing at Omaha

Beach. As a First Lieutenant, Teno led a platoon from C Company onto Omaha Beach. Cornelius Ryan wrote, "They came ashore on Omaha Beach, the slogging, unglamorous men that no one envied."[2]

It was near midday on June 6, when they landed in a second wave of U.S. troops. They were assigned the elimination of a deadly Nazi machine gun pill box blocking the Americans from reaching the St. Laurent Draw, which would allow them to pursue the Germans inland. In the fog of war, they landed too far west of the objective and were forced to make their way across a bloody beach to a place where they could join the battle to take out the pillbox.

Most Americans today know what it was like only because they saw the realistic movie version. *Saving Private Ryan*. Strewn along their path were mutilated American bodies, parts of heads, hands, and legs. Blood everywhere. Explosions to the left and right, front and back, and often walking across the bodies of dead, dying, or frightened soldiers. There were disabled tanks, tractors, bulldozers, trucks, and soldiers from the 2nd battalion in whose wake Teno and his compatriots landed. At long last, between the infantrymen and artillery fired from the U.S.S. Frankford, the German machine gun nest was destroyed. Now Teno and the other officers could lead their troops up the draw, which was lined with enemy mines.

While mine detection squads cleared a narrow path, Teno's platoon walked over and around the dead bodies of the infantry soldiers who trod that same, narrow path earlier and set off some of the mines. Lt. Roncalio's platoon included a mix of hardened combat veterans and soldiers entering combat for the first time. All were frightened. Most were brave. Shells were landing too close for comfort as his unit ducked and covered. It took hours but eventually the beach landing became a slow crawl up the draw and into the hedgerows lining the fields atop the hill. Teno and the others were ready to chase the Germans to Berlin.

For his gallantry on D-Day, Teno Roncalio was awarded a Silver Star. Given what it takes to earn it, the lapel pin is a decidedly understated one-eighth by five-eighths of an inch red, white, and blue treasure. Teno never talked about Omaha Beach or what it took to win the medal, but he proudly wore the small, unassuming lapel pin every day of the rest of his life.

Germany surrendered on May 8, 1945. After years of leading troops into some of the heaviest combat of the war, invading North Africa and Sicily, D-Day, and the push into Germany to end the war, the realization that it was over slowly swept over now Captain Roncalio. He was filled with an unsteadiness about his future. Joseph O'Mahoney was a father figure to Roncalio, whose parents were, like Teno's, both dead by now. Teno wrote the Senator on June 14 seeking advice. He said he was unsure of what to do next. He worried about his temper. "I find myself doing and saying things I shouldn't."

He was unsure whether what he felt was an addiction to the adrenaline of combat or simply the weariness one would expect after many months of war. Part of him wanted to transfer to a China-Burma-India unit that was still fighting as the Japanese hung on.[3] The other alternative was going home, becoming a civilian, and starting a new life. "And I feel a bit befuddled."

> *"Senator, you see on the one side, Roncalio, the ambitious, Roncalio, the bachelor and orphan wanting immediate duty in the Pacific, and on the other side, Roncalio the veteran, Roncalio the weary, wanting to 'serve it out' at home. The point then, is just what should I do? What action should I take to bring about something certain?"*[4]

The Senator replied on the 4th of July. O'Mahoney acknowledged "this war will leave a deep imprint on all the boys who have participated." Speaking to his protégé, he assured him every "soldier will find himself somewhat at a loss when he resumes complete control over his activities." O'Mahoney urged Teno to come home where things might look clearer as he decided what's best for his future.[5]

In his book *The Dead and Those About to Die: D-Day: The Big Red One at Omaha Beach*," historian John McManus described the D-Day experience.

> *"All the beauty of the world was gone. Nothing mattered now except this brutal moment and survival. It was almost as if everything that came before; home, childhood, family * * * had never really happened."*[6]

Roncalio's "home, childhood, family" had really happened, the good with the bad. As he led Company C onto Omaha Beach, his father had been dead for five years, having succumbed to a lengthy illness. It had been little more than four years since Teno's mother Ernesta Roncaglio had been murdered. The Sweetwater County coroner ruled she died in a murder-suicide in her home in Rock Springs, at the hands of her second husband, Domenic Melli.[7]

She had lived in Rock Springs since 1903, after coming to the United States from her birth home in Piacenza, Provincia di Piacenza, Emilia-Romagna, Italy. Ernesta and her first husband Frank Roncalgio, of Lombardia, Italy, were among four million Italians emigrating to the U.S. between 1890 and 1920. They left Italy's poverty in the hope of a better life in the United States.[8] Because of the Union Pacific Railroad and its mining operations, Rock Springs was seen by many immigrants, Italian and others, as a place of opportunity. In addition to his work as a miner, Teno's father Frank could be seen pulling a cart through town collecting junk, which he sold to raise extra cash. Ernesta raised their children and took care of the many boarders, mostly World War I veterans and Italian immigrants, with whom they shared their home.

Celeste Domenico Roncaglio was born in that home on March 16, 1916. "Few babies were so happily received in this world as that little bundle of joy," recalled older sister Julia.[9] A four-year-old brother, Domenic, and eight-year-old sister Elvira had recently died of the Spanish Flu. "Our parents," Julia wrote, "with their great capacity for love, courage and cheerfulness, consoled us by telling us that God would send another child soon to brighten our lives and here he was at last." Schoolmates nicknamed him "Teno." He dropped the hard "g" in Roncaglio and was, therefore, known for the remainder of his life as Teno Roncalio. Most knew him simply as "Teno."

For Christmas when he was ten-years old, his mother gave him a concertina, an accordion-like musical instrument. On Christmas morning, he opened the present, picked up the concertina and promptly broke into a rendition of "O Solo Mio." Writing to Julia from Ft. Benning, Georgia, in December 1942, Teno remembered that Christmas morning. "Mom wondered how the hell come I could play the damn thing when I apparently hadn't seen it before." Julia had disclosed the gift weeks before and Teno taught himself to play so that he could surprise his mother with a song on Christmas morning. The Army veterans among the boarders taught Teno naughty songs like "Mademoiselle from Armentieres," which he happily sang "in a manner that would put a Frenchman to shame."

> *Oh Mademoiselle from Armentieres. Parlez-vous*
> *She'll do it for wine, she'll do it for rum*
> *And sometimes for chocolate or chewing gum*
> *Hinky-dinky parlez-vous*

> *Oh Mademoiselle from Montparnasse. Parlez-vous*
> *As soon as she'd spy a Colonel's brass*
> *She'd take off her skirt and roll in the grass*
> *Hinky-dinky parlez-vous*

During the difficult days of the Great Depression, Ernesta "was notorious for feeding what were, in those days, called 'hoboes.' They used to get off the trains when they stopped at the chutes and his mother would be found taking food out to them on the bench that ran along the front of our house." It was the source of Teno's empathy for hungry working people when he served in Congress. One morning while he was being driven by a young staffer to Laramie, he pulled his schedule from a briefcase. As he looked it over, Teno noticed he was to speak at the Laramie Chamber of Commerce monthly luncheon. He was outraged. "I told Marietta (his scheduler) I never want to speak to a Chamber of Commerce." He realized it was too late to cancel and so he arrived a bit irritated at the Laramie hotel where they met.

It was the fall of 1978, after the historic Camp David Accords between Israel and Egypt. After his short speech, he asked if anyone had a question. There was one. He was asked why he voted to allow striking workers to receive food stamps. Congressman Roncalio slammed his papers on the table and said angrily, "Jimmy Carter is working to make peace in the Middle East and you don't ask a single question about that. All you want to know is why your congressman voted to give food to children whose daddy's you can't get along with." He then stormed out of the room. Teno didn't stew long. Once in the car, he asked his driver to go by the flower shop at the old Connor Hotel. There he bought a bouquet of fall flowers and delivered them to an old friend on Grand Avenue. The day ended well.

The renowned consumer advocate Ralph Nader called Teno, "the prototype of America's self-made man, who pulled himself up by his bootstraps."[10] Teno passed the state's barber licensing exam at 16 and received his first union card. He learned barbering as a shoeshine boy in Jack Vicar's Rock Springs barber shop. His political career was bolstered by the "bootblack to banker" legend that had its genesis in those years. One of Teno's contemporaries later joked, "All I hear is about how tough Teno had it. Well, I remember those winter days, snow blowing in my face, temperatures below zero freezing my hands and feet as I walked my paper route. I'd look through the window and see Teno in that warm barber shop shining shoes and I thought he had a pretty damned good job."[11]

Before the war, Teno enrolled at the University of Wyoming where he studied journalism and took pre-law courses. To make ends meet, he "ran a snack bar in a dormitory, waited tables and washed dishes, at Annie Moore's boarding house, tended furnaces, shoveled snow, and scrubbed 'acres' of floors."[12] During his sophomore year, he was elected student body president while working as the business manager for the campus newspaper, the *Branding Iron*. Shortly before Pearl Harbor, Teno went to Washington, where he took a job as an intern for Wyoming's U.S. Senator Joseph C. O'Mahoney and enrolled in law school at Catholic University.

After the war, Teno returned to Laramie and resumed his studies. Within the coming decade, Teno received a law degree, opened a private practice in Cheyenne, served as assistant Laramie County prosecutor, was elected president of the Laramie County Bar Association, edited the *Wyoming Labor Journal*, and founded the Cheyenne National Bank. In his spare time, Teno learned how to ski and to fly an airplane. As one political observer noted, "Ambition and drive have stamped Roncalio's life since he was five-years-old."[13]

1958 was a major milestone in the life of the one-time Rock Springs bootblack. That year, he was elected chair of the Wyoming Democratic Party, leading the party to an historic electoral victory and establishing himself as a major player in Wyoming politics for the next twenty years. It was also the year Teno established a lifetime bond with the Kennedy family of Massachusetts. The three Kennedy brothers, John, Robert, and Ted, each came to the state at Teno's invitation to rally support for the 1958 Democratic ticket.

In the 1958 Wyoming general election, the voters elected a governor, a U.S. senator and representative, and the four other top state elected official including the state school superintendent. A little-known Rawlins attorney named Joe Hickey ran for governor against an incumbent Republican, Milward Simpson. Dr. Gale McGee, an egg-head liberal college professor who had been in the state for fewer than a dozen years, was running against the incumbent Republican senator Frank Barrett. Barrett was intensely popular having served previously as attorney general, U.S. representative, and governor before being elected to the senate six year earlier. Jack R. Gage who served as state superintendent of public Instruction two decades before, was the Democratic candidate for secretary of state. His opponent, Everett Copenhaver, was the Republican incumbent. The only incumbent Democrat was Velma Linford, then finishing her first term as superintendent of public instruction.

Teno coined the motto, "Give 'em the gate in '58," but not a lot of pundits predicted that would happen. Dr. McGee could have been speaking of the entire Democratic ticket when he said of his own candidacy, "I was not even a dark horse. I was a hopeless horse."[14] When votes were counted on November 4, Democrats won the governorship, the U.S. senate seat, secretary of state, and superintendent of public instruction." Milward Simpson knew who deserved the "credit" for his defeat and held a grudge. He'd get his revenge eight years later.

McGee and the other victorious Democrats gave the credit to the state Democratic Party chair. "The luckiest thing for us," said senator-elect Gale McGee, "was that Teno Roncalio was the state chairman. Teno had bounce and fire." Journalist and fellow Sweetwater County alum, Paul Krza, was a young man when Teno was firing up the Democrats to achieve those 1958 wins. He reminisced about it forty years later.

> *"I remembered it as always the biggest rally before the general election, over at the Slovenski Dom, the Slovene lodge's meeting home in my hometown of Rock Springs. Democrats from Sweetwater County, the party's big, reliable stronghold in Wyoming, showed up to drink beer, eat kranske klobase and hear the speeches. For the always-minority Democrats, this was a last shot of adrenaline from the coal miners and all the other blue-collar folk in southwest Wyoming who didn't think it was strange to belong to a labor union. At the lodge he gave one of his fiery blasts about the corporate-loving Republicans and their exploitation of the working people. It was liberal Democratic stuff delivered by an earthy guy who knew the Kennedys. Everybody loved it."*[15]

It was that "bounce and fire" that Senator John F. Kennedy saw in Teno that caused him to recruit Teno for the tough 1960 presidential campaign. Little did Kennedy know at the time that this decision would turn out to be responsible for giving him the nomination and open the door for him to become President of the United States.

"Will the delegates please take their seats?" Paul Butler, chair of the Democratic National Committee, announced that the 1960 Democratic National Convention was underway. It was Monday, July 11 when they gathered in the spacious Los Angeles Sports Arena. Wyoming's delegation was seated center right, near the back of the room. Only New Jersey was farther from the podium. There were 1,521 delegates from around the country. Fifteen were from Wyoming, less than one percent. Nonetheless, they would have an oversized impact of the proceedings.

Teno and Jack Kennedy first met when Senator Kennedy spoke at the 1956 Wyoming Democratic Party convention in Thermopolis. A delegate to the 1956 Democratic National Convention, Teno voted for JFK's opponent for the vice-presidential nomination, Senator Estes Kefauver of Tennessee.[16] Over the next year, Teno warmed to Kennedy. In 1957, while in DC on business, Teno visited Kennedy's senate office. He left a business card on which he wrote, "Sign me up to help you get elected President."[17] Kennedy speechwriter and biographer Theodore Sorenson recalled that JFK was intentional about enlisting people like Teno "long before their talents were equally recognized throughout their home state."[18] In his post-assassination biography of Kennedy, "Johnny, We Hardly Knew Ye," aide Kenneth P. O'Donnell remembered people like Roncalio were "invaluable" to the election of President Kennedy in 1960.

Throughout 1959 and 1960 and through the nominating convention, Teno worked tirelessly to secure Wyoming's delegation for the Massachusetts senators' candidacy. He traveled the state, buttonholing anyone who might end up a delegate to the coming national convention. No one in Wyoming worked harder or more effectively to make the case for a Kennedy nomination. It was not an easy chore. Labor unions, then a powerhouse in state Democratic politics, were uneasy about the man whose brother had attacked Jimmy Hoffa ruthlessly. Kennedy's Catholic faith was a major issue. As Teno courted potential delegates, he ran into "a rather vehement objection to Catholicism." Indeed, when Kennedy came to Wyoming to campaign, Teno had difficulty convincing Protestant ministers to offer a blessing before the meal.[19] By the time of the Los Angeles convention it appeared uncertain whether JFK could win even four of the 15 Wyoming delegate votes.

On the third day of the convention, nine men were nominated for president. Wyoming governor Joe Hickey surprised the state's delegation by seconding the nomination of Lyndon Johnson because Hickey was a devout Catholic. Hickey told them that even his wife was angry with him. After LBJ, Kennedy's name was placed in nomination, followed by senators George Smathers of Florida, and Stuart Symington of Missouri. Eleanor Roosevelt urged a third nomination for the Party's 1952 and 1956 candidate Adlai Stevenson. Finally, the governors of New Jersey (Robert B. Meyner), Iowa (Herschel C. Loveless), Kansas (George Docking), and the segregationist governor of Mississippi, Ross Barnett, were placed on the ballot. Then the roll was called.

In those days, there were few primaries and most delegates came to the convention uncommitted. Thus, the outcome of the first ballot was unpredictable. Most pundits believed Kennedy would amass a plurality of the first ballot vote, but not the majority needed to secure the nomination. Joe Hickey told Johnson Kennedy would fall about 100 votes short and would have even less support on subsequent ballots. Many believed that if Kennedy did not win the nomination on the first ballot, he would eventually lose, most likely to Johnson. Thanks, in large measure to Teno and Wyoming Senator Gale McGee, that did not happen.

As the clerk called on the states in alphabetical order, the tension built. Alabama was first. Twenty of its 29 votes went to LBJ. Kennedy received only three and a half. As the states continued announcing their tallies, Kennedy began to mount an expected but not insurmountable lead. By the time the roll call reached Illinois, Kennedy had 100 of the 760 votes the nomination required. He hit the 200 mark at Iowa. Massachusetts brought JFK's total to 300. As the roll call reached the state before Wyoming, Kennedy had 735 votes to LBJ's 405.

The day before, Teno asked the Wyoming delegates whether they would vote for his man if, by the time the count reached Wyoming, Kennedy could be nominated with their votes. Someone made a counteroffer. They would make that commitment if Roncalio committed to voting for LBJ if he was within 15 votes of the nomination when Wyoming was called. Teno declined. The discussion ended. So, that night in LA that when the clerk called "Wyoming" no one was certain of the outcome.

Ted Kennedy spent his time hanging around the Wyoming delegation so that he'd be there if this moment came. Before West Virginia's vote was announced, the candidate's youngest brother could sense how critical Wyoming was about to become. "I shouted to (Tracy) McCraken (the delegation chair)," He later recalled, "If Wyoming will make the difference in giving John Kennedy the nomination, will you give us the whole fifteen?" Ted Kennedy said it seemed McCraken "thought he was agreeing to something that he never believed was going to happen, so he said, "Sure." Just then, West Virginia, where Kennedy won a dramatic primary a few months earlier, awarded him 15 of their 25 votes. Now, Kennedy was, as Ted predicted, only 11 votes shy of the magic number.

The convention clerk called, "Wyoming?" Although among the state's delegates was a governor who had just nominated Lyndon Johnson and it wasn't altogether clear all the remaining 14 agreed, McCraken grabbed the mic and shouted, "Mr. Chairman, Wyoming's vote will make a majority for Senator Kennedy." The younger Kennedy recalled the entire arena erupted into bedlam. It took more than 15 minutes for the convention chair to restore order. "Can we get the vote from Wyoming?" he demanded. McCraken said, "Wyoming votes, we have 15 votes. There are 15 votes for Kennedy."[20]

Without Teno's political acumen and hard work, it may well be that John F. Kennedy would not have been nominated. JFK's younger brother certainly believed that. In the eulogy he wrote for Teno's 2003 memorial service, Senator Edward Kennedy said, "We all knew that if Jack couldn't win on the first ballot, he probably wouldn't win at all. So, in a very real sense, Teno didn't just deliver the delegates—he delivered the whole New Frontier."

As JFK was being elected President on November 8, Wyoming voters were electing Republican congressman Keith Thomson to the U.S. Senate. The Senator-elect suffered a massive heart attack a month later. Now it fell to Governor Joe Hickey to appoint a successor. The choice was obvious to everyone except the Governor. Teno Roncalio was promptly endorsed by 10 of the 23 county Democratic central committees and the University of Wyoming Young Democrats. The chair of the Wyoming Citizens for Kennedy endorsed Teno, most likely not without the approval of the President-elect.[21] Perhaps it was a hangover from the Kennedy-Johnson battle or some other grudge or slight. Hickey refused to consider Teno, instead asking Tracy McCraken to take the job. McCraken considered the offer but declined. A few days later, McCraken died.

The Kennedy family was grateful to Teno for his critical role in securing the nomination for JFK in 1960. They came to Wyoming often to support Teno's campaigns. Sen. Robert Kennedy, center, Wyoming Senator Gale McGee, left, campaign for Teno, right, in 1966. Sen. Edward Kennedy's rally for Teno in Casper in 1972 was one of the largest political gatherings in Wyoming history. Photo from Kathy Karpan's personal collection. Used with her permission.

Governor Hickey first told reporters he was not interested in becoming a senator. However, Hickey made a deal with his secretary of state, Jack Gage. Hickey would resign the governorship, which would make Gage governor and then the newly installed Governor Gage would appoint Hickey to the senate. Gage and Hickey served in their new offices only until the next election. In 1962, the voters punished both for their antics.

Perhaps it was three years of non-stop, grueling political campaigning. Perhaps it was the loneliness of bachelorhood. Regardless, by the time the 1960 election ended and gave way to another Wyoming winter, Teno was melancholic. He was feeling the sting of having not been appointed to an open senate seat by the governor whom he had worked so hard to elect two years earlier. He had a law practice and owned a bank. "I was well taken care of. But I was not very happy in Wyoming in those years. I was a bachelor and not yet married when the call came."[22]

President Kennedy was on the line. He wanted Teno to be part of his administration. Teno suggested the ambassadorship in Italy. It was decided that "a fellow who was not quite what you would call a devout Catholic, a little on the backsliding side, worshipping in the Congregational church" might not be welcomed by the Vatican.[23] Kennedy appointed Teno to chair the International Canadian-US Joint Commission on Water Rights. It was what Teno called "the cream plum job in Washington," an ambassador-rank diplomatic position that paid $22,000 a year, just $500 less than the salary of a U.S. senator.

On June 22, 1962, Teno married Cecelia Waters. They made their home in an elegant two-story home in the tree-lined avenues of Cheyenne. It was at the corner of Pershing Boulevard and Capitol Avenue but would not have been out of place in the pre-war South with its white exterior and large columns. It was a lively place. Teno and Ceil entertained, welcoming visitors from presidential candidates to schoolmates of their young boys to the ordinary friends he and Ceil made part of their lives. On entering, you'd be welcomed warmly while listening to a Mozart opera or a Beethoven concerto. Ceil graciously offered a beverage while Teno showed you around. Walls were lined with books, the great classics as well as contemporary fiction and non-fiction. If you said you'd like to read one, more often than not, the generous Teno gifted it to you on the spot because he and Ceil had already read it. Most days, Teno sat at his desk reading the *New York Times* or the *Washington Post*, or the *Wyoming Eagle*.

Young protégés weren't allowed to be simply impressed. They would be quizzed what they were doing with their lives, why they weren't in college, why they weren't in law school. The words were never judgmental. Only encouraging. Once you heard them coming from a man you knew had brought himself up by his bootstraps, you knew what you had to do. For some, it was a turning point in their lives.

Then came November 22, 1963. Dallas. Teno was visiting Cheyenne's newspaper offices when the teletype alarm began to ring. Ding, ding, ding, ding, ding. Roncalio, the old newspaperman knew the sound of five dings meant something serious had happened. This was not an ordinary bulletin. He headed to the teletype machine and lifted the rolled-up paper and read the horrific news.

> *President Kennedy Shot / Dallas -AP- President Kennedy was shot to / day just as his motorcade left downtown Dallas–/Mrs. Kennedy jumped up and grabbed Mr. Kennedy–/ She cried Oh No–The motorcade sped on [sic] / AP photographer*

> *Jeams W. Altgens said he saw / blood on the President's head / Altgens said he heard two shots but thought / someone was shooting fireworks until he saw / the blood on the President / Altgens said he saw no one with a gun / AP reporter Jack Bell asked Kenneth O-Donnell / Presidential Assistant if Kennedy was dead–O-Donnell gave no answer / Kennedy was reported taken to Parkland [sic] Hos- / pital*

near the Dallas Trade Mart where / he was to have made a speech / Bell said Kennedy was transferred to an / ambulance / He lay on the seat of the car / Bell reported three shots were fired as the / motorcade entered the triple underpass which / leads to the Stemmons Freeway route to / Parkland Hospital / Pandemonium broke loose around the scene / The Secret Service waved the motorcade on / at top speed to the hospital / Even at high speed it took nearly five / minutes to get the car to the ambulance entrance / of the hospital / -v- /

A few minutes later came the dreaded news.

ADD- Kennedy / Dallas -AP- Kennedy died of a gunshot / wound in the brain at approximately 1 p m / -CST-[24]

The day before, Teno predicted Kennedy would be re-elected in 1964.[25] Now he could only cover his face with his hands and along with millions of Americans, he wept. The President of the United States and his friend was dead.[26]

Teno Roncalio was committed to public service. The tragedy in Dallas would not be permitted to change that. In the Spring of 1964, less than six months after the assassination, Robert F. Kennedy and Teno, perhaps not so coincidentally, both announced their candidacies for congress. RFK was running for the senate in New York and Teno for Wyoming's lone seat in the U.S. House of Representatives. Kennedy ran against a popular Republican incumbent as did Teno. As the state Democratic Party chair looked ahead, he saw a primary that would pit Roncalio against several tough opponents. Walt Phelan estimated the field would include U.S. Marshall John Terrill, the Natrona County Attorney Harry Leimback, State Senator Ed Kendig, and State Representative Ed Herschler.[27] But, when Teno announced in May, the others opted out. "Sweetwater County's first native to seek election on either the Democratic or Republican ticket," was immediately endorsed by the state party and the largest newspaper in the state, the *Wyoming Eagle*.[28] In the end, Teno had only token opposition and was nominated with more than 70% of the Democratic vote.

Teno's Republican opponent, William Henry Harrison, was the great-grandson of the 9th President of the United States, his namesake. His grandfather, Benjamin Harrison served as the 23rd U.S. President, known for the longest inaugural address and the shortest presidency in American history. His one hour forty-five-minute inaugural address was delivered on a biting cold day in March 1841. He contracted a bad cold and died a month later.

Harrison was born in Indiana in 1896. He served briefly in the Indiana legislature before moving to Wyoming in 1937. He was elected to the Wyoming legislature, representing Sheridan County for eight years, until 1950, when he was elected to the U.S. House of Representatives. After two terms, Harrison sought the senate seat held by Republican Ed Crippa, who did not seek election after having been appointed to serve the remainder of Lester C. Hunt's term following Hunt's suicide in June of 1954. Harrison was defeated by former Senator Joseph C. O'Mahoney. By the time he ran against Teno in 1964, he had been re-elected to another two terms in the House.

It was clear very early the Republicans were going to nominate the archconservative senator from Arizona, Barry Goldwater, for president. Harrison and Goldwater were politically in sync. Harrison supported prayer and Bible reading in public schools as did Goldwater. Both men opposed Medicare and federal aid for education. Harrison opposed foreign aid and believed the United Nations was controlled by Communists. Goldwater didn't disagree. Both men thought LBJ's civil rights legislation would, as Harrison told a constituent, destroy "the rights of all Americans to engage in business" and create "special rights for certain people."[29] Goldwater and Harrison both voted against the Civil Rights Act of 1964. Despite the political synchronicity between the party's presidential favorite and the Wyoming Republican Party, there were signs of trouble early on. By July, a year before the election, state party fundraising was at such a crisis level, party chair John Wold told Sam Lopez the GOP could not afford a $20 ad Lopez pitched annually for inclusion in the Wyoming Federation of Latin American Groups convention program.

This wasn't Teno's first campaign, but it was the first time his name was on the ballot. The people of Wyoming quickly learned he was not an ordinary politician. A "Meet the Candidates" event in Sheridan County near the end of the campaign became part of the Roncalio mythos. After Teno spoke, he asked whether there were questions. An old man near the back of the barn in which the forum was held, stood. "Roncalio!" he said, "With a name like that, you must be a member of the mafia?" The audience laughed nervously, expecting Teno would offer a politically correct response like, "Well sir, not all people of Italian descent are members of the mafia." Instead, they learned a first lesson about Teno's blunt honesty. He walked briskly from the stage to where the old man stood, got in his face, and said, "If you weren't so damned old, I'd mop this barn floor with you." That was the Teno Roncalio Wyoming came to know and admire.

In November, while Lyndon Johnson's national landslide engulfed even Republican Wyoming with LBJ winning the state by almost 19,000 votes, Teno scraped by with a 2,211-vote edge. It would not be Teno's closest margin of victory.

In January 1965, Teno joined his friend Robert Kennedy in congress. Johnson was still stinging from Roncalio's role in Los Angeles 1960 and had been feuding with Robert Kennedy since shortly after Dallas. LBJ lumped Teno into "a liberal Kennedy bloc," believing the two, along with congressmen John Tunney of California and Joseph Tydings of Maryland, were "gunning to embarrass the Administration at every turn."[30] The only "conspiracy" Teno was involved in was planning to run for the U.S. senate in 1966. He wasn't the first politician representing Wyoming in the U.S. House of Representatives to covet a senate seat. In states like Wyoming, whose population qualifies it for only a single house seat, candidates are required to cover the same land mass and persuade the same voters to win a six-year senate term as it takes to win a two-year house term. Congressmen William Henry Harrison and Frank Mondell before had been lured into that trap. Beyond the benefit of a six-year term, Teno was also excited about the prospect of working side by side with his friends Robert and Ted Kennedy in the senate.

Less than two months before someone leaked Johnson's concerns about and the supposed RFK / Teno "liberal Kennedy bloc," there was another leak, hinting that Mike Manatos, a top LBJ aide from Wyoming, might challenge Roncalio for the U.S. Senate.[31] The *Rocky Mountain News* reported that by July, Manatos, a boyhood Rock Springs playmate of Roncalio's, claimed to have raised $290,000, a huge sum for the times. Hinting that an LBJ staffer might run closed off several sources of funds that might have gone to Roncalio early. Washington donors were slow to cross the president. Teno, it was said, would run even if it meant a difficult primary. The *Washington Post* saw the publicity value of setting it up as a "Kennedy versus Johnson" grudge match.[32] The analogy was supported by the history between the President and Roncalio.

Manatos and Johnson remembered how Teno controlled the Wyoming delegation when it put JFK over the top on the first ballot in 1960. They also remembered how Teno attempted to prevent Manatos from being seated in the place of an ailing Joe O'Mahoney at the Democratic National Convention. "We were asked to substitute Mr. Manatos for Mr. O'Mahoney and I objected," Teno recalled, "knowing full well that Mike Manatos was coming as a Lyndon B. Johnson delegate and not as an O'Mahoney vote." When Teno's challenge came to a vote, his objection was overruled.[33] Manatos became a delegate. The bad blood congealed.

As support for Teno grew through 1966, Manatos continued to toss out hints that he might run. It was not until July, four months before the general election, that he withdrew. Teno was now alone in the Democratic Primary and, after token opposition in the GOP primary, the sitting governor, Cliff Hansen, was chosen as his November opponent. The senate seat for which they vied was open because it had been vacated by Milward Simpson, the man who had been "given the gate in '58," largely because of the brutal campaign waged against him by then state Democratic Party chair, Teno Roncalio. Now it was Milward's turn. His son Alan remembered both campaigns. "He helped engineer my father's 1958 defeat in a bid for a second term as governor. In 1966, Dad had the opportunity to return the favor." Alan described the constant barrage of attacks Simpson meted out on Teno.

> "For a while Teno ignored Dad, taking aim only at Hansen. But eventually he exploded. Roncalio called the attacks 'vicious.' He said he 'welcomed Simpson's return to his traditional role as the hatchet

man for the Republican Party.' The next day, a reporter asked Dad, 'Are you really nothing more than a hatchet man for Cliff Hansen?' 'You bet I am,' grinned Dad. 'And I am never any happier than when my little old hatchet is banging down on Teno's bald head.' Teno lost and he knew what hit him."[34]

Teno loss to Hansen was a close 4,407 votes out of the 122,689 votes cast. A slender loss can be blamed on many things. Perhaps it was Milward Simpson's hammer "banging down on Teno's bald head." Republican chairman Stan Hathaway, who was elected governor in 1966, might have been right when he called Teno "an accident of Wyoming politics," alluding to his congressional victory enabled by the LBJ landslide of 1964. Wasn't it Teno who said to the voters, "I want to go back to congress, but you can't blame me if I decide to go to a different part of the building?"[35] It could be they did "blame" him as they had others who lost elections when trying to move from the house to the senate, including the Republican Teno beat for the U.S. House two years earlier. Maybe people were not pleased that a one-term congressman was leaving that office for a higher one. More likely, however, the slim margin was the result of Teno's bold but risky decision to support the Fair Housing Act of 1966.

President Johnson proposed the civil rights legislation in his 1966 State of the Union message. He asked congress to ban discrimination in the sale, rental, and financing of housing by tract developers, apartment house owners, and mortgage lenders. Together with bankers and realtors, those groups made up a large, powerful, and influential voting bloc in Wyoming. Stirred by the National Association of Real Estate Brokers, they launched an all-out campaign to persuade Wyoming's congressional delegation to vote against LBJ's proposal. In the summer of 1966, they flooded Teno's office with preprinted postcards, letters, and phone calls. They feared the Fair Housing Act would destroy property values. They were offended that a property owner could not decide who to sell to and who not to sell to, arguing that "a man's home is his castle."

The 1966 election was only a few months away when Teno decided he needed to respond to what he saw as racist opposition to the legislation. He told the realtors, bankers, and builders who asked him to oppose the bill that "the right to sell your property to whomever you wish is not a legal right I find existing in property law." He said it was "a privilege too easily equated with liberty in our peaceful pursuit of life." Teno explained how the abuse of that "privilege" led to the isolation of communities of color in substandard housing. Their congressman said it came down to a "basic consideration and that basic consideration is whether or not Negroes should be allowed to live in certain parts of town where they are able to afford the homes available."

He talked about growing up in Rock Springs where in "the immediate neighborhood where was born and raised, there were three homes; a Negro lived in one, across the creek from the Roncalio home, and next door was a Chinese family of the Lion Hand Laundry." Teno recalled how these, and other diverse families lived "in harmony, and in friendship and in fulfillment of the American dream." Finally, Teno accused Wyoming realtors of stirring up opposition to the Fair Housing Act, led by fear, to judge a person "by the color of skin." He closed by saying, "For these reasons, I have made this reply to your letters a 'Credo' of my life's work."

Few professionals speak to more people in a day than realtors, bankers, and builders combined, and, while the letter was courageous, it is more than a little possible that Teno's "Credo" letter motivated the 3-4 votes per precinct that made up the total of his 1966 loss.

It was a crushing defeat. Teno was uncertain what was next. He had a successful law practice to which he returned. He owned banks in Cheyenne and Gillette. Years later he'd laugh when telling of the day during these times when his old friend Bill Daniels came with a proposition. Cable TV. Daniels explained how he planned to run cables down every alley in Wyoming. People could plug into them and receive cable television in their homes. They would be billed a monthly charge. He wanted Teno to invest on the ground floor. "Why the hell would anyone pay you to run a cable into their homes so they can watch," Teno asked skeptically, "when they get it free from that antenna on their roof?" By 1986, Daniels banked millions from the 31 cable systems he owned in 10 states.

Teno was an entrepreneur, but it was public service that he loved. He often said, "good public service is its own reward," and he wasn't done with it. He spent much of 1967 tending to business and enjoying family. By then he and Ceil had two young sons and she brought four children from a previous marriage to their home. In the spring of 1968 Robert Kennedy called. He had decided to run against Lyndon Johnson for the 1968 presidential nomination. RFK knew of Teno's political acumen and wanted him to manage the campaign in the eleven western states. Teno was back in the game. Only three of those states had held primaries before June 5. Kennedy lost in Oregon on May 28, but Teno helped him win South Dakota and California on June 4. Minutes after declaring victory in Los Angeles, Robert Kennedy, like his brother five years earlier, was murdered.

Inconsolable by the sheer madness of an awful event that would defy a Shakespearian tragedy, Teno watched the television coverage into the night. When a reporter called at 7 AM the following morning, with "a voice cracked with emotion," he said simply, almost hopelessly, "I can't think of anything appropriate, newsworthy, or decent to say."[36]

There seemed little left to do. More than a year before his assassination, Bobby Kennedy told a writer for *Look* magazine, "Politics can hurt badly but there are lots of other ways of getting hurt in life."[37] Kennedy and Roncalio shared the life sentence that accompanies memories of the loss of a loved one to gunfire. Death had taken much from both. The murderer who killed Teno's mother had taken a big piece of his past. Death tried its damnedest to take his life at Omaha Beach. Now, John and Bobby Kennedy's murderers threatened to take his future and that of the country.

At the end of August, having been chosen a delegate to the Democratic National Convention in Chicago, he watched sorrowfully as it turned into a police riot and nominated a candidate promising to follow Johnson's policies in Vietnam. In November, Richard Nixon was elected president.

Was this the reward for "good public service?" Teno wondered. In the darkness of these long days, State Representative Ed Herschler told Teno he planned to run for congress in 1970 but would not enter the race if Teno planned to run. Teno assured Herschler he had no plans to run for public office again. Herschler announced his candidacy. Teno grieved.

But a story circulated among the Kennedy circle about an evening in June of 1968 when they carried the Senator's coffin to the grave. "The pallbearers," the story went, "were not sure where to place the coffin (and) walked on, uncertain in the night. Averill Harriman finally said to Stephen Smith (Kennedy's brother-in-law), 'Steve, do you know where you're going?' Smith said, 'Well, I'm not sure.' Then Smith said, 'I distinctly heard a voice from the coffin saying, 'Damn it. If you fellows will put me down, I'll show you the way.'"[38] Teno listened to Kennedy aides tell the story and he immediately knew. Public service was the way.

Teno grieved that he was unable to help deliver a second Kennedy presidency, but he knew it could not end that way. His Republican friend and journalist Roy Peck wrote about those difficult days in Teno's life. "A man's ego is not fed by telling others how to whip dragons, but by taking a crack at the dragon yourself. And Teno had his dragon."[39] It was an insatiable need, instilled from his childhood along Bitter Creek in Rock Springs. It was the need to serve.

On June 24, 1970, little more than two years after Robert Kennedy died, Teno announced he would seek the Democratic Party's nomination for his old seat in the U.S. House of Representatives.

It was clear from the earliest days of that campaign. Teno was heartened by the prospects of being back on the campaign trail and perhaps returning to Congress. He drove a van around the state, stopping in supermarket parking lots, setting a table with cold water, lemonade, and iced tea. Ceil and their young sons Frank and John invited passersby for a cold glass on those warm Wyoming summer days. Teno would engage them in conversation. He was as happy as he had been for a long time.

Republicans tried to persuade the voters that this was just another effort to get back in their good graces as a prelude for another senate race against Cliff Hansen in 1972. Not so, said Teno. With a well-aimed offside, he noted that John Wold, the GOP nominee running that year against the incumbent Democrat Gale McGee, had run against McGee six years earlier. Teno replied to his critics with a smirk. "If anyone in Wyoming thinks Cliff

Hansen is going to be lucky enough to draw the same opponent twice in a row, they are mistaken."[40]

In the August primary, Teno defeated Ed Herschler for the nomination. Although unhappy that Teno jumped into the race after telling him he wouldn't, future three-term governor Herschler endorsed Teno in his general election match-up against Harry Roberts. In a November squeaker, the voters gave Teno another term in Congress. Out of 116,304 votes cast, Roberts received 57,848 to Teno's 58,456 tally, a slim margin of 608 votes. After a recount, Teno was certified and was on his way back to what he called "my beloved House."

With no designs on any other office, Teno adopted what he called "the Warren Rule." He read Lewis L. Gould's book, *Wyoming: From Territory to Statehood*. Gould described how Francis E. Warren survived in the senate for so many years (1890-1893 and 1895-1929). The formula was how Warren "set about making arrangements for the smoother flow of federal largesse." There were no thoughts of presidential politics or seeking another office. Being an effective member of the U.S. House of Representatives consumed his professional life. During that first term back in the House since losing to Hansen in 1966, Teno arranged or announced grants for agriculture, education, airports, roads and highways, water projects and hospitals. He made certain there was federal "largesse" for tennis courts in Cody, work study programs at the University of Wyoming, a sewer for Chugwater, and money for the Big Horn Canyon Highway. He spent at least every other weekend back in Wyoming, traveling the entire 100,000 square miles, top to bottom, corner to corner, meeting and speaking in every community to large groups and small, listening to Republicans as well as Democrats and responding to every request.

He also began to openly break with his Democratic colleague, Senator Gale McGee, on Vietnam. McGee remained an outspoken defender of the war. By June of 1971, Teno decided to go public with his opposition. He called the war "an unspeakable tragedy" and voted to cut off all funds president Nixon needed to continue to wage the war after January 1, 1972.[41] While the effort failed, Teno had separated himself from both of Wyoming's senators (McGee and Cliff Hansen) on the issue. The break was especially pronounced when the *New York Times* published "The Pentagon Papers."[42] The leaked documents were entitled, "Report of the Office of the Secretary of Defense Vietnam Task Force." It was an inside-the-government secret review of the conduct of the war from 1945-1967. The heretofore secret documents disclosed how the U.S. government had consistently lied about the war and the prospects of a U.S. victory. In a highly controversial and litigated move, the *New York Times* published the papers in their entirety and the U.S. Supreme Court upheld their decision to do so. Senator Hansen said the *Times* had "flaunted the law." McGee "questioned the judgment" of the newspaper. Teno called the publication of the secret report "essential to a democratic society" and a matter of the freedom of the press.[43]

Speaking to a Memorial Day observance in Rawlins, Teno noted, "the majority of the general public looks on Vietnam veterans with indifference and sometimes antagonism." The WWII Silver Star hero comfortably distinguished support for veterans from opposition to the war, adding "the sooner we get out of Vietnam, the better."[44] In time, Teno became the only Wyoming political leader to call for amnesty for Vietnam era draft dodgers.

As Stan Hathaway before, most of the GOP leadership considered Teno "an accident of Wyoming politics." After all, he won in 1964 because

Congressman Teno Roncalio, 1974, chairman of the House Indian Affairs Subcommittee of the House Committee on Interior and Insular Affairs. Photo from Kathy Karpan's personal collection. Used with permission.

of LBJ's landslide coattails. He'd barely survived in 1970. A year ahead of the next election, they could be excused for making Teno their "prime target."[45] As they looked ahead to 1972, they saw a Republican ticket with the popular Richard Nixon at the top and the even more popular Cliff Hansen on the second line. Both were sure bets to win the state by wide margins. By the time the voters got to the U.S. House race, they figured, the voters would be well on their way to creating a Republican sweep. They were two-thirds right. Nixon won the state by 55 thousand votes, Hansen by a 61-thousand vote margin. But, the GOP house candidate, Bill Kidd, a 28-year-old Casper stockbroker, lost to Teno by 4,965 votes.

Teno could only look forward to another tough election campaign in 1976. To make it more politically difficult, the House would have to decide whether to impeach Richard Nixon who increased his margin of victory in Wyoming in 1972 over his landslide in 1968. Teno knew the hearings of the senate's select committee investigating Watergate had produced evidence that even die-hard Nixon supporters would find troubling. His staff tracked the phone calls and mail received on the issue. Early in the hearings, a slight majority opposed impeachment. By the late spring of 1974, that slowly began to change. By summer, Teno's staff recorded 919 messages in support of Nixon's impeachment, 909 opposed. He was confident enough that Wyoming opinion had shifted against the president that he invited House Majority Leader (soon to become speaker of the house) Thomas P. "Tip" O'Neill to come to Wyoming to support his hotly contested 1974 reelection campaign. Legendary journalist Jimmy Breslin accompanied O'Neill to take the impeachment temperature of a heavily Republican Western state. Breslin wrote about the night in his book "How the Good Guys Finally Won."

"The dinner (at the historic Hitching Post Inn in Cheyenne) drew a crowd of 500 people, the backbone of influence in Cheyenne," Breslin reported. Teno introduced O'Neill, referring to him as "one of the two or three men in whose hands rest the impeachment process in the House of Representatives." Toward the end of his speech, O'Neill sensed this crowd was ready to hear what he wanted to say about the fate of the President. "You could feel the tension run through the room," reported Breslin.

"Ranchers who had flown in for the meeting, big, long armed westerners, put their coffee cups down without causing the slightest clinking sound. Bankers held their cigarettes near the ashtrays and leaned forward. The woman seated next to me held her breath. It was the first time any audience in Wyoming heard impeachment discussed by anybody involved in it."

O'Neill began, "Justice Brandeis said, 'Decency, security, and liberty alike depend on the system in which no one is above the law.'" Breslin could see nearly every head in the big room nodding in the affirmative. "You've got to be kidding me," O'Neill told himself. "Nixon doesn't have a vote in this room. If he doesn't have a vote here, how the hell can he hope to get one anywhere?" Later that night, as Teno and the majority leader flew back to Washington, O'Neill observed, "Wyoming! He doesn't have a vote in Wyoming. This thing has been over for months."[46] Indeed, it was over less than two months later. Before Teno had to cast a vote on impeachment, Nixon resigned on August 9, 1974.

Teno had finally persuaded the Republicans he was who even they wanted in congress. He won re-election in 1974 by 12,000 votes and in 1976 by more than twenty thousand. During these years in the House, Roncalio's courage and abilities will be remembered for three especially historic accomplishments. He led the effort to end an ill-conceived and dangerous plan to detonate nuclear bombs under the ground of Northwest Wyoming to free deep natural gas deposits. He played a major role in the enactment of significant federal laws limiting the environmental impact of strip mining in Wyoming and the West. Working with Senators Cliff Hansen and Gale McGee, he played a key role in increasing Wyoming's share of federal mineral royalties, causing untold millions of dollars to flow to the state yet today.

As three 33-kiliton nuclear bombs were detonated under the Colorado ground below, Roncalio flew above the explosion with Dixie Lee Ray, the director of the Atomic Energy Commission and Colorado Governor John

Love. They watched the ground shiver in an awesome and frightening undulation. It was the third such test for what was called "Project Plowshare," a cynical play on words from Isaiah where the Hebrew prophet promised that someday, "they will beat their swords into plowshares." The Wyoming congressman was there to observe because an even larger detonation was planned for Sublette County in his state.

El Paso Natural Gas Company intended to set off a series of nuclear explosions under Sublette County of many times greater strength than a combination of the bombs dropped on Hiroshima and Nagasaki. It was a sort of atomic fracking. Supporters believed it would be an economic boom for Wyoming's natural gas industry. Opponents thought it would unleash earthquakes, contaminate ground water, and do extensive damage to the entire Yellowstone geologic region.

While Senator Cliff Hansen and Governor Stan Hathaway initially supported "Project Wagon Wheel," Senator Gale McGee took a "watch and wait" stance, saying he "wanted to make a scrupulous assessment of what was at stake."[47] Teno was more impulsive. He decided the moment he flew over the Colorado detonation. The project in Wyoming needed to be stopped. John Perry Barlow was a Pinedale rancher who later wrote songs for the Grateful Dead. Barlow recalled years later, "Teno was on our side from the beginning."[48]

In January of 1973, as he began his third term, Teno persuaded Speaker of the House Carl Albert to appoint him to the Joint Committee on Atomic Energy. He used the position to launch a successful campaign to halt funding for Wagon Wheel. Just a few days after his appointment to the committee, Roncalio announced that the Atomic Energy Commission budget for Plowshare, thus Wagon Wheel, did not "include funds for any test events in fiscal 1974."[49] Employing scientists to review the planned detonation, Teno penned a 47-page scholarly review of nuclear excavation projects like Wagon Wheel for the *Atomic Energy Law Review*. He described how such "nuclear excavation technology had been proposed for 'digging canals, harbors, mountain passes and underground reservoirs." He concluded the use of nuclear power in this manner was "politically unwise, technically hazardous, and economically questionable."[50]

Debating with congressional colleagues and industry lobbyists, he provided an impressive academic argument based on science and economics. He employed sound economic, technological, and environmental arguments to gradually persuade colleagues the project should be derailed permanently. Eventually the idea dried up and blew away like a tumbleweed on the Wyoming prairie. Writing in the *Wyoming Almanac*, historian Adam Lederer observed, "While the exact date of Wagon Wheel's death is murky, the direct cause appears clear." It was Teno Roncalio in the House and Gale McGee in the Senate.

Wyoming history doesn't begin with the cowboys. Not even with the Native Peoples who were here before them. It begins tens of millions of years earlier with the dinosaurs. Some were small. Others quite large. Some swam. Others flew or simply walked. A cataclysmic event triggered when a giant meteor struck the earth, put an end to them and started a long geologic process converting decomposing plants into coal. Billions of tons of it ended up barely below the surface of the arid Great Plains of Wyoming.

Fast forward to the 1970s and America's energy crisis. In 1974, the U.S. Bureau of Mines estimated that as much as 137 billion tons of coal could be harvested by simply removing the thin, grass covered surface and mining the coveted low-sulphur coal. It was a process known as surface mining or strip mining. In those years coal and other minerals such as trona and uranium, oil and gas, and the construction of large power-producing plants created a modern-day version of the Old West. Virtually unregulated, out of state entrepreneurs made huge amounts of money removing nearly untaxed chunks of the state's mineral wealth and taking it elsewhere to meet the needs of an energy thirsty nation.

Rock Springs, Teno's hometown, suffered under the impact of energy development and power plant construction projects. In the short four-year-span between the 1970 census and 1974, the community grew from 11,674 to a population in excess of 20,000. The *Rocky Mountain News* told its readers about what was happening in the small Southwest Wyoming community. "Burglaries, thefts, assaults, and barroom brawls have become common. A small brothel is rumored to be operating out of one hotel."[51]

Historian Phil Roberts recalled those days. Dr. Roberts was there and saw how Wyoming communities were unprepared "for the onslaught of miners, construction workers, and employees for support companies that descended on Wyoming in a brief period of time."[52] People were forced to live in man camps. Trailer houses accounted for a fifth of the housing. There were workers living in tents, campers, and their pickup trucks. Schools were overwhelmed as teachers left the classroom for better paying construction or mining jobs. Social services and law enforcement resources were stretched to the breaking point. City services including sewer and water, solid waste control, streets and road maintenance was a daily struggle for municipalities.

As ranchers and farmers who owned the right to make a living on the surface of the land battled mining companies that owned the rights to minerals below the surface, a National Academy of Sciences report suggested that certain parts of the country "must be given up as impossible to reclaim or even rehabilitate." They were talking about huge swaths of Wyoming and the people whose lives were at stake when they said their land should become a "National Sacrifice Area."[53] In other words, while some became wealthy off the minerals, a lot of Wyoming people would lose their way of life.

It reminded Teno of the old company store scenario he watched play out during his childhood in Rock Springs. The congressman pleaded his case. "My colleagues," began his speech in favor of the Surface Mining and Reclamation Act of 1974, "Do not mortgage our souls to the company store. That is what will happen if we do not get some considerate, fair, decent strip-mining legislation." He decried the profiteering of the companies that opposed any regulation. "Last year the profits of Consolidated Coal Company were not 700%," Teno roared, "but 7800%."[54]

President Richard Nixon called for legislation to rectify the abuses of the mining companies in his 1973 State of the Union message. He resigned before a bill could pass. The new president, Gerald Ford, was not a proponent of the legislation. Teno and the other legislators who favored the law found it impossible to reach a compromise with Ford. He vetoed the 1975 act. Teno did not lose heart. He and others continued to push for the law. It was not until after Jimmy Carter defeated Ford in 1976 that congress was able to secure the president's signature on tough strip-mining regulation by passing a law Carter referred to in his 1978 State of the Union speech as, "one of the most significant environmental statutes in recent years."

Nonetheless, if you could ask Teno what achievement he was most proud of in his ten years in the house of representatives, it would likely be increasing the share of mineral royalties returned to the state after he and the other members Wyoming's congressional delegation teamed up to make it happen. To this day, Teno and Senators Cliff Hansen and Gale W. McGee are remembered for the bipartisan success they achieved in the enactment of the Federal Land Policy and Management Act.

For years, congress toyed with the idea of updating the laws directing management of federal lands. When the effort to do so became serious in 1976, Teno recognized the momentum behind the reforms was an opportunity to address Wyoming's need for funds to meet the costs of energy development. As a senior member of the House Interior Committee, he successfully proposed amendments providing a significant increase in the state's share of federal royalties. For decades, private companies producing minerals on federal land paid a royalty or tax ranging from 5 to 12.5 percent, of which the state received 37.5%. Teno argued the state share should be increased to 50%.

With Roncalio taking the lead in the House, Democrat McGee and Republican Hansen teamed up in the Senate. The three recognized this was a once-in-a-lifetime opportunity. The bill passed with the increase, but the day before the nation celebrated its Bicentennial, President Ford crushed the hopes of many in Wyoming by vetoing the legislation even though the bill passed the House 344-51 and the Senate by an 84-12 margin. Congress overrode the veto the following month and ever since then, Wyoming has been on the receiving end of hundreds of millions of dollars for schools, roads and highways and other needs.

The voters of Wyoming "celebrated" this crowning demonstration of bipartisanship by never again electing another Democrat to congress after Teno's last election in 1976.

On a warm September day after the Wyoming Cowboy football team defeated the University of Texas at El Paso 27-17, Teno walked slowly out of War Memorial Stadium. A reporter came up beside him. Almost casually, Teno told him he would not seek re-election in 1978. It was Teno. "Predictably unpredictable," the reporter called him.[55] Teno said it was time for someone else. "The same old horses cannot always be called on to haul the coal."[56]

He served until December 31, 1978, resigning a few days before his term ended, graciously allowing his Republican successor, Dick Cheney, to be sworn in before other freshmen, giving Cheney a higher rung on the seniority ladder.

In 1979, Governor Ed Herschler named Teno the Special Master to adjudicate a historic water rights dispute between ranchers, farmers, municipalities, and the Eastern Shoshone and Northern Arapaho Tribes of the Wind River Indian Reservation. "This contest," Teno recounted, "produced a trial nearly two years in length, a transcript of over 15,000 pages, over 2,300 exhibits admitted into evidence, and a 450-page report."[57] Teno's analysis of complex water law and Indian rights issues resulted in lower court decisions affirmed by the United States Supreme Court a decade later.[58]

Teno lived the remainder of his life mostly out of the public arena. Ceil died of cancer in March of 1997. Teno passed away six years later, also in the month of March. In a eulogy he wrote to be read by the priest at Teno's memorial service, Ted Kennedy recalled the Kennedy family friendship with Roncalio as well as the decade they served together in Congress. Kennedy reminded the gathered mourners of Teno's "golden tenor voice and the beautiful songs he loved to sing from opera at the drop of a hat and above all, his enduring friendship and the powerful voice he always was for progress and opportunity and the great ideals we share as a country."[59]

A longtime political adversary and longer time friend Robert Peck, publisher of the *Riverton Ranger* memorialized Teno in an April 3, 2003, editorial. Mr. Peck called Roncalio "a prime example of a public servant embraced by the majority of Wyoming voters regardless of party affiliation. He leaves behind a legacy of service and a broad base of sincere respect, crossing political lines and embracing a wide slice of Wyoming people from every walk of life."

Teno Roncalio comes to mind when reading Clarence Darrow's story of his friend, the courageous governor of Illinois and leader in the American Progressive Movement, John Peter Altgeld. Among Altgeld's bold work were the pardons he issued to three of the men convicted in the Haymarket Affair. When Altgeld died, Darrow asked several clergymen to preside at the funeral. They shied away, fearing it would cost them their pulpits. The chore fell to Darrow. He was more eloquent than usual. "In the great flood of human life that is spawned upon the earth," the renowned orator said, "it is not often that such (an authentic human) is born."[60]

Indeed, let it be said of Teno Roncalio.

Endnotes

1. McManus, *The Dead and Those About to Die*, 8
2. Ryan, *The Longest Day*, 196
3. The China-Burma-India Theater served two purposes during the war. It opened air routes over the Chinese mountains to move supplies and it built a key road to move Chinese armies to fight battles against the Japanese. The second purpose for the units was to provide a bas eof operations for air attacks against Japan
4. Letter Roncalio to O'Mahoney, June 14, 1945, Box 359, Folder: "Personal Papers-Correspondence 1945" O'Mahoney Papers, AHC
5. Letter O'Mahoney to Roncalio, July 4, 1945, Box 359, Folder: "Personal Papers-Correspondence 1945" O'Mahoney Papers, AHC
6. Id., 7
7. "Rites Held for Victims of Murder-Suicide," *Rock Springs Rocket Miner*, February 20, 1940, 7
8. "Italian Immigration In The 1900s," *Researchomatic*, https://www.researchomatic.com/Italian-Immigration-In-The-1900s-54077.html, accessed November 23, 2021
9. Unless otherwise indicated, the source of Roncalio's early family history is an unpublished ten-page memoir written by Julia Roncalio Peterson in the mid-60s. It is part of a private collection held by Kathy Karpan, Cheyenne, WY
10. "Citizens Look at Congress," Ralph Nader Congress Project, 1972, 6
11. The Chamber of Commerce and barber shop stories are from the author's personal recollections from times when he was a member of Teno's congressional staff and accompanied him on trips across the state
12. Mabel Brown, "Teno Roncalio: Congressman from Wyoming," *Bits and Pieces*, Vol. 2, No. 5, http://www.roncalio.com/Teno/index.htm, accessed December 1, 2021
13. "Teno Roncalio: Ex-Dishwasher, Now Wyoming's Whirlwind," *Billings Gazette*, May 10, 1964, Roncalio Papers, AHC, box 7
14. McDaniel, *The Man in the Arena*, 84, citing Gale McGee, recorded interview by Sheldon Stern, November 16, 1982, JKK Library Oral History, 6
15. Paul, Krza, "Democrats struggle to regain a foothold," *High Country News*, July 6, 1998, https://www.hcn.org/issues/134/4288, accessed December 6, 2021
16. Grele, transcript of recorded interview with Teno Roncalio, John F. Kennedy Library Oral History Program, December 20, 1965, 3, JFKCAMP1960-0975-020-p0001
17. Edward M. Kennedy, Written eulogy for Teno Roncalio, April 5, 2003, from author's private collection
18. Sorensen, *Kennedy*, 115
19. Grele, 23, 48
20. Official Proceedings of the 1960 Democratic National Convention, 167
21. "Roncalio Gets Support Here in Bid for U.S. Senate," *Casper Star Tribune*, December 18, 1960, 26
22. Grele, 54
23. Id., 53
24. Original Associated Press, UPI and Dow Jones Teletypes-Kennedy Assassination, https://www.baumanrarebooks.com/rare-books/kennedy-assassination/original-associated-press-upi-and-dow-jones-teletypes-kennedy-assassination/56902.aspx,

accessed December 4, 2021

25 "Roncalio sees JFK-McGee Wins," *Rock Springs Daily Rocket*, November 21, 1963, 1
26 "Cheyenne Remembers Kennedy as Smiling, Vivacious Man," *Wyoming State Tribune*, November 24, 1963, 3
27 "Democratic candidate list," *Casper Star Tribune*, January 30, 1964, 1
28 "Teno Roncalio Throws Hat in Ring," *Jackson Hole Guide*, April 30, 1964, 13; *Wyoming Eagle*, May 13, 1964, 5
29 Letter from Harrison to Mr. and Mrs. Donald D. Pellatz of Bill, Wyoming, June 26, 1963.' Harrison papers, Box 14, AHC
30 Bohrer, "The Revolution of Robert Kennedy," 182, citing Allen L. Ottesen, *Wall Street Journal*, June 17, 1965
31 "LBJ Aide is Hinted as Senate Candidate," *Rocky Mountain News*, April 27, 1965, 8
32 "1966 Primary Could Have Johnson versus Kennedy Overtones," *Washington Post*, July 5, 1965, A4
33 Grele, Roncalio Oral Interview, December 20, 1965, 16, https://www.jfklibrary.org/sites/default/files/archives/JFKOH/Manatos%2C%20Mike%20N/JFKOH-MNM-01/JFKOH-MNM-01-TR.pdf, accessed December 6, 20
34 McDaniel, *Dying for Joe McCarthy's Sins*, Introduction by Senator Alan K. Simpson, ix
35 "Teno to run for senate, he admits," *Sheridan Press*, June 14, 1966, 1
36 "State Leaders Shocked by News Kennedy Shot," *Casper Star Tribune*, June 5, 1968, 8
37 Oriana Fallaci, "Robert Kennedy Answers Some Blunt Questions," *Look*, March 9, 1965, 62
38 Schlesinger, *Robert Kennedy and His Times*, 916
39 "Teno has a hole card over his opponents," *Riverton Ranger*, undated newspaper clipping, Roncalio papers, box 8, AHC
40 "Teno Won't Run Against Hansen," unidentified newspaper clipping, Roncalio papers, box 9, AHC
41 "Roncalio to Support Move to Cut-off Viet War Funds," *Casper Star Tribune*, June 19, 1971,
42 "The Pentagon Papers," https://www.archives.gov/research/pentagon-papers, accessed December 9, 2021
43 "State Newspaper Editors Support High Court Rule," *Laramie Daily Boomerang*, July 1, 1971,
44 "Roncalio Praises Men in Uniform," *Rawlins Daily News*, June 2, 1971,
45 "Both Parties Concerned on Building Candidates," *Casper Star Tribune*, November 25, 1971, p.
46 Breslin, *How the Good Guys Finally Won*, 160-164
47 Letter from McGee to Floyd Bousman, reprinted in the *Pinedale Roundup*, August 24, 1972, 14
48 Oral Interview of John Perry Barlow, conducted by C.L. Rawlins, January 3, 1994, box 13, folder 9, Wagon Wheel Information Committee papers, AHC
49 Adam Lederer, "A Nuclear Plowshare for Wyoming," https://wyomingalmanac.com/?p=939, accessed December 14, 2021, citing "AEC budget has no test funds," *Casper Star Tribune*, Jan. 31, 1973, 11; "Nixon budget delays Wagon Wheel

plans," *Casper Star Tribune*, February 3, 1973, 7
50 Teno Roncalio, "Plowshare-A Technology in Search of a Use," *Atomic Energy Law Journal*, Vol. 16, No. 1, Summer 1974, 93-140
51 "Wyoming offers Colorado a glimpse of shale difficulty," *Rocky Mountain News*, February 19, 1974,
52 McDaniel, *Man in the Arena*, 264, citing Phil Roberts, "Boom and Bust in Wyoming," http://www.uwyo.edu/ahc/energybboom/boom-bust.htm, accessed November 3,2015, page removed since accessed
53 Helena Huntington Smith, "The Wringing of the West," *Washington Post*, February 17, 1975, *Congressional Record*, February 18, 1975, 3345
54 *Congressional Record*, (1975), 1798
55 "Teno Calls it Curtains," *Casper Star Tribune*, September 20, 1977, 4
56 "Teno Roncalio explains his reasons for quitting," *Jackson Hole Guide*, October 27, 1977, 4
57 Teno Roncalio, "The Big Horns of a Dilemma," https://open.uapress.arizona.edu/read/indian-water-in-the-new-west/section/901f1314-3ff3-4936-b463-55fed1272b15, accessed December 17, 2021
58 *Wyoming v. United States*, 492. U.S. 406 (1989
59 Edward M. Kennedy, Written eulogy for Teno Roncalio, April 5, 2003, from author's private collection
60 Irving Stone, *Clarence Darrow for the Defense*, Doubleday, Doran & Company, Inc., Garden City, New York (1941), 126

Chapter 9

THE SIMPSONS

"if you believe it's right, you do what is right"

When Milward Simpson ran for re-election for Governor in 1958, he became only the second Simpson to lose an election in Wyoming. The first was Milward's father Billy. Billy chaired the Park County Democratic Party in 1905. He was also a candidate for county attorney at the time. A part owner of the bank where the Democrats kept their money was a fellow named W. Dean Hays. Hays didn't like Democrats. To irritate and embarrass the local Democrats, he began bouncing their checks even though the Party had sufficient funds to cover them. One thing led to another, and the day came when Billy Simpson brought a gun to the bank to confront Hays. Billy fired the gun and, as grandson Alan K. Simpson tells it, "The bullet grazed the side of Hays's head and nearly blew his ear off, probably 'deafed' him too."[1]

The incident cost Billy the election, but, by only three votes.

Some years later, Billy, by then a 55-year-old attorney, found himself in a vicious fistfight with a man named Edward Uriah Raines. Raines, nursing an old grudge from the time Simpson represented the other side in a lawsuit, attacked Simpson. Billy was armed and ended up killing Raines. A judge found the evidence unable to support a premeditated murder charge and the jury deadlocked on a verdict of manslaughter. Billy was unhappy with the result, saying I am not altogether satisfied with the vindication of the dismissal of the case." He didn't feel his friends would "look upon it in view of the situation without particular reference to myself or any disposition to censor myself or my family." Even so, the county attorney and the trial judge agreed there would not be a second trial.[2]

"Broken Ass Bill," they called this rough, tough, hard drinking, gambling man, was Milward's colorful father. Milward came into the world in a log cabin in Jackson on November 12, 1897. Later the family moved to Cody where Milward graduated from high school in 1916. He attended a prep school in Maryland, leaving to join the Army, expecting to fight in World War One. Son Al said, "His only combat was being seriously injured by an attacking bulldog."

After the war, Milward returned home, graduating from the University of Wyoming in 1921. He worked briefly as a coal miner in Red Lodge, Montana, joining the United Mine Workers Union, before deciding he'd rather practice law. Then he was off to study law at Harvard before being admitted to the Wyoming Bar in 1926, the same year he was elected to the Wyoming House of Representatives. He was appointed to the board of trustees of the University of Wyoming in 1939, becoming a leading force in the development of the state's only university for 15 years.

As Milward approached voting age, he sought his father Billy's advice about which party he should join. "Democrats are fine," he told his boy, "but Republicans always win."[3] Billy was, therefore, the last Democrat in the Simpson family tree until Pete's son and Milward's namesake, Milward Allen Simpson. The younger Milward was asked about being a Democrat among a long line of Republicans. He said his political values are identical to those of his grandfather who "instilled in us, that it's important to be who you are and stand up for what you believe and be honest and truthful. It doesn't really matter what your party stripe is, if you love the state and you want to serve it, that's what you've got to do." He added, "Blood's much thicker than partisan politics."[4]

The elder Milward Simpson's first foray into statewide politics was an unsuccessful campaign for the United States Senate in 1940. He was soundly defeated by Joseph C. O'Mahoney. Fourteen years passed before Simpson made another attempt. In 1954, he was elected Governor.

As his grandfather Fincelius Grey Burnett lay on his death bed, he called Milward and the other grandchildren together to leave behind some advice. "My children," Grandpa Fincelius said, "the circle is about completed. Don't try to be too good. Don't be too bad. Stay in the middle of the road and go as far as you can."[5] It could never be said that Simpson walked the middle of the road. Once he decided which side of the road he'd walk, he walked straight and tall.

Milward Simpson died on June 10, 1993, at the age of 95. Son Al recalled the family gathering at the funeral home in Cody a few days after his death and just before his earthly remains were cremated. Lorna's wheelchair was positioned in front of Milward's body, his sons listening as their mother prayed.

> *"I pray, God, for his integrity and his character and I ask that those traits and attributes be passed down through the generations.*

This is the story of how his integrity and his character guided him as it was "passed down through the generations" and how he courageously risked his political fortunes by modeling those traits and attributes.

It appeared the man they nicknamed "Tricky" had come to grips with the idea that he was about to pay the ultimate price for killing two people in cold blood. Clay "Tricky" Riggle lay on his bunk at the Wyoming State Penitentiary. He read for a while and then wrote a few last words to his family, a couple of friends, and his attorneys. Of those at the center of the storm, the convicted murderer was the more relaxed of the three.

Meanwhile, down the hall from Riggle's cell, the warden scurried around nervously making sure everyone knew his or her role and that the standard operating procedures were in place to put a man to death within the next 24 hours. He checked the old gas chamber. There were no leaks. It would hold enough gas long enough to kill Riggle. The execution was on.

One hundred forty miles away, the Governor of Wyoming was still mulling the decision he had to make before midnight tomorrow. Volumes have been written about how elected officials disappoint their constituents. Little is ever said about constituents disappointing their elected officials. "At the next election," the letter from Bruce Jennings, a Casper constituent, read, "I will vote for the blackest Negro in Natrona County in preference to a person that has proved himself twofaced by betraying his office to which the people elected him."[6] The Governor, who had just pushed a civil rights bill through the legislature, cringed as he read it.

Having made his decision, the burden didn't get any lighter. Milward Simpson leaned back in his chair and stared at the ceiling, contemplating the troubling, racist letter. Heaving a heavy sigh, the governor, tossed Jennings's correspondence to the top of one of two stacks of other letters telling him what they would do if they had this burden on their shoulders. That stack consisted of letters opposing any decision to commute Riggle's

Governor Milward Simpson. Photo courtesy of the Wyoming State Archives.

sentence. It was side by side with another stack of letters from people who thought commutation was the right thing. The two stacks appeared to be about the same height.

Absent the racist tone, most of the letters opposed to commuting the sentence said much the same thing. Riggle was a murderer. He had been tried and convicted by a jury of his peers. His lawyers had appealed the case all the way to the United States Supreme Court and lost. A governor's personal feelings about the death penalty, many told him, were irrelevant. His job was to carry out the law. He should allow the execution to go forward. Riggle should die.

His attorney general, George Guy, told him the same thing. George Guy was an old school, by-the-numbers, sort of fellow. To him, this was an easy question. Riggle got a fair trial. He had competent attorneys representing him. The verdict was "guilty." The sentence had been lawfully handed down. Riggle's day in court continued through the Wyoming and the U.S. Supreme Court. Case argued. Appeals denied.[7] In George Guy's mind, it was simple. The time had come to put "Tricky" Riggle to death.

From the moment he first heard of the double murder in Wheatland, the Governor followed the case closely. From the moment he heard the verdict and the death sentence pronounced, he knew the day would come when he would have a tough choice to make. The facts of the heinous crime played on a loop in Governor Simpson's head. He knew how awful it was and he knew that those who would decide whether he was reelected next year also knew.

Tricky Riggle and his girlfriend Frances Williamson were small-town celebrities of sorts. Tricky got his nickname as a trick roper, performing at small rodeos and county fairs. He entertained circus audiences with his rope tricks and an exciting knife throwing act. While Frances stood 30 feet away, Tricky would throw his long knife at her with sufficient accuracy to have never been charged with manslaughter. He and Frances combined to do their knife throwing act at the 1952 Platte County Fair and Rodeo, which gave them both some degree of notoriety in Wheatland, the county seat.

Tricky was under the mistaken impression that he and Frances were in love with one another and were going to be married on March 28, 1953.

Frances was not under the same impression. When he got off work that day, Riggle went to his apartment, took a shower, and put on "a striped pair of brown pants, a blue shirt, and a clean jacket with a fur collar. These were my best clothes," he told the jury. "I also had my hat and was going to pick Frances up and go to Lusk." That's where, he figured, they planned to be married.[8]

Frances's plans, on the other hand, differed considerably. She scheduled her evening to include hanging out at the Top Hat Bar in Wheatland and drinking with a fellow named Walter Ackerblade. When Riggle walked through the door and saw the woman he thought he was about to marry with another man, he "laid his hand on Ackerblade's shoulder and said, 'You son-of-a-bitch, I told you to stay away from her or I would kill you.'" Ackerblade didn't respond. Riggle turned to Frances. Unable to persuade her to leave with him, he threatened that if she didn't "quit fooling around with this guy, evidently meaning Ackerblade, he would kill her."[9] Riggle went to his car, retrieved his gun, and followed through on both threats. Finding the couple in the Angle Café, Tricky first targeted Ackerblade. "Damn you, I told you I would get you and now I am getting you." He then shot Ackerblade four times before turning the gun on Frances and pumping four bullets into her. "The bullets entering the hearts in both bodies were practically identical. Death was instantaneous in both cases because of the extensive damage to the aorta and the left ventricle of the heart."[10]

The defendant's guilt was evident and beyond any reasonable doubt. The jury took little time to convict Clay "Tricky" Riggle. A judge decreed he should die in the gas chamber at the Wyoming State Penitentiary. Riggle's attorneys appealed to the Wyoming Supreme Court. In a 53-page decision, the Court announced its decision.

> "We have made the most careful examination of the record and of the briefs of counsel for the defendant and have been unable to find any reversible error, and the judgment of the trial court is affirmed."

Denying Riggle's petition for a rehearing, the Justices, just a stone's throw away from the Governor's office but a light year away from his thinking, spoke less to the condemned man and more to the Governor who was now left alone with the constitutional authority to save Riggle's life.

> "The defendant is guilty of a serious crime. He killed not only one person, he killed two. That accentuates the fact that if the defendant had a fair trial, as we think he had, no sentiment or sympathy on our part should permit him to escape the penalty which the law decrees. It is not he alone whom we must consider. We must consider society as well. A warning must be given that to take another's life is dangerous to the one who takes it. We have too many killings. If capital punishment is to be abolished, that must be done by the legislature. We have no power to do so. We but follow the law and must do so. It is not this court that is sending the defendant to his death. That was done by the jury, and unless we find a prejudicial error of law, as we have not found, we have no right, privilege, or power to interfere with its province, centuries old as that province is."[11]

The Wyoming Supreme Court set September 5, 1956, for the execution of the sentence pronounced in the trial court. The Court was unwilling to save Milward Simpson from having to make the hardest call of his political life. It seemed they intended to provide him a legal roadmap to justify a politically correct decision to allow the execution to proceed. The Governor could simply adopt the rationale of their ruling and announce, "If capital punishment is to be abolished, that must be done by the legislature. A governor has no power to do so. My obligation is to follow the law, and I must do so. It is not I that is sending the defendant to his death. That was done by the jury, and unless the attorney general or I find a prejudicial error of law, as we have not found, a governor has no right, privilege, or power to interfere with the jury's province."

It was not like Milward Simpson to take the easy way out.

Although Riggle's lawyers were planning an appeal to the U.S. Supreme Court, Simpson was an astute enough of a lawyer to know the high court would not likely overturn either the conviction or the sentence for some obscure reason they might find was overlooked by the Wyoming court. The Governor knew the verdict and death sentence would survive the last chance appeal. Weighing on Simpson was the fact that it wasn't only Tricky Riggle.

Twenty-four-year-old Ernest Lindsay was likewise awaiting death in a cell at the Wyoming Penitentiary. The young man had been convicted of murder. Two years earlier, Lindsay botched an attempt to burglarize what he thought was an abandoned pickup near Shawnee, Wyoming, along a state road east of Douglas. Later, the Wyoming Supreme Court recounted the facts. Lindsay was surprised by the owner, "who turned, swung his arm, and hollered, and the Defendant shot him. The Defendant testifies, 'I don't know if he was fixing to hit me with something or shoot me or whether he was as scared as I was. I don't know, and I shot him.'" He drove to Casper. There he bought a shovel and took Herbert A. Diester's body out into the prairie and, after taking a couple of traveler's checks and two one-dollar bills from his pockets, buried him.[12]

A third man also faced the gas chamber under Simpson's watch. Joe Cruz Martinez was convicted of first-degree murder. After a night of drinking on New Year's Eve 1957, Martinez and his bunkmate, Ramon Gonzalez, with whom he worked on a ranch near Lander, got into a fight. It culminated with Martinez retrieving a gun and shooting Gonzalez. Martinez was tried and convicted of first-degree murder. Along with Riggle and Lindsay, he anticipated his last breath would come in the gas chamber at the Wyoming state penitentiary.

Standing between Tricky Riggle's date with death and that of Lindsay and Cruz were two lifelines. First was a long-shot appeal to the Wyoming Supreme Court that Riggle had already lost. Second was the Governor's constitutional prerogative. Final court decisions for both Lindsay and Cruz would likely be handed down long before Election Day 1958. The Governor was now on the clock.

It wasn't as though Milward Simpson needed more trouble as he headed into the final year of his first term, planning to seek re-election. Shutting down illegal gambling in Jackson Hole and the location of an interstate highway in northern Wyoming stirred up more than enough trouble for the Governor.

Those who knew Milward Simpson during his first term in the state legislature might not have expected him to take illegal gambling in bars seriously. During Prohibition, Governor Frank Emerson proposed making the possession of a liquor-producing still punishable by a severe prison sentence. In the House debate, State Representative Milward L. Simpson, then of Big Horn County, was reported to have said, "My county is sopping wet and the saloons run wide open." Juries, he said, would not convict if conviction meant a jail term.[13] Thirty years later and now serving as governor, Simpson learned several bars, as well as law enforcement officers and city officials in Jackson Hole were flaunting illegal gambling operations in violation of state law.

Historian T.A. "Doc" Larson chronicled Wyoming's colorful history struggling to handle the gambling issue. Before statehood, gambling was "a favorite pastime. Men were excited to bet on everything from poker hands to foot and horse races to shooting live pigeons on the wing." The 1888 Territorial legislature attempted unsuccessfully to ban gambling. One lawmaker called gambling "an inherent attribute of the human heart." Politicians who interfered with that inherent attribute, risked not only their jobs but their lives. Frank Mondell served Wyoming in the U.S. House of Representatives for 26 years, during which time he was twice elected Majority Floor Leader. None of that would have been possible had he not survived being shot when, as mayor of Newcastle, he attempted to run 20 gamblers out of town.[14]

In 1901, the legislature finally outlawed gambling, but the law was mostly observed in its breach and enforced in few communities. In 1935, Governor Leslie Miller vetoed a bill repealing the ban. He admitted, "No act of mine since I have been in office brought to my desk such a flood of communication."[15]

Two decades later, Milward Simpson waded into the Jackson Hole gambling controversy with eyes wide open. In August of 1956, Governor Simpson ordered Attorney General George Guy to investigate those rumors he'd heard about illegal gambling activities in the small northwest Wyoming town. On the recommendation of the Colorado Attorney General, Guy contracted with James Lail and his associate Robert Roberts, a former F.B.I. agent from Denver to carry out the inquiry.[16] Upon completion of his seven-day investigation, Mr. Lail sent the state of Wyoming a bill for $632.85, which included $6.50 for "illness as result of certain investigation." Lail left us wondering what kind of an illness could arise from that investigation, but concluded, "I consider it very fortunate that nothing of a more serious nature occurred and that no one's health was impaired."

Governor Simpson was attending the 1956 Republican National Convention in San Francisco when a registered letter arrived at his room in the Whitcomb Hotel.[17] The August 23, four-page letter was Attorney General Guy's report on the Roberts investigation. It included some startling recommendations. Guy said the investigation demonstrated the county sheriff "has completely failed to enforce the law and should be removed from office." He alleged the local police had, likewise, failed in their responsibilities to enforce the law "for some time." Guy reported to the governor:

> *"Suffice it for me to say that law enforcement with respect to gambling and liquor law violations has completely broken down. All the bars in Jackson stay open as long as they feel like it and as long as there is still a customer to buy another drink."*

Guy reported that since the investigation had been made known "open gambling has subsided," but some gambling was still ongoing and "the crap tables and 21 tables are merely shoved to one side and covered over with cloths, apparently ready for immediate use should the proprietors decide that it is time to put them back in business." He said investigators had found "the bars stay open beyond closing time and (allow) minors and even children in the bars." Guy named the offenders and, despite their influence in the community, recommended their liquor licenses be revoked.

> *"Perhaps if their licenses were revoked and the establishments in question abated as public nuisances, and a new county attorney and a new sheriff installed in Teton County, we would have an atmosphere under which law enforcement may proceed in the normal channels."*

Forebodingly, the Attorney General said he had already obtained the permission of the district court judge to declare martial law and use National Guard troops to enforce the law during legal proceedings. Within a few days, the September 13 front page of the *Jackson Hole Guide* blared a headline telling the people of Teton County that the "Governor Threatens to Impeach Our Sheriff." The story said, "A United Press release of September 11 says that Governor Milward Simpson stated he is asking for the impeachment of Teton County Sheriff Olin Emery because of continued gambling law violations in Jackson and the revocation of liquor licenses of Jackson bar owners selling liquor after legal closing hours.

"This latest outburst," the story continued, "came as a result of so-called photographs which appeared in the *Deseret News* and *Salt Lake Tribune* supposedly taken here last Saturday night showing 'open gambling.' There is no proof of when or where the pictures were taken, and the people are unrecognizable."

A few weeks later, the Wyoming Liquor Commission, chaired by the Governor, found evidence of illegal gambling was compelling. After a hearing during which city officials pled for the Commission to show mercy for the town's economy, the liquor licenses of the offending bars were suspended for forty-five days.[18] By now, the county sheriff and county attorney had been forced to resign and the rest of the county was resigned to the fact that the Governor would no longer tolerate illegal gambling.

It was the last time the gambling controversy appeared in a Teton County newspaper before the 1958 election, when Simpson's vote total dropped more than 200 votes over his 1954 numbers. Democrat Joe Hickey came within 10 votes of carrying the small but heavily Republican County.

A few days after the election, the *Jackson Hole Guide* observed, "More Democrats came out from under the rocks and bushes in Teton County than anyone had dreamed existed here."[19]

It is impossible for most of today's Americans to imagine a country without interstate highways. Most have never known anything else. They take for granted the four-lane thoroughfares allowing them to drive safely at rather high speeds, stopping only for gas and fast food at stores bordering the highways, allowing for minimum down time as they make their trip. Other than folks like Henry Ford, those who lived in the days and months leading up to the passage of the "Federal Aid Highway Act of 1956," could envision neither the blessings nor the curses of an Interstate Highway system. A notable exception was Lewis Mumford, the American historian and social critic.

> *"When the American people, through their Congress, voted…for a twenty-six-billion-dollar highway program, the most charitable thing to assume about this action is that they hadn't the faintest notion of what they were doing."*[20]

In the years before interstate highways, "smaller towns in sparsely populated areas looked to their local highway that served as their main street to bring them commerce and connect them to the world."[21] In those days, a drive from Cheyenne to Casper didn't just take you from Cheyenne to Casper. The trip forced you to drive through the hearts of Chugwater, Wheatland, Glendo, Douglas, and Glenrock, where you might buy gas at a locally owned filling station in Wheatland, stop for lunch at a main street "Mom and Pop" café in Douglas, or mosey into the Glenrock shoe store to make an impulse purchase of a new pair of cowboy boots. As the federal government partnered with state highway departments to build an Interstate highway system, it began to dawn on small town folks that they would pay a heavy price. "Now planners were telling them that the new Interstate would bypass their highway and their businesses."[22]

The law creating the interstate system was signed on June 29, 1956, by President Dwight D. Eisenhower. A month before the bill became a law, news broke in Wyoming. Under a front-page banner headline reading "Direct-line Route Ok'd for Highway," it was revealed that the Wyoming Highway Commission was considering a direct route from Gillette to Buffalo bypassing several small communities. The *Casper Tribune Herald* said the Wyoming Highway Commission and the U.S. Bureau of Roads concurred.[23] It took the Buffalo Chamber of Commerce only 48 hours to let the decisionmakers know they disagreed.[24]

James Cagney's movie "Run for Cover" was playing at a Sheridan theater as the Highway Commission began backtracking from its earlier recommendation. By the end of June, the Wyoming Highway Commission was backing off its position. They issued a statement saying "There appears to be some confusion" about the Commission's earlier support of the route. The Commission says they are taking into account the views of every effected Wyoming community and that several possible routes will be considered before a final decision is made."[25]

Communities throughout the state worried theirs would be bypassed as the reality of the Wyoming portion of the interstate highway system became more and more clear. A member of the Buffalo Chamber of Commerce spoke aloud what was on the minds of businesspeople in every community along any proposed route. "It is a fight for survival."[26]

A writer in the Sheridan newspaper summed it up. "You cannot wander into the remotest corner of Wyoming without running into a heated discussion about interstate highways and bypasses. And there's a good reason." The article said the new federal interstate highway system is bringing about a "revolution in the sphere of public roads." The dilemma faced by highway planners was how, on one hand, to avoid doing economic harm to communities that grew up around the old roads that led travelers through their business districts and how, on the other hand, to provide a modern, convenient highway system throughout the nation. The inconvenient truth was that "In almost every Wyoming case, the ultimate solution will be a by-pass."[27]

Newspaper coverage was extensive as public interest grew and northern Wyoming communities took sides. By the time 1956 ended, the controversy was voted top news story of the year.[28] In 1957, the U.S. Bureau of Roads and the Wyoming Highway Commission made the only sensible decision. The route was more direct. The nature of the land would result in smaller costs of construction. Interstate Highway 90 would run direct from Gillette to Sheridan bypassing Buffalo to the north by a couple of miles.

By then, the harsh debate had taken a toll on Governor Simpson's support in the region. He wrote an old friend that community leaders in towns that were left off the newly beaten path threatened him with "political reprisal if I did not overrule the Highway Commission with respect to the location of interstate highway systems." Characteristically, Simpson said, "I think you know me well enough to know that I would not arbitrarily overrule any state commission or agency when they had made investigations and those investigations proved conclusively that they were right." He then addressed the fear shared by many small towns.

> *"The philosophy that any of our towns are about to dry up and blow away is pure poppycock. The economy of Wyoming is in the best condition it has ever been in, and the next ten years will see an era of prosperity that will be unprecedented."*[29]

While that highway in the northeastern corner of the state gave Simpson heartburn, it was the road Charles Starkweather traveled when he came into Wyoming that doomed the Governor's chances of being re-elected.

Her boys called her "the Velvet Hammer." On Lorna Simpson's funeral program, son Al wrote that she was a "dear and graceful woman of powerful faith."[30] Son Pete remembered how his father relied on Lorna as a political adviser. Milward sought her advice on the decision he had to make about the life and death of the three men on death row. He almost seemed to be seeking her permission to avoid the matter. He told Lorna Riggle they had been legitimately convicted and maybe he should carry out the jury's wishes. Pete recalls Lorna's response. She quoted scripture. "Vengeance is mine, sayeth the Lord." It wasn't Milward's. Lorna was fully aware that her husband did not believe in the death penalty. She waited until he asked her for advice as he usually did on weighty matters. "If you believe it's right," she said of the choice to commute the sentences, "you have to do what's right."[31] And so, he did.

On March 26, 1957, Simpson commuted Riggle's death sentence to life in prison 13 hours before the scheduled execution. The Governor removed Ernest Lindsay from death row the following November. He promised to nullify the death sentence given Joe Cruz Martinez on January 24, 1958. While a large number of people disagreed with the Governor's decision, they admired him for following his convictions. That changed when Charles Starkweather went on a late January killing spree through Nebraska and into Wyoming.

"Six Murdered, Giant Manhunt Underway." It was the first time anyone heard the name of Charles Starkweather. But his dastardly deeds quickly occupied every conversation as the details of his grisly Nebraska murders were revealed.

> *A serial killer was loose for the first time in the television age and no one knew where or when he might strike next. The seemingly random nature of Starkweather's victims, young and old, male and female, rich and poor, acquaintances and strangers, added to the terror.*"[32]

The January 29, 1958, story on the front page of the *Wyoming Eagle* struck fear in the hearts of many across Wyoming and the region and for good reason. By that time, Starkweather, 19 years old, had brutally murdered his 14-year-old girlfriend's (Caril Ann Fugate) stepfather, mother, and 2-year-old sister as well as a family friend, and two strangers, ages 16 and

17 who offered him and Fugate a ride. Before heading west to Wyoming, Starkweather killed three more people in Lincoln, Nebraska.

After committing one more murder, this time near Douglas, Wyoming, the two were captured five miles east of the small central Wyoming town. The January 30 *Wyoming Eagle* announced in large black letters on its front page "Mad Dog Killer Nailed at Douglas." People following the news, as most had been, breathed a sigh of relief before venting their anger at Starkweather and his young girlfriend. The Converse County Attorney quickly announced he would file first degree murder charges against the pair. A few hours later, he reversed himself and said the two would be returned to Nebraska to stand trial. With a noticeable whiff of bitterness, he asked rhetorically, "How can I dare try the man here, knowing the governor has come out against capital punishment?"[33]

The same newspaper story quoted Governor Simpson as promising to commute Starkweather's death sentence if he was tried and convicted in a Wyoming court.

It was a fair warning to the prosecutor, which the governor uttered gratuitously.[34] An editorial in the January 31 *Wyoming Eagle* suggested that the Governor's commutation of Riggle, Lindsay, and Martinez now coupled with his promise to commute any potential death sentence given to the most notorious mass murderer of the times, "may not have been the politically expedient thing to do." Indeed. The editor of the *Rock Springs Rocket* was more direct. He defined Simpson's opposition to the death penalty as a "stand on whether or not a ruthless killer should receive the death penalty if convicted." The attack added, "Wyoming peace officers wonder if it is worth the risk to capture a killer who is guaranteed clemency in advance."

Milward Simpson announced he would seek a second term on March 27. That same day, an editorial in the *Casper Star Herald* mused in a column entitled "Justice or Vengeance," that "there will be no executions at the Wyoming penitentiary while Mr. Simpson is governor, even though the law sometimes calls for them." The implication was clear. The voters would be deciding whether that restriction would apply for the remainder of this year or for five more years.

Without naming names, the editor of the Rock Springs newspaper offered, "Republicans are becoming increasingly doubtful about Governor Milward Simpson's chances for re-election and are looking for a suitable candidate to replace him." It acknowledged Simpson caused himself trouble with the highway controversy, but it was "the statewide disgust over this incident" that caused the editor to suggest an alternative nominee. The editorial said the Governor had, in effect, repealed the death penalty. "His stand on whether or not a ruthless killer should receive the death penalty if convicted has caused many to wonder."[35]

They did come up with a primary opponent, but Simpson easily won the GOP nomination in August. His Democratic opponent was John J. Hickey, chairman of the state Democratic Party and an attorney who served as President Harry Truman's appointee as United States Attorney for the District of Wyoming. The matter of Milward Simpson's views on the death penalty was not a major issue in the back and forth between the two candidates. It didn't have to be after Starkweather. It was one thing to commute the sentences of Riggle, Lindsay, and Martinez. To have announced preemptively, less than eight months before the election, that he would save a "Mad Dog Killer" like Starkweather from the gas chamber was a deal breaker. Undoubtedly, as astute a politician as he was, Milward Simpson knew that when he took the risk.[36]

Simpson had been elected governor in 1954 by a mere 1,112 votes. He started his first term with slim support. Four years later, he lost by 2,582 votes in an election where more than 112,000 voted. Wyoming historian T.A. "Doc" Larson blamed the Gillette-Sheridan Interstate highway controversy. Doc Larson said, "A highway-location squabble hurt him more than anything else."[37] Others point to Simpson's anti-gambling crusade in Teton County, where his 1958 vote total dropped by 200 votes from four years earlier.

Simpson and Hickey had an unexpected rematch in 1962. When the U.S. Senator-elect, Keith Thomson died before he could be sworn in, Governor Hickey arranged to resign and have his successor, Secretary of State Jack R. Gage, appoint him to the Senate. The voters seem to have been satisfied they had punished Simpson sufficiently with the 1958 loss. This time, Simpson defeated Hickey by 18,714 votes.

It is tricky to blame one issue alone for losing an election by as small a percentage as Simpson's 1958 loss. It can be argued that in the absence of one of the three controversies, Simpson might well have been re-elected. However, all three exposed Simpson as a person of principle. Milward Simpson's handling of illegal gambling in Jackson and the highway controversy in Northeastern Wyoming said a great deal about his integrity. When combined with his decision to risk re-election by commuting the sentences of convicted killers and committing himself to commuting Starkweather's probable conviction in advance of a trial, Milward Simpson was a profile in courage.

Doc Larson acknowledged as much, quoting with approval an editorial in the *Casper Star Herald*, which he claimed, "voiced an opinion that was often heard on the street."

Simpson family around dining table in Governor's mansion 1955-1959. Left to right Lorna, Alan and Ann, Milward, and Pansy Wyman. Photo courtesy of the Wyoming State Archives.

"Governor Simpson was undoubtedly a victim of his own complete frankness and independence. He never withheld an opinion or reserved an act in consideration of the political consequences."[38]

Milward Lee Simpson died on the 10th of June 1993. He had been Wyoming's 23rd governor and served in the United States Senate. More significant to him was that he had been Lorna's husband and Al and Pete's father. In a biography, *Shooting from the Lip: The Life of Senator Al Simpson*, author Don Hardy describes the moment Al and brother Pete told Lorna of Milward's passing. "No! No! It cannot be," she cried. She gathered herself and "began to speak of what an inspiration her husband was, that he was 'a man of such courage.'"

Later Pete and Al and their spouses accompanied Lorna to the funeral home. She sat in her wheelchair and asked the group to pray. They said the Lord's Prayer first. Al wrote in his diary that her voice was as strong as it had been for a long time when she then asked the Divine that "his integrity and his character…be passed down through the generations."[39] Lorna Helen Kooi Simpson's prayer was answered, her supplication granted.

She and Milward's eldest son, Peter K. Simpson is a successful educator, a respected thespian, and a former Wyoming state legislator. He holds a bachelor's degree from the University of Wyoming and a PhD from the University of Oregon. At UW, he served as vice president for development and alumni affairs and vice president for institutional advancement. After retirement in 1997, Simpson taught history at UW and in 1999 and 2000 was recognized as the Milward Simpson Distinguished Visiting Professor.

Pete's brother Al likewise served in the Wyoming legislature. He was there for a dozen years before being elected three times to the U.S. Senate, where he served in the Republican Party leadership. One of President George H.W. Bush's closest allies, Simpson was expected to be named to the ticket as the vice-presidential candidate in 1988. In July a popular national commentator urged Bush to choose Simpson. Mark Shields said that even though the Wyoming senator could bring only three electoral votes from his home state, he had "an irreverent, earthy, and irrepressible sense of humor, capable of eliciting feelings of respect and admiration or trust or confidence" of the voters.⁴⁰

The Bush campaign team vetted Simpson. The Senator understood he had a political career filled with baggage. "There are nine years of collected mutterings in the *Congressional Record*," he told Bush adviser James Baker. "I have taken on every sacred cow in America. They would wrap those things around George Bush and me in thirty-second television spots."⁴¹ Simpson took an enormous amount of time filling out a 16-page "Confidential Personal Data Questionnaire" required of all VP hopefuls. It was learned he was a member of an organization that recognized his outsized sense of humor. The Royal Order of Jesters was named for the court fools in medieval times known as jesters, who not only amused the patrons whom they served, but also assisted in intellectual and cultural development.

However, his support of LGBTQ rights and reproductive freedom threatened a war with the religious right if Bush named Simpson. All acknowledged "a considerable number of GOP delegates were prepared to disrupt the convention" if Simpson were selected. The Wyoming Senator appeared on NBC's *Face the Nation* and expressed his frustration with how the party conservative wing assessed his potential nomination. "I never understood that," he said. "I can vote with the President. I can assist the President. I have a good record in that. But once you flunk that (abortion) litmus test, you're doomed. It's crazy." Simpson suggested his friend find someone "whose laundry has been washed."⁴²

Thus, the idea of inviting Al Simpson to the ticket was nixed while an actor who made a name for himself as a playacting gunslinger and rogue police detective cleared the party's litmus tests. Jim Baker later admitted consideration was given by the Bush team to nominating Clint Eastwood. Baker said the possibility was "suggested in not an altogether unserious" manner. When the dust settled, Senator Dan Quayle of Indiana won the sweepstakes.⁴³

In the final analysis, Al Simpson refused to do what George H.W. Bush did to win the vice-presidency under Ronald Reagan, i.e., change his position on abortion to conform with that of the party. Even so, as a candidate and as president, Bush relied heavily on Senator Simpson for advice and to advance his political agenda.

Curiously, among Alan Simpson's official papers at the University of Wyoming is a campaign button prepared by someone looking ahead four years with optimism. It reads, "Bush-Simpson 1992."[44]

His public service never ended. In December 2018, he joined 43 of his former colleagues warning the country of Donald Trump, saying the U.S. is "entering a dangerous period" with challenges to "the rule of law, the Constitution, our governing institutions and our national security."[45] The prescient warning, largely unheeded by his fellow Republicans, came two years ahead of the attempted insurrection of January 6, 2021.

On July 7, 2022, the Republican received the Presidential Medal of Freedom from President Joe Biden, a Democrat. Biden called Simpson "one of the most decent, stand up, genuine guys that I've ever served with," saying to Simpson, "We need more of your spirit back in the United States Senate, on both sides of the aisle."[46]

Al Simpson's support for gay rights and women's rights cost him a shot at the vice-presidency. It was just the kind of risk he watched his father Milward take before. It sprang from the well of courage he inherited from a father who was always willing to put his principles above political expediency.

Endnotes

1. Hardy, *Shooting from the Lip: The Life of Senator Al Simson,* unless otherwise noted, the book is the source of much of this brief biography of Milward Simpson.
2. Letter from William L. Simpson to Grace Raymond Hebard, March 9, 1925, Hebard papers, box 45, folder 2 "Simpson, William Lee, AHC
3. Gressley Papers, Box 5, Folder: "Writings: Papers about Robert T. Rose," AHC, citing Olga Curtis, "Milward Simpson: Wyoming's Fiery Petrel is Still Alive," Empire Section, *Denver Post*, October 31, 1976
4. Jeremy Pelzer, "Wyoming Simpson family out of politics but not for long" *Casper Star Tribune*, January 1, 2011, https://trib.com/news/state-and-regional/govt-and-politics/wyoming-s-simpson-family-out-of-public-office-but-probably/article_20cb1170-cac9-52e2-9f69-3087d5cfbb87.html, accessed March 25, 2022
5. Letter from Milward Simpson to Grace Raymond Hebard, June 22, 1934, Hebard papers, Box 45, file 1, AHC
6. Letter to Governor Milward Simpson from Bruce M. Jennings, Jr., December 18, 1957, Box 181, Folder 3, Milward Simpson Papers, American Heritage Center, University of Wyoming (hereinafter "Simpson Papers, AHC")
7. Kirk Knox, *The School of Hard Knox*, page 1
8. *State of Wyoming, Plaintiff and Respondent vs. Clay Riggle, Defendant and Appellant*, 76 Wyo. 1 (1956), 25
9. *State of Wyoming, Plaintiff and Respondent vs. Clay Riggle, Defendant and Appellant*, 76 Wyo. 1 (1956), 21
10. Abstract of the record, *State of Wyoming, Plaintiff and Respondent vs Clay Riggle, Defendant and Appellant*, Docket 2666, Wyoming Supreme Court, R-44-45
11. Petition for Rehearing, *State of Wyoming, Plaintiff and Respondent vs. Clay Riggle, Defendant and Appellant*, 300 P2nd 567 (July 31, 1956), 567
12. State of Wyoming, Plaintiff and Respondent vs. Ernest Lynn Lindsay, Defendant and Appellant, 77 Wyo. 410, 415-416, 317 P2nd 506 (1957)
13. Larson, *History of Wyoming, Second Edition, 441*
14. Id. 214
15. Supra., 446
16. Letter, George Guy to Milward Simpson, September 5, 1956, Milward Simpson papers, AHC, Box 164, Folder 7
17. Letter, George Guy to Milward Simpson, August 23, 1956, Simpson paper, AHC, Box 164, Folder 7
18. "Local Bars Given Forty-Five Day Suspension at State Board Hearing," *Jackson Hole Guide*, December 6, 1956, 1
19. "Hickey Defeats Simpson in Close Race for Governor, Democrats Sweep Nation" *Jackson Hole Guide*, November 6, 1958, 1
20. Mumford, *Highway and the City, 234*
21. Lewis, *Divided Highways, 141*
22. Id., 141
23. "Direct-line Route Ok'd for Highway," *Casper Tribune Herald,* May 22, 1956, 1
24. "Road Decision Being Opposed by Sheridan Chamber of Commerce," *Buffalo Bulletin*, May 24, 1956, 1

25 "Road Relocation Still Wide Open," *Sheridan Press*, June 29, 1956, 1
26 "Present US 14 Route is Backed," *Sheridan Press*, September 28, 1956, 1
27 "New Interstate Highway Program Creates Dilemma," *Sheridan Press*, May 6, 1956, 1
28 "Highway, Stone Controversies Top News Review of 1956," *Sheridan Press*, December 31, 1956, 1
29 Letter, Simpson to Frank Norris, August 5, 1957, box 189, folder 18, Simpson papers, AHC
30 Hardy, *Shooting from the Lip*, 426
31 Author's interview with Pete Simpson, August 23, 2020
32 Lesley Wischman, "The Killing Spree that Transfixed a Nation: Charles Starkweather and Caril Fugate 1958," *wyohistory.org*, https://www.wyohistory.org/encyclopedia/killing-spree-transfixed-nation-charles-starkweather-and-caril-fugate-1958, accessed August 20, 2021
33 "Nebraska to Get Killer," *Wyoming Eagle, January 23, 1958*, 1
34 "Governor Says He Will Commute Sentence," *Wyoming Eagle, January 23, 1958*, 27
35 "Call for Norman Barlow," *Rock Springs Rocket Miner*, February 9, 1958, 4
36 On June 25, 1959, Charles Starkweather died in the electric chair at a minute after midnight in the Nebraska State Penitentiary. According to Nigel Cawthome's book, *Serial Killers and Mass Murderers* (Ulysses Press 2001) his companion, Caril Ann Fugate, was the youngest female to ever be tried for first degree murder. She was convicted by a jury and ordered to serve a sentence of life without parole. Nonetheless, she was paroled in June of 1976, seventeen years after her conviction.
37 T.A. Larson, *History of Wyoming*, 551
38 Ibid., *p 527*
39 Hardy, *Shooting from the Lip*, 412-413
40 Mark Shields, WMAL Commentary, July 13, 1988, Simpson papers, box 59, folder 8, AHC
41 Id., 267
42 Michael Tackett, "Vice Presidential Hopefuls Air Their Support for Top of Ticket," *Chicago Tribune*, August 15, 1988, https://www.chicagotribune.com/news/ct-xpm-1988-08-15-8801220922-story.html, accessed March 26, 2022
43 Brian Browdie, "Clint Eastwood almost chosen to be George H.W. Bush's Vice President in 1988," *New York Daily News*, October 15, 2011, https://www.nydailynews.com/news/politics/clint-eastwood-chosen-george-h-w-bush-vice-president-1988-article-1.964613, accessed March 26, 2022
44 Simpson papers, box 624, folder 1, AHC
45 "Wyoming's Al Simpson among former senators who warn U.S. 'entering a dangerous period," *Casper Star Tribune*, January 16, 2019, https://trib.com/news/state-and-regional/govt-and-politics/wyomings-al-simpson-among-former-senators-who-warn-u-s-entering-a-dangerous-period/article_0c166ece-8baf-57f6-9f56-0103589517c1.html, accessed July 7, 2022
46 "Former Sen. Al Simpson receives Presidential Medal of Honor," *Casper Star Tribune*, July 7, 2022, https://trib.com/news/state-and-regional/govt-and-politics/former-sen-al-simpson-receives-presidential-medal-of-freedom/article_a7d02168-fe2f-11ec-ad63-8f097c03d01a.html, accessed July 7, 2022

Chapter 10

THE PEOPLE OF THE WIND RIVER INDIAN RESERVATION

"it was not a sale but the conquerors' will that deprived them of their land"

If you are reading this anywhere in the United States, you are on stolen ground. Before the colonizers arrived, it all belonged to Indigenous tribes. *"From California to the New York Island, from the Redwood Forest to the Gulf Stream waters."* This land was their land. Gradually, by "discovery and conquest," or through the signing of and reneging on treaties, Native lands diminished. Today's total tribe-owned acreage is about 56 million acres, approximately 90% the size of the state of Wyoming. Land alone wasn't taken, but also a way of life. Shoshone Chief Washakie explained, "The white man who possesses this whole country from sea to sea, who roams over it at pleasure and lives where he likes, cannot know the cramp we feel in this little spot, that every foot of what you proudly call America not very long ago belonged to the Redman."

As a white man, it is impossible for me to fully understand the Native American experience. I don't pretend to do so in these pages. One of the characters in Dan Nerburn's classic book "Neither Wolf nor Dog," says, "White people shouldn't write books about Indians."[1] I get it. Yet, with regret for any mistakes or misunderstandings, it was not possible to write this book without including the history of the courage of the people of the Wind

River Indian Reservation. They have stood against the Wyoming wind since long before Wyoming became Wyoming, and they face it daily even yet.

Dan, the Lakota elder at the heart of Nerburn's book, asked the author to write his story despite the admonition about white people writing books about Indians. "Turn on the tape recorder," he instructs. "Let me tell you how we lost the land. Let me tell you the real story." Dan explains the land belonged to the Creator. It was simply where Indians lived, hunted, and buried their ancestors. Then white men came, first a stream, then a river. They had no respect for the sacred nature of the land or the animals. "And here was what was really happening. Your people did not know about the land being sacred. We did not know about the land being property." Dan asked, "How could we people even talk together when we each believed our God had told us something different about the land? We couldn't and we never did."[2]

The colonists saw land as real estate. For Indigenous Peoples, who lived on the land for centuries before, the land was "identity, the connection to our ancestors, the home of our non-human kinfolk, our pharmacy, our library, the source of all that sustained us. Our lands were where our responsibility to the world was enacted, sacred ground."[3]

From the beginning of the colonization of the continent, European settlers sought to exterminate the Indians so that they could have the land. They used violence, laws and policies, papal edicts, and broken treaties. They used reservations and boarding schools. They slaughtered the buffalo, wiping them from the face of the grasslands of the plains once they understood their centrality to Native culture. They left a trail of tears but did not achieve their goal. Even a white writer can recognize the courage it took for Indigenous Peoples to survive the onslaught.

Some heirs of the colonizers like to think the history of the Americas started with the arrival of their European ancestors. They speak of Columbus "discovering" America and an American exceptionalism that, they say, started with the events of 1776 and 1787. The powerful Kentucky Senator Mitch McConnell says those dates are more important to the American story than, for example, 1619, when the first slaves arrived on the shores of what the colonists called "the New World." Teaching 1619 as a starting place, he says, is denigrating American history.[4] McConnell, therefore, attributes no significance whatsoever to dates thousands of years earlier when the ancestors of the Eastern Shoshone, Northern Arapaho, and other Native Peoples first appeared on land that would, centuries hence, be known as the United States of America.

In the last days of his term in office, President Donald Trump created what he called "The 1776 Commission." Its purpose was to "enable a rising generation to understand the history of the founding of the United States in 1776 and to strive for a more perfect Union."[5] Not a single Native American was part of the Commission and its report mentioned Native Americans only once, and then casting them in negative terms, quoting from a list of grievances set forth in the Declaration of Independence.

> *"He (King George) has excited domestic insurrections against us and has endeavored to bring on the inhabitants of our frontier, the merciless Indian Savages, whose rule of warfare is an undistinguished destruction of all ages, sexes and conditions."*[6]

The 1776 Report spawned bills in dozens of state legislatures, including Wyoming's, banning the teaching of Critical Race Theory and dictating what teachers may and may not teach. With no sense of the historic irony arising from the Indian Boarding School history, many of the bills required teachers to assure, "No person shall be made to feel discomfort, guilt, anguish, or any other form of psychological distress on account of his (sic) race."[7]

Ignoring the truthful history of the clash between colonizers and Native Peoples is one way to avoid "discomfort, guilt, anguish, or any other form of psychological distress." Honest study will not permit that.

The extraordinary courage of the people of the Wind River Indian Reservation is incomprehensible unless you know the historic winds against which they stood. They were biblical. Literally. Prerequisite to understanding the conspiracy to ethnically cleanse the country of its Native Peoples is an awareness of the religious building blocks. First was how the Bible was interpreted by the colonists. Second was the papal edict ordaining the Doctrine of Discovery. Working in tandem, they provided the legal and moral authority necessary to establish "the West's first modern settler-state society," with a "white racial identity."[8]

The myth underpinning the Hebrew Bible (the Old Testament) is God's promise to give away land that already belonged to someone else. In Genesis 12, the Lord said to Abram (whose name God later changed to Abraham), "Go from your country, your people and your father's household to the land I will show you. I will make you into a great nation, and I will bless you; I will make your name great, and you will be a blessing. I will bless those who bless you, and whoever curses you I will curse." Later, the Israelites were enslaved in Egypt. It takes God 400 years to hear their cries. God sent Moses to free the people. They wander in the desert for four decades before reaching the promised land. God instructs them to invade. Following divine orders, Joshua and his troops, "defeated the whole land, the hill country and the Negeb and the lowland and the slopes, and all their kings; he left no one remaining, but utterly destroyed all that breathed, as the Lord God of Israel commanded." *Joshua 10:40*. Thus, according to scripture, land belonging to tribes of Hittites, Amorites, Canaanites, Perizzites, Hivites, and Jebusites was ethnically cleansed.

It didn't actually happen that way. Robert Alter is a renowned Hebrew scholar and philologist. Among his works is a three-volume, 3100-page treatise translating the Hebrew Bible and commenting on its meaning by way of thousands of scholarly notes including this one. "The bloodcurdling report of the massacre of the entire population of Canaanite townsmen, women, children, in some cases livestock as well, never happened."[9]

The genocide narrative was invented. The story was written centuries later, after the Babylonians destroyed Jerusalem and forced thousands of Israelites into exile where they had time to contemplate what had happened. Rationalizing their fate led to conjuring a memory of conquest. The archeological truth tells of a rather peaceful assimilation. They suffered the Babylonian defeat, later writers reasoned, because they had become unfaithful. However, violent taking through conquest was more dramatic and allowed them to "re-member," or recreate a past when God rewarded their faithfulness with military victories.

> "This story of annihilation of the Indigenous population of Canaan belongs," according to Alter, "not to historical memory but to cultural memory."[10]

The Biblical account was problematic when religious zealots became colonizers and lived out that cultural memory with the Indigenous communities they encountered. They saw themselves as God's chosen people and the North American continent as the "New Jerusalem." They believed they had, as did Abraham, a covenant with God awarding them the land. Once when early colonizers came upon a mass grave filled with deceased Native Peoples who succumbed to a plague, they fell to their knees, not to pray for the souls of the deceased, but to give thanks to God for clearing the land of "these savages" so they could occupy it.[11] John Winthrop, known for his famous lay sermon entitled "A Model of Christian Charity," said the dead Indians were evidence of a "Puritan destiny," that God "hath hereby cleared our title to this place."[12]

Scripture provided the colonizers another assist as well. One Native American scholar referred to it as a "manifestation of literary chauvinism." In this context, it is "the fabrication of racial stereotypes to set the proper mood for conquest."[13] Biblical writers showed how it was done when God promised the Israelites someone else's land. After setting out a list of sins that could get the sinner stoned or banished, God is quoted as telling those about to enter the promised land that God is dispossessing the owners of the land because "all these things they have done, and I loathe them." *Leviticus*

20:23. In other words, the owners of the land were stereotyped as "savages" and "pagans," and therefore, were deserving of having their land taken.

Likewise, the Eurocolonizers were granted the legal right to take the land and slaughter its inhabitants under the terms of a 15th century edict issued by the Pope. It had the force of law in the Catholic Church, a major political player when Pope Alexander VI signed the Doctrine of Discovery. It provided "general and indefinite powers to search out and conquer all pagans, enslave them and appropriate their lands and goods."[14] Complementary to the Doctrine of Discovery was the principle of *terra nullius*, Latin for "nobody's land," an invention of the British monarchy. It allowed for the taking of lands that were unoccupied or lands that were occupied but "not being used in a fashion that European legal systems approved."[15]

Thomas Jefferson, in his capacity as secretary of state, pronounced the doctrine applicable to the United States.[16] Its authority was extended when two non-Indians took their dispute over a piece of land that once belonged to Native Peoples to the U.S. Supreme Court in 1823. The high court didn't blink an eye when it voted unanimously to incorporate the racist doctrine into U.S. property law. Chief Justice John Marshall opined for the court, writing that once "discovered" by Europeans, the title to Indian-occupied lands belonged "to the government, by whose subjects, or by whose authority, it was made against all other European governments, which title might be consummated by discovery."[17]

Employing words that define "white supremacy," the Chief Justice said, "The character and religion of the New World's inhabitants afforded them an apology for considering them as a people over whom the superior genius of Europe might claim an ascendency."[18] Marshall used the term "an apology," not to express guilt, but rather as a defense of something in which he and his fellow justices and the colonizers felt strongly, i.e., institutionalizing white superiority and Native inferiority. Eventually the Supreme Court took it farther, ruling the Constitution's Fifth Amendment protection against taking property without "just compensation" didn't apply to Indians. Voluntary "contributions" of "blankets, food, and trinkets" were sufficient. "Discovery and conquest" were all the law required.

> "Every schoolboy knows the savage tribes of this country were deprived of their ancestral ranges by force, and that when the Indians ceded millions of acres by treaty in return for blankets, food, and trinkets, it was not a sale, but the conquerors' will that deprived them of their land."[19]

Ironically, the year after Marshall's words stirred those harsh winds to blow from east to west across the entire continent, the Shoshones were welcoming the first Euromerican trappers to South Pass City while many of the nomadic Arapaho were timing their lives around changes in animal migration routes rather than the migration routes of the millions of settler-colonizers who would soon be coming.

―――

The Reservation covers a large portion of the Wind River Basin, which includes the Wind River Mountains and the southern portion of the Big Horn Mountain range.[20] The rocks of the Wind River tell the story. Translated by geologists is a history receding more than 350 million years. During the Paleozoic Era, the Reservation and much of Wyoming was "covered by seawater and the climate was tropical."[21] It was 110 million years later before some of Wyoming began to emerge from the waters. What geologists call "the Laramide orogeny" was a time of "mountain building." It continued for 30 million years and birthed the Wind River mountains.

Overlying all of this was the Mesozoic period during which dinosaurs roamed the earth including what became the Wind River Indian Reservation (WRIR). Fossils inform us that there were as many as 40 different types of dinosaurs, large and small. They had names like "Diplodocus, Apatosaurus, Stegosaurus, Allosaurus, and Dryosaurus." The bison, around which Indians constructed a way of life, were more than 200 million years in the future.

A process of millions upon millions of years and better described by geologists gave the world the WRIR's extraordinary mountain views, granite outcroppings, canyons, freshwater lakes and rivers, forests, grasslands, mineral deposits, and glaciers. These landscapes have not changed appreciably in the last two centuries although the cartographers have been kept busy adjusting to the changing boundaries imposed on the nomadic First Peoples.

Because the Shoshone were first to settle on what became the Wind River Indian Reservation, this discussion begins with them. Adam Hodge's seminal study of the Shoshone people, *"Ecology and Ethnogenesis: An Environmental History of the Wind River Shoshones, 1000-1868,"* develops ethnogenetic theory to explain their culture. Hodge emphasizes the importance of the pre-contact period, i.e., before contact with white people, and by stressing the "environmental dimensions of Eastern Shoshone history."[22] Hodge starts with their creation myth.

As Euro-Americans have their creation stories, so do the Shoshones. They began with the "moon people," when the great inland sea covered Wyoming's Big Horn Basin. The people were unable to kill animals roaming near the shore nor catch the fish in the waters. They grew more and more hungry. At their behest, Creator lowered the water. Fish were gathered. People were fed. The sea retreated. A river full of fish was left behind. Life was good. The legend informs a future when the Shoshone "stayed that way until the white men came."[23]

Many Shoshone are convinced their people lived there always, "as long as the mountains." This belief challenges an assertion to the contrary that the Shoshone came to the Great Basin in just the last millennium, a view employed by Anglo-Americans to rationalize "Shoshone dispossession."[24] It's one of many misconceptions Hodge felt the need to correct.

By studying the "environmental history" of the land and the Shoshonean peoples of the Great Basin who occupied those lands, he finds several portrayals of early Anglo-American visitors erroneous. They saw the land as "deficient" and referred to the people on it derogatorily as "digger Indians," who subsisted on the "desert" by "digging up roots and begging emigrants for food." Hubert Howe Bancroft was an example. An early historian, Bancroft, described what he saw in 1886, setting a world's record for stereotyping.

"Lying in a state of semi-torpor in holes in the ground during the winter and in spring, crawling forth and eating grass on their hands and knees, until able to regain their feet, having no clothes, scarcely any cooked food, in many instances no weapons, with merely a few vague imaginings for religion, living in utmost squalor and filth, putting no bridles on their passions, there is surely room for no missing link between them and the brutes."[25]

To the contrary, archeological analyses demonstrate a "detailed ecological knowledge (that was) always the secret of survival in the Great Basin from the earliest human sentiment of this varied region before 9000 B.C."[26] Native Peoples understood their environment enough to give heed to the seasons of life, knowing when to be where they could reap the harvest of hard-shelled grass seeds, wild beans, berries, pinion nuts, acorns, and other natural foods and to follow the game migrations. They adjusted to their environment and did not expect it to adjust to them. In contrast to the

Shoshone and Arapahoe Indians in front of J.K. Moore's Post Trader's Store, Haynes photo. Photo courtesy of Wyoming State Archives.

"digger Indian" misperception, "they did much more than merely survive in the Great Basin."[27]

The Numic-speaking Shoshone, Paiute, Ute, and Comanche dialects lived throughout the Intermountain West from their earliest identifiable homelands in the southern Sierra Nevada.[28] The Numu developed "a well-tuned cycle of seasonal migrations." Each tribe had an area where "they typically wintered and enjoyed uncontested access to resources." Occupancy was shared with other Numic speaking peoples and migratory patterns were traversed on foot long before the acquisition of horses.

The Shoshone are thought to have lived on the edges of the Wyoming Basin and the Great Plains for centuries. The Basin functioned as a corridor through the Rocky Mountains. It included the Green, Big Horn, Wind, Snake and North Platte River basins. There were then, as now, rugged mountains and flowing plains, hot summers and cold winters, sage brush and grass-covered lands supporting "significant populations of big game animals, especially bison and pronghorn, in addition to jack rabbits and other small game that the Numu pursued."[29] A broad-based diet and the use of plant-based medicinal practices contributed to an healthily increasing population.[30] Hodge surmises that a growing population during the pre-horse "pedestrian era," meant larger gatherings, larger villages and thus the development of stronger leadership. "Larger communities required strong leaders to organize and direct them as they engaged in bison hunts and raids on other peoples, as well as to ensure order within villages and protection from outside threats."[31]

And there were significant outside threats even before the introduction of the horse. "Pedestrian warfare" usually began when a war party from another tribe lined up opposite the village. They were armed with bows and arrows to which poisonous rattlesnake venom had been applied. At first arrows flew. When one side was weakened, hand-to-hand combat followed. In the seventeenth century, the enemies of the Numu were "the Algonquian-speaking tribes of the Blackfeet Confederation, which would dominate the northern Great Plains until the late eighteenth century."[32] By 1730, the Blackfeet acquired horses and, as their range grew, they fought incessantly with the Shoshone and other tribes.[33]

The cultural and ecological impact of acquiring horses from Spanish colonizers spurred the "greatest period of transformation for the Numu," a new era that altered tribal relationships with the land and among themselves and other Native Peoples. These animals changed the way they found food and fought battles. The conquistador Herman Cortez brought them with him to what is now Mexico in 1519. Trade between the Spaniards and Indians and then among tribes meant the expansion of the availability of horses. Eastern Shoshones likely acquired their first horses in the last decade of the seventeenth century, probably during the annual rendezvous in the upper Green River Basin.[34] They immediately became more effective hunters and warriors enjoying a vastly expanded range from the South Platte River on the south to an area north of the South Saskatchewan River and from the Salmon River in present day Idaho to the Black Hills. The ability to cover more ground led to the historically significant friendship between the Shoshone and Bannock tribes. Horses, and then guns, changed the dynamics of war on the frontier.

What became an annual rendezvous began along the Green River in the mid 1820s. Trappers and white traders met Indians to exchange goods. Here, the Shoshone were able to acquire guns. Now they were mounted and well-armed, a combination assuring they were a force to be dealt with on the Great Plains.[35] Historian David Treuer, an Ojibwe from the Leech Lake Reservation in Minnesota, suggests the tribes of the Great Plains such as the Shoshone ironically survived the determination of Euromericans to eradicate them because they acquired guns and horses from the Europeans. "Despite their later losses, the Plains tribes are, quite likely, around today only because they fought, armed with guns and mounted on horses, in the eighteenth and nineteenth centuries."[36]

By the middle of the 19th century, a stream of settler/colonizers became a raging river. Ray A. Billington was a mid-20th century American historian and an advocate for Frederick Jackson's Turner's "Frontier Thesis."

It was through Billington's classic *America's Frontier Heritage* that tens-of-thousands of college students became acquainted with a decidedly racist explanation of what the Native Peoples began to experience in the 1800s. "Manifest Destiny" explained that "continuous expansion was God's will."

> *"Nothing must stand in its way, neither Indian barbarian nor Mexican peon nor British tyrant on his London throne. The red men could be pushed aside, or assigned to the barren waste of reservations, for they had abandoned all rights to justice by hindering the march of progress."*[37]

What began with fur traders and trappers evolved into a headlong rush for free land, wealth, and adventure. Wagon trains and overland stagecoaches disrupted game habitat, trampling the grass on feeding grounds and driving away the buffalo the tribes depended on for their survival. Plans were underway to build a railroad from coast to coast and tracking it through the heart of the tribe's hunting grounds. To reap profits from passengers, the railroads mounted a mass marketing campaign. After running the Indians off the land, they lured white settlers by telling them the Wyoming plains were as fertile as 'the prairies of Illinois," though "it was 5,000 feet higher and had a third as much rain and a growing season two months shorter."[38] So, they came with visions of wealth in their minds.

The government built the forts and the soldiers came to make safe the path of the white colonizers. Priests and other religionists arrived to baptize "the heathens." From time to time, gold was discovered in this place and that, motivating thousands to come to the lands that just a few years earlier provided community, shelter, and sustenance to the First Peoples.

Some of the Native leaders looked into the future and envisioned the soul-crushing environmental and cultural destruction ahead. They could foresee a time in the not-too-distant future when tribes would be forced to compete with one another for dwindling resources. The result would be heightened tribe-on-tribe and Indian-versus-white violence. Government negotiators cleverly employed threats inherently obvious in more and more whites coming to the land as they prophesied continuing violence to persuade the Indians that a treaty was in their best interest. Of course, the threat was not disingenuous. "During the course of the nineteenth century American Indian wars, the U.S. government authorized more than 1,500 wars, attacks, and raids on Indians, the most of any country in the world against its Indigenous people."[39] These invaders were made legendary as the cowboys and cavalry who "saved the settlers" while white kids cheered during mid-twentieth century movies.

The Superintendent for Indian Affairs, D.D. Mitchell, convened a peace conference at Fort Laramie in the summer of 1851. Thousands of Indians and hundreds of soldiers gathered along with bureaucrats from Washington, D.C. Ahead of the gathering, the "Great Father" sent runners to scour the lands "from the Missouri River to Fort Bridger and from Canada to Arkansas," to invite as many tribal representatives as they could find in that vast stretch of land.[40] Thousands came. There were so many that the convocation had to be moved from the Fort to the place where Horse Creek flows into the North Platte River. Thus, the agreement negotiated there is often called the Horse Creek Treaty of 1851. As many as 60,000 spent days in ceremonies, battle reenactments, and dialogue about how the tribes could "make peace with one another" and "fix up matters so that there would be no friction between tribes, nor between the various tribes and the government."[41]

The largest contingents were Sioux, Arapaho, and Cheyenne. The Snakes (or Shoshone) also came, though they had not been invited. In his book *Five Years a Dragoon* Percival C. Lowe described their grand entrance. "They were dressed in their best, riding fine war horses, and made a grandly savage entrance." This greatly annoyed the Sioux, especially one whose father had recently been killed by a Snake. A threatened attack on the Shoshone was narrowly averted. The Shoshone also had a score to settle. As they traveled to Fort Laramie, two of their entourage were killed in an attack by a group of Cheyenne warriors. The dispute was resolved when the Cheyenne agreed to pay reparations, conduct a ceremony of apology, give gifts, and return the dead men's scalps.[42]

Famed trapper Jim Bridger accompanied Shoshone Chief Washakie, of whom Bridger was an admirer. Bridger told Percival Lowe that Washakie and the Snakes were "awful brave fellows" and that he "can take their word for anything; trust 'em anywhere." Nonetheless, Washakie was snubbed during the peace conference at Horse Creek. The Chief politely waited his turn to speak. It never came as "government officials divided up the Wyoming Basin east of the Divide among other Indian groups."[43] The word "Shoshone" was not even mentioned in the treaty.[44] Washakie left disappointed that he had not been able to protect the interests of his tribe.[45] He would have to wait a dozen more years before the reserve of a Shoshone land would be addressed.

In the meantime, game herds were becoming scarcer as settlers moved into and across Shoshone hunting grounds en route to new gold discoveries near Denver and in Nevada and Montana. The ambiguities of the Horse Creek Treaty, likely intentional on the part of the government negotiators, led to "the invasion of Shoshone country and the depletion of resources they depended upon, (which) precipitated conflict that hastened the dispossession of their lands."[46] The government was struggling to find a final solution to what they called "the Indian problem." They had legal authority under the Indian Removal Act of 1830 to drive Indians from their ancestral lands. It was exercised in the tragic "Trail of Tears." But if the Plains Indians were removed, where would they go?

Another quarter of a century of history shrouded what became the Fort Bridger Treaty of 1863. While the Civil War raged between the North and the South, in the American West, Indians, mountain men, fur traders, westward bound colonizers, and soldiers from the U.S. Army were a constant presence at Bridger's trading post along the Black Fork of the Green River in what became southwest Wyoming. In 1863, General Christopher C. Augur invited leaders of the Shoshone and Bannock Tribes to meet at Fort Bridger to discuss a range of issues including challenges faced by the Indians because of growing competition between tribes for diminishing bison herds and the escalating conflicts with white settlers.[47] The discovery of gold nearby and the building of the transcontinental railroad promised the conflict would worsen unless the U.S. could reach an agreement with the tribes.

The Shoshones, by 1862, were "in a destitute condition" due mainly to the absence of game.[48] The "fierce winds driving snows, terrible storms and intense cold that prevails here" was tough on Benjamin Davies, Superintendent of Indian Affairs for the Utah Territory. Yet, his concern was not so much for himself, as for the "hostile savages, sleeping all the time upon frozen ground without tents."

> "The poverty, misery, and wretchedness of the poor creatures men, women, and children who crowd the wayside on my return trip to shake hands and beg me to 'come again with presents from the great chief in Washington' is beyond conception, much less description."[49]

Davies said, "These are unquestionably the poorest Indians on the continent." He assured his boss, "The Indians are now all peaceable and entirely friendly with the whites and are likely to remain so, unless the interference of white men causes disturbances to spring up among them." Contrary to that assurance, many of the starving Shoshones were compelled to raid settler camps for the food. Sometime later, when "14 snows gone by," a Shoshone elder told the story of the time they camped along the Green River, resting after "robbing the emigrants, stealing their horses and cattle, and burning their wagons." As they danced and sang songs, a scout arrived from Fort Bridger, reporting "soldiers there were pretty mad and that the 'Big Chief,' meaning General (Patrick E.) Connor was going to try to punish the Indians." Washakie, the youngest chief around the campfire spoke first. He suggested they "leave the white people alone" and go to the Wind River Valley. He said there they'd have plenty of game and fish "and we will be happy and will disturb no one."

One chief called Washakie "an old woman." An elder among the tribe's prominent chiefs, Old Bear Hunter, also challenged Washakie, intimating he was afraid. Washakie met the challenge forcefully. Old Bear Hunter "very wisely held his peace." About half of the tribe left for the Wind River

Valley with Washakie. The others remained in the camp where they were that late January morning when General Connor made good on his threat.[50] On January 29, 1863, Connor's troops attacked the Shoshone camp along Bear River, leaving 200-250 Indians dead, perhaps more. The women and children watched helplessly as the soldiers destroyed their provisions and killed the men; "soldiers reportedly raped multiple women and slaughtered infants."[51] Survivors were left to starve to death in the winter cold.[52]

The tragedy created a renewed sense of urgency among government and military officials as well as Washakie, all of whom were desperate to put a halt to the violence. In October 1861, Henry Martin, Superintendent of Indian Affairs, reported he had spoken to Washakie and other chiefs. All were ready to enter into a treaty whereunder they would "hold themselves responsible for any depredations committed by any of their bands" in exchange for "annual presents of blankets, beads, paint, calico, ammunition, etc., with occasional supplies of beef and flour sufficient to make them comfortable."[53]

A year later, the government's Indian Agent at the Fort Bridger Agency connecting the dots to draw a line from hunger to violence, informing Washington there was insufficient game in the area to feed the tribes. As a result, "Large numbers of Shoshones, along with the Bannocks, who range along the southern boundary of Washington Territory, have begun committing upon the emigrants traveling to California and Washington some of the most brutal murders ever perpetrated upon this continent."[54] Earlier reports of hunger and misery among the Indians hadn't raised an alarm in Washington. This report of murdered white colonizers did. The following July they met at Fort Bridger.

The U.S. had three goals in mind as they sat with the tribal chiefs at Fort Bridger to negotiate a treaty. The Transcontinental Railroad had been funded by Congress and the government needed assurances workers would not come under attack or be harassed by Indians. Second, they considered it a priority that stagecoach routes would not be targeted by warriors. Third, the government sought promises from the tribes that telegraph lines would be left alone. Chief Washakie agreed to each.

Unlike the 1851 Fort Laramie negotiation when Washakie was denied an opportunity to speak, the Eastern Shoshone chief played a key role in developing the 1863 pact. By then, Washakie had achieved a dual reputation. Among Indians he was one of three Shoshones "at whose names the Blackfeet quaked in fear."[55] Among whites, he was respected for having once said with pride, "I have never in my life shed the blood of a white man."[56] While that assertion on Washakie's part may have been an exaggeration, he developed and maintained good relationships with whites in an era of upheaval. In the mid-1860s, when the Lakota attempted to organize Plains Indians around the goal of eliminating "the white man from the face of the earth," Washakie refused, citing the pledge he made at Fort Bridger to remain at peace with the whites.[57]

Washakie's influence during the Fort Bridger talks was aided by the intention of government officials to promote the leadership of this particular Chief. Motivated by Washakie's "friendly disposition toward Anglo-Americans," Frederick W. Lander, the Superintendent of the Overland Road urged the Commissioner of Indian Affairs to advance "any steps which could be taken to augment the power of Washikee (sic) who is perfectly safe in his attachment to the Americans."[58] What he wanted for his people now was a reservation where they could live unmolested by whites and Indians alike, where his people would have adequate hunting grounds and be assured of government annuities. What the U.S. government wanted was an end of the violence and they were willing to over promise in order to get it.

In exchange for the promises sought by the government, the Shoshones were promised annuity payments for the next 20 years with an upfront payment of $6,000 in "presents and goods" upon signing the document.[59] In exchange, the 1863 treaty "identified a vast Shoshone territory" as belonging to "the Waushakee (sic) Bands of Shoshones."[60] It was 44,672,000 acres, a number so large that in retrospect it seems, as it turned out to be, disingenuous. It stretched from north of the Snake River (in present day central Idaho) and the Wind River on the north to the Uinta Mountains of

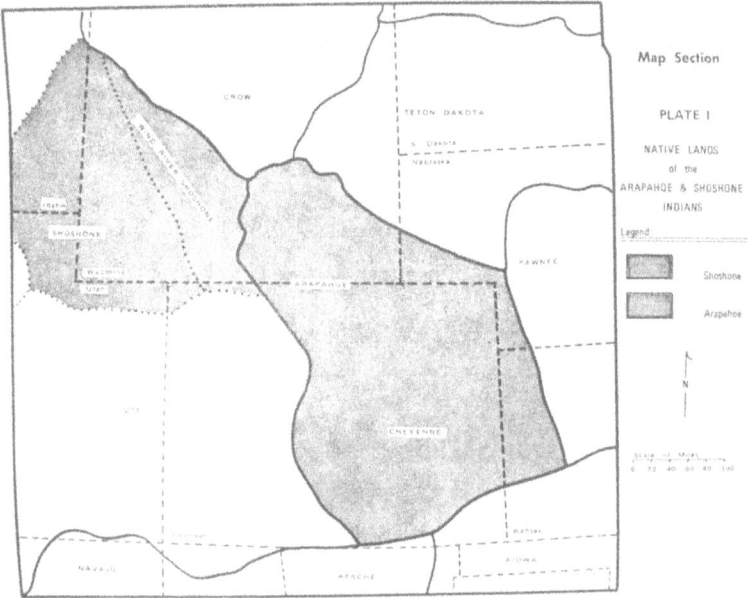

the Utah Territory on the south and from the North Platte in present-day eastern Wyoming to near the edge of the border between Idaho and Utah.

The huge land mass was awarded the Bannock and Eastern Shoshones, the Northwestern Shoshones, the Western Shoshones, the Goshutes, and the Washakie Band of Shoshones touched five states. The size of the set-aside land promised each nomadic tribe sufficient area to roam, as they had always, to follow game migrations and the natural food harvest of the region.

Despite his leadership in bringing about the 1863 agreement, Washakie was disappointed. He fervently desired land that would provide his people protection "from encroaching whites and their Indian enemies alike as they learned to farm and ranch. The 44-million-acre set-aside had not done that. The treaty included no provisions protecting the tribes from non-Indians and changed their lives little in terms of the day-to-day struggle for food and safety. The year following the treaty, Washakie refused to move his tribe from Fort Bridger to their hunting grounds as they were expected to do in the fall. The Chief feared the Sioux and decided to remain in the shadow of the Fort for safety. Washakie told officials that white men drove the game away and his people were dependent on the annuities they were promised for survival.[61] While the Shoshone refrained from attacking wagon trains in the face of their hunger, Euromericans complained often about Shoshones begging for food.

Government officials continued to talk among themselves about the need to identify a reservation exclusive for Washakie and his followers. "Indian agents recommended various areas for an Eastern Shoshone reservation during the early 1860s, including Elk Mountain (north of the Medicine Bow Range in southeastern Wyoming) as well as multiple locations in the Green River Country."[62] They knew the Wind River Valley to be one of their favorite hunting grounds but needed to know first whether the site would "be found to be rich in mines of silver and gold and springs of petroleum." If so, the government would not allow it to be designated a reservation.[63]

By 1867, prospectors flooded the area looking for gold. The onslaught caused conflicts with the Indians and further depletion of game resources. In the end, the two groups came to understand each served the interests of the other. The presence of the miners often persuaded attacking tribes to stay away. The presence of the Shoshone, likewise, kept the miners safer. The miners joined the voices calling for the Shoshone to have a reservation at that site.[64]

In 1868, it finally happened. Washakie and his people, who had spent centuries roaming freely, were now confined to a reservation, and Washakie was happy to be there given the alternative, which included continued violence, death, and upheaval. The 44,672,000 acres awarded to all the various Shoshone groups in the region became a 3,054,182-acre home for the Eastern Shoshone. Although the agreement included a clause opening the door for the Bannocks to join them, they never did. Washakie's peoples' new home was called the Shoshone Indian Reservation until 1937 when it became the Wind River Indian Reservation.

Wyoming writer Geoffrey O'Gara notes the historic significance. "Only in a few instances, the Shoshone at Wind River are one, were reservations demarked on a people's ancestral land." O'Gara observed poetically that "the Shoshone passed through the Wind River Valley like birds through a field."[65]

The ink on the Treaty of 1868 was barely dry when the U.S. government decided it needed some of that land back. Another group of colonizers had come down with "gold fever" and began moving into the southern portion of the reservation in violation of the treaty. The government needed something palliative to make reopening of negotiations less painful for Washakie. The pretext was a claim that part of the Popo Agie (poe-poe-ghah) Valley was never intended to be part of the reservation.

"Mistaken" maps were not an uncommon justification for promising the Indians one thing and giving them another. One historian called the strategy, "a cartographic equivalent of a Freudian slip."[66] After one 1808 treaty, white squatters moved illegally into territory given the Indians at a place called Boon's Lick, Missouri. In 1816, William Clark of the Lewis and Clark Expedition, had become governor of the Missouri Territory. He unilaterally altered the map to benefit squatters. Brian Oaster described the far-reaching impact. "Boon's Lick spontaneously went from being an illegal squatter camp on Native land to a part of the Missouri Territory. A massive land grab followed, with colonizers flooding the area and establishing plantations fueled by slave labor."[67]

In the case of the Shoshone Reservation, Indian Commissioner Felix R. Brunot represented to Washakie and the others that, "The mistake arose from the inaccuracy of a map" relied upon by government negotiators during proceedings leading to the Fort Laramie Treaty of 1868.[68] The Commissioner proposed a land swap as a way of resolving the "mistake." If the Shoshone would cede 700,000 acres that included the mines and the mining district, they could have a like amount of unoccupied land some 30 miles north. Washakie was unimpressed with the Commissioner's sales pitch. The land he was being asked to relinquish had "plenty of berries, prairie squirrel, and fish, plenty of everything." Besides that, the Chief observed, the land the government was offering already belonged to the Crow. The Commissioner said he could show Washakie a map to prove him wrong.

Washakie was uninterested in another government map. "The land belongs to the Crows," he retorted, "the Sioux and everybody. If we went there, the Sioux might come and scalp us."

Washakie made a counteroffer. The Shoshone wanted nothing to do with the land up north. However, they were willing to sell the land the government wanted. Any agreement reached between the Commissioner and the tribe was subject to approval or veto by Congress. Congress enacted "the Brunot Cession" two years later, taking, not selling, 710,600 acres of the Shoshone land the government coveted and giving the Indians $25,000 in provisions.[69] Thus, the size of the reservation was diminished significantly when, in 1878, the Eastern Shoshone learned they would be sharing it with another tribe.

It wasn't supposed to be permanent. The Northern Arapaho were promised their own reservation. The stay at the Shoshone Indian Reservation[70] was to last only until General George Crook could arrange for the Tribe to have its own reservation "somewhere in east central Wyoming, between present-day Casper and Sheridan."[71] Until then, the Arapaho needed a place to set their tipis.

Chief Washakie didn't trust the Arapaho. The two tribes were, off and on, bitter enemies. After years of ministry on the Reservation, the Reverend John Roberts knew the two tribes as well as anyone. Roberts said, "No people could be more unlike each other."[72] It had been less than four years since the two tribes engaged one another in war. Nonetheless, with no apparent concern about the tribes' troubled history, nearly a thousand Northern Arapaho were escorted by the Army, "in starving condition," to the Shoshone's reservation in the early months of 1878.[73] Though it's not clear he was given a choice, Chief Washakie, the peacemaker, eventually accepted the inevitable, conceding temporarily to share the Shoshone Indian Reservation, though he pointedly refused to call them anything but "visitors."[74] The Arapaho could camp on the reservation in 1868-1869, just until the government could make good on General Crook's promise.⁷⁵ Believing they would soon move onto their own reservation, the Arapaho set up where the Popo Agie meets the Little Wind River and flows into the Big Wind River.⁷⁶ They never left.

The "interethnic" nature of the reservation worked when longtime friends shared the land, but the idea would be put to the test in coming years when longtime enemies were asked to share the Shoshone Reservation.

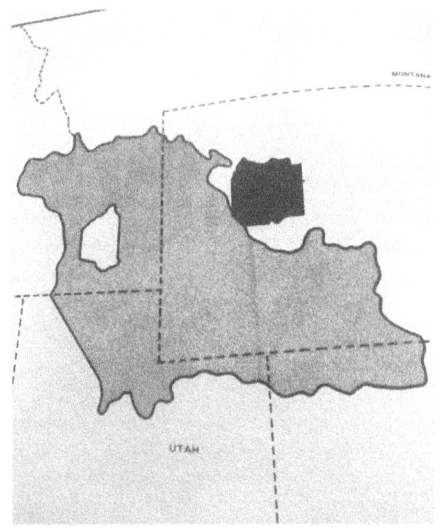

The Shoshone Reservation under the Treaty of 1863 in gray. Today's Reservation, after other treaties, is shown in black.¹⁵⁶

Historical summary: The Fort Bridger Treaty of 1863 designated 44.6 million acres for the Shoshone. An 1868 treaty reduced the reservation to 3,054,182 acres. In 1872 Congress voted to take another 710,642 acres for which the Shoshones were not compensated until 1957 when paid $443,013 for that land. The McLaughlin Agreement of 1898 transferred 55,040 to the U.S. government. A second "McLaughlin Agreement" ceded 1,480,000 acres to the U.S. government, lands restored to the Reservation in 1938. Today the Reservation encompasses approximately 2.2 million acres of land. In addition to these diminishments, the Northern Arapaho Tribe was placed on the Shoshone Reservation in 1878. It was not until 60 years later that the Shoshones were compensated for this taking. Today the Shoshones "principally occupy the western area of the reservation including Ft. Washakie, Crowheart, and Burris. The Arapaho Tribe principally occupies the eastern segments of the reservation at Ethete and Arapaho.¹⁵⁷

"*Buffalo were dark rich clouds moving upon the rolling hills and plains of America. And then the flashing steel came upon bone and flesh.*"[77]

The "starving condition" in which the Arapaho and Shoshone found themselves in the 1870s was not happenstance. It was the result of the institutionalized poverty imposed on the Plains Indians by U.S. Army policy. Some saw the reservation system as a humane alternative to the brutality of the Indian wars and to some extent, it might have been had promises been kept. At its core was a strategy "to gather them all into a small district which we can really police and protect, and there teach them the arts of civilized life."[78] There was a certain level of cynicism behind treaty provisions that assured the tribes a right to hunt buffalo on lands shared with white settlers and miners "so long as the buffalo may range thereon in such numbers as to justify the chase." That provision was boilerplate language in treaties including the Fort Laramie Treaty of 1868.[79] The government knew the hunting grounds would be opened to hide hunters and others on whom they would rely to destroy the Indian's buffalo-centered way of life. The Army had already decided that it would make sure the herds were not of "such numbers." Killing off the buffalo was the key to bringing the Indians to their knees and forcing them onto reservations even as the government reduced the size of those enclaves through treaty violations and treaty renegotiations.

The buffalo herds were central to Native American culture. Every part of a harvested buffalo was put to a use central to Indigenous life on the plains. Hides became water-proof tipi covers and clothing. Shields were made of toughened rawhide. The meat was eaten fresh or "jerked" and stored for lean days. Parts of the animal were turned into utensils and containers. Even the buffalo "chips" or dung was put to use; some in making fires where they were preferable to cottonwood, and some pounded into a fine powder and sifted, before being poured into the pouch of a baby's cradleboard where they made excellent baby diapers.[80]

Above all, the animals were sacred, part of religious ceremonies, a cherished symbol of their way of life. Watching their genocide, Indians experienced an "apocalyptic dread. For the Plains Indians, extermination of the buffalo meant death, both physical and spiritual."[81] As they looked across the plains, they could see the future held the end of their culture as the lands of their ancestors were littered now with the carcasses of millions of dead bison. Indian hunters like General Philip Sheridan also sensed an apocalypse, one he welcomed and had helped usher in. "These men," he said referring to the hunters, "have done in the last two years, and will do more in the next year, to settle the vexed Indian question, than the entire regular army has done in the last thirty years."[82]

Historian David Smits makes the case that "the United States Army was primarily responsible for the destruction of the bison."[83] The Army didn't do it alone. It had eager accomplices. Not only did the Army organize large-scale hunting trips for wealthy Easterners and others, but it also refused to enforce treaty provisions designed to limit the hunt to Indians on reservation lands. Some came simply to kill the animals. Others were in the business of providing buffalo hides for commercial enterprises back east. Hunters could average as many as 50 kills per day, taking the hide and leaving the remainder of the animal to rot on the prairie.[84] From 1872 until 1874 alone, 1,378,359 hides were shipped by rail.[85] That number, staggering as it may be, does not reflect the total kill. Buffalo hunters were notoriously wasteful, killing five bison for every hide they shipped.

Between those who slaughtered the animals to wreak vengeance on the Indians and those who made money off the hides, the creature that had been central to Indigenous lifestyle and culture was mostly gone by 1890. The iconic Wyoming environmentalist Tom Bell, who lived most of his life near the Wind River Indian Reservation, repeated the legend he'd been told of the last buffalo. "Two cowboys ran four bison past the camp of emigrants heading for South Pass City. Somewhere south of Oregon Butte, the cowboys shot the bull, yearling, and a calf. They roped the cow and tied her to one of the emigrant's wagons. They said they wanted to sell her to a circus, but she laid down and died on them. It was the last known wild bison to be killed in the (Great Divide) Basin."[86]

As the buffalo disappeared, tribes competed with one another for the dwindling resource. Violent clashes among them were followed by an increasing number of attacks on the white colonizers, which required counterattacks by the army. The cycle of violence ravaged the plains while the Indians could see they could no longer remain nomadic and withstand the onslaught. Tribe by tribe, they retreated to the reservations. Historian Andrew C. Isenberg summed it up. "The engine of the advancement of Euromericans into the plains was the ability of an industrial society to thoroughly destroy the bison herds and thus deny their use by the nomads." They waged a "scorched earth campaign against the Indians" because they "impeded" white expansion across the continent.[87]

The Arapaho among other Indians had yet to hear about social Darwinism when they became its victim.

Goes-in-Lodge listened as General George Crook asked the Arapaho chiefs which land they would like for a reservation. Ground Bear told him their choice was the land on Tongue River not far from Sheridan. White Horse confirmed the choice. "This is the land we like best." The General ceremoniously set a stake in the ground "as a sign that we picked this land for our reservation." However, Goes-in-Lodge admitted, "No definite time was set when we should get this reservation."[88]

The mid-nineteenth century witnessed a debate between views expressed by General Philip Sheridan and those of Ulysses S. Grant; the former having said, "The only good Indian is a dead Indian," the latter, "Let us have peace."[89] The middle ground was the policy decision to force tribes onto reservations. President Grant "began steering the federal government away from a policy of war toward one of peace. This was not a new idea. George Washington hoped he could avoid exterminating Indigenous Peoples by "civilizing" them. Washington saw that their culture and lifestyle necessitated roaming across large swaths of land. It was how they hunted migrating game and found plants growing in diverse locations as the seasons changed. It was how they traveled for ceremonial purposes. However, he reasoned, if they could be "civilized" and become farmers like the Euromericans who needed more Indian land, the Native peoples could survive on less.[90] Grant adopted Washington's philosophy with a twist. Grant added the goal of "civilizing" them within the confines of reservations. That didn't necessarily mean Sheridan's philosophy had been abandoned by Grant. In her book *An Indigenous Peoples' History of the United States*, Roxanne Dunbar-Ortiz notes, "Many of the intensive genocidal campaigns against Indigenous civilians took place during the administration of President Grant, 1869-1877."[91]

The "peace-making" policy required treaties between the tribes and the government. However, treaties collided with colonizer expansion. The *Cheyenne Leader's* April 3, 1868, headline succinctly explained what the collision meant to the tribes. "Though the government proposes, the pioneer disposes." The Manifest Destiny of the colonizers demanded an evolving imposition on the rights of Indigenous Peoples. What a treaty gave the Indians one day could be taken back the next when gold was discovered or there was an intercontinental railroad to build or a wagon trail and the Overland Stage to protect.

The Northern Arapaho learned this lesson after the Fort Laramie Treaty of 1851 awarded them and the Southern Cheyenne a vast territory from the North Platte River and Arkansas River eastward from the Rocky Mountains to western Kansas. This area included present-day southeastern Wyoming, southwestern Nebraska, most of eastern Colorado, and the westernmost portions of Kansas. In exchange, the tribes promised safe passage for white migrants and assured the government's right to build roads and forts on their land. The congressional creation of the Colorado Territory intervened. Settlers and gold miners soon flooded the lands covered by the 1851 agreement.[92] Whites were hastily "staking out ranches and land claims on territory assigned by the Fort Laramie treaty to the Southern Cheyenne and the Arapaho."[93] So an 1861 agreement, the Treaty of Fort Wise, became necessary. "What they were told would be in the treaty and what was actually written into it, were quite different," according to the chiefs of both tribes. In any event, the new treaty significantly reduced the lands of the Arapaho and Cheyenne to a small tract in eastern Colorado. Its northern boundary ominously encompassed Sand Creek. It was called "the Sand Creek Reservation." Government negotiators told the Indians this treaty would enable them to "settle down, engage in agriculture," though there was disagreement about whether the tribal negotiators were told of the rich mines located in the lands they were "voluntarily" ceding.[94]

As expected, the arrangement caused increasing hostilities between the tribes and ever-increasing numbers of white setters. 1863 was known among the Arapaho as "the year of hunger."[95] Whites were multiplying. Buffalo were disappearing. "Coloradoans grew less and less tolerant of the Native Americans more and more eager for war."[96] Some whites would eventually come to view what happened at Sand Creek on November 29, 1864, as the final solution to Colorado's Indian problem.

While wolves and wild dogs ate the mutilated earthly remains of Indians massacred at Sand Creek, the Methodist preacher who led the cavalry of 650 men in killing an estimated 150 Indians, two-thirds of whom were women and children, turned his attention to finding the Arapaho who had somehow escaped. Colonel John Chivington tracked them as far as the Kansas border. With the soldiers' horses in bad shape and his men in worse condition, he returned to Denver.[97] The surviving Arapaho contemplated their future. They were now even more determined to have a reservation of their own as they left their ancestral land, in what is now known as Estes Park, to live in Wyoming after the Sand Creek holocaust. On February 17, 1870, the Arapaho and the Shoshones reached an agreement whereunder each could travel and hunt on the lands of the other. Nonetheless, the Shoshone were adamantly opposed to sharing their reservation.

Unable to get any traction for their request for a reservation, many of Arapaho volunteered to serve as U.S. Army scouts. Many of these warriors achieved status and recognition for their bravery. In early 1877, several Arapaho scouts aided General Crook in forcing the legendry Sioux Chief Crazy Horse to surrender. When Crazy Horse defied orders by leaving Fort Robinson to care for an ailing wife, Crook dispatched Arapaho scouts to bring him back.[98]

Shortly after, the Army commander of the Indian scouts, Lieutenant Philo Clark, secured an agreement for a delegation of Arapaho to take their case to Washington. Black Coal and Sharp Nose went to speak for their people. In a meeting with President Rutherford B. Hayes, the Arapaho chiefs reminded the President of the faithfulness of his people, arguing they deserved a reservation.

> "These two sitting here, General Crook and Lieutenant Clark, will remember what we were promised. It was settled quietly and it is all over and this day I have come down to talk about it. You ought to take pity upon us and give us good land so that we can remain upon it and call it our home. If you give us a good place to stay where we can farm, we want wagons and farming implements of all kinds, provisions, and annuities of all kinds, all to be given to us as we want them."[99]

President Hayes agreed to allow the Arapaho to move temporarily to a winter range on the Sweetwater.[100] Without much of a dialogue with Chief Washakie, the Arapaho were almost surreptitiously, step-by-step moved to the Shoshone Reservation. Between the fall of 1877 and spring of 1878, they migrated from Fort Robinson to Fort Fetterman to the area around Independence Rock before arriving at the Shoshone homelands.[101] It was a quintessential reservation-era decision; made with little or no dialogue with the Indians and with no regard for Native history or culture. Just the year before, the Indian agent received an assurance that "the government had not the slightest intention of placing the Arapaho" on the Shoshone Reservation.[102] "The arrangement proved distasteful to both tribes, for the two had nothing in common except a bitter hatred."[103] Outraged by the imposition on his people, Washakie asked to meet with an ally, Wyoming's Territorial Governor John W. Hoyt. By now, the treaty system had taken the Shoshones from a more than 44-million-acre reserve to a reservation of fewer than 2.5 million acres. Now they would be required to share that space with a second tribe. Washakie, who had been known among whites as soft-spoken unloaded decades of grievance.

> "He spoke first of the wretched lives of the Indians who had once roamed over the country from sea to sea, and reminded the governor that every foot of what he now proudly called 'America,' had belonged to the red man not very long ago. Then came the white hordes of them from beyond the sea who finally cornered the 'sorry remnants of tribes

once mighty in little spots of the earth, where they were watched over by men with guns who were more than anxious to kill them all.'[104]

Washakie did not mention the 44 million acres his people were allowed to hunt as a result of the Fort Bridger Treaty of 1863. He started his lecture with the Treaty of 1868, which, he reminded the governor, promised the Shoshone "the little patch" of land together with food and other necessities, much of which never arrived. The treaty promised white men would not be allowed to do what they did regularly, i.e., trespass on their land, "kill our game, capture our furs, and sometimes feed his herds upon our meadows." The Chief said, "The white man does not keep his word." The governor was moved enough to promise "that justice would be done." However, justice was not part of the federal government's strategic plan.

The following years were challenging times for the chiefs of these two tribes. Washakie of the Eastern Shoshone and Sharp Nose of the Northern Arapaho were beset with trying to keep government agents happy while serving the best interests of their own people. At the same time, Washakie was determined to push the Arapaho off the Shoshone Reservation. Sharp Nose was equally determined to stay.

Forcing them from their nomadic lifestyle and culture onto reservations was not an end to itself. A series of genocidal policy decisions followed the otherwise illogical decision to force the Shoshone to share a reservation with their enemy. Hostilities between the two tribes continued. When the following spring, seven miners were killed in an Indian attack, "a mob of 250 white vigilantes, together with some Shoshones, attacked two groups of Arapaho moving from their camp on Wind River to trade in nearby Lander. About a dozen Arapahos were killed, including Black Bear."[105] Yet, the two tribes continued to share a common enemy, broken U.S. government promises.

The onslaught was relentless. A policy of enforced hunger leading to deficient diet and disease was followed predictably by depopulation. The government instituted a campaign to undermine the authority of the chiefs. There were continued demands for land concessions. Traditional practices were discouraged or outlawed altogether. Indians were forced to use Anglicized names. White-settler intrusion on Indian lands was ignored even as it was accompanied by theft of equipment and supplies intended for the Indians. Then came the boarding schools and the General Allotment Act. Some defended all of this as necessary for assimilation. Others viewed it as genocide.

The destruction of the buffalo was calculated to cause the suffering that accompanies hunger. It was hunger, the government accurately predicted, that would bring the Indians in from the vast plains to the limiting reservations. If the Indians went peacefully to the reservation, the government assured them of annuities, i.e., food. Once the gate closed behind them, the government shorted them the promised food or denied it altogether. Arapaho Chief Black Coal complained to Wyoming's Territorial Governor John W. Hoyt, "The government has been slow in fulfilling its promises to us. My people are hungry and must sell furs and even their ponies for food that was promised us."[106] By 1889, the rations promised under prior treaties were unilaterally decreased and later the rations for Indian children were eliminated under the supposition that Indian parents would thereby be forced into self-sufficiency. To make matters worse, game was scarce on the reservation and the Wyoming legislature prohibited Indians from hunting on non-reservation lands.[107]

The delay in complying with treaty obligations to provide food to the Indians was not simply inept bureaucracy. It was intentional. It was designed to cause suffering. When a reporter asked General William Tecumseh Sherman whether the government was obligated to feed the hungry reservationists, he replied, "Should the government support 260,000 able bodied campers? No government the world has ever seen has done such a thing."[108]

John Steinbeck believed, "The Indians survived our intention of wiping them out, and since the tide turned, they have even weathered our good intentions toward them, which can be more deadly." When the religionists teamed up with the government to "save the Indian," they proved Steinbeck's point. It's 1803. President Thomas Jefferson is the first to envision the use of boarding schools to destroy Indian culture. He coupled it with the goal of dispossessing Indians of their land. In a confidential message to Congress, the man who drafted the Declaration of Independence said it should be policy and practice "to encourage Indian Tribes to purchase goods on credit so as to likely fall into debt, which would cause Indian Tribes to cede their lands to the United States with the proceeds of such cessions predominately funding the Federal Indian boarding school system."[109]

Fast forward to 1875. That old dark and dank prison is the Fort Marion prison in St. Augustine, Florida. Richard Pratt marched 72 Plains Indians into its cells. Their native clothing was confiscated as their long traditional braids were sheared. They were given military clothing to wear. They received new names. Anglicized. From the top of their heads to the bottom of their feet they were made white in the hope that this would give them new hearts and minds. Richard Pratt coined the phrase, "Kill the Indian and save the man." That was the philosophy he applied to those 72 Indians.

Pratt was so enamored with his idea that he proposed experimenting with Indian children. He, therefore, established the Carlisle Indian Industrial School in Pennsylvania.[110]

> *"Carlisle, the boarding school where Little Chief (the son of Sharp Nose) and other Northern Arapaho and Eastern Shoshone children were sent, along with children from as many as 140 other tribes – set the standard for Indian boarding schools. Life was highly regimented. Children who arrived in their finest traditional clothing, often bearing pipes and other gifts, were stripped of their tribal possessions and their hair was cut short. Their days were divided between academic classes – intensive English classes when they arrived, and*

then math, physiology, geography, and U.S. history – and a half day working at trade skills, such as carpentry and agriculture. The children also lived and worked for periods with white families in surrounding communities on 'outings,' ostensibly for them to experience a non-Indian family and workplace, but sometimes merely providing their hosts inexpensive farm and domestic labor."[111]

This was called assimilation. In hindsight, it looks more like another exercise in white supremacy. With enrollment enforced, the policy "compared to slavery and other methods of subjugation."[112] Still hoping to prove themselves good enough Indians to be given their own reservation, the Arapaho sent 13 of their children to Carlisle, including Chief Sharp Nose's son, Little Chief. These fathers believed a stint at Carlisle was key to their survival. The government had failed to provide the promised resources to help the Indians make the transition to farming. Sharp Nose told the Indian agent, "There are not enough good men to show us how to plant and cultivate our crops." He hoped Indian children would "learn to do as the white men do," at the boarding school nearly 2,000 miles from Wind River.[113] Of the 13 sent to Carlisle, only five returned.[114] Little Chief was not one of them.

It wasn't only Carlisle. Episcopal clergyman John Roberts was assigned to minister to the Indians at Wind River. He stayed 66 years and was widely known as a compassionate man who deeply cared for the Native peoples. In the 1880s, he too was convinced boarding schools offered the best hope for reprogramming Indian children. With all good intentions, Rev. Roberts oversaw the construction of a school along the banks of Trout Creek in 1884.[115] The single-story adobe building had few windows. Iron bars were put across them to prevent the children from escaping to go home to be with their families. The Arapaho and Shoshone youngsters who attended the school could look out the barred windows and see their homes but were not permitted to visit them. Federal policy prohibited the government from providing furniture apparently to force the child students, who had no furniture building skills to learn self- sufficiency.

Despite Rev. Roberts' good intentions, fifty percent of the children in his school died while attending in the early years. Roberts' papers provide statistical evidence of the death toll but do not list causes of death. However, in 1901, the Reverend wrote to the distant bureaucrats who established boarding school rules. He blamed "the effect of civilization."

> *"The heavy death rate of the pupils is undoubtedly due to the effect of civilization upon them. In school, they have food, care, wholesome food, well cooked. They have plenty of fresh air, outdoor exercise, and play. Yet, under these conditions, in school they droop and die."*[116]

Roberts compared his students with "their brothers and sisters" in the Indian camp nearby, whom he saw "live and thrive." He proposed allowing the students "to spend time at home, at intervals." The bureaucrats eventually acquiesced in the request, though they took their time doing so, just as historians have taken their time to acknowledge the hurt and historical trauma caused by the boarding school experiment. Elinor Markley's biography of John Roberts says that after his suggestion that the children be allowed occasional home visits, "Today, all is well in school." She claimed the schools improved the lives of the children. Her measuring stick? "Practically all the young people were baptized and confirmed. Most of the old people, who are fast passing away, have learned the truths of the Gospel through their children." Most Wyoming history books ignored the schools altogether.[117]

Among the first to acknowledge that Ms. Markley's assessment was off the mark and that the schools were "quite oppressive to Indian youth," was another Episcopal clergyman. The Reverend Warren Murphy wrote a book entitled *On Sacred Ground: A Religious and Spiritual History of Wyoming*. He criticized the "civilizing" protocols visited on the children including enforced enrollment, required haircuts to make the Indian children look like whites and the imposition of name changes. "Some were given names of the local white settlers, while others were simply assigned famous names like Shakespeare."[118]

Some historians noted the irony of U.S. policy choices. The Indian Removal Act of 1830 was used to remove Indians from their land to reservations and then the government "proceeded to remove them from reservations." Boarding school horrors have been slowly revealed. "An untold number of Native children were murdered, and generations traumatized, tortured, raped, and beaten as a result of this removal program."[119] Children were programmed to demonstrate disdain for their elders. "And so, after a while we also began to say Indians were bad. We laughed at our own people and their blankets and cooking pots and secret societies and dances."[120] All of this was documented by the Indigenous coalition called "The Boarding School Healing Project," who gathered testimony about the generational trauma still today ruining lives in the Native community. "My mother lived with rage all her life," reported one Native woman, "and I think the fact that they were taken so young was part of this rage and how it, the fallout, was on us as a family."[121]

The experiment backfired, ripping families apart in the context of a cultural structure that was built on interfamilial and tribal relationships and obligations. For hundreds of years before Richard Pratt and Rev. Roberts, Indian villages had established norms and obligations to their children. From pre-birth expectations to naming the newborns and celebrating their first steps, teaching youngsters to hunt and respect their elders, the entire tribe guided their offspring through "the four hills of life," i.e., childhood, youth, adulthood, and old age.[122] Now the government and the church combined to deny Native parents the right to raise their own children. "It was just like a defeated nation," Pius Moss, an Arapaho and former boarding school student, reflected. "There wasn't much they (parents) could say."[123] Helen Cedartree ran away from the St. Stephen's Mission boarding school three times. Imprinted on her memory is how she was chained to the floor and handcuffed to other runaway children afterward. The priest said, "That's for runaway girls so they don't jump out."[124]

In the wake of the boarding schools, parents were left with the psychological damage inherent in having been rendered unable to protect their children while their children were taught to disrespect their elders. The U.S. Department of Interior issued a Federal Indian Boarding School Investigative Report in May 2022. Its findings include the existence of "quantitative research" demonstrating that "the Indian boarding school system continues to impact the present-day health of Indians," and that the experience led to "an intergenerational pattern of cultural and familial disruption.[125] Psychologists predict the ghosts of the boarding schools will haunt Native families for generations. It isn't only the children who were forced to attend and their parents from whose lives they were taken. The same ghosts haunt the government and the religious institutions overseeing this failed and harmful experiment.

Today, apologies for the boarding schools are ubiquitous, though not nearly so ubiquitous as the intergenerational trauma they caused Indian people. A variety of religious and governmental organizations have awakened from bad dreams and are living with self-doubt and deep regret about their roles. Among those who haunted are the government of Canada and Pope Francis who said:

> *"I feel sorrow and shame for the role that a few Catholics, particularly those with educational responsibilities, have had in all these things that wounded you, the abuses you suffered and the lack of respect shown for your identity, your culture and even your spiritual values."*

The Presbyterian Church (USA) apologized to what they called "the stolen generations during the Indian assimilation movement."[126] On behalf of the Anglican Church, Primate Archbishop Michael Peers announced, "I am sorry, more than I can say, that we were part of a system which took you and your children from home and family. I am sorry, more than I can say, that we tried to remake you in our image, taking from you your language and the signs of your identity. I am sorry, more than I can say, that in our schools so many were abused physically, sexually, culturally, and emotionally. On behalf of the Anglican Church of Canada, I present our apology."[127]

Debra Ann Haaland is the first Native American to serve as Secretary of the Interior, where she has authority over the Bureau of Indian Affairs. Secretary Haaland also has personal knowledge of the boarding school history. Her grandfather was forced to attend the Carlisle school. She ordered the Department to investigate the schools and to literally find out where the bodies are buried. Until then the federal government didn't have a complete list of all the schools much less a complete picture of who established the system and who was responsible for the abusive practices they employed.

The Department identified "408 Federal schools in 37 states or then-territories." The Department of Interior's 2022 report identified 53 marked and unmarked gravesites used by these schools to bury Indian children. They expect to find more as their work continues.[128] But it was not only boarding schools. There were "Indian day schools, sanitariums, asylums, orphanages, and stand-alone dormitories that involved the education of Indian people, mainly Indian children," whom the report said "were induced or compelled by the Federal government" to attend.[129] There were six such schools in Wyoming.[130]

The boarding schools on the Wind River Indian Reservation were among the longest surviving. St. Stephens last boarded kids in 1939; Roberts' school for girls closed in 1949. The Government Boarding School shut its doors in 1955.

In 2017, a delegation from the Wind River Indian Reservation traveled to Carlisle. They hoped to find the remains of Little Chief, Little Plume, and Horse, three of the Northern Arapaho children who died and were buried in unmarked graves at Carlisle in the 1880s. But officials at Carlisle cared so little for the children under their care that they failed to document who was buried in which grave. Expecting to find a child of Wind River, the delegation dug up the grave of a child other than the one they expected in that plot. A film, *"Home from School: The Children of Carlisle,"* documented the way in which yet another failure of the boarding school experiment exacerbated the generational trauma scores of years after the death of these children.[131]

Arapaho elder Sherman Sage watched as hundreds of Paiutes danced. He was part of a delegation sent to Mason Valley, Nevada in 1889, to learn about a new religion that was being spoken of by Indigenous peoples. These were years of "epidemics, meager rations, poverty, poor housing" and "a death rate higher than the birthrate."[132] Throughout history, dire conditions like those facing the people of Wind River have always piqued interest in a new way of understanding the divine. This one incorporated the story provided by the Christian missionaries who ceaselessly streamed into the reservation.

The new religion, about which they learned from a visiting Bannock in 1889, promised a return to life of those who had died. The resurrections would be followed by a time of peace. Sage was invited to visit the Paiutes to learn about this rekindling of the Ghost Dance. He watched the dancers with curiosity and skepticism. They wore eagle feathers and claws and what they referred to as "ghost shirts." They said the attire would protect them from the white man's bullets. Hundreds of dancers held hands and swayed and shuffled around the Sacred Pole as the Medicine Man chanted. Some appeared to be in a trance, drifting off from the circle. A few fell to the ground seemingly unconscious. Others "wailed cautiously and in awe, feeling their dead were close at hand."[133] They were told to dance for five days, after which they would bathe ceremoniously. This was to happen every six weeks for the prophecy to be fulfilled.

After several trips, Sage became the link between the Paiute adherents in Mason Valley and several of the Plains tribes including the Lakota. Kicking Bear, a Lakota, traveled to Mason Valley following an 1889 conference with Sage at Wind River. In May 1924, he was interviewed by Tim McCoy, a Hollywood cowboy who became an adopted Arapaho. Kicking Bear told McCoy about his journey to Mason Valley. "We went to the Messiah. He had scars on his hands and said he was the same man who had come down to see the white man a long, long time ago. But the white man stuck him on a tree. Those scars were the places where they had nailed him to that tree. Wovoka (the prophet) said he had died and gone back to his father but now he was here on earth to help his children, the Indian."[134]

Later Sage told McCoy, "Yes we found the messiah." Yellow Calf, an Arapaho, affirmed Sage's story. "I saw him die and come back to life." The resurrected messiah told them, "Soon, a Great Cloud will come and on it will be all the Indians who ever lived on their war ponies and all the buffalo, elk, antelope, and deer. This Great Cloud will cover over the white man and then everything will be as it always had been.[135] This was to happen, "two years from when we saw him, when the leaves turned. Autumn 1891." McCoy recorded that, having said that, "Yellow Calf nodded and turned away. His shoulders trembled. He was crying." Yellow Calf, by then, knew the rest of the story.

The U.S. government was fearful a revolt could be stirred by the Ghost Dance and outlawed it, which Peter Cozzens likened to "banishing Christ from Christian churches."[136] In the last month of 1890, the Standing Rock Indian Agent ordered the arrest of Sitting Bull. In the chaos that resulted, two Indigenous police officers assassinated the Chief. One shot him in the chest, the other scalped him,[137] leading to the infamous Wounded Knee slaughter on December 29.[138]

As Dan, the Lakota elder told Kent Nerburn in *Neither Wolf nor Dog*, "The government got angry. They had killed us because we wouldn't believe in Jesus. Now they were going to kill us because we did."[139] Dan remembered, "the Night of the Popping Trees," Lakota speak for the night in December 1890 when the wind was so cold it made twigs snap and trees made popping sounds. "Wind that will kill you. Freeze off your toes and fingers in minutes. Snow that will blind you. Ice on everything and the trees split. But they were outside, running from soldiers in the wind and cold. They had children, women. Babies wrapped in blankets."[140] As many as 350 Indian men, women, and children were killed. The "torn and bleeding bodies (of the wounded) were carried into the candlelit church," where a Christmas banner hung across the chancel. "Peace on Earth, Goodwill to Men," it read.[141]

The Arapaho continued participating in the Ghost Dance ceremony long after Wounded Knee, "some years after the prophesied date of the apocalypse."[142] The members of the American Indian Movement led the "Second Wounded Knee" more than 80 years later, occupying the small South Dakota town of Wounded Knee. The protest began on February 27, 1973, and lasted until May 8. The occupiers danced the Ghost Dance, as Russell Means explained in his autobiography, "to acknowledge the spirits present there and call out to them to help and protect us."[143]

The government continued to chip away at the Shoshone Reservation. As the acreage shrunk, the temporary sharing with the Northern Arapaho became *de facto* permanent. Two tribes with a historic dislike for one another were sharing less and less land. Even when the government tried to give, they couldn't help but also try to take.

The Eastern Shoshone never stopped objecting to the intrusion. Finally, in 1937, nearly six decades after the Arapaho moved in, Congress passed the Jurisdiction Act of March 3, 1927. It allowed the Shoshones to present a claim for compensation. Initially, the government argued "the Shoshones had consented, without consideration, to give away a half interest in their beautiful home to their ancient enemies, the Arapahoes."[144] The government abandoned that argument and told the court the land had been forcibly taken. There was Supreme Court precedent under the Doctrine of Discovery upholding "taking" the land. In its decision in this case, the court acknowledged the government "could have adopted the original appropriation as a forcible taking in the exercise of the power of eminent domain," thus avoiding the requirement to pay damages to the Shoshone. But, there was an intervening treaty obligation.

In writing for the court, Justice Benjamin Cardozo provided a comprehensive history lesson of the period from the Fort Bridger Treaty of 1863 to the Fort Laramie Treaty of 1868, the arrival of the Arapaho in 1878, and the land cessions from then until the Supreme Court decided the government was liable for taking Shoshone land when it moved the Arapaho onto their reservation.[145] Justice Cardozo traced the diminution of the reservation from the

44,672,000 acres the Shoshone and other tribes were initially given to hunt, fish, and roam through Colorado, Utah, Idaho, Montana, and Wyoming, to the 3,054,182 the Shoshone were given in 1863 for their Wind River reservation in Wyoming." He recounted the day in March 1878, when a band of Northern Arapaho was brought to the Reservation of the Shoshones under military escort. By then, the Reservation had been reduced to 2,343,000 acres by the 1874 cession. Washakie agreed that they could remain temporarily to rest their horses and themselves.

> *"The famished Arapahoe and their horses had been fed and cared for, but they did not move away. Instead of moving away, they came in increasing numbers. As early as April 8, 1878, nearly the whole tribe was on the scene."*[146]

The Justice added, "The Treaty of 1868 charged the Government with a duty to see to it that strangers should never be permitted without the consent of the Shoshones to settle upon or reside in the Wind River Reservation." The Supreme Court recognized the ownership of the Shoshones and asked lower courts to determine the compensation for which the government would be liable. That question ended up back in the lap of the Supreme Court in 1938.

Having conceded the Shoshones had a legal right to compensation, the government then sought to "take back" the rights to the reservation's valuable mineral and timber resources. If they prevailed, the Indians would be denied millions in past compensation and millions upon millions in future income. The Court rejected the government's argument, holding, "Minerals and standing timber are constituent elements of the land."[147] It is the royalties and other income from these resources, not welfare as many believe erroneously, that provide Tribal members with monthly per capita income yet today.

The government was assessed damages for taking Shoshone treaty lands in the amount of $4,408,444.23 and the name of the Shoshone Reservation was changed. The Eastern Shoshone and the Northern Arapaho now formally shared the Wind River Indian Reservation.

A 2012 *New York Times* exposé concluded, "The difficulties among Wind River's population of about 14,000 have become so daunting that many believe that the reservation, shared by the Northern Arapaho and

Eastern Shoshone Tribes is haunted — the ghosts of the innocent killed in an 1864 massacre. 'Anywhere, there are good spirits and bad spirits around,' said Ivan Posey, a former member of the Eastern Shoshone Business Council. 'But when people are struggling in their lives, those bad spirits come around more often. It's kind of a yin and yang.'"[148]

The bad spirits came for Andy Antelope. Mr. Antelope, an Arapaho, was shot and killed by a Riverton policeman on September 21, 2019. Andy Antelope was eating a hot dog near the vendor's food truck. "I don't believe the male was bothering anyone or being disruptive," a witness told investigators. He couldn't have been causing much trouble with a blood alcohol content of .258, which would have rendered him near unconscious. Lloyd Larsen, a Fremont County state legislator who knew Mr. Antelope told the Riverton newspaper:

> "He was a gentle person who nevertheless had addiction issues and had been committed involuntarily to the Wyoming State Hospital in Evanston. However, due to limited space, he was released from the state hospital, after which he spent time receiving mental health care in Lander, was released, and stayed at Sage West Health Care in Riverton. His stay in Sage West was cut short because he hadn't had a current psychological evaluation. So, he was released from the hospital. There's more history to that afternoon in a Walmart parking lot. He shouldn't have been there. The system failed him. I'm not judging whether he had the right to be at Walmart, but I am saying that he should not have been released from mental health care that he had been receiving prior to the incident at Walmart. That the system failed him is why he shouldn't have been there."

On that afternoon, instead of medical assistance, a policeman was called. He arrived at the Walmart parking lot with no backup and no body camera. It was, coincidentally or not, the same officer who, two days earlier responded to Mr. Antelope's report that he had been brutally raped. The officer was aware of the severe injuries Andy received in the attack and his mental health and addiction problems. According to a subsequent report of the Division of Criminal Investigation, Andy Antelope had 296 police contacts between 1995 and the day he died. Emergency Medical Services were needed 66 times and 77 contacts resulted in hospitalization. He was arrested 130 times and cited 113 times. His average blood alcohol content for the 95 times detailed was .254%. He was taken to a detox facility 12 times.

This day, Andy Antelope asked to be taken to the hospital. The officer told him he was going to jail. There's a scuffle. The nearly unconscious Indian waves a knife in the direction of the officer, striking him on his ceramic-plated bullet-proof-vest protected chest. The officer fired a bullet into Andy Antelope's head from pointblank range. Seven minutes, 14 seconds after the officer arrived on the scene, Andy is dead. The county coroner believed a public inquest necessary to learn the truth about the fatal encounter. The county attorney used his position to thwart the inquest. As of this writing, local officials have also refused to make public the records of the investigation of Mr. Antelope's rape allegation. He was buried along with the facts of the killing.

Andy Antelope's death is a metaphor for the social, economic, and political winds against which Indigenous Peoples have stood since the first white men came to the Wind River. Addiction. Mental illness. Violence. Inequality in healthcare. Discriminatory law enforcement. A biased criminal justice system. Deprivation. Unemployment and economic disparity. Lack of safe housing. Stereotyping. Injustice. Indignities. Through the 1960s, storefronts and restaurants in white-dominant communities surrounding the reservation posted "No Dogs or Indians Allowed" signs.[149] Many Native Peoples have stories to tell today of the discrimination they suffer in Riverton, the Wind River Indian Reservation border town they must visit at least occasionally to buy groceries and other necessities.

All of this accounts for a deficit of 15 years between the life expectancy across Wyoming compared to that of Native Americans in the state, as does the perniciousness of historical trauma, infecting each generation of Native Peoples.

> *"Historical trauma differs from other types of trauma in that the traumatic event is shared by a collective group of people who experience the consequences of the event, as well as the fact that the*

impact of the trauma is held personally, and can be transmitted over generations."[150]

The destruction of the Native American culture is not ancient history. Those who lived in the generation of our great-grandfathers and grandmothers were perpetrators, others eyewitnesses or victims of "the deterioration, and at times complete loss, of original languages, traditional and sustainable economies, governmental structures, kinship systems, religious ceremonies and social ordering mechanisms."[151] It is not difficult to consider the medical science that concludes those events created a traumatic path to the present. Nonetheless, we can't understand the historical trauma unless we know the full extent of the historical losses suffered by Native Peoples. Calling it the greatest story left untold, one observer admitted, "No historian has been or ever will be able to properly capture the nuanced detail of Native American culture from the perspective of Native peoples from antiquity up until the present day."[152] However, victims understand. "Indigenous 'First Nations' communities have consistently associated their disproportionate rates of psychiatric distress with historical experiences of European colonization."[153]

The hurricane-like winds of genocide howled through times of "discovery and conquest," war, removal, reservations, hunger, epidemics, allotments, and the assimilation movement of the boarding schools. And yet the people of the Wind River Indian Reservation stood courageously and they survived. While the colonizers claimed they wanted the nomadic tribes to become farmers, "the United States built projects for the settlers, while little was spent for Indian irrigation." That was the opinion of former Wyoming Congressman Teno Roncalio, the Special Master appointed to hear evidence about the competing claims among Indians and non-Indians to water rights in the Big Horn Basin in the late 1970s.[154]

Under Wyoming law, the first to claim a right to use water has priority. This lawsuit was filed by the state to undermine the rights given the Native peoples in the Treaty of 1868. To their surprise, Roncalio's decision, upheld by the U.S. Supreme Court, precluded non-Indians from claiming a priority for Indian water. It meant that the Shoshone and Arapaho will have the water they need well into the future. After the legal dust settled, Roncalio explained the process and its conclusion this way:

> "Except for two landmark United States Supreme Court decisions, this historic pattern might well have survived to the present. Each set of citizens would have enjoyed state-issued water rights, most of which carried a 1905 priority date for the tribes and a 1906 date for settlers, the year the land sales began. The famed Winters case of 1908, however, said simply that Congress, when it created an Indian reservation in Montana, intended to grant a water right at that time also, since it was untenable that Congress intended to leave Indians without the water needed to sustain life, particularly in the arid West. In Wyoming, first in time is first in right, and the 1868 priority date became a beacon to Indians."[155]

At long last, a treaty designed to take Indian land was interpreted to protect their future. It was a good omen. The Indigenous survivors are re-introducing buffalo to the grasslands, reviving Native languages, practicing ancient dances and ceremonies, listening to the wisdom stories of their elders, and raising their children with a sense of pride for what they endured. Despite the historic cross winds and cross purposes, they are standing against the Wyoming wind.

Endnotes

1. Kerburn, *Neither Wolf nor Dog*, dialogue 241, 237
2. Kerburn, *Neither Wolf nor Dog*," 45-51
3. Kimmerer, *Braiding Sweetgrass*, 17
4. "McConnell says he's 'concerned' schools are denigrating American historical events," *Fox News*, https://www.foxnews.com/politics/mcconnell-schools-denigrating-american-historical-events, accessed March 19, 2022
5. "The 1776 Report" The President's Advisory 1776 Commission," January 2020, 1 https://documents2.theblackvault.com/documents/The-Presidents-Advisory-1776-Commission-Final-Report.pdf, accessed March 19, 2022
6. "The 1776 Report," 23
7. Senate File 103, 2022 Wyoming Legislature, https://wyoleg.gov/Legislation/2022/SF0103, accessed march 19, 2022
8. Williams, *Like a Loaded Gun*, 48
9. Alter, *The Hebrew Bible*, Vol. 2, "Joshua: Introduction," 3
10. Alter, *The Hebrew Bible*, Vol. 2 "Joshua Introduction," 5
11. Roy Harvey Pearce, *The 'Ruines of Mankind': The Indian and the Puritan Mind*, Journal of the History of Ideas, Vol. 13, No. 2 (April 1952) published by the University of Pennsylvania Press,
12. Takaki, *A Different Mirror*, 39-40
13. Peyer, *The Tutor'd Mind*, 1
14. "Papal Bulls," *Doctrine of Discovery Project* (30 July 2018), https://doctrineofdiscovery.org/papal-bulls/, accessed April 4, 2022
15. Miller, *Native America, Discovered and Conquered*, 21
16. Dunbar-Ortiz, *An Indigenous People's History of the United States*, 199
17. *Johnson v. McIntosh*, 21 U.S. (8 Wheat.) 543, 572-573 (1823)
18. Williams, *Like a Loaded Weapon*, 52, citing *Johnson v. McIntosh*, 21 U.S. (8 Wheat.) 543, 573 (1823)
19. *Tee-Hit-Ton v. United States*, 348 U.S. 272, 289-290 (1955)
20. Overview: Wind River Indian Reservation, "Petroleum System Overview, *Bureau of Indian Affairs*, https://www.bia.gov/sites/bia.gov/files/assets/as-ia/ieed/ieed/pdf/DEMD_OG_WindRiver_OilGasPlays_508_0.pdf. Accessed March 8, 2022
21. Knight, et al, *Mountains and Plains*, 12
22. Hodge, *Ecology and Ethnogenesis*, 4-5
23. Clark, *Indian Legends*, 215-216
24. Hodge, *Ecology and Ethnogenesis*, 19, citing Brewster, Numu Views, 1-43, 80-120
25. Trenholm and Carley, *The Shoshonis*, 7
26. Hodge, *Ecology and Ethnogenesis*, 47; citing Fagan, *Ancient North America*, 219
27. Hodge, *Ecology and Ethnogenesis*, 56-57
28. Hodge, *Ecology and Ethnogenesis*, 45
29. Hodge, *Ecology and Ethnogenesis*, 81
30. Anonymous Interview, Demitri Boris Shimkin papers, collection no. 09942, Box 1, Folder 1"Eastern Shoshoni," 317, AHC
31. Hodge, *Ecology and Ethnogenesis*, 90
32. Hodge, *Ecology and Ethnogenesis*, 96

33 Treuer, *Heartbeat of Wounded Knee*, 238
34 Hodge, *Ecology and Ethnogenesis*, 110-111
35 "Coming to Wind River: The Eastern Shoshone Treaties of 1863 and 1868, *wyohistory.org*, May 23, 2018, https://www.wyohistory.org/encyclopedia/coming-wind-river-eastern-shoshone-treaties-1863-and-1868, accessed March 19, 2022
36 Treuer, *Heartbeat of Wounded Knee*, 88
37 Billington, *America's Frontier Heritage*, 202
38 Woodard, *American Nations*, 248
39 "When Native Americans Were Slaughtered in the Name of Civilization," October 25, 2021, original March 2, 2028, https://www.history.com/news/native-americans-genocide-united-states, accessed March 21, 2022
40 Lowe, *Five Years a Dragoon*, 1; Hebard papers, box 10, File: Indian Treaty-Fort Laramie 1851, AHC
41 Lowe, *Five Years a Dragoon*, 1
42 Lesley Wischmann, "Separate Lands for Separate Tribes: The Horse Creek Treaty of 1851," *WyoHistory.org*; https://www.wyohistory.org/encyclopedia/horse-creek-treaty, accessed March 14, 2022
43 Hodge, *Ecology and Ethnogenesis*, 237
44 "Indian Affairs: Laws and Treaties," Complied and edited by Charles J. Kappler, Clerk, Senate Committee on Indian Affairs. https://americanindian.si.edu/static/nationtonation/pdf/Horse-Creek-Treaty-1851.pdf, accessed March 21, 2022
45 Trenholm and Carley, *The Shoshonis, Sentinels of the Rockies*, 121
46 Hodge, *Ecology and Ethnogenesis*, 238
47 Hodge, *Ecology and Ethnogenesis*, 246-247
48 Letter to the Superintendent of Indian Affairs, 1862, Hebard papers, box 60, Folder 3, AHC
49 Memorandum to "Office of the Superintendent of Indian Affairs, Salt Lake City, Utah Territory, June 30, 1861, Hebard papers, box 60, folder 3, AHC
50 Farlow, *Wind River Adventure*, 64-65
51 Hodge, *Ecology and Ethnogenesis*, 238-239; also see "Coming to Wind River: The Eastern Shoshone Treaties of 1863 and 1868," *wyohistory.org*, https://www.wyohistory.org/encyclopedia/coming-wind-river-eastern-shoshone-treaties-1863-and-1868/, accessed March 9, 2021; also see Farlow, Wind River Adventures, 66
52 Farlow, *Wind River Adventure*, 66
53 Memorandum to "Office of the Superintendent of Indian Affairs, Salt Lake City, Utah Territory, October 1, 1861, Hebard papers, box 60, folder 3, AHC
54 Memorandum to "Superintendent of Indian Affairs, Salt Lake City, Utah Territory, September 20, 1862, Hebard papers, box 60, folder 3, AHC
55 Trenholm and Carley, *The Shoshonis*, 98
56 Undated notes from "Conversation with Attorney J.R. Dixon, Hebard papers, box 46, folder 18, AHC; referenced in General Order No. 2, issued February 22, 1900, by 1st Lt. Clough Overton, announcing Washakie's death; "It was his pride that he had never allowed a white man's blood to be shed when he could prevent it." Hebard papers, box 46, folder 17, AHC
57 Hodge, *Ecology and Ethnogenesis*, 243
58 Morgan, *Shoshonean Peoples*, Letter from Frederick W. Lander to the Commissioner

for Indian Affairs, February 11, 1860, 255
59 "Coming to Wind River: The Eastern Shoshone Treaties of 1863 and 1868," *wyohistory.org*, May 23,2018, https://www.wyohistory.org/encyclopedia/coming-wind-river-eastern-shoshone-treaties-1863-and-1868, accessed March 20, 2022
60 Hodge, *Ecology and Ethnogenesis*, 239
61 Letter from O.H Irish, Superintendent of Indian Affairs, Salt Lake, to William T. Dole, Commissioner of Indian Affairs, Washington, D.C., October 13, 1864, Hebard papers, box 40, folder 3, AHC
62 Hodge, *Ecology and Ethnogenesis*, 237
63 Letter from Commissioner of Indian Affairs F.H. Head to Superintendent of Indian Affairs, Salt Lake City, September 20, 1866, Hebard papers, box 60, folder 3, AHC
64 Hodge, *Ecology and Ethnogenesis*, 246
65 O'Gara, *What You See in Clear Water*, 5
66 Brian Oaster, "Missing map by William Clark turns up an unflattering revelation," *High Country News*, March 2, 2022, https://www.hcn.org/articles/indigenous-affairs-history-missing-map-by-william-clark-turns-up-with-an-unflattering-revelation/print_view, accessed March 30, 2022
67 Id.
68 "Report of the Commission Appointed Under Act of Congress Approved June 1, 1872," Washington: U.S. Government Printing Office (1873) 6, Note: all the quotes in this pericope are from that document
69 "The Wind River Reservation Yesterday and Tomorrow," papers of Virginia Trenholm, box 3, folder 8, AHC
70 The "Shoshone Indian Reservation" was renamed the "Wind River Indian Reservation" in 1937
71 Dorsey and Kroeber, *Traditions of the Arapaho*, ix
72 Robert's handwritten notes, John Roberts papers, box 2, folder 26, AHC
73 Trenholm and Carley, *The Shoshonis*, 278
74 Hebard, *Washakie*, 148
75 Hodge, *Ecology and Ethnogenesis*, 251
76 Anderson, *One Hundred Years of Old Man Sage*, 51
77 Ortiz, *Sand Creek*
78 Isenberg, *The Destruction of the Buffalo*, 147, citing an 1870 *New York Times* editorial
79 Isenberg, *The Destruction of the Buffalo*, 124-125
80 "Disposable diapers, 'nothing new under the son…and daughter," *Wind River Rendezvous*, 7, (undated) Trenholm papers, box 2, folder 3, AHC
81 Cozzens, *The Earth is Weeping*, 156
82 J. Weston Phippen "Kill Every Buffalo You Can! Every Buffalo Dead is an Indian Gone," *The Atlantic*, May, 13, 2016, Can https://www.theatlantic.com/national/archive/2016/05/the-buffalo-killers/482349/, accessed March 29, 2022
83 David D. Smits, "The Frontier Army and the Destruction of the Buffalo," *Western Historical Quarterly*, 24 (Autumn 1994), 312-338
84 J. Weston Phippen "Kill Every Buffalo You Can! Every Buffalo Dead is an Indian Gone," *The Atlantic*, May, 13, 2016, Can https://www.theatlantic.com/national/archive/2016/05/the-buffalo-killers/482349/, accessed March 29, 2022

85   Isenberg, *The Destruction of the Buffalo*, 136
86   Reflections of Tom Bell, February 2006, Bell papers, box 9, folder: "1946-2014," AHC
87   Isenberg, Id., 163
88   Fowler, *Arapahoe Politics*, 63
89   Chernow, *Grant*, 657
90   Nikole Hannah-Jones, *The 1619 Project*, 145
91   Dunbar-Ortiz, *Indigenous Peoples' History*, 146
92   "Colorado Territory Created," *Colorado Encyclopedia*, https://coloradoencyclopedia.org/timeline-date/colorado-territory-created, accessed March 28, 2022
93   Brown, *Bury My Heart at Wounded Knee*, 68
94   Trenholm, *The Arapahoes*, 162
95   Anderson, *One Hundred Years of Old Man Sage*, 33
96   Id., 33
97   Trenholm, *The Arapahoes*, 195
98   Anderson, *One Hundred Years of Old Man Sage*, 57
99   Fowler, *Arapahoe Politics*, 65
100 "The Arapaho Arrive: Two Nations on One Reservation, *wyohistory.org*, June 23, 2018, https://www.wyohistory.org/encyclopedia/arapaho-arrive-two-nations-one-reservation#_ftnref4, accessed March 29, 2022
101 Anderson, *One Hundred Years of Old Man Sage*, 59
102 Trenholm, *The Arapahoes*, 261
103 Trenholm and Carley, *The Shoshonis*, 279
104 Id., 279
105 "The Arapaho Arrive: Two Tribes on One Reservation, *wyohistory.org*, June 23, 2018, https://www.wyohistory.org/encyclopedia/arapaho-arrive-two-nations-one-reservation, accessed April 5, 2022
106 Fowler, *Arapaho Politics*, 73
107 Fowler, *Arapaho Politics*, 88
108 Vizenor, *Native Liberty*, 143-144
109 President Thomas Jefferson, "Confidential Message to Congress Concerning Relations with the Indians," January 18, 1803, National Archives and Records Administration, Record Group 233, Records of the U.S. House of Representatives, Presidential Messages, 1791-1861, President's Messages from the 7th Congress
110 Dunbar Ortiz, *Indigenous Peoples' History*, 151
111 Geoffrey O'Gara, "From Wind River to Carlisle: Indian Boarding Schools in Wyoming and the Nation," *wyohistory.org*, May 28, 2019, https://www.wyohistory.org/encyclopedia/wind-river-carlisle-indian-boarding-schools-wyoming-and-nation, accessed April 6, 2022
112 Geoff O'Gara, "From Wind River to Carlisle: Indian Boarding Schools in Wyoming and the Nation," id.
113 Geoffrey O'Gara, "From Wind River to Carlisle: Indian Boarding Schools in Wyoming and the Nation," Id.
114 Fowler, *Arapaho Politics*, 74
115 The information in this section about the boarding schools on the Wind River Reservation, unless otherwise noted, comes from the manuscript for a biography of Rev. John Roberts written by Elinor R. Markley entitled *Sixty Six Years on the Wind*

River Reservation: A Ministry. The manuscript is found in John Roberts papers, box 3, folder 11, AHC. It was subsequently published as *Walk Softly, This is God's Country: 1883-1949 Among Shoshone and Arapaho Indians*, written by Markley and Beatrice Crofts, listing John Roberts as a "Contributor," Mortimer Publishers (1997)

116 Markley, *Sixty Six Years on the Wind River Reservation*, 31, Roberts papers, box 3, folder 11, AHC
117 Those interested in understanding the historic trauma caused by the Indian boarding schools, should read *The Wolf at Twilight: An Indian Elder's Journey Through a land of Ghosts and Shadows*, by Kent Nerburn, New World Library (2009)
118 Murphy, *On Sacred Ground*, 79
119 Estes, *Red Nation Rising*, 27
120 Nabokov, *Native American Testimony*, 222
121 Yvonne Leif, *All Things Considered*, National Public Radio, October 14, 1991, cited in Dunbar-Ortiz, *An Indigenous Peoples' History of the United States*, 212
122 Anderson, *One Hundred Years of Old Man Sage*, 7 (See chapters 2 through 7 for a detailed description of Tribal and familial obligation for raising Indian children)
123 Wiles, *The Arapaho Way*, 49
124 Id., 55
125 Federal Indian Boarding School Investigative Report, May 2022, 87-90; citing Ursula Running Bear, et al; "The Impact of Individual and Parental American Indian Boarding School Attendance on Chronic Physical Health of Northern Plains Tribes, 42 Fam and Community Health 1 (2019)
126 "PC (USA) leaders issue apology to Native Americans, Alaska natives, and native Hawaiians," February 9, 2017, https://www.pcusa.org/news/2017/2/9/pcusa-leaders-issue-apology-native-americans-alask/, accessed April 14, 2022
127 "The Churches Apologize," https://www.facinghistory.org/stolen-lives-indigenous-peoples-canada-and-indian-residential-schools/chapter-5/churches-apologize, accessed May 16, 2022
128 Id., 89
129 Federal Indian Boarding School Investigative Report, May 2022, 95- 96
130 Id., 6, 83
131 Christine Casatelli, "Long Journey Home for the Children of Carlisle," https://www.wgbh.org/long-journey-home-for-the-children-of-carlisle, accessed April 5, 2022
132 Anderson, *One Hundred Years of Old Man Sage*, 60
133 Dunbar Ortiz, *Indigenous Peoples' History*, 153
134 Anderson, *One Hundred Years of Old Man Sage*, 62
135 Anderson, *One Hundred Years of Old Man Sage*, 65
136 Cozzens, *The Earth is Weeping*, 423
137 Connell, *Son of the Morning Star*, 392
138 Treuer, *The Heartbeat of Wounded Knee*, 4-6
139 Nerburn, *Neither Wolf nor Dog*, 210
140 Nerburn, Id., 290
141 Brown, *Bury My Heart at Wounded Knee*, 445
142 Anderson, *One Hundred Years of Old Man Sage*, 66
143 Means, *Where White Men Fear to Tread*, 285-286
144 *Shoshone Tribe of Indians v. United States*, 299 U.S. 476, 499 (1937)

145 Justice Cardozo's opinion in *Shoshone Tribe of Indians v. The United States* is an excellent summary of the treaty history involving the Eastern Shoshone and Northern Arapaho. Readers can find it at 299 U.S. 484-498
146 *Shoshone Tribe v. U.S.*, 299 U.S. 476, 488 (1937)
147 *United States v. Shoshone Tribe of Indians*, 304 U.S. 111, 116 (1938)
148 Timothy Williams, "Brutal Crimes Grip an Indian Reservation, *New York Times*, February 2, 2012, https://www.nytimes.com/2012/02/03/us/wind-river-indian-reservation-where-brutality-is-banal.html, accessed April 8, 2022
149 Wiles, *The Arapaho Way*, 181
150 Chris Engel, "Historical Trauma and Microaggressions," *PACES (Positive and Adverse Childhood Experiences)*, https://www.pacesconnection.com/blog/historical-trauma-and-microaggressions, accessed April 9, 2022
151 Twiss, *Rescuing the Gospel from the Cowboys*, 196
152 "Understanding the Destruction," *Native Hope*, https://pages.nativehope.org/native-american-life-today, accessed April 9, 2022
153 Joseph P. Gone, Redressing First Nations historical trauma: Theorizing mechanisms for indigenous culture as mental health treatment, May 28, 2013, https://journals.sagepub.com/doi/abs/10.1177/1363461513487669, accessed April 9, 2022
154 Teno Roncalio, "The Big Horns of a Dilemma," https://open.uapress.arizona.edu/read/dc19d40e-ae7d-4010-a72b-337de7467d64/section/901f1314-3ff3-4936-b463-55fed1272b15#page_209, accessed April 14, 2022
155 Id.
156 "The Wind River Reservation: Yesterday and Today," Trenholm papers, box 3, folder "Shoshone," AHC
157 "Wind River Reservation Resume," Trenholm papers, box 3, folder: "Wind River Reservation," AHC

Chapter 11

THE PEOPLE OF HEART MOUNTAIN

...a battle between racism and reason. Racism won.[1]

"For some Mexican Americans, the war brought unhoped for opportunity. The playwright Luis Valdez, born in Delano, California in 1940 of American-born parents, recalled his early childhood. The Army, after it removed Japanese American farmers in 1942, replaced them with Mexicans like his father. 'Suddenly, we were rancheros! So, World War II was very prosperous for my family. But a strange and tragic thing happened on our ranch before we got it. The Japanese farmer who lived on it refused to go to a concentration camp. So, he hanged himself in the kitchen. In 1945, the G.I.'s came back, and the Mexican American farmers began to lose their farms and my family fell into utter poverty."[2]

Wyoming calls itself "the Equality State," but had to be publicly shamed into becoming the next to last state to recognize Martin Luther King's birthday as a holiday and then only after a compromise with the conservatives, casting it as "Martin Luther King/Equality Day." They didn't note the irony, nor do they recognize the irony of the Equality State being the only state in the union refusing to sign a refugee resettlement agreement with the federal government. In 2022, its governor said that even the refugees who helped American soldiers survive the war in Afghanistan were not welcome here. Nor are Ukrainian refugees. It is still one of the four holdouts among the

50 states refusing to criminalize hate crimes and firmly resists the enactment of laws protecting lesbians, gays, bisexual, Transgender, and other non-binary human beings from discrimination in housing, employment, or other basic human rights.

This is the state where the Chinese Massacre took place in 1885, and where Matthew Shepard was brutally murdered more than a century later because he was gay. It's where 14 Black football players were ostracized by the governor and kicked off what could have been a national championship football team because they objected to the racist policies of an opponent. It's a state where most people wanted the U.S. government to build an immigrant prison to incarcerate undocumented persons who came to the U.S. seeking a safe and better life because concentration camps create jobs.

It is a place where the winds of hate blow strong. Standing against them takes extraordinary courage. In 1942, the winds of hate blew across the nation. This is the story of the Japanese Americans who withstood those winds.

As the construction team inspected the completed barracks at Heart Mountain Relocation Camp (or what some called a concentration camp) ahead of the arrival of thousands of internees, the team looked at cracks in the tarpaper buildings through which they knew the harshest winds of a Wyoming winter would howl, making life miserable for the Japanese Americans who were coming to that remote place from California. "Well," said the construction foreman, "I guess those Japs will be stuffing their underwear in there to keep the wind out."[3]

There would come significantly greater suffering after their arrival at Heart Mountain but there had already been so much suffering from the day the Japanese government bombed Pearl Harbor. Before Pearl Harbor, there was half a century of anti-Asian hate on the West Coast and elsewhere across America. There was no "give me your, tired, your poor, your huddled masses, yearning to be free" message greeting Japanese immigrants as they arrived on the West Coast of the United States in the mid-19th century.

The Chinese came first and in far greater numbers than Japanese. They were imported as cheap labor to lay track for the transcontinental railroad. That's why they were in Rock Springs on September 2, 1885, when a labor dispute between the Union Pacific Railroad and white workers belonging to the Knights of Labor became "a day of violence and black injustice, when the blood of innocent men soaked (Rock Springs) soil and the stench of burning flesh arose from smoking ruins."[4] In the weeks before, a cache of guns was smuggled into the mining camp, having been "brought from Chicago to Cheyenne, and then from Cheyenne to Rock Springs" by "the news boys on trains."

Before the white mob was done firing those guns, twenty-eight Chinese workers were dead and the shanty town in which they lived was near totally burned to the ground. "Everything was quiet after the shooting, and they had burned down every semblance of a home that the Chinese might have had."[5] It is what Wyoming historians call "The Chinese Massacre."

As Chinese workers were forced to leave the U.S., the Japanese were their "logical successors."[6] But, disdain for the Chinese was projected easily on the Japanese since many thought they differed little in appearance. Discrimination against those coming after those who were the first "others," is as American as apple pie, oddly baked into the DNA of the settler/colonizers of North America. "No Irish need apply" signs predated "No Chinese need apply" signs, which came before the "No Japs need apply" placards. The obvious differences in appearance made acceptance considerably more of an issue for Asian newcomers. "With Europeans, a generation or two was all that was needed for immigrants to be absorbed into the American scene."[7] Not so with those from China or Japan. For decades ahead of Pearl Harbor, American politicians made these immigrants their "whipping boy," while labor organizations employed boycotts and other forms of economic intimidation including violence to dissuade employers from hiring Japanese workers. Politicians built careers choosing the road most traveled, that of demagoguery.

By the time the Empire of Japan carried out its attack on Pearl Harbor, there were 126,947 first or second-generation Japanese living in the United States, a fraction less than one percent of the nation's total population. The

1940 census showed a significant decline from the nearly 140,000 living in the U.S. a decade earlier. "Their average age was ten years."[8] Still, by December 7, 1941, fear and loathing of these people was imprinted on the American psyche. The events of that day galvanized the racism.

Despite the hardships visited on them by bigotry, prior to the "day that will live in infamy," many Japanese Americans were thriving. "American farmers envied how the Japanese turned marginal land profitable through intensive farming techniques that required them to tend each plant by hand."[9] Many owned homes and businesses. Nearly all of them (96.7%) were employed.[10] Significant numbers worked as civil servants. Others were commercial fishermen, shop owners, teachers, lawyers, doctors, nurses, insurance agents, and hoteliers. Japanese entrepreneurs and families carved out "a seventy-three-block enclave west of San Francisco's financial district."[11]

> *"Economic advancement for the (Japanese) immigrants was built on hard work, frugality, and willingness to invest and save. Individual effort was aided by stable family structure."*[12]

The publisher of the *Sacramento Bee*, V.S. McClatchy, advocated for cutting off Japanese immigration, arguing "the immigrants were superior workers against whom West Coast whites could not compete."[13] A Japanese immigrant who came to Wyoming to help build the Union Pacific Railroad provides a representative glimpse into how hard work translated into success. Rokuazem Matsumura ("Roy") and his wife, Takeko, gave birth to son Clarence in Bryan, Wyoming, now a ghost town 12 miles east of Green River. Daughter Susan was born on the other side of the Utah line in Devil's Slide, another mining town that has ceased to exist. Roy and Takeko decided their children needed a better education than what was available in those rough and tumble railroad and mining towns. In 1935, the Matsumuras moved to the Silver Lake neighborhood of Los Angeles where Walt Disney had recently built his first large studio. By December 1941, Roy and Takeko owned a market they named "Wyoming," a demonstration of loyalty to the state that had given them a start.¹⁴

Pearl Harbor came as a surprise. The war, not so much. Tension had long been building between Japan and the U.S. Though much of Congress was isolationist and hoped to avoid becoming involved in the war, President Franklin Roosevelt knew it was inevitable and his intelligence agencies had long been preparing. As the Japanese Americans raised families and worked and operated businesses, they "had no inkling of how much of a spot they were in." In her book "Setsuko's Secret," Shirley Ann Higuchi, who, along with her mother survived Heart Mountain, documents how "the FBI was already compiling lists of suspect members of the community, starting with the Buddhist priests, Japanese-language teachers, and leaders of various organizations."¹⁵

A few years later, the U.S. government revealed in a brief filed before the U.S. Supreme Court that the backdrop to surveilling Japanese Americans was "the common knowledge that the Nazi invasions of Norway and Western Europe had been aided by agents and sympathizers within the country under attack, the so-called fifth column."¹⁶ FDR felt it would have been a dereliction of his duty not to gather intelligence on those of Japanese descent. He was told, "There will be no armed uprising of Japanese." Roosevelt was informed that while there may be some who help the Empire's cause, "For the most part the local Japanese are loyal to the United States or, at worst, hope that by remaining quiet they can avoid concentration camps or irresponsible mobs."¹⁷

In the end, remaining quietly loyal saved them from neither.

As the Mineta family sat in church the morning of December 7, 1941, saying the prayers, singing the hymns, and listening to scripture read, they could never have anticipated the events that would unfold in the coming hours, weeks, months, and years. They would soon be dispossessed of their property and living in the harshness of Heart Mountain, accused of being disloyal though their son would, one day, become a member of the United States House of Representatives and member of the cabinet of two presidents, Bill Clinton and George W. Bush.

After church, ten-year-old Norman Mineta changed out of his Sunday "going to church" clothes and went out to play. He heard a scream coming from the house next door. It was his young friend, the daughter of the Mineta's next door neighbors. She cried out to no one in particular, "They're taking papa away. They're taking him away." When Norman and his father ran next door, they found a "horrified family [who] did not know who the men were who had handcuffed him, forced him into a car, and driven off."[18] It was four months later until the man's family learned he had been imprisoned 1,600 miles away in Bismarck, North Dakota. It was two more years before this family was reunited.

Throughout the West Coast, FBI agents ransacked Issei and Nisei[19] homes, terrorizing the occupants and confiscating items such as gardening implements they thought could possibly be used by an invading force. Young Norman's neighbor was one of the 736 Nikkei, i.e., Japanese Americans, who were arrested and jailed in secrecy within 24 hours of the Japanese Empire's attack on Pearl Harbor. While the Mineta's neighbor was being arrested, the head of the Japanese American Citizens League was hauled from a passenger train by a Wyoming policeman during a brief stop in Cheyenne. Mike Masaoka was one of more than twelve thousand community leaders whose names were compiled in that list of "Suspect Enemy Aliens" during the buildup to the war. Nearly 2,200 were arrested within days of Pearl Harbor.[20] The list of those who were to be arrested included Germans and Italians. When FBI agents attempted to arrest Joe DiMaggio's parents in San Francisco, director J. Edgar Hoover realized that the Italian and German population were too sizeable to sustain an arrest rate equivalent to that visited on the Issei and Nisei.[21]

Wyoming Governor Nels Smith wired every sheriff in Wyoming before the fires were extinguished at Pearl Harbor. He demanded they "contact all alien Japanese and require their registration."[22] Sheriff Frank Narramore of Uinta County informed the governor "we have only one in the county." George Yamada was, wrote the sheriff, "employed as section foreman for Union Pacific Railroad at Antelope, Wyoming. Age 45 years, born in Japan, in United States since 1914, has made two trips to Japan, one in 1922, and again in 1936. Has five children all born in this country, now living in Japan. Taken there after the death of their mother." Other reports identified families living in Wyoming for as long as 50-60 years. Many had adult children who had been raised in the state and some were currently serving in the U. S. Army.

The absence of any reports of sabotage in Wyoming didn't preclude discriminatory conduct. The only incidents of attempted sabotage came later in the war and not from Japanese Americans but from 9,000 balloon bombs launched by the Japanese military from outside U.S. borders in 1945. Only eight of the so-called "Fu-Go balloon bombs" landed in Wyoming. They were found near Thermopolis, Basin, Manderson, Kirby, Powell, Glendo, Newcastle and Gillette. None did any damage.[23]

But, in the wake of the Pearl Harbor attack, federal orders were issued requiring law enforcement to seize cameras, short-wave radios, and firearms from Japanese American citizens. Wyoming railroads discharged all workers of Japanese descent as "a precautionary measure."[24] Even so, there were those encouraging tolerance. The editor of the *Rawlins Republican Bulletin* asked, "Who are there among us who should take it upon themselves to condemn, belittle, criticize, persecute, or hold up to ridicule our more recent citizens from the old countries."[25]

Governor Smith said, in effect, "I will," using strong words to tell Milton Eisenhower how he felt about "our most recent arrivals from the old countries" As the Wyoming Governor "shook his fist in my face and growled through clenched teeth," he told General Dwight Eisenhower's brother, the director of the U.S. War Relocation Authority, "The people of Wyoming have a dislike for any Orientals. If you bring Japanese into my state, I promise you they will be hanging from every tree."[26] Despite Smith's threats, the Japanese Americans came to Wyoming.

As December 1941 turned into the early months of 1942, Japanese victories in the Pacific dominated the news, demoralized Americans, and raised their anxiety about the possibility of an attack on the West Coast and other parts of the continental U.S. Physical attacks on citizens of Japanese descent and vandalism of their property increased daily. "Restaurants posted signs claiming they poisoned 'both rats and Japs.' Barbershops promised 'All Japanese shaved free; not responsible for accidents.'"[27] Then the gathering rain clouds burst. On the 19th of February, President Franklin Roosevelt signed Executive Order 9066. The Secretary of War now had the authority to remove Japanese Americans from their homes in areas rumored to be at risk. Soon, more than 100,000 people were told they had to move. Removal was initially voluntary. While some acquiesced, that strategy failed. Removal was made mandatory, and the families given deadlines.

Most of those targeted were home and/or business owners. With deadlines of a few days or a couple of weeks, they were forced to sell their property, becoming prey for predators who saw an opportunity to acquire valuable land and personal property at less-than-bargain prices. Japanese Americans were forced to sell farms and homes and automobiles, furniture, jewelry, tools, and equipment that had sustained their lives, trades, and occupations. There was a pattern. Official looking men would show up one day, informing a family they would be forced to leave within a few days. The following day, people would come to the door offering to buy their property for pennies on the dollar. From thousands of homes, the post-Pearl Harbor arrests removed male decision makers from the home. Spouses and children with no experience maneuvering business decisions were left to confront these predators. One of the community leaders, Dr. Yoshihko Fujikawa, described the scene.

> *"It was during these 48 hours that I witnessed unscrupulous vultures in the form of human beings taking advantage of bewildered housewives whose husbands had been rounded up by the FBI within 48 hours of Pearl Harbor."*[28]

The greatest losses were experienced by farmers. Hard working Nikkei farmers dominated the pre-war market for vegetables and fruit. As they succeeded, these farmers invested in more land and equipment. "With the war sending demand soaring, fortunes were to be made.[29] As orders for removal were posted, a bumper crop was in the ground. The managing secretary of the Western Growers Protective Association admitted white farmers would reap the harvest and the profits as they benefited from the "most satisfactory prices on all commodities shipped from California and Arizona" after the "Japanese were evacuated from Military Zones."[30]

Homes were lost, farms sold for a fraction of value, personal property abandoned, stolen, or sold to "vultures." The Commission on Wartime Relocation of Internment of Civilians later found the value of the lost property and income to be "incalculable." San Francisco's Federal Reserve Bank estimated "evacuee property losses ran to 400 million." That equates to $6,899,337,423 in 2022 dollars.[31] The latter number represents lost generational wealth. Neither number includes the priceless value of lost dignity.

On March 31, 1942, the mass evacuation of Issei and Nisei began. Soon more than 120,000 Japanese Americans would be displaced by the exclusion order. Some were spared from the displacement but not the prejudice. In his book, *Beyond Heart Mountain*, Alan O'Hashi, who grew up in Cheyenne, said, "The few Japanese who lived in the-middle-of-nowhere places, like my family in Wyoming, were interned in place." They didn't have to be exiled to experience the "xenophobia, racism, and distrust" which affected them and their children profoundly.[32]

Little Norman Mineta and his family, like all the others on the West Coast, were ordered to board a train. The Minetas, and those who did not yet know they would end up in Wyoming, headed for the Santa Anita Racetrack, a stopover before Heart Mountain. They weren't told to go to the passenger station but to the freight yard, each man, woman, and child required to wear a number on their baggage and their person. By then most of the valuable property had been sold or given away, like the Mineta's "prized Packard Clipper, which they bought for $1,100 in November 1941" sold for $3 before the family boarded the train.[33] "My dad's proudest possession," Norman recalled, "was his car." Norman's proudest possession was his baseball bat. Norman prepared to board the train that morning dressed in his scout uniform, shouldering his favorite baseball bat. A military policeman demanded he hand it over. His father watched helplessly. Norman "fought down the lump in his throat as he gave his bat to the officer. It had been a gift from Papa and now it was gone."[34] The soul-crushing indignities would only increase.

> *"One day these Japanese Americans were free citizens and residents of communities: law-abiding, productive, proud. The next, they were inmates of cramped, crowded American-style concentration camps, under armed guard, fed like prisoners in mess hall lines, deprived of privacy and dignity, shorn of all their rights."*[35]

That morning they left their comfortable home in San Jose. That evening found them in a horse stall at the Santa Anita Racetrack where nearly 19,000 evacuees lived until the end of October. They were given mattress covers and told to stuff them with the straw on the ground of the stall, still reeking of the foul odor of horse manure. Toilets were communal, toilet paper rationed. They showered in the same facility used to clean the horses.

South Pacific Railroad Car with Japenese people leaning out window, cart and group of men in foreground, nd. Photo courtesy of Wyoming State Archives.

Sparse meals were made more so by kitchen staff who stole food supplies.³⁶

Meanwhile, workers were laboring to build barracks and other facilities on a forlorn piece of land in Northwest Wyoming. A sewage and electrical power system had to be speedily installed to serve the Heart Mountain Relocation Center, what would be the third largest community in Wyoming, smaller only than Casper and Cheyenne. As if to intentionally introduce the internees to Wyoming during the harshest weather of the year, the last train from Santa Anita to Heart Mountain, by way of El Paso, left on October 27. Three nights and four days later, they arrived. The armed guard who greeted the train taunted them with a weather report. "The wind chill is well below zero," he said as they "climbed aboard trucks where we sat on open benches in the wind."³⁷ Literally standing against the Wyoming wind, they were processed. Then each family was escorted to their assigned barracks where metal cots, the only furnishings, were illuminated by a single light bulb perilously hanging by a wire from the ceiling. With no insulation beyond the tarpaper haphazardly nailed to the walls, the cold wind came through the walls and surrounded them as if to say, "Welcome to your new life."

By the time the last train arrived from California, the people of Heart Mountain had established a newspaper. On October 24, 1942, the *Sentinel* published its first edition. The paper's name was derived from the mountain from which the camp got its name. The *Sentinel* said Heart Mountain "looms like a sentinel over the vast plains, vigilant and immovable, undisturbed by the elements."

The camp newspaper had much the same appearance as any contemporary publication attempting to appeal to tourists and other consumers. It advertised movies. Admission 10 cents. The birth of two babies was announced. It reported a court had been established to hear misdemeanor cases. The first two, for assaults, were dismissed. The schedule for the Buddhist and Catholic churches was included as was the blossoming of a "pre-evacuation romance." Mary Teresa Hiratsuko and Kazuo Otshsi were wed. A grocery store advertised its specials as did a clothing mercantile. Boy Scouts and Girl Scouts were meeting and sports page banners announced results for girls' softball and six-man football games. There were classes for everything from English to embroidery, shorthand to bookkeeping.

Without a hint of the irony, the newspaper told readers the camp planned to celebrate Armistice Day on November 11. Speakers from the local American legion would be on hand and patriotic music would be performed. Not until a reader got to the opinion page and read editor Bill Hosokawa's column, did one see a display of righteous anger.

> *"It started softy at first, just a supposition. 'Do you suppose they will put us in camps?' It grew from a supposition to a question to an answer, from an answer to reality – evacuation. All because God gave us yellow skin, black hair, and slant eyes."*[38]

The juxtaposition of announcements of normalizing activities with this expression of resentment demonstrates the courage it took for the evacuees to begin to build a new life in the confines of what many considered a concentration camp. Men, women, and children were surrounded by barbed wire and armed guards, sentenced without due process to an indeterminate term for crimes they did not commit because the leaders of a free country imagined that, because of their ethnicity, they might possibly commit those crimes.

Their Wyoming home was a barracks, subdivided into single-room apartments. Floor space for two people was 10 feet by 20; three people 15 x 20; four to six people, 20 x 20. If the family included five or more, they received a space of 24 x 20. None of the "apartments" had running water. Bathhouses and latrines were used in common and were in buildings separated from the living space.[39]

Two-thirds of what the *Sentinel* called "the colonists," were U.S. citizens. To achieve that status, they had to prove they understood the U.S. Constitution. They understood it well enough to know it had been violated by those responsible for their predicament. When 3,000 "colonists" petitioned the War Relocation Authority to dismantle the barbed wire fences, their petition challenged their captor's own sense of patriotism. "For what shall it profit the citizens of the United States if they save the whole world and lose their own freedom?"[40] Enough of the Japanese Americans "living under abnormal conditions" required mental health services that the Park County attorney was forced to sound the alarm. The relocation center had no such services, and the county could no longer afford the costs of placing inmates in the "Wyoming State Hospital for the Insane" or the Wyoming State Training School.[41]

Everyday life took over. There were children to raise and educate. The sick needed care as did elderly grandparents. Focusing on these things was one way of forgetting what they had been forced to leave behind, though simply waking up in one of the stark barracks would have made it impossible to forget. That first winter, the Japanese Americans experienced subzero temperatures for the first time in their lives. The thermometer dropped to as low as 30 degrees below zero. Snow blew across the plains and into their poorly insulated homes. Some of the men organized a Saturday workday to "winterize" the barracks "by shoveling dirt against the walls so the wind couldn't blow under the floors."[42]

The stoves moderately warming the barracks were installed hastily and fires were a constant hazard as were the frozen pipes of a water system that had been installed as though those responsible had never endured a Wyoming winter. On too many occasions when fire broke out, frozen pipes denied firefighters the water they needed to extinguish the blaze.[43]

Families culturally accustomed to sharing a meal, were forced to walk through the snow and wind to a mess hall and stand in long lines waiting to be served the less than appetizing meals. One Nisei son said he will be forever haunted by the picture in his mind of his elderly grandmother standing there with her metal bowl in hand, waiting patiently to be served. However, on their first Thanksgiving at Heart Mountain, internees were treated to a traditional feast. The WRA provided 7500 pounds of turkey, 600 gallons of ice cream and "traditional Japanese foods as long as the necessary items are available."[44] For the most part, they weren't. Even the Army Quartermaster Corp, which was responsible for providing supplies for the camp, called the food "edible offal," referring to the low-quality pork, liver, beef heart, and tripe usually on the menu.⁴⁵

Day by day, the "colonists" courageously adapted to the harsh reality. Evidence was found in an editorial in the *Sentinel* in November 1942. "Here in the camp, we are all one big family, and happy most of the time," wrote Bill Hosokawa. "Differences in wealth, influence, and position are a part of the past and mean nothing in the simple life we are forced to lead here." On New Year's Day 1943, Hosokawa went farther. He said the camp was a "smooth running, orderly, and progressive city. Many of the evacuees will enter the new year with little or no nostalgia for things and friends left behind in their pre-war homes." Though the Heart Mountain prisoners may have been among the few who saw the irony of the so-called "Zoot-Suit riots," during which white soldiers attacked Mexican Americans back home in California simply because they didn't like the clothes they wore. During several days of violence in Los Angeles, Americans saw "American soldiers pausing *en route* to fight a racist enemy in order to indulge in racist violence" even as they guarded the internment camps to enforce their country's racist policy.⁴⁶ Thus, the reality of life inside the camp was made more difficult by the bigotry outside it.

Governor Nels Smith had been clear about how he felt about Japanese Americans being imprisoned in Wyoming. Having lost his re-election campaign in 1942, he took the opportunity of a farewell speech to offer a parting shot. Smith warned there would be "a serious social problem" if the Japanese Americans were permitted to remain in Wyoming following the war.⁴⁷ The pot, having been stirred by Smith, boiled over at times after he departed. Some in the surrounding communities of Cody and Powell and elsewhere wanted the evacuees to be treated as prisoners of war. They suggested they be placed under constant armed guard. Others wanted them for farm labor and to build highways. A constituent who ranched near Split Rock asked Governor Lester Hunt's help to "get a Japanese girl to work for me." He was specific. "I would like a girl around twenty-years-old."⁴⁸ The Governor declined to accommodate the rancher.

Some merchants invited Heart Mountain residents into their stores, welcoming the money they spent, which was an economic boost during these tough times. Others, however, wanted them banned from entering the nearby towns. One of Wyoming's U.S. senators, Edward V. Robertson, took up their cudgel. Robertson had an unusual resume for a Wyoming politician. He was born in Wales and served in the Second Boer War from 1899 to 1902. Robertson, himself an immigrant, settled in Park County in 1912 where he ranched 14 miles from Heart Mountain. He was elected to the senate in 1942, when Lester Hunt was elected governor. This Welsh American had shockingly little compassion for Japanese Americans.

Robertson told reporters the evacuees were "coddled" and "pampered," were served wine with their meals and hoarded food that was denied to average American citizens during rationing.[49] He encouraged the *Denver Post* to "investigate the conditions" at the relocation center.[50] "Here, at Heart Mountain Relocation Center, where the War Relocation Authority is host to (thousands of) men and women of Japanese blood," The *Post* reported, "the pampered and petted charges of the government are not only being politely asked to work but

Heart Mountain Relocation Center, WWII. Photo courtesy of Wyoming State Archives.

are being flooded with offers of gainful employment far better than most of them, before coming to the center, ever knew."[51]

In addition to being fake news, there was another way to view that "gainful employment." First, it was not "better than most of them" had ever known. Many had been forced to leave far better jobs in California. The gainful employment in which many were now engaged was "contributing their strength and energy towards saving this year's precious war-time crop of sugar beets."[52] And there were any number of local farmers petitioning the governor to have some of the internees assigned to work on their farms, particularly after so many of Wyoming's farm boys had been drafted to serve in the war.

The facts didn't matter so much as a *Denver Post* story of Japan's well-publicized summary executions of American airmen. Their planes crashed while participating in Jimmy Doolittle's famous air raid on the Japanese mainland on April 18, 1942. The reports stirred anti-Japanese passions. The Cheyenne Lodge No. 89 of the International Association of Machinists was incensed by the report. The labor union told Governor Hunt, "We do not profess to know the actual facts," but "the present management is not satisfactory." They wanted "strict military management" for "these undesirables."[53]

Governor Hunt decried the *Denver Post* story as "political." The reporter relied, according to the governor, on a "disgruntled employee who was discharged about two weeks ago and went direct to the *Denver Post*."[54] The Governor defended the camp. "If you can picture a town of 13,500 people and only one actual arrest in such a community over a period of several months duration, you can realize how orderly and well managed the camp is."[55]

Senator Robertson insisted on a much more divisive narrative. He bootstrapped the *Post's* article into a set of false facts he used to support his claim that "disloyal Japanese are being pampered" at Heart Mountain while Americans are being "murdered or mistreated" by Japanese soldiers. Internees were harshly critical of Robertson's role in the *Denver Post* article telling the *Laramie Daily Bulletin*, "Despite repeated invitations both before and after his election, Senator Robertson has not seen fit to visit the Center. Now in the nation's capital, Senator Robertson sets himself up as a fountain of information about this Center."[56] The editor of the *Sentinel* made sure his audience knew that although Robertson had spent time in nearby Cody, he couldn't be bothered to visit the camp to learn the truth.[57] The Japanese Americans at Heart Mountain were not Robertson's only critics. In nearby Lovell, the editor of the *Lovell Chronicle* was less tactful. He called the Senator's speech "tommyrot."[58]

Robertson, like Governor Smith before him, openly advocated that all Americans of Japanese descent should be sent "back to Japan."[59] *Sentinel* editor Bill Hosokawa was speaking of politicians like Robertson when he said, "the fascist-like attacks on us by fellow citizens" have shaken "faith in the principles of American democracy." Hosokawa said the community especially resented "the professional race baiters, the economic interests, the pressure groups, the native fascists, and others who continue to keep alive race hatred at the expense of an American minority."[60]

For his part, Governor Hunt found the internees caused "no trouble and very little concern" to civilian authorities.[61] Nonetheless, he found himself in the middle of quarrels about the camp and its residents. In May of 1943, the town councils of nearby Powell and Cody petitioned the Governor to bar internees from visiting their communities.[62] Hunt asked camp director Guy Robertson (no relation to Senator Robertson) to "restrict permission allowing evacuees to visit Powell and Cody."[63] Robertson politely resisted his boss. "There are two sides to the question and I am sure that you will soon find a lot of the farmers and businessmen insisting that we allow the evacuees to go to work."[64]

The Governor began hearing from those who disagreed with their town councils. "As you no doubt are aware of the Anti-Heart Mountain War Relocation Camp Mayor we have," wrote A.R Fryer of Fryer's Pharmacy in Powell, "there happen to be a few other details which I think should be brought to your attention at this time since our Honorable Mayor and City Council are again trying to kick up more trouble concerning said Camp and its citizens."[65] Fryer informed the Governor the camp provided an economic boom to the businesses of Park County, explaining "90% of the merchants here in Powell have been able to pay off their old debts and now buy War Bonds since this Relocation camp was built two years ago." To make himself clear this was an economic and not a social justice issue, Fryer assured Hunt the business community favored the evacuees over "these Mexican Nationals brought up from Mexico that can't even talk United States (sic), then steal you blind the minute they come into your store."

Other merchants agreed. They appreciated the extra income received from the internees and hastened to assure the Governor the town council did not speak for the majority. Nevertheless, the mayor continued to insist the evacuees not be permitted to visit Powell. In August 1944, Hunt commissioned a private investigator to determine which side was right. Hunt made this promise to the mayor. "If his report substantiates your position, I will immediately follow your suggestions with reference to asking the Heart Mountain authorities to discontinue allowing the Japanese to visit Powell."[66] The mayor felt certain that if the inquiries were "thorough and unbiased" his position would prevail. He agreed to Hunt's strategy.[67] Captain William Bradley of the Wyoming Highway Patrol was dispatched to Powell. He interviewed "perhaps twenty people" at random. Many didn't care one way or another, Bradley reported to the Governor. Some told him, "Every Jap should be taken out and shot." Others raised no objection. Bradley reported, "I was given the impression that the larger majority of the townspeople were in favor of having the Japs (sic) come to Powell to trade." He estimated the split to be about 65% to 35% opposed to the mayor's position.[68]

Hunt told the mayor he was "more stymied than ever on what I should do." He promised to take "drastic action to see that the Japs (sic) leave the relocation Center and Wyoming immediately after the termination of the war." In the meantime, the Governor bowed out of the community controversy.[69] Regardless, the presence of so many Japanese Americans in Park County continued to stir controversy. The Governor received countless petitions and letters demanding he assure them all the evacuees would be required to leave Wyoming at war's end.

Of course, a governor had no such authority. Nonetheless, the question of whether any of the evacuees would be allowed to remain in Wyoming had long been an issue. During the 1942 gubernatorial campaign, Governor Smith told a Cody audience he received written assurance from the U.S. government that all internees would be required to leave Wyoming at the end of the war.[70] No such document was ever located.[71] Governors Smith and Hunt refused to acknowledge that after the war, as American citizens, the evacuees were free to live anywhere in the country they might choose.

Some, not many, chose Wyoming.

In July 1945, with the war nearly over, the Powell Chapter of American War Dads petitioned the Governor to "not impose these people on the Fathers and Mothers of this community now at a time when many of them are being advised of the death of their sons and daughters in our war against Japan." Governor Hunt forwarded the petition to Guy Robertson, who, by now, had run out of patience with Park County complainers. The camp director replied angrily. He referred to his wards as "peaceful, law-abiding citizens and aliens who are guaranteed protection by the Constitution of the United States" and told the Governor that there would have been no such petition in the first place "if some fanatical, race baiting, unthinking and unprincipled individual did not instigate the petition and by canvassing the highways and byways of Powell and by cajolery and false information prevail upon these people to sign something that sober reflection and study might cause them to hang their heads in embarrassment and shame."

Robertson said he knew nothing about the group calling itself the Powell Chapter of War Dads but said "Heart Mountain also has its War Dads and War Mothers. 758 boys from families in Heart Mountain are now fighting in our armed forces all over the world, and I venture to suggest that these boys are just as dear to their War Dads and Mothers as are the boys from Powell or any other community to theirs." The camp director singled out the "442nd Combat Unit who fought in Italy and France," composed "entirely of American boys of Japanese ancestry."72

Many Heart Mountain internees showed their courage during the war, some by serving in the armed forces, others by refusing to serve.

On Christmas Eve, 1942, a headline in the *Sentinel* advised internees that all males, 18-years-of-age and older, were required to register for the draft. Furthermore, failure to do so would result in prosecution. Another headline appeared in the *Sentinel* on January 29, 1944, speaking to what was an ongoing conversation in every barracks at Heart Mountain. "Nearly 2,000 Draft-age Evacuees Giving Deep Thought to Future."

The news was disorienting. Forcefully removed from their homes with no evidence of disloyalty, they were now required to demonstrate their loyalty to the nation that had deprived them of their rights. From the outset of the war, even those who were U.S. citizens (two-thirds of the Heart Mountain residents) had been considered "an enemy race."[73] Before Pearl Harbor, 5,000 Nisei were serving in the armed forces. By March 1942, the War Department discontinued inducting Japanese Americans. Many of those already in uniform were ordered discharged. The Selective Service then classified all "registrants of Japanese ancestry IV-C, the status of enemy aliens."[74] In January 1942, that changed. Now they were subject to conscription.

Among the more than 33,000 Japanese Americans who wore their country's uniform during WWII, two all-Nisei Army combat units were fighting in Europe with great success; the 100th Infantry Battalion and the 442nd Regimental Combat Team. The heroism of the 100th was thought to have motivated the change in policy, opening the door for more Japanese American conscripts.[75] But, the government created a conundrum for itself. Having declared Japanese Americans disloyal per se, but now needing them to fight for America's freedoms, they needed to manufacture a rational basis for the change. It was decided that most would be reclassified as I-A, subject to a loyalty review.

Of the nearly 120,000 evacuees, 1,500 were Japanese nationals who happened to be in the U.S. when war was declared. Thirty-three were in the camp at Heart Mountain. There were Westerners interned in Japan under the same circumstances. An agreement was negotiated. On August 29, 1943, all were taken to Goa, a Portuguese colony west of India, where an exchange was consummated.[76] Others were determined to be "troublemakers" and removed from camps like Heart Mountain and assigned, as part of a policy segregating "disloyals" to the Tule Lake Camp.

The remainder of those living at Heart Mountain and now eligible for the draft split into factions based on whether they would comply with the order to register for the draft. One faction believed voluntary compliance would prove their loyalty. Another faction, i.e., "the majority of prisoners, opposed drafting young people while the government denied them their rights as Americans. The resisters formed the 'Fair Play Committee.' Most were not willing or prepared to go to prison over their views."⁷⁷ However, a few were willing and courageously prepared themselves to take the risk.

Ernest Goppert was a Cody lawyer who later enlisted in the Navy and fought in the Pacific. Before that he was a member of the local draft board. Goppert was invited to the camp to talk to the Fair Play Committee. He warned them sternly against advising others to resist the draft. "That's sedition," he said, "and there's a heavy penalty for it."⁷⁸ The American Civil Liberties Union provided much the same legal advice. The ACLU attorneys warned, "They doubtless have a strong moral case, but no legal case at all."⁷⁹

The *Heart Mountain Sentinel* waved the flag of patriotism with daily front-page stories about plans for Victory Gardens, War Bond campaigns, USO fund drives, young Heart Mountain men lining up to serve, and "stories recounting the bravery of Nisei soldiers."⁸⁰ The death of camp director Guy Robertson's nephew was reported. He had been fighting in Sicily. The Heart Mountain Community Council sent condolences. "May you find comfort," the internees wrote, "in that his life was heroically given in service to his country."⁸¹

Sentinel editor Bill Hosokawa warned that a "life-long stigma awaits Nisei who fail to serve."⁸² The newspaper's editor urged federal officials to treat draft resisters harshly, to arrest them and lock them up, as had been done elsewhere."⁸³ In the environment created by the drumbeat coming from the *Sentinel*, the camp director and the War Relocation Authority, among others, taking a path less traveled would have required a great deal of personal fortitude. By the end of February, 90% of those eligible had registered.

In May, the *Sentinel* announced that 25 Heart Mountain men were headed for Army units. Another 100, deemed "troublemakers," were going to Tule. The large banner headline informed readers that federal grand juries in Cheyenne and Denver had indicted 75 Nisei, among them three women who assisted German prisoners of war in an escape from a POW camp in Trinidad, Colorado. They were charged with treason, while the others, 63 of whom were from Heart Mountain, were charged with failure to appear as ordered for pre-induction physicals.⁸⁴

The lawyer given the chore of representing the Nisei once represented a group of Jehovah's Witnesses who lived in Rawlins, Wyoming. In 1940, it appeared likely the U.S. would end up in the war. Patriotism intensified. Upon learning people of their faith would not pledge allegiance to the American flag, a mob attacked a group of Jehovah's Witnesses while neighbors jeered." One identified as a "pioneer Rawlins businessman," was dragged from his home and forced to kiss an American flag. Others were beaten. Some had their homes burned.[85] The Japanese resisters were Samuel D. Menin's clients now. He was experienced in trying cases that aroused community righteousness.

Courtrooms are not designed to lift your spirits. They are dreary places. Nothing grows there. No flowers. Only dark wood. Drab paint. No spirit-moving works of art on the walls. If anything, there will be large black and white photos of old, dignified, unsmiling, white men (most often) who once sat on the throne-like structure occupying much of the front of the cavernous room. The architecture is intended to intimidate. Federal Judge T. Blake Kennedy was an imposing figure. He had served since President Warren Harding appointed him in 1921. He had a reputation for giving the benefit of the doubt to "the home team," i.e., the insiders or members of the political and economic power structure. Not long before the case of the Heart Mountain resisters was set for trial, Kennedy upheld the validity of the oil leases at the center of the Teapot Dome scandal. Even though there was sufficient evidence of fraud that a cabinet secretary and an oil executive eventually went to prison and Harding escaped impeachment over the matter by dying before charges were brought, Kennedy ruled there was no fraud in the lease scheme.[86] Although his decision was overturned, Judge Blake's decision should have given pause to attorney Menin when he advised his clients to waive a jury trial and let Kennedy alone determine their guilt, though Menin can't be faulted for having even more concern about finding 12 impartial jurors during wartime.

That morning the bailiff called out, "All rise," and the judge entered the courtroom to add more darkness through the authoritative nature of his flowing black robe. On June 12, 1944, it was made more intimidating when, soon after telling the defendants they may be seated, Judge Kennedy convened the court to hear the case of *United States v. Shigeru Fujii, et al*, and eliminated any question about his prejudice. They immediately regretted their choice to allow Blake alone to determine their fate when the man in the black robe referred to them as "you Jap boys."[87] What they never knew about Kennedy, however, is how steeped in bigotry were his private thoughts and public words. He once adjourned an important New York trial for which he was sitting as a visiting judge in 1950 to travel to Philadelphia to watch the Yankees and the Phillies play a World Series baseball game. He reasoned that since his Jewish colleagues take of "all those Jewish holidays," he shouldn't be denied a baseball game.[88]

The jurist spoke openly about his disdain for African Americans in a paper he delivered to the Young Men's Literary Club of Cheyenne. He lamented there hadn't been more support for the idea of returning the slaves to Africa. Kennedy told the club that requirements imposed for voting should be onerous enough "that the rank and file of the negros (sic) are thereby disenfranchised." Otherwise, Kennedy worried aloud that whites would "be overcome and dominated by the ignorant and illiterate black."[89] He believed Blacks to be inherently lazy, unintelligent, and wanting only "a life of ease and sloth." How did he feel about Japanese Americans? Kennedy openly expressed his preference for immigrants from Northern Europe, who, he said, "seemed to more quickly catch the American perspective and the American ideal."[90]

These 63 young men who had been held by armed guards behind barbed wire fences in a concentration camp without due process for the last two years were about to learn what it means to be imprisoned with due process. The trial lasted a week. It was tense. Both attorneys were passionate in their cause. During closing arguments, the prosecutor, Assistant U.S. Attorney John C. Pickett and defense counsel Menin nearly came to blows. During Pickett's closing, Menin stood to object. "Sit down," Pickett commanded, "or I'll sit you down." Menin dared him to try. Pickett asked to court to allow him to follow through on his threat. "If the court will allow me, I'll do it in short order." The judge silenced Menin and Pickett continued.[91]

All 63 of the defendants were sentenced to three years in a federal prison after receiving a tongue lashing from Judge Kennedy. "If they are truly loyal Americans," Kennedy said, "they should at least, when they have become recognized as such, embrace the opportunity to discharge the duties of citizens by offering themselves in the cause of national defense."[92] An appeal to the 10th U.S. Circuit Court of Appeals was unsuccessful. Appellate judges found violation of the Nisei's constitutional rights irrelevant. It didn't matter that they had been imprisoned at Heart Mountain, perhaps illegally. It was sufficient to support their conviction and sentence that they were ordered to report for military physicals and refused to do so."⁹³

In *Setsuko's Secret*, Shirley Ann Higuchi wrote of her affection for those she called "the no-no people' who resisted the draft." She said, "I don't blame them. It took a lot of guts to come out and do something that the majority did not agree with. It takes a lot of courage. But these men stood their ground, and they got their views across."⁹⁴

While these men were fighting for their rights in a Wyoming courtroom, other Japanese Americans were fighting for our freedoms on battlefields around the globe.

Stanley Hayami sat on his bed at the Heart Mountain Relocation Center studying the questionnaire the soldiers handed out earlier that day. "Statement of United States Citizens of Japanese Ancestry." Question 28 asked, "Will you swear unqualified allegiance to the United States of America and faithfully defend the United States from any and all attacks by foreign or domestic forces and foreswear any form of allegiance or obedience to the Japanese emperor or any foreign government."⁹⁵ We know enough about young Stanley to make an educated guess that he answered, "Yes."

The so-called "loyalty questionnaire" was conceived as a simple way to determine who among the internees were committed to the United States during the war. It was not that simple for the Japanese Americans whose loyalty was being questioned. The interrogatory asked whether Nisei saw their country the way they did before they were forced from their homes into "the squalid injustice" of concentration camps.⁹⁶ For many, it was not as simple as answering "yes" or "no." For some, the question presented an opportunity to vociferously decry the way they had been treated. Young Stanley saw it differently.

After being told he and his family must leave their San Gabriel home in California, he shared thoughts about what he and the others experienced in evacuation and imprisonment with his diary. "I think the whole mess was unnecessary and a lot of trouble could have been avoided. I personally will proceed to forget the whole mess, will try to become a better man from having gone through such experience, keep my faith in America, and look forward to relocation and the future."⁹⁷

Born in 1925, Hayami was a 16-year-old facing a very uncertain future as he and his family were in the process of being "relocated" to Heart Mountain in 1942. He was a good student, a good son, and an optimist. At the end of his first year in the camp, he still had not lost hope. "Well, today is the first day of the year nineteen hundred and forty-three," he wrote in his diary. "I wonder what it has in store for me. Wonder what it has in store for everybody? Wonder where I'll be next year? Wonder when the war will end? Last year today, I said I hoped that war will end in a year. Well, it didn't, but this year I say again, I hope the war ends this year. Another thing is, I hope I'm out of here and a free man by '44."

The war did not end by the last day of 1944, which disappointed him, but did nothing to deprive Stanley of his inherent optimism. A January 31, 1944, entry in his diary proclaimed, "So the world better watch out. Hayami is going to the top." An Army recruiter came to visit the draft-age men at Heart Mountain. "The army man says that if we volunteer, it'll do a lot to show our loyalty and improve the relations and opinions of the American people toward us. It'll show that we are truly Americans because we volunteered despite the kicking around we got." Stanley soon became Pvt. Hayami and was assigned to the 442nd Regimental Combat Team.

The 442nd was a segregated Japanese American unit, legendary for becoming the most decorated unit in U.S. military history, given its size and length of service. In 2010, congress awarded all the unit's members the Congressional Gold Medal for their heroism in World War II. Their accomplishments were rewarded during the war with 4,000 Bronze Stars, 560 Silver Star Medals, 21 Medals of Honor, seven Presidential Unit Citations, and more than 4,000 Purple Hearts. Pvt. Stanley Hayami was posthumously awarded a Bronze Star and a Purple Heart for his heroism as told in the medal's citation, characteristic of so many of the other Japanese Americans who served.[98]

> "Pvt. Hayami left his covered position and crept toward the wounded men. Despite the hostile machine gun and sniper fire directed at him, he reached the first casualty. Exposing himself in a kneeling position, he administered first aid and then proceeded to another man and rendered first aid without regard for the heavy fire. While engaged

in this act he was mortally wounded. Pvt. Hayami's unselfish courage under such hazardous combat conditions reflects credit upon the finest traditions of the United States Army."

On May 9, 1945, the day after the war in Europe ended, Stanley's parents received the dread telegram. Their son had been killed in Italy on April 23. Other Nisei died before Hayami. Others would die after. The first Heart Mountain alum to die in battle were Yoshiharu Aoyama and Kei Tanahashi. Both men won Silver Stars for bravery. As he left for the war that would take his life, Teruo Fujioka wrote about the country for which he was going to war with the 442nd.

> *"America is far from perfect—contradictory in oh so many ways—imperfect as far as democracy goes. We have endured many bitter, heart-breaking experiences ... and so have all other minorities—but if we become cynical and bitter, we'll never improve our situation. We've got to keep plugging."* And later, *"I'm not fighting for the pre-war America, the America with prejudice, intolerance, greed. I'm fighting for a better America, striving always to improve this land to a real democracy."*[99]

Pvt. Fujioka was killed in France on November 6, 1944. Some 900 Heart Mountain residents served during WWII. Fujioka was one of 22 who died protecting American freedom. Two were awarded the Congressional Medal of Honor. "They were not only fighting America's enemies, they were fighting for acceptance as American citizens."[100]

In his book *Looks Back*, Father John Meyer remembered being at Heart Mountain during the war, watching "young, bright men, clad in the uniform of our country, passing through the barbed wire gate to visit loved ones." The Catholic priest recalled how the gates were guarded by other bright, young men wearing the same uniforms.

By early 1945, few in the U.S. government could articulate a rationale for keeping the Japanese Americans incarcerated. Fewer yet could articulate a reason for their incarceration in the first place. Knowing the U.S Supreme Court would hand down a decision the next day that might force their hand, the Army announced the end of the Japanese American exclusion order on December 17, 1944, little more than four months after America dropped atomic bombs on Japan.[101] However, on December 18, the Supreme Court issued a decision affirming the conviction of Fred Korematsu, who refused to leave his home in violation of the 1942 exclusion order. Many of the justices agreed that "martial necessity arising from the danger of espionage and sabotage" warranted the military's evacuation order.[102]

Justice Robert Jackson, nominated to the Supreme Court by FDR five months before Pearl Harbor, wrote a harsh dissent. He called the exclusion order "the legalization of racism" that violated the Equal Protection Clause of the Fourteenth Amendment. He compared the exclusion order to the "abhorrent and despicable treatment of minority groups by the dictatorial tyrannies which this nation is now pledged to destroy." He concluded that the exclusion order took America "into the ugly abyss of racism." This Justice worried that the court's decision in the Korematsu case would lay around "like a loaded gun, ready for any authority that can bring forward a plausible claim of an urgent need."

The Supreme Court's decision differed sharply from the conclusion reached less than two years later by the Committee on Civil Rights appointed by President Harry S. Truman. In October 1947, the presidential commission confessed, "The most striking mass interference since slavery with the right to physical freedom was the evacuation and exclusion of persons of Japanese descent from the West Coast during the past war."[103] The Committee called for reparations.

Despite the Supreme Court's ruling in *Korematsu*, most were now free to return home, such as it was. Many were required to rebuild from scratch. "Some Issei, then in their late fifties or sixties, never regained lost momentum and stayed impoverished, dependent on their children, for the rest of their lives." Most had no home to return to, while others found their property vandalized or stolen. Their release from confinement had not released some Americans from their prejudices. Daniel Inouye, who later became a United States Senator, told of his return to Hawaii. When he stopped in for a haircut, the barber asked whether he was Chinese. Inouye told the man, "My father was born in Japan. I am an American." The barber huffed, "Don't give me that American stuff. You're a Jap and we don't cut Jap hair."[104]

Certainly, this was not universal. Some were welcomed home and received the help of friends and community in reestablishing their lives. Still, over time, the trauma was inescapable. In *Setsuko's Secret*, Shirley Ann Higuchi describes the generational trauma that led her mother and so many former internees of that generation to avoid even talking of the ordeal for the remainder of their lives.

Little by little, the evacuees who lived three long years behind barbed wire at Heart Mountain were allowed to return home. The last train, filled with more than 400 Japanese Americans, left for the West Coast on November 9, 1945. All the former residents had now been relocated. The water was turned off, the boilers drained, the windows boarded up and the mess hall closed. One of the sorriest chapters in Wyoming and U.S. history came to an end.[105]

In 1986 a simple plaque was placed at the site of the Heart Mountain Camp. It reads, "May the injustices of the removal and incarceration of 120,000 persons of Japanese ancestry during World War II, two-thirds of whom were American citizens, never be repeated."

> *"Prophet!" said I, "thing of evil! – prophet still, if bird or devil! –*
> *Whether Tempter sent, or whether tempest tossed thee here ashore,*
> *Desolate yet all undaunted, on this desert land enchanted –*
> *On this home by Horror haunted – tell me truly, I implore –*
> *Is there – is there balm in Gilead? – tell me – tell me, I implore!"*
> *Quoth the Raven "Nevermore."*[106]

"Nevermore," they said. "Never again." But in 1986, the Reagan administration considered a plan to round up "thousands of Muslims" in the event of an attack. The idea was on the table until former evacuee, Congressman Norman Mineta learned of the scheme, "exposed and killed the plan." That didn't discourage others who revisited the possibility after September 11. But President George W. Bush made it clear that would not happen this time. During a White House meeting, "Bush nodded at Norman, adding, 'We don't want to have happen today what happened to Norm in 1942.'"[107]

Nonetheless, these ideas are always just below the American surface. In 2017, President Donald Trump ordered a widespread round up of those he called "illegal aliens." Trump, who ignited anti-Asian animus during the COVID-19 pandemic by calling the virus "the China Flu," proposed building internment camps around the nation to house undocumented persons, mostly Hispanics. Public officials were immediately excited by the idea, calling it an "economic opportunity." In Wyoming, the Uinta County Commissioners donated land for the 500-bed immigrant prison, the proposal for which was subsequently amended to require capacity for a thousand inmates.

Wyoming's Governor refused to oppose the project and his Attorney General said the governor could ignore a state law requiring his consent and that of the other four state elected officials prior to the construction and operation of the private prison. Though the facility would have a wall and armed guards, they reasoned it was something other than a prison. The legislature refused to prohibit it. "Never," it seems, is not forever. It has an expiration date tied to the demagoguery of politicians and shifting public opinion. The company planning to build the concentration camp pulled the plug on the project when it became clear in early 2020 Trump would not likely be re-elected and Joe Biden planned to end private prisons as had Barack Obama before Trump's 2016 election victory. Otherwise, Heart Mountain II would now be part of Wyoming's landscape.

The Report of the Commission Wartime Relocation and Interment of Civilians, which is quoted often herein under the report's title, *Personal Justice Denied*, laid the foundation for the Civil Liberties Act of 1987. The federal law awarded reparations in the amount of $20,000 per survivor and provided a formal presidential apology to every surviving incarcerated

U.S. citizen or legal resident immigrant of Japanese ancestry. The act was sponsored by California's U. S. representative Norm Mineta and Wyoming Senator Alan Simpson. The two became friends while each was a member of a Boy Scout Troop, one inside Heart Mountain barbed wire, the other on the outside.

On August 2, 2011, the Heart Mountain Interpretive Center was formally dedicated. Senator Inouye joined Al Simpson and Norman Mineta among hundreds in attendance. Mineta told the large crowd, "This is not about the past. It is about the future because it is the future that always has the capacity to repeat the past."[108]

Endnotes

1. Higuchi, *Setsuko's Secret*, 28
2. Nugent, *Into the West*, 284-285
3. Kashima, "Personal Justice Denied," Supra., 159
4. Anonymous Authors, *History of the Union Pacific Coal Mines*, The Colonial Press, Omaha Nebraska (1940), 75
5. Interview with "Mrs. Thayer of Rock Springs, Wyoming, August 29, 1921" conducted by Dr. Grace Raymond Hebard, Hebard papers, box 3, Folder 2 "Chinese Massacre-Rock Springs-1885," AHC
6. Bill Hosokawa, *Nisei: The Quiet American*, William Morrow and Company-New York (1969), 44
7. Id., 107
8. Id., 151
9. Shirley Ann Higuchi, *Setsuko's Secret*, University of Wisconsin Press (2020), 13
10. *Personal Justice Denied*, 44
11. Higuchi, *Setsuko's Secret*, 15
12. *Personal Justice Denied*, 44
13. Id.
14. Clarence Matsumura, Roy and Takeko's son, served in World War II, helping to liberate Dachau at the war's end, https://mycountry955.com/powerful-book-tells-the-story-of-heroic-former-heart-mountain-incarceree/?fbclid=IwAR1JRlCHDhNVF4By7W7_6t6tf9g8A8BpnQZ_I0ls6IscKVyEc3d03FYi554, accessed April 7, 2022
15. Higuchi, Id., 26
16. *Personal Justice Denied*, 51, citing *Kiyoshi Hirabayashi v. United States*, 380 U.S. 81 (1943)
17. Curtis B. Munson, Report to FDR, "Japanese on the West Coast," November 7, 1941, FDR Library, cited in *Personal Justice Denied*, 52-53
18. Andrea Warren, *Enemy Child*, 25
19. The term "Issei" refers to immigrants who were born in Japan; their children born in the new country, are "Nisei; and their grandchildren are referred to as "Sansei."
20. Pearson, *The Eagles of Heart Mountain*, 23
21. Reeves, *Infamy*, 2-5
22. Copy of telegrams and correspondence, dated December 7, 1941, box 3, folder "Correspondence re: Japanese Interment," Nels Smith papers, AHC
23. "Japanese balloon bombs fall" *Douglas Budget*, April 12, 1995, 4; also see "Wyo Weatherman Don Day Featured in WWII Documentary Japanese Balloon Bombs," *Cowboy State Daily*, November 29.2021, https://cowboystatedaily.com/2021/11/29/wyoming-weatherman-don-day-featured-in-doc-about-wwii-balloon-bombs/#:~:text=One%20bomb%20exploded%20near%20Thermopolis%20In%20December%201944%2C,for%20psychological%20warfare%20than%20as%20truly%20devastating%20weapons, accessed March 12, 2022
24. Larson. *The War Years*, 8
25. Id., 9
26. Reeves, *Infamy*, 98; also Pearson, *The Eagles of Heart Mountain*, 128
27. Pearson, *The Eagles of Heart Mountain*, 93

28 *Personal Justice Denied*, 108
29 Pearson, *The Eagles of Heart Mountain*, 89
30 *Personal Justice Denied*, 124-125
31 https://www.usinflationcalculator.com, accessed February 27, 2022
32 O'Hashi, *Beyond Heart Mountain*, Introduction
33 Higuchi, *Setsuko's Secret*, 48
34 Warren, *Enemy Child*, 53
35 Hosokawa, *Nisei*, 329a
36 *Personal Justice Denied*, 138-144
37 Warren, *Enemy Child*, 75
38 Sentinel, October 24, 1942, 5
39 Memorandum from War Relocation Authority, Hunt papers, box 1, Folder: "Heart Mountain," AHC
40 "Removal of barbed wire fence asked," *Sentinel*, November 21, 1942, 1
41 Letter from Sarah Donley Steadman to Governor Lester Hunt, January 8, 1943, Hunt papers, box 1, Folder: "Heart Mountain," AHC
42 Hosokawa, *Nisei*, 351
43 Mackey, *Heart Mountain*, 48
44 "Heart Mountain residents join Thanksgiving Day Feats," *Sentinel*, November 27, 1942, 1
45 Hosokawa, *Nisei*, 351
46 Newton, *Justice for All*, 175
47 "Hunt Takes Oath as Governor" *Wyoming State Tribune* January 4, 1943, 7
48 Letter to Governor Hunt, March 6, 1943, box 1, File: "Heart Mountain," Hunt papers, AHC
49 Ehrlich, *Heart Mountain*, 179
50 *Congressional Record*, Vol. 89, Part 3, p. 4040, May 6, 1943
51 *Denver Post*, April 24, 1943
52 "1128 Leave for Harvest," *Sentinel*, October 24, 1942, 8
53 Letter from Harold A. Waechter, Recording Secretary to Governor Lester Hunt, May 8u, 1943, Hunt papers, box 1, Folder: "Heart Mountain," AHC
54 Letter from Governor Hunt to William J. Stone, dated April 26, 1943, File: "Wyoming-World War II-Gov. Hunt Correspondence" Box 36, Papers of T.A. Larson, AHC
55 Letter from Governor Hunt to Ella W. Hise, July 3, 1943, T.A. Larson papers, AHC
56 "Heart Editor Says Robertson Has Not Visited Jap Camp" *Laramie Daily Bulletin*, May 12, 1943, 1
57 "Senator Robertson, in Cody, declines invitation to center," June 12, 1943, 1
58 "Which War is Most Important" *Lovell Chronicle*, May 27, 1943
59 "Wyoming Senator Would Deport All Japs From US" *Rock Spring Rocket-Miner*, February 23, 1944
60 "Still strong, straight, and smiling," *Sentinel*, January 1, 1943, 5
61 Letter from Governor Hunt to US Senator A.B. Chandler, dated March 31, 1943, File: "Wyoming-World War II-Gov. Hunt Correspondence" Box 36, Papers of T.A. Larson
62 "Resolution of Policy Toward Japanese at Heart Mountain Relocation Center" File: "Heart Mountain" Box 1, LCH Papers

63 Letter from Hunt to Guy Robertson, May10, 1943, File: "Heart Mountain" Box 1, LCH Papers
64 Letter from Guy Robertson to Hunt, dated May 13, 1943, Id.
65 Letter from A.R. Fryer to Governor Hunt, June 21, 1944, Id.
66 Letter from Hunt to mayor O.E. Bever, dated August 8, 1944, File: "Heart Mountain Relocation Project" Box 1, LCH Papers
67 Letter from O.E. Bever to Hunt, August 12, 1944, Id.
68 Letter from Captain William R. Bradley to Hunt, dated August 22, 1944, Id.
69 Letter from Governor Hunt to Mayor Bever, dated August 31, 1944, Id
70 Letter from Milward Simpson to Governor Hunt, dated April 13, 1944, Id.
71 Letter from described above returned to Simpson with handwritten note from Hunt, "Dear Milward, We can find no record of any kind in this office." Id.
72 Letter from Guy Robertson to Governor Lester Hunt, August 2, 1945, Hunt papers, box 1, Folder: "Heart Mountain," AHC
73 *Personal Justice Denied*, 66
74 *Personal Justice Denied*, 187
75 "Selective Service Opens for Nisei," *Heart Mountain Sentinel*, January 22, 1944, 1
76 Mackey, *Heart Mountain*, 84-85
77 Higuchi, *Setsuko's Secret*, 123
78 "No Rules Prohibit Nisei from Any Service Branch," *Heart Mountain Sentinel*, February 26, 1944, 1
79 "ACLU Takes Issue with Okamoto," *Heart Mountain Sentinel*, April 15, 1944, 1
80 Higuchi, *Setsuko's Secret*, 122
81 "Robertson's Nephew Killed in Sicily," *Heart Mountain Sentinel*, August 21, 1943, 1
82 "Life-long Stigma Awaits Nisei Who Fail to Serve," *Heart Mountain Sentinel*, March 6, 1943, 1
83 "Our Cards Are on the Table-Editorial," *Heart Mountain Sentinel*, March 11, 1944, 5
84 "Jury Indict Delinquents as 25 Leave for Service," *Heart Mountain Sentinel*, May 13, 1944, 1
85 "Members of Religious Sect Made to Kiss Flag in Wyoming," *Corpus Christi Times*, June 19, 1940, 1.
86 "The Teapot Dome Scandal," *wyohistory.org*, https://www.wyohistory.org/encyclopedia/teapot-dome-scandal, accessed March 24, 2022
87 Muller, *Free to Die for Their Country*, 104
88 Kennedy, *Memoirs*,615, Kennedy papers, Box 1, AHC
89 Kennedy, "The Race Problem in America, Kennedy Papers," Undated Manuscript of speech delivered to the Young Men's Literary Club of Cheyenne, Kennedy papers, Box 3, Folder: "Papers and Addresses 1906-1930, AHC
90 Kennedy, "Will the New immigration Policy Improve American Citizenship?" May 16, 1924, Box 3, Folder: Papers and Addresses 1906-1930, Kennedy papers, AHC
91 "Judge Kennedy's Decision Slated Monday Afternoon," *Heart Mountain Sentinel*, June 24, 1944, 1
92 Higuchi, *Setsuko's Secret*, 130-131
93 White, *Wyoming in Mid-Century*, 126
94 Higuchi, *Setsuko's Secret*, 266
95 *Personal Justice Denied*, 93

96 *Personal Justice Denied*, 245
97 http://cgm.smithsonianapa.org/stories/stanley-hayami.html, accessed March 4, 2022 (all quotes from Stanley Hayami's diary are found at the same link)
98 "Going for Broke: The 442nd Regimental Combat Team," September 24, 2020, https://www.nationalww2museum.org/war/articles/442nd-regimental-combat-team, accessed March 4, 2022; also http://cgm.smithsonianapa.org/stories/stanley-hayami.html, the source for the description of Pvt. Hayami's bravery in action
99 http://cgm.smithsonianapa.org/stories/ted-fujioka.html
100 Mackey, *Heart Mountain*, 109
101 Higuchi, *Setsuko's Secret*, 153
102 "Facts and Case Summary – *Korematsu v United States*, https://www.uscourts.gov/educational-resources/educational-activities/facts-and-case-summary-korematsu-v-us, accessed March 7, 2022
103 "To Secure These Rights," Report of President Harry S. Truman's Committee on Civil Rights, published in 1997, Bedfords/St. Martin's 71
104 Higuchi, *Setsuko's Secret*, 167-168
105 "Special Instructions for Next Week" *Heart Mountain Sentinel Supplement*, November 2, 1945, final bulletin issued.
106 Edgar Allan Poe, *The Raven*
107 Higuchi, *Setsuko's Secret*, 254
108 "Heart Mountain Interpretive center Dedication Ceremony, American History TV, C-SPAN, August 20, 2011, https://www.c-span.org/video/?301340-1/heart-mountain-dedication-ceremony, accessed March 12, 2022

Chapter 12

"McCARTHYISM, THE JOHN BIRCH SOCIETY, AND THE GREEN BAY SWEEP"

"what you're seeing in your rearview mirror is closer than you think"

Wyoming was Trump before Donald Trump was conceived or conceivable. There was the anti-democratic attempt to repeal women's suffrage only a year after it was enacted. There was the Ku Klux Klan in the early 20th century. Joe McCarthy's witch hunts visited themselves tragically on Wyoming, targeting supposed Communists and homosexuals and taking the life of a United States Senator in the 50s. The John Birch Society followed McCarthy's tracks into the Cowboy State with its conspiracy theories through the 1950s, 60s and 70s. Other religious and political extremists followed into the 80s and 90s and on into the 21st century, opening a path for Trumpism today. There has always been a political subculture in Wyoming defined by conspiracy theories, which formed their politics and their views of government. Until now, the Republican Party was careful to keep the extremists in the shadows, distancing itself from them while subtlety taking advantage of votes they produced for GOP candidates.

With the election of Donald Trump in 2016, it became clear that the anti-democracy authoritarians many believed were in our rearview mirror were closer than we thought. This is the story of three Wyoming politicians who volunteered for the frontline to steer our democratic Republic on a course away from the authoritarian goals of McCarthyism, Bircherism, and Trumpism.

All who knew him would have been surprised when the mild-mannered Lester Hunt courageously became one of the first U.S. senators to challenge Joe McCarthy, exposing McCarthyism for the demagoguery that it was. No one who knew him was surprised when Gale McGee went toe to toe with the John Birch Society, warning Republicans in the 1960s that their Party had been invaded by extremists. On the other hand, anyone familiar with Liz Cheney's pro-Trump record expected her to join colleagues John Barrasso and Cynthia Lummis and others in backing Donald Trump's "big lie" even after the attempted coup of January 6, 2021. It stunned Donald Trump when she didn't. Once Ms. Cheney realized Trump posed a clear and present threat to the Republic, she risked both her career and her life to do what her conscience commanded.

In the beginning, as a group of powerful white men gathered in Cheyenne to create Wyoming, the 1890 Congress considered whether to make Wyoming the 44th state in the Union. Those who supported statehood advised their colleagues Wyoming would most certainly become "a strong, prosperous, and progressive state."[1] In the intervening years, it has, at times, been strong and, between the inevitable economic busts, even prosperous but seldom progressive, more often displaying a tendency to toward right-wing populism.

The first time Wyoming politicians dipped a big toe in the icy waters of progressivism, they pulled it back quickly, as if it had been caught in a beaver trap. It was 1869. Wyoming's 1st Territorial Legislature took the bold step of granting women the right to vote. A year later, Wyoming's 2nd Territorial Legislature was determined to take that right away. Women, some men felt, abused their right to vote by supporting Sunday closing laws imposed on saloons, "a very unpopular move in the hard-drinking railroad towns in southern Wyoming."[2] The 1870 election sent several suffrage opponents to the Capitol. A repeal measure passed 9-3 in the House and 5-4 in the Council (later renamed the state senate). Governor John Campbell vetoed the bill. The House voted to override his veto, which would have ended Wyoming's two-year-old experiment with women's suffrage had it not been for the failure of the Council to follow suit. There the veto was sustained by a single vote.[3] That, however, didn't mean it was settled.

Twenty years later, when delegates expected statehood to be conferred soon, they convened in Cheyenne to draft a constitution. By then Wyoming women had been voting for two decades. Many asked, "How could suffrage still be on the chopping block?" Yet, it was the first debate of any significance at the 1889 Constitutional Convention, opening with delegate A.C. Campbell's proposal to remove suffrage from the draft constitution and put it to a vote of the people. He recounted attending a women's convention in Omaha when "a young lawyer" cited Cheyenne, Laramie, and Rawlins as "three of the most lawless communities in the country." He blamed women voters. Campbell assured his colleagues he disagreed but, even so, felt the matter should be decided by the voters, not the delegates.[4] When Campbell's proposal was rejected, a second amendment was offered to strictly limit the right to vote to men. Eventually, the convention determined the right to vote "shall not be abridged on account of sex," but not before the debate turned to dog whistles about race and whether voters should successfully complete literacy tests.

A.C. Campbell, now a full-fledged supporter of extended suffrage, argued vehemently that if a citizen was required to pay taxes and fight for his or her country, they should be allowed to elect those who made decisions about their lives. Convention President M.C. Brown injected race into the debate. "The welfare of the entire South," he cried, "was in danger as a result of ignorant Blacks being allowed to vote."[5] Brown was apparently not distracted by the irony that Southern states enacted laws preventing the education of slaves. He thought it appropriate to use freed slaves' lack of education to keep them from voting in the Equality State. In his retort, Campbell observed that the provision limiting the vote only to those who could read and write would have eliminated two-thirds of those who signed the Magna Carta since they were only able to scribble an "x" on the document.

As the debate continued, it was clear that the views of most of the delegates were rooted in racism masked as xenophobia. Some were concerned that the "foreign element" should be kept from voting. John Hoyt admitted to harboring a fear that a "tide of people who did not understand our customs" would move into the state. The education requirement "would help to control that element." Campbell's effort to stop it was defeated 22-12.[6] And so it was that, from the beginning, Wyoming's first Constitution included a suffrage provision to keep "the foreign element" out of the voting booth. It read:

> *"No person shall have the right to vote who shall not be able to read the Constitution of the State."*

Although such limitations to the right to vote were ended three quarters of a century later when Congress passed the Voting Rights Act of 1965, the 1889 debate demonstrates Wyoming's origin story is rife with flirtations with right-wing ideology and its characteristic racism and xenophobia witnessed to this very day. Chart the political winds against which only the most courageous men and women were able to stand. They have blown across Wyoming since Territorial days, most always from the far right.

Anyone arriving in Wyoming after the mid-1970s might think the state was always dominated by the extreme side of conservatism. It wasn't. After 1913 when the U.S. Constitution was amended to allow voters rather than state legislators to choose United States senators, Wyoming voters were as likely to elect a Democrat as a Republican. However, when Gale McGee lost his bid for a fourth term in 1976, he became the last Democrat the state ever elected to the Senate. In their book *Right-Wing Populism in America*, Chip Berlet and Matthew N. Lyons document how, "Since the 1970s, the political center of gravity in the United States has moved dramatically to the right."[7] Wyoming's experience tracks that trend.

The year McGee was defeated, Teno Roncalio was easily re-elected to a fifth term in the U.S. House of Representatives (56%-44%). In the process of winning, he became the last Democrat Wyoming ever sent to Congress. In the years since, Wyoming has taken a sharp turn to the political right *en route* to becoming a one-party state. The numbers tell the story. When Roncalio was last elected to Congress, there were 63,752 registered Republican voters and 56,359 Democrats, a margin of less than 7,400 votes. As of primary election day 2022, the difference grew to more than twenty-four times greater than it was in 1976; 215,195 Republicans and 36,403 Democrats. The ideological divide is even greater than those number reveal. As a result, you must go back to 2006 to find a statewide election won by a Democrat. Since then, with one exception, Republican candidates amassed no fewer than 67% of the vote, most capturing at least seven out of ten votes cast.

The reversal of fortunes is further confirmed in state legislative contests. In 1976, a respectable 29 of the 62 state house seats were taken by Democrats who also held 12 of the 30 senate seats. That was the Democrats' high-water mark in the 44 years that have come and gone since. Republican majorities steadily increased election after election until 2020, when the GOP won 28 of the 30 senate seats and Democrats held only six of the 60 house seats. Percentages of Republican office holders at the county level were even higher.[8] In presidential contests since 1976, Jimmy Carter scored higher than any Democratic Party nominee, receiving 39% of the vote, losing the state's three electoral votes to Gerald Ford. In 2020, Donald Trump won 70% to Joe Biden's meager 26.5%.

This didn't occur in a vacuum. It wasn't only in Wyoming that "the political center of gravity moved dramatically to the right."[9] Many of the most powerful and notable members of the United States Senate before the mid- 1970s were Westerners and Democrats. Mike Mansfield and Lee Metcalf of Montana. Frank Moss of Utah. George McGovern and James Abourezk of South Dakota. Frank Church of Idaho. All gone and each replaced by senators committed to far-right ideology with the exception of Montana's centrist Democrat, Senator Jon Tester. In Wyoming, the center of gravity shifted on ground that had been plowed much earlier. The clouds hanging over Wyoming politics started gathering long before 1976. What was referenced in the first chapter of this book is worth repeating. A panel of Wyoming's most esteemed historians reviewed Wyoming's 20th century to identify the "top 10 stories" of that 100-year period. Their conclusions demonstrate a historic pattern of acting out biases against women and social, cultural, and racial minorities. They cited glaring events in the state's history; the "Equality State's unequal treatment of women" and its "lack of commitment to women's rights throughout our whole history." Heart Mountain made their list as did, "violence against Jehovah's Witnesses,"[10] the Black 14 scandal, the murder of Matthew Shepard, and "the mistreatment of Indians."[11] That's a lot to cram into a single century.

The list could have been longer, more complete if it included all the years since Wyoming was colonized. It could have included the tragedy of 1885, when a group of white workers unhappy because the Union Pacific Railroad used Chinese workers as strike breakers, "killed twenty-eight Chinese, wounded fifteen others, chased several hundred other Chinese out of town and destroyed property valued at $147,000 in what's known as the Rock Springs Massacre."[12]

The panel of historians didn't include their colleague Todd Guenther's research, reviewing the tragic lynching chronicles. Guenther concluded, "A black man's life wasn't worth much in Wyoming." He calculates that between 1910 and 1920, blacks were lynched in Wyoming at a per capita rate higher than in the state of Mississippi.[13] The historian told of Ku Klux Klan operations throughout Wyoming in the 1920s and documented that, "All across the state" businesses posted signs in their front windows saying, "No Indians, No Mexicans, No Negroes."[14]

Political scientists describe attitudes leading to these behaviors with the term "producerism." John "Chip" Berlet is an investigative journalist and research analyst who focuses on conspiracy theorists. Historian Matthew Lyons has written extensively about right-wing movements. In their book *Right-Wing Populism in America: Too Close for Comfort*, Berlet and Lyons describe the core of right-wing political ideology as "producerism." It sees society as consisting of two kinds of people, i.e., "producers" and those who are "unproductive." In their minds, producers are generally white middle-class males. They are contrasted against low-income workers, women, people of color, those on welfare, government employees or "bureaucrats," and "elites" such as bankers and corporate executives. "In this way, producerism bolstered white supremacy, blurred actual class divisions, and embraced some elite groups while scapegoating others."[15]

Producerism is the lens through Wyoming viewed the economic collapse known as the Great Depression. Historian T.A. Larson says Wyoming adopted President Herbert Hoover's position that "it is not the function of the government to relieve individuals of their responsibilities to their neighbors." Wyoming held to that approach "longer than elsewhere in the country."[16] Wyoming refused to accept millions in federal funds that could have alleviated the suffering.

An editorial in the December 8, 1933, *Wyoming Eagle* called economic conditions confronting the state, "the most serious situation in its history." By then, most were painfully aware that "thousands of cases of undernourished children" filled every community. As a special session convened on December 4, 1933, to deal with the problems, Governor Miller told the Republican-dominated legislature about those kids and the suffering of their families.

> *"There is abroad in our state a condition arising from long continued unemployment and the ravages of drouth more acute than generally realized, and I am convinced as of late that, as public servants, we have failed to measure up to our responsibilities in these matters."*[17]

While the GOP-led legislature refused Reconstruction Finance Corporation funding for relief projects, balances of the "Poor and Pauper Funds" in every county were exhausted. The Democratic Governor begged the legislature for $75,000 to "provide food, clothing, fuel, and shelter to the needy and deserving in this period of great need." He proposed it be paid for with a four cent per gallon tax on beer. It would be the last time the legislature ever raised the beer tax but not the last time the legislature took pride in refusing federal funds to help low-income citizens. While refusing funds to help people, Wyoming accepted "millions of dollars as her share in farm aid."[18] That is producerism, as is contemporary Wyoming farmers and ranchers receiving 38.2 million dollars for agricultural subsidies in

2020, $1.17 billion between 1995 and 2020, while the legislature refuses to expand Medicaid, denying healthcare to thousands of working families and threatening financial ruin for rural hospitals. State Senator Lynn Hutchings speaks fluent "producerism." A military veteran whose healthcare has been paid entirely by the taxpayers for much of her life, opposes Medicaid for low-income constituents because, she argues, the taxpayers should not have to pay for everyone's healthcare. She says government is getting too big and costing too much. Sociologist Sara Diamond sees through that argument, calling it a guise.

> *"To be right-wing means to support the state in its capacity as enforcer of order and to oppose the state as distributor of wealth and power downward and more equitably in society."*[19]

Beret and Lyons understand what is going on in Wyoming and believe we should take the threat seriously. "The scapegoating and conspiracism of right-wing populism, exploiting anti-elite resentments inextricably rooted in social inequality and oppression, is not on the margins of U.S. political traditions, but it too close for comfort."[20]

Long before Congressman Liz Cheney stood courageously against Trumpism, U.S. Senator Lester Hunt stood tall against the harsh Wyoming winds created by McCarthyism as U.S. Senator Gale McGee did against the John Birch Society.

McCarthyism[21]
n.
1. The practice of publicizing accusations of political disloyalty or subversion with insufficient regard to evidence.
2. The use of unfair investigatory or accusatory methods in order to suppress opposition.

On the night he died, Socrates bathed and then gathered his closest friends around him. They urged him to flee into exile to avoid the death sentence he'd been given. He always counseled others to follow the law and he would do so as well, even unto his own demise. Many around him wept loudly. It fell on the man who was about to drink the poisonous hemlock to reassure them. "Calm yourselves and try to be brave." Plato reported Socrates "quite calmly and with no sign of distaste, drained the cup in one breath."[22]

In the ancient world, it was considered noble to take control of one's life in the face of tyranny even unto a self-induced death. After Socrates beathed his last, the jailer testified, "Such was the end of our comrade, who was, we may fairly say, of all those whom we know in our time, the bravest and also the wisest and most upright man."

Ironically, those lofty words spoken of Socrates substantially mirror the words of the eulogies uttered by two of the three men whose tyrannical behavior was responsible for the suicide of Wyoming's U.S. Senator Lester Hunt. Senator Herman Welker of Idaho said Hunt "was truly emblematic of all that was good in America."[23] Senator Styles Bridges of New Hampshire observed that Hunt "demonstrated the best qualities that could characterize an American. He was loyal and true, and he served his State and Nation well."[24]

In the year before he took his own life, Styles and Bridges, aided by Senator Joseph McCarthy, made Lester Hunt's life a living hell in one of the most vicious scandals never investigated by the United States Senate.

It was a warm Washington evening in June 1953. Senator Hunt's twenty-five-year-old son Buddy made his way through Lafayette Park across the street from the White House. He made eye contact with a man who "was swaggering." It appeared to Buddy that he was "trying to get my attention."[25] Buddy was a seminary student at the time. He was also experimenting with bisexuality. Buddy knew Lafayette Park was a place frequented by gay men looking to hook up and it seemed obvious to him the fellow he encountered was interested in just that. What he didn't know was that the park was crawling with undercover agents who were part of the District of Columbia's "Pervert Elimination Campaign."[26] The conspiracy to blackmail Senator Hunt into resigning from the Senate began within hours of Buddy's arrest.

The impetus behind the Pervert Elimination Campaign was Joe McCarthy's claim that homosexuals were as much a security risk to the country as Communists. The campaign was organized for the purpose of entrapping homosexuals so that when they turned out to be government employees, they could be fired. The fear that caused the removal of thousands of men and women rumored to be homosexuals started with a 1947 letter to Secretary of State George Marshall cautioning of the "extensive employment in highly classified positions of admitted homosexuals, who are historically known to be security risks."[27]

Central figures in the tawdry blackmail scheme perpetrated against Lester Hunt seized on this issue. When he realized McCarthy may have bitten off more than he could chew, claiming the government was teeming with Communists, Senator Styles Bridges used the cause of removing homosexuals from government to distract the public from the fact that McCarthy could not find many Communists.[28] The argument began with a bizarre conspiracy theory. Nebraska Congressman Arthur L. Miller, a self-proclaimed expert on homosexuals, claimed the C.I.A. informed him that Adolf Hitler and Herman Goering had a "complete list of homosexuals in the State Department, the Department of Commerce, and the Department of Defense, and they knew whom to contact when they came over here on espionage missions."[29] After Hitler and Goering died, the ominous list, the conspiracists continued, fell into the hands of Stalin who was now busily recruiting Soviet agents from among the names.[30]

A careful search of the correspondence received by Senator Hunt during these years failed to turn up a single letter expressing concern about whether homosexuals were employed in the State Department. Though it might not have been an issue yet back home, it was becoming the focus of McCarthyism in Washington. Bridges cried that the State Department purposely recruited "homosexuals and subversive agents" because, he alleged, "Russia wanted them there."[31] So it was that when Bridges and Welker learned of young Hunt's arrest, they saw an opportunity to force the Democrat Hunt from office. They surmised the Republican governor of Wyoming would replace him with a Republican, thus shifting control of the Senate to their party.

After charges against Buddy were dismissed, Bridges asserted his power to have them reinstated. Buddy was tried and convicted of a misdemeanor and paid a $100 fine. The ordeal took a terrible toll on the family, but it had just begun. In the coming months, Welker sent word to Hunt that if he didn't resign, the Republicans would use Buddy's conviction as a political weapon in Hunt's 1954 re-election campaign. Hunt refused to resign. The onslaught worsened. Someone broke into his District of Columbia home and ransacked it while the Hunts were in Wyoming over the Christmas holiday. The following spring, Senator Welker let it be known that while many Wyoming newspapers had refused to run the story of Buddy's trial,[32] he would make sure the information found its way into every mailbox in the state.[33] He printed 25,000 flyers to send to Wyoming voters.

Despite it all, Hunt formally announced he was a candidate for reelection. Then President Eisenhower got involved. A note found among Eisenhower's official papers is headed "L.C. Hunt, Senator-Possibilities." The document bears a notation verifying it was "Received May 3, 1954 – Central Files." It lists eight executive branch jobs. Someone who likely had the authority to commit to a presidential appointment placed a mark near "Tariff Commission: $15,000—Six-year term."[34] (In 1954 a senator was paid $12,000 a year.) If Hunt would leave the senate race, the President offered to appoint him Chairman of the Federal Tariff Commission.

After his staff and his wife persuaded him to reject Eisenhower's overture, the walls closed in around Lester Hunt. He was publicly committed to a re-election campaign. Friends had already contributed thousands of dollars. It was too late for the party to recruit a replacement. Still, he knew the campaign risked exposing his wife and son to an ordeal he could not willingly permit them to suffer. Initially he decided to push forward with his plans to seek reelection. He flew to Cheyenne with the announced intentions of filing his formal candidacy with the Secretary of State's office. He returned to Washington having not done so. "Something must have taken place in Cheyenne," his administrative aide Mike Manatos said years later. "The only explanation Hunt had was that he just wanted to get away from it all."[35]

On June 4 Hunt sent a letter to Joe Hickey, the Wyoming Democratic Party chairman. "Regret exceedingly at this date to advise you that," he wrote, "due to personal reasons beyond my control, namely health, I am compelled to withdraw my announcement as a candidate for reelection to the United States Senate."[36]

A few days later, Hunt asked Leslie Miller to come to his office for a visit.[37] He began by sharing polls to assure Miller he could be reelected. Fear of losing was not the reason he'd withdrawn. Neither was his health. Hunt explained. Buddy's trial and the ongoing threats "almost killed" his wife Nathelle and him. Hunt told Miller the whole story of how he was being pressured by Bridges and Welker. He called it "blackmail." Hunt was also aware the two senators were spreading another conspiracy theory, claiming the detective who initially dismissed the charges had taken a bribe to halt Buddy's prosecution. The following Thursday, Hunt's old friend Joe O'Mahoney dropped by for a visit. He found Hunt "pale and depressed."

The following day, Senator McCarthy informed the press he intended to open hearings to investigate a fellow senator "who had fixed a case."[38] Lester Hunt recalled his son had told him an elevator operator in the Senate Office Building had overheard the Wisconsin Senator and another man talking. "McCarthy was on his way down (riding the elevator) and he was talking about you and this and that," said the elevator operator, "and he's about to take your father on because of you and your activities."[39]

The Wyoming Senator knew immediately what the coming days of his life and the lives of his wife and son would be like. McCarthy hearings had ruined the lives of many innocent people, driving some to suicide. The truth didn't matter. Hunt witnessed McCarthy's hold on Wyoming voters two years earlier. McCarthy was largely responsible for his colleagues 1952 defeat, when the Wisconsin Senator attracted one of the biggest crowds for a political rally in Wyoming history where he brutally attacked Joe O'Mahoney. More troubling was that he, his wife, and his son would be dragged through the mud by a cruel demagogue who was willing to say anything. The accusations would be headlines, Hunt's rebuttal buried in a follow-up story.

The next morning, June 19, 1954, Lester Hunt rose from bed early after a sleepless night. He kissed his wife goodbye and drove to his Senate office. There, seated at his desk, Hunt killed himself for much the same reason Socrates did centuries earlier, to take control of his own life in the face of tyranny. But McCarthy's life had begun to spin out of control.

A year later the Wisconsin Senator was formally censured by his Senate colleagues and his life began a slow certain decline into the depths of alcoholism, which ended with his death on May 2, 1957.

But old demagogues never die. Under the laws of political evolution, they quickly morph and find new life in the skewed thinking of others. Much like the process of "cooking" dead leaves and grass clippings into compost, eventually the old movement becomes fertilizer for future extremists. Within a few years, McCarthyism became Bircherism.

Bircherism[40]

n.

Bircherism (the teaching of the John Birch Society) expressed a belief in domestic communist conspiracies. They went so far as to accuse President Dwight Eisenhower and Chief Justice Earl Warren of being Communist dupes and agents – building on the legacy of Sen. Joseph McCarthy whose movement of predominantly Midwestern Republicans found the society's agenda appealing.

Post-World War II America was ripe for conspiracy theorists. Communist boogeymen were perceived to be hiding behind every bush. With Joe McCarthy fully discredited, the right needed another bugler. The heir of Joe McCarthy's brand of anti-communism was the John Birch Society (JBS). They worried about the loyalty of FDR, Eisenhower, and Truman. They saw anti-American plotting in the New Deal, the Second World War, the Korean War, universal healthcare, and federal housing programs, as well as McCarthy's 1954 censure. Robert Welch founded the organization, which reflected his "tendency toward melodramatic, if not apocalyptic, rhetoric and a firm belief in the revelatory power of the conspiratorial."[41]

The JBS origin myth is an example of Welch's skills. Welch happened to be in a Senate Office Building committee room listening to a discussion of foreign policy when he first heard John Birch's name. His ears perked as he learned of a young man born to missionary parents, raised on a Georgia farm, who volunteered for General Claire Chennault's Flying Tigers mission to save some of "Doolittle's Raiders" who had ditched their planes during a bold raid inside China in 1942. Welch created a myth of how Birch was involved in a dispute with a squad of Chinese guerillas. It ends with Birch's dramatic death. A Lieutenant Tung, a member of JBS, claims to have been a witness as Birch was bayoneted to death, proclaiming with his last breath, "It doesn't make much difference what happens to me, but it is of utmost importance that my country learn now whether these people are friend or foe."

Welch recognized immediately what could be done with a story like that. It had all the elements to motivate a conservative audience. A boy with a rural, Christian upbringing, grows into a courageous young man, finds himself cast against a larger-than-life conspiracy, left alone to fight the good fight, bravely martyring himself to expose the truth. It was the central plot in Welch's 1954 book *The Life of John Birch: The Story of One American Boy, the Ordeal of His Age*. John Birch became, in the words of Robert Welch, "the first American casualty of World War III."[42]

The John Birch Society was not well enough organized to have a role in Dr. Gale McGee's 1958 campaign for the U.S. Senate. But a university professor with expertise on the Soviet Union and other foreign policy matters whose campaign was backed by Eleanor Roosevelt and the Council on Foreign Relations was the sort of target that could not avoid the scrutiny of JBS plotters. The fact that McGee was an articulate opponent of Soviet aggression did not shield him from Welch's sense that "in the conspiracy of history, things are never what they seem, and are often the opposite."[43]

As he began thinking about his 1964 re-election campaign, McGee took note of "the hardening of lines" and the "emergence of name-calling." He didn't see it as coincidental that John Birch chapters were popping up across Wyoming. He saw the ubiquitous billboards along Wyoming roads urging, "Get US out of the UN" and "Impeach Earl Warren." He read full-page ads soliciting JBS membership and was aware of how saturated local radio stations were with far-right programming. With little television coverage across much of the state, and with only weekly newspapers in most communities, radio provided most of the electronic entertainment and news. Though it would become more vitriolic later with talk show hosts like Rush Limbaugh and Cable TV stars like Sean Hannity and Tucker Carlson, even in the early 1960s, the radical right dominated the air. Most station owners offered it to their listeners as "a public service." A few radio stations were paid to run the programming. H.L. Hunt, for example, was a billionaire who owned the Hoodoo Ranch near Cody.[44] Hunt pedaled a fifteen-minute daily dose of extremism called "Lifeline" to radio stations across Wyoming.

Senator McGee warned President John Kennedy, who was also thinking ahead to his own 1964 campaign, "It would be difficult to exaggerate how the concentration of these programs in limited population areas ultimately captures the public mind, even among well-meaning citizens."[45]

McGee knew a confrontation with JBS was unavoidable. He made the strategic decision to be intentional about placing himself directly in their crosshairs. In turn, the Wyoming chapters of the John Birch Society set a goal to defeat McGee in 1964. They knew how to play hardball. In an article titled "Conspiracy USA," published in *Look* magazine, one of McGee's colleagues, Senator Frank Church of Idaho, described the confrontations his Wyoming colleague experienced. "In Wyoming, Sen. Gale McGee, an outspoken critic of the Radical Right, found youngsters in Laramie and Cheyenne on a house-to-house canvas distributing mimeographed leaflets. They were instructed to say, 'This man is an enemy agent. Here are the facts about Communist McGee.'"[46]

The JBS state president, whom McGee did not name in an interview recalling this incident, was an old duck-hunting friend of the Senator. Though they'd spent hours chattering away in duck blinds, his friend now refused to accept McGee's phone calls. After McGee's 1964 reelection, the fellow apologized. "I was sure taken in by those rascals," he told his friend. "I thought they were good Americans trying to find spies and Communists and I was helping. They just took me in, and I want to apologize."[47]

Others weren't nearly so kind as to simply refuse to take his phone calls. In Big Piney, a JBS member spat in the Senator's face. Mrs. McGee said, "They stole things from our car." On a freezing late fall night in Douglas, while McGee spoke to a local gathering, someone squirted shaving cream on the windows of his station wagon. It froze and they spent hours removing it so that he and Loraine could drive on to the next rally.

Kathleen Karpan, Wyoming's Secretary of State from 1987-1995, then a reporter for the *Cody Enterprise*, recalled the time Senator McGee came to speak to Park County businesspeople in the early 1960s. When word got out that McGee was coming, a group of Birchers, mostly local ranchers, made plans to confront the Senator. They were angry about McGee's support for social programs, what they deemed socialism. McGee supporters told him to be prepared. He was. No sooner had he been introduced than several in the crowd began stomping their feet and creating a disturbance. McGee asked them to relax, assuring them he'd take their questions and hear them out. He wanted to make a few remarks first. The crowd settled as McGee pulled a stack of papers from his briefcase.

"I have here some public records. No secrets here. All of these are open to anyone who wants to see them. What I have is a list of Park County folks who are receiving money from the federal government, agricultural subsidies." Their Senator began reading names and amounts received. McGee confronted the hypocrisy of Bircher claims that the federal government interfered in people's lives and wasted tax dollars on the poor and disadvantaged, while many of them "were usually the first in line to get federal funds."[48] Several of those on the list were in the room preparing to attack McGee for his "socialist" votes. Many quietly left. The threatened protest dissipated.

On another occasion in Cody, a group of JBS supporters threatened physical violence. "Several of my former students in the audience, three or four of them had been football players at Wyoming…put together a flying wedge…in order to get me out of there safely."[49] In the lobby of Casper's Henning Hotel, the Senator was physically grabbed "by some husky cattlemen. They were very threatening." They raised their voices and clenched their fists. McGee's staff intervened "and made sure there was no violence, but it was sure a hairy moment."[50]

The JBS whispering campaign coloring McGee a "pinko" got louder and concerns about physical violence heightened as the John Birch Society made the defeat of the Wyoming Senator its number one national goal. It led McGee to warn President Kennedy of what he thought was the insidious nature of the right wing's appeal to "our population in the West (who) already believe the extreme right-wing line before the current group of extremists invented it."[51] In early 1963, JFK asked McGee to study the impact of groups like the John Birch Society on both men's chances for reelection. Kennedy told McGee his plan was to use Congressional investigations to marginalize them long before the November election. McGee suggested otherwise.

"One word of caution, it seems to me, is in order," McGee's memo to the President warned. "It revolves around the question of timing. A wide-open investigation in the Congress of the right-wing groups now might have the effect of killing them dead before next fall." McGee thought that making the extremists the issue in 1964 was preferable to running them off the playing field too early.[52] McGee's relentless attacks on the right wing were paying off. Even his conservative colleague Senator Milward Simpson was forced to deny he was a member of the John Birch Society. Using language evoking memories of the victims of Joe McCarthy's attacks a decade earlier, Senator Simpson said, "I am not now, nor have I ever been a member of the John Birch Society."[53]

McGee thought the behavior of the John Birch Society "may well turn out to be the winning issue for 1964. He and the President began coordinating a response. Then came November 22, 1963, in Dallas. McGee immediately knew who was to blame.

Senator Gale McGee accompanied President Kennedy on JFK's September 1963 visit to Wyoming. Photo courtesy of Robert McGee and used with permission.

During a Democratic Party dinner as the 1964 campaign got underway, McGee took off the gloves. He said those who "continually downgrade the American government" are enemies of freedom. Referring to Kennedy's murder, the Senator said, "We have paid a heavy price for permitting the erratic, the distorted and the hateful among us to determine the climate of American opinion."[54] The federal lawmaker took the unprecedented step of going after state lawmakers, charging they were overly influenced by JBS. As if determined to prove McGee's point, conservative state legislators introduced resolutions expressing their right-wing mood on national issues. One reaffirmed "support for the House Committee on Un-American Activities and the Senate Internal Security Committee."[55] A second opposed any future increase in social security.[56] They called for the end to all foreign aid,[57] and asked Congress to repeal the Arms Control and Disarmament Act.[58] The legislature went on record opposing any additional wilderness land designations in the state.[59] State lawmakers passed another resolution asking for the establishment of a "Court of the Union" to review decisions made by the U.S. Supreme Court.[60]

McGee had a nose for these things. He sniffed out the influence of the John Birch Society and openly criticized conservative state legislators with being a part of a scheme "to destroy democracy as we know it." He called them "gullible" and said they were too quick to adopt ideas thoughtful people ridiculed.[61]

John Wold, McGee's 1964 opponent, said McGee should take a "loyalty oath" because of his criticism of right-wing influence in the state.[62] Democratic Party Chairman Walter Phelan counterpunched. "If Mr. Wold thinks everyone in Wyoming is supposed to agree with the right-wing record of the 37th Legislature and deny the existence of right-wing groups in Wyoming, it seems far more appropriate to ask a sanity oath of Wold than a loyalty oath of Senator McGee."[63]

With many Democrats reluctant to take the Birchers head on, McGee provided liberals with a powerful voice, exposing the Society in televised debates across the country. He crisscrossed the nation, debating dozens of JBS officials throughout 1964. He exposed Bircher tactics in Senate speeches and before any audience that would listen. As he celebrated his 1964 re-election McGee knew the battle with rightwing extremism had not been won. McGee's aggressive approach in the 1964 campaign worked in the short run but, as the Wyoming Senator predicted in 1965, his victory and Lyndon Johnson's landslide only served to whet the appetite of conspiracy theorists.

Looking back from where Wyoming politics are today, it can be said Senator Gale McGee was indeed prophetic. On July 15, 1965, McGee told an auditorium filled with Georgetown University students that "Goldwater's defeat served to reinforce their view that America is awash in a tide of Communism." The right had come to believe that mainstream Republicans were part of the problem they wanted to solve. As the right turned to conspiracy theories about Goldwater, McGee predicted LBJ's victory would serve to recruit at least a 50% increase in Bircher membership in the coming year.

The Senator had a sober mind and a crystal ball. Appearing on an NBC special report investigating fringe groups in June 1966, McGee said the rightwing extremists were a great danger, not to liberals, but to "the constructive voice of conservatism at a time when we need that voice expressed as articulately as possible."[64] In August 1966, McGee told an Indiana convention the Bircher strategy of infiltrating school boards and Parent Teacher Associations was working to strengthen their organization. He said Robert Welch's "finger was pointing in only one direction," i.e., "seize control of the PTA and the school boards." McGee explained the plan was "integrated, organized, and directed by the John Birch Society." In October, McGee told the Minnesota Education Association that while it was popular to say that after Goldwater's landslide defeat, the "extremists backs were broken," it was not true. He said the 1964 election was taken by the right to mean they could not count on mainstream Republicans, who they now believed were as much of an enemy as Democrats. McGee warned Republicans that they would suffer the consequences of failing to rid their party of the rightwing extremists.[65] The warning went unheeded.

After McGee's 1976 defeat, Wyoming conservatism continued its journey toward extremism. As the 1970's gave way to the 1980s, the popularity of JBS waned nationally but held steady in Wyoming. The state and every surrounding state except Colorado remained among the top ten nationally in percentage of population still claiming JBS membership.⁶⁶ In time, the label "John Bircher" fell out of mode but the conspiracy theorists and scapegoaters did not. The new right emphasized social issues such as abortion, education, crime, and homosexuality. As the 20th century came to a close and the 21st began, Wyoming politics was an incubator for Trumpism.

Trumpism⁶⁷

n.

A social/political movement based on elements of (a) racism, (b) religious bigotry, (c) demeaning attitudes towards women, (d) attempts to intimidate the press, (e) economic uncertainty, (f) rejection of scientific findings, and (g) general expressions of hatred that are reminiscent of German National Socialism of the Hitler era. It is often characterized by completely baseless, false statements.

This is not Liz Cheney's biography. It is the story of the events that led her from the politics of acquiescence to the politics of personal courage. A raw survey of Wyoming's political history allows for full appreciation of the strength of the political winds blowing against Liz Cheney when she decided Donald Trump was unfit to be President. Looking back, you can see that the Klan begat McCarthyism, which begat the John Birch Society. The John Birch Society begat the Liberty Lobby. The Liberty Lobby begat the Christian Right and the Moral Majority, which, in turn, begat a plethora of rightwing crusaders like WyWatch, CROW, the Wyoming Liberty Group, and the Right to Life Movement. In time, they begat Donald Trump. Donald Trump begat Trumpism and QAnon, the Proud Boys, and the Oath Keepers. The cycle continues from one generation to the next. The Old Right finds a way to become the New Right and, ironically, as if to substantiate Darwin's theory, each evolutionary transition begats a better organized, more sophisticated, though distorted but increasingly effective, appeal to white male grievances. Today, they are aided by a Cable TV and social media cabal with enhanced ability to sow the field with conspiracy theories, harvesting the fruits of producerism, scapegoating, and "alternative facts." The result includes manufactured culture wars, enlisting those with the inevitable fears arising from economic, social, and political trends and natural demographic changes.

After the waning of the Klan, McCarthyism, and the John Birch Society, Wyoming's hard right was relatively quiet during the 80s but was reawakened by the nationalization of Wyoming politics and a "purity movement." During the 1990s, Wyoming's extremists came under the spell of Congressman Newt Gingrich of Georgia. Wyoming Congressman Barbara Cubin was an acolyte. John Barrasso joined later, followed by Cynthia Lummis. As Gingrich became the national voice of conservatism in the mid-1990s, he "set the United States on a course toward the ruinous politics of today."[68] Politicians watching him lie, be called out for lying, and doubling down on the lie, took notice. In his book *The Destructionists: The Twenty-five Year Crack-up of the Republican Party*, reporter Dana Milbank said Gingrich set a standard for Trump by employing political attacks which were not supported by evidence, repeating such attacks even when disproven, using the most incendiary language and demonstrating no shame when his charges were exposed as lies or hypocrisy.[69] During this time, the political rhetoric in Wyoming began changing to match that coming from the national stage as it provided a foundation for the purity movement. It started to become "my way or the highway" for not only democrats but moderate, fellow Republicans.

While conservatism in Wyoming always teetered on extremism, the genesis of today's rendition of the far-right GOP can be found in a Defense Department employee named Harlan J. Edmunds. He was transferred to Wyoming in 1993, just before Gingrich's rise to power. He thought he was moving to "a conservative sanctuary," but found Wyoming conservativism "to be lousy with liberals and political opportunists."[70] Seeing the Republican Party goal of building a "big tent" as "insidious," Edmunds founded a new organization in 2012. He called it CROW, an acronym for Conservative Republicans of Wyoming. Its purpose was to close the flaps of the Republican Party's "big tent" to "all but true red, white and blue conservatives." Edmunds and his wife Amy served brief stints in the Wyoming legislature, where they honed their sense of self-righteousness and worked in tandem to unmask moderate Republicans. The two slowly disappeared from politics but the purity movement strategy they perfected to identify those Republicans who didn't toe the line 100% of the time remains. Today the state and local party regularly censures or officially condemns fellow Republicans who stray.[71]

Wyoming historian Phil Roberts once headed the University of Wyoming's history department. The professor believes CROW was an evolutionary product of the John Birch Society. He accurately predicted CROW's purity campaign would infect Wyoming politics with the dysfunction of national politics "because of the stridency and refusal to compromise" that Edmunds brought to Wyoming.[72]

By then, mainstream Wyoming Republicans were in the crosshairs of a movement characterized by a group calling itself WyWatch. It was, according to journalist Kerry Drake's salty description, "an anti-abortion, anti-gay, Bible-thumping, gun-toting, homeschool-supporting, keep-transgendered-people-out-of-women's restrooms group."[73] Republican State Representative Dan Zwonitzer, one of the purity movement's targets, said WyWatch was Wyoming's "first threatening organization." Zwonitzer said it was "a lot more 'my way or the highway.'"[74] Though WyWatch exercised considerable influence in Wyoming elections, engineering the defeat of "RINOs,"[75] while exercising an outsized voice in matters before the state legislature, it unexpectedly closed its doors in 2016. The ultra-conservative Wyoming Liberty Group took up the right-wing cudgel and guided the state Republican Party through its full conversion to the far right's tool.

Throughout the early years of the 21st century, they took a page from the Bircher playbook. Conservatives, particularly evangelical Christians, recruited like-minded Republicans to fill open seats on the county central committees. Soon they were the majority not only at the county level but in the state GOP central committee as well. In 2017, they elected one of their own as chair. Frank Eathorne, an evangelical Christian, had been an influential WyWatch organizer and is currently a member of the Oath Keepers, whose leaders were charged with "seditious conspiracy" in the January 6,

2021, insurrection.[76]

Eathorne is unapologetic about limiting who can be considered a good Republican. "In Wyoming, we don't necessarily embrace the idea of a big tent," he said on Fox News in 2022. Mary Martin, chairman of the Teton County Republicans and an Eathorne supporter, admitted her "disappointment in Frank is that he hasn't been able to come up with a process to keep the Republican Party with more of a big-tent approach." She acknowledged another problem. "We have a couple of people who come to the Wyoming party meetings who are absolute bullies."[77]

Under Eathorne's leadership the party earned a thuggish image. In 2018, the party's elected secretary was forced to take a plea bargain after he allegedly assaulted a woman serving as GOP executive director during a party function, "touching her in a rude, insolent manner by pushing her from behind and grabbing her clothing."[78] Gillette police later cited one the Republican Party's county chairmen after a fistfight with another county chairman at a GOP convention in 2020. The victim was hospitalized with serious injuries.[79] A Park County central committee member made the news when he sent an obscene letter to a Republican state senator in 2021. The letter was signed "Troy Bray, Precinct Committeeman, Park County (9-7)" and noted his official position as "Secretary, Park County Republican Men's Club." Bray told Senator Tara Nethercott, "If I were as despicable a person as you, I would kill myself to rid the world of myself. You sicken me." The email finished with four-letter words, one starting with the letter "f", the other "specifically derogatory towards women."[80]

Not one of these party officials was censured while it continued its condemnation of those they determined to be "Republicans in Name Only," including a nearly successful attempt to censure Matt Mead in 2014, while he was serving as Governor. By 2022, the definition of the term RINO had been further narrowed. "In a reflection of the GOP's murkier ideological grounding in the Trump era, it's a term reserved almost exclusively for lack of fealty to Trump." To be clear, no matter how loyal one was to the Trump agenda, anyone questioning Trump's contrived claims that he won the 2020 election was relegated to RINO status.[81] In Wyoming, Republicanism became Trumpism.

Nevertheless, in 2016, as he campaigned for president, Trump was not particularly popular in Wyoming. He was handily defeated by Texas Senator Ted Cruz in the state's GOP delegate contest.[82] As the results were announced, Trump test-marketed his now signature assertion that he could not possibly lose unless his opponent cheated. According to a CNN report, "Trump started calling foul well before votes were cast, saying on Fox and Friends *Saturday Morning* that states like Wyoming and Colorado show the system isn't fair. 'I don't want to waste millions of dollars going out to Wyoming many months before to wine and dine and to essentially pay off all these people because for a lot of them it's a pay-off,' Trump said. 'You understand that they treat 'em, they take 'em to dinner, they get 'em hotels. I mean the whole thing's a big pay-off, has nothing to do with democracy.'"[83]

Harriett Hageman was an early "never Trumper." In 2016, she was a close confidant of Liz Cheney and a Cruz supporter, lining herself up to run for Governor in 2018. A member of the GOP hierarchy, Hageman condemned Trump as a bigot who would repel the voters Republicans needed to win a national election, warning the GOP that if Trump was the nominee, it would be saddled with a "racist and xenophobic" candidate.[84] Despite such vitriol and a lopsided defeat for Trump, judging by the party platform, the Wyoming GOP was already more Trump than not. In 2016, Wyoming Republicans went on record supporting an isolationist foreign policy; opposing gays in the military; supporting reneging on the Iran agreement; demanding the U.S. withdraw from the United Nations, calling it a "socialistic organization;" denying citizenship to "anchor babies;" repealing or nullifying the Affordable Care Act; and opposing "resettlement of refugees in Wyoming."[85] The Wyoming Republican Party was hard-wired for Trump. After Trump won the nomination, he defeated Hillary Clinton 68%-22%, picking up Wyoming's three electoral votes with the strong support of Harriet Hageman and Liz Cheney.

Although Trump harshly criticized her father, former Vice-President Dick Cheney, Liz endorsed Trump, calling Hillary Clinton a "felon" with a "long history of not abiding by the law and getting away with it." Cheney asserted against Clinton words similar to those she would use four years hence to describe Trump. "There is just a level of slime and sleaze associated with the Clinton family, and we know in Wyoming we've gotta do everything possible to make sure they never get anywhere near the Oval Office," adding, "She would be the most corrupt individual ever to sit in the Oval Office, if she's elected."[86]

By then, Liz knew who Trump was. She listened in silence as Trump ridiculed John McCain's military service and the years he spent in a North Vietnamese prisoner of war camp. She heard him say McCain "is a war hero because he was captured. I like people who weren't captured." Liz watched him mimic a disabled man and said nothing when Trump implicated Ted Cruz's father in the assassination of JFK and offered multiple disgusting observations about various women. She knew his fraudulent Trump University had been exposed and repeatedly that Trump made continuous racist claims including alleging the Hispanic judge presiding over the fraud trial regarding his "university" could not be fair because of his ethnicity. As much as Liz had come to know about the GOP nominee, she was motivated more by the need to be a loyal Republican and supported Trump.

She was a faithful party member, whose impeccably partisan credentials as a conservative were well documented to include an occasional flirtation with a return to McCarthyism. She refused to denounce the false birtherism narrative that Barack Obama was a Kenyan Muslim and not an American Christian. She claimed lawyers representing GITMO prisoners were disloyal, while supporting the Bush-Cheney administration's use of torture.

In March 2019, Special Prosecutor Robert Mueller issued a "Report on the Investigation into Russian Interference in the 2016 Presidential Election." Mueller's report documented how Trump's campaign manager shared "internal polling data with a Russian agent,"[87] that in the summer of 2016, the Trump campaign was planning a press strategy, a communications campaign, and messaging based on the possible release of Clinton emails by WikiLeaks, that within five hours of Trump asking Russia 'to find the 30,000 emails that are missing,' Russian intelligence agents targeted Clinton's personal files,[88] and that Trump and his close aides and family had obstructed justice.[89] Willfully overlooking the serious red flags raised by the Mueller Report, Liz Cheney loyally participated in a campaign orchestrated by the President and his Attorney General William Barr to neutralize the impact of the findings. She issued a statement, mirroring the party line. "As the Attorney General's letter revealed a month ago, the release of this report confirms that Democrats have perpetuated a fraud on the American people for the last two years. There was no collusion."[90] She steadfastly protected the leader of her party until January 6, 2021.

A lot of brackish water would flow under the bridge before Cheney could see Donald Trump in a different light.

Cultism[91]

n.

The practices and devotions of a cult, creating an idealized and heroic image of a leader by a government, often through unquestioning flattery and praise. Historically, it has developed through techniques of mass media, propaganda, the big lie, fake news, spectacle, the arts, patriotism, and government-organized demonstrations and rallies.

"We need to get the ladies away from the aisle," Congressman Jim Jordan of Ohio, a Trump ally, said patronizingly. It was January 6, 2021. Members of the House of Representatives were hurriedly evacuating the chambers to find safety from the insurrectionists who could be heard chanting "Hang Mike Pence" and calling out threateningly, "Nancy, oh Nancy, where are you?" Jordan, whom Cheney called, "that son-of-a-bitch," reached out his arm to help a female colleague. "Let me help you." Jordan had chosen the wrong "lady" to lend his hand. Wyoming Congressman Liz Cheney was in no mood for Jordan's charity. She recalled the moment the following day. "That fucking guy," Cheney said. "I smacked his hand away and told him, 'Get away from me. You fucking did this.'"[92]

As attempted coups go, the plotters gave this one a cringe-worthy, frat-boy-like name. "The Green Bay Sweep." Legendary football coach Vince Lombardi drew it up for his Green Bay Packers. Lombardi explained to his team that the success of the play depended on the ability of the offense to overpower the defense as the quarterback takes the ball and runs parallel to the offensive line. He either keeps the ball or hands it to a running back as his linemen block defenders out of the play to enable the ball carrier to turn up field, find the weakness in the defense and run the ball into the end zone for the score.

Team Trump's version of the Green Bay Sweep started when they drafted members of Congress including Senators Ted Cruz, Josh Hawley, and Cynthia Lummis to block on January 6 as the House and Senate met to certify the electoral college results. Although Biden's victory was certified by the proper authorities in every state, it was their duty to raise objections claiming falsely that his victories in battleground states were produced by fraud as they tried to block the peaceful transfer of power. Peter Navarro, White House economic adviser turned political plotter, explained Vice-President Mike Pence was the quarterback. Head coach Donald Trump expected Pence to either carry the ball into the end zone himself or hand it off to the Republicans in swing states. They could then reverse the Biden win and keep Trump in power. The success of the Green Bay Sweep depended on whether Pence would accept the pretext that he had the legal authority to reject electors certified by states like Arizona, Michigan, Wisconsin, and Pennsylvania. If Pence played the game, those electors would be rejected, the path to the end zone would be clear.

There was only one problem. When the team huddled on January 6, quarterback Pence refused to call the Green Bay Sweep. Pence audibled. When Trump saw what was happening on the field, he called his own number, suited up and went into the game as a linebacker with the intent of sacking the quarterback and inflicting damage on his own teammate.

Donald Trump once said in Orwellian fashion, "What you're seeing and what you're reading is not what's happening." As the riot was brought under control, he and his supporters began a campaign to prove what Americans had seen with their own eyes and heard with their own ears was not what happened. As she was led from the Senate chambers amidst the turmoil of January 6, Wyoming Senator Cynthia Lummis said, "I hope it's not Trump supporters that are involved in the mayhem. In my previous experience with these Trump supporters, they have been peaceful demonstrators, happy people, very patriotic, pro-America, and I feel like other forces like Antifa were advocating violence."[93]

Liz was neither that clueless, nor that devious. The *Casper Star Tribune* noted all three members of Wyoming's congressional delegation "condemned the siege, albeit to varying degrees," but only Cheney condemned both, the attempted insurrection, and the President.

Cheney tired of Trump's antics earlier than most, criticizing some of his Tweets, his decision to reduce troop numbers in Europe, and his invitation to the Taliban to come to Washington for peace talks. By July of 2020, CNN noted that Cheney "increasingly breaks with Trump." Three weeks after the 2020 election, she demanded Trump produce evidence supporting his unsupported claims of fraud. By then, the definition of RINO had narrowed precipitously to the point where the only metaphorical camels who could pass through the eye of that needle were those who accepted Trump's lie that the 2020 election was stolen. In a brief two months from Election Day 2020 until January 6, 2021, the party ceremoniously shed itself of all others, even those like Cheney who had strong conservative Republican resumes.

The party had become a one-man band. Cults are made up of excessively zealous followers exhibiting a commitment to a single leader. Experts find them unquestioning about his beliefs, values, ideology, and practices. They defend him against any effort to test the truth. Questioning, doubt, and dissent are discouraged, even punished. Trump offered bizarre conspiracy theories to support his claim the election was stolen. He said a long-dead dictator in Venezuela rigged the voting machines, that Trump votes were changed to Biden through smart thermostats, that thousands of dead people had voted. Trump claimed various state election officials had "trucked in" suitcases full of Biden votes. Those conspiracy theories were debunked. Yet, when he said illegal votes had been shipped in from China, Republicans in Arizona inspected the ballots searching for bamboo. He had no evidence to prove any of the assertions, but the absence of truth didn't sway his ardent backers. If Trump said it, that was sufficient unto itself.

When he made unsubstantiated claims that certain states, only ones he lost, had violated federal law, the Attorney General of Texas filed a frivolous lawsuit in the U.S. Supreme Court seeking to nullify the votes cast by millions of Americans. The suit was so clearly without merit that the Justices promptly dismissed it with three-sentence order. The Texas Bar Association lodged ethics charges against the Texas Attorney General. Yet nearly three dozen Wyoming Republican legislators including the president of the state senate, Dan Dockstader, and senate majority leader Ogden Driskill endorsed the lawsuit. The state Republican Central Committee also signed on.[94] As the big lie gripped Trump supporters in Wyoming, they inexplicably demanded the three-to-one Trump victory margin be audited after hearing their cult leader demand audits in other states.[95] Fortunately for Wyoming election officials, there were but three electoral votes at stake and the popular vote was not close. They were, therefore, spared the death threats and harassment visited on election officials and poll workers in states where the results were closer.

Cheney came to recognize the Wyoming GOP had become a "cult of personality." Intent on proving her point, an influential member of the legislature denounced Cheney after the GOP vote to expel her from the party. "She essentially left the party and bad mouthed the party," said State Representative Rachael Rodriquez Williams of Cody, although Liz had only "bad mouthed" one member of the party, Donald Trump.[96] Cheney had simple decided she wasn't interested in being a member of the cult.

As she watched the mob raid the Capitol Building, Congressman Cheney was forced to ask herself whether she was an American or a Trump supporter. It was no longer possible to be both. She wrestled with how to respond to what she had just experienced. Her own safety and that of her congressional colleagues had been put at risk along with the Republic itself because of a reckless President's plot to stop the peaceful transfer of power. She witnessed Trump place his own Vice-President in danger of being hanged from gallows erected on the Capitol grounds. Liz Cheney knew the leadership of her own party would side with the insurrectionist President over her. Indeed, the state party chair joined his fellow Oath Keepers at the Capitol that day.[97] Liz determined the seriousness of the times demanded her to test the truth and require Republican voters to face it.

Cheney knew how the country had arrived at this dangerous place. She realized this was no longer the Wyoming Republican Party that elected her father to congress five times and awarded her nearly 70% of the vote only a few weeks earlier. "Trump had not only taken over the Republican Party. He transformed it into its own opposite."[98] Longtime GOP operative Stuart Stevens wrote a book in 2020 he titled, *It Was All a Lie: How the Republican Party Became Donald Trump*. More than four years of accepting the President's lies about big things and small rendered false claims of a fraudulent election believable. By one account, that of the *Washington Post*, Trump told 30,573 lies while in the Oval Office.[99] It had taken a toll on public trust while somehow immunizing Trump from truth tellers. Even as Americans watched the riots unfold on January 6, Trump took advantage of the fact that he could rely on his cult-like followers and a massive rightwing media complex to tell them that "what they were seeing was not what was happening."

Cheney knew what was at stake and that the risk was both political and personal. She had witnessed others crushed by Trump's hyperbolic and dishonest responses to criticism. She watched as other Republicans put a toe in those icy waters only to draw it out quickly as the onslaught began. Yet, on January 6, 2021, unwilling to wait another day to tell the truth, the incensed Wyoming Congressman declared, "The President summoned this mob, assembled this mob, and lit the flame of this attack. Everything that followed was his doing."

Her sentiments were no different from those of the House Republican Leader Kevin McCarthy. In the early morning hours after the day on which the Capitol building was desecrated, McCarthy spoke. "The President," he cried bravely, "bears responsibility for Wednesday's attack on Congress." Within hours, McCarthy sought Trump's forgiveness and pledged himself to the big lie that the 2020 election had been stolen. Unlike McCarthy and a long line of other Republicans, Liz never backed off and she suffered the political and personal consequences she must have known would follow. Despite a solid pro-Trump, conservative record, Liz Cheney was now a pariah to the Right.

A month after the attempted coup, the House Republicans punished Cheney for her vote to impeach Trump by stripping her of her credentials as the third ranking House GOP leader. In November 2021, af-

Profiles in Courage

The Cheney family at the 2nd Inauguration of George W. Bush. Photo of Dick Cheney being sworn in as Vice-President. Left to right Vice President Cheney, wife Lynne, daughters Mary and Liz. Shutterstock photo.

ter Cheney accepted Speaker Nancy Pelosi's overture to join the Select Committee Investigating the January 6 Attack on the U.S. Capitol, Wyoming Republicans became dissatisfied with their earlier censure of the Congressman. Lacking any legal authority to do so, they voted to expel her altogether from membership in the party.

Donald Trump obsessed with finding a candidate to run against Cheney. At Mar-a-Lago, he entertained a state senator who quickly volunteered to be that candidate. Then it was discovered that Anthony Bouchard had impregnated a 14-year-old girl who subsequently committed suicide after he married her. Bouchard called it "a Romeo and Juliet thing." Trump called it a deal breaker. He looked elsewhere. Ultimately, he chose Harriet Hageman, the one-time "never Trumper," who had supported Liz Cheney as recently as when she won reelection by a 69-25% margin two months before the January 6 attack.

As the January 6th Select Committee opened public hearings on June 9, Liz Cheney didn't flinch despite "consistent and credible death threats" which caused the Capitol Police to assign a fulltime personal security team to the Congressman more than a year ahead of the Wyoming primary. The death threats were so frequent that they limited her ability to campaign as she always had, meeting voters face to face. Cheney was "forced to abandon traditional retail campaigning," and hold almost private meetings with smaller groups of constituents that could not be publicized until after the fact.[100] Colleagues John Barrasso and Cynthia Lummis abandoned her rather than risk their own standing with Trump. Liz had a message for them. "I say this to my Republican colleagues who are defending the indefensible. There will come a day when Donald Trump is gone, but your dishonor will remain," Liz said of those Republicans who she viewed as choosing Trump over the Constitution.[101]

In June of 2022, a poll of Republican voters found Hageman leading the incumbent 56% to 26%. "Liz Cheney given 10% chance of winning re-election," blared a June 16, 2022, headline in the *Washington Examiner*. The article noted that "prior to her vote to impeach the 45th president, Cheney had a 26% disapproval rating. That number now sits at 72%." Harry Enten, CNN's senior data reporter, told "AC–360" moderator Anderson Cooper, "If you look at the betting odds, whether or not she'll win reelection, (there's) only about a 10% chance she'll win." Cooper invoked the memory of her father who was elected to Congress five times by Wyoming voters and twice as Vice-President, and Liz's three landslide wins, with both Cheneys always garnering 60-70% plus of the Wyoming vote. "Given the political dynasty she's from, that's incredible."[102] But not so incredible in the context of today's Wyoming politics.

Less than a month before the August 16 GOP primary would determine whether Cheney was to be punished or rewarded for her courage, a poll of likely voters told her that six of every ten voters found her service on the January 6 Select Committee reason to vote against her.[103]

Andrew C. McCarthy is hardly a "never Trumper." He wrote a book arguing, "The real collusion in the 2016 election was not between the Trump campaign and the Kremlin. It was between the Clinton campaign and the Obama administration."[104] However, writing for the conservative *National Review* in June 2022, McCarthy suggested that regardless of what happens in the Wyoming Republican primary, Liz Cheney is the winner.

> *"Liz Cheney has used her platform to make a powerful showing that Trump is unfit, and that Republicans would be on a suicide mission*

if they nominated him again. Democrats wanted to make Trump relevant in the hope that he gets the Republican nomination in 2024. Cheney wanted to make Trump relevant to illustrate that he can't be nominated because it would mean certain defeat. She's winning."[105]

Epilogue

"And so, my fellow Americans: ask not what your country can do for you—ask what you can do for your country." Most Americans are familiar with this iconic phrase from President John F. Kennedy's 1961 Inaugural Address. When Liz Cheney received the JFK "Profiles in Courage" Award on May 22, 2022, she quoted a line Kennedy used in the preceding paragraph.

"In the long history of the world, only a few generations have been granted the role of defending freedom in its hour of maximum danger."

Our generation is one of the few and at a time when our Constitutional Republic was in "its hour of maximum danger," the JFK Presidential Library determined Liz Cheney deserved its Profiles in Courage Award because she "broke with most in her party, urged fidelity to the Constitution, and stood her ground with honor and conviction," that despite "numerous death threats" and being "stripped of her leadership position in the GOP caucus," Liz Cheney "refused to take the politically expedient course that most of her party embraced."[106] As she accepted the award she had so courageously earned, Liz Cheney said, "Let us resolve to do what is right, that we will be able to look back on these days and say, in our time of testing we did our duty and stood for truth."

On August 16, 2022, Wyoming voters went to the polls to vote in the Republican primary in a contest between the truth and the big lie, between honoring demagoguery or rewarding courage.

We end where we started, with a quote from John F. Kennedy's *Profiles in Courage*, even more relevant nearly seven decades later. "A nation which has forgotten the quality of courage which in the past has been brought to public life is not as likely to insist upon or reward that quality in its chosen leaders today."[107]

Endnotes

1. Congressional Record, June 25, 18980, 6472
2. "Wyoming Almost Repealed Women's Suffrage," *Wyoming Almanac*, https://wyomingalmanac.com/?p=904, accessed June 6, 2022
3. Larson, *History of Wyoming*, 2nd Edition, 87
4. Mackey, *Meeting in Cheyenne*, 106
5. Id., 111
6. Supra., 112
7. Berlet and Lyons, *Right-Wing Populism in America*, 16
8. https://sos.wyo.gov/Services/docs/LegComposition.pdf, accessed June 22, 2022
9. Id., 16
10. Refers to a 1940 incident in Rawlins, Wyoming, when a mob of more than a thousand men and boys terrorized a group of Jehovah's Witnesses for their beliefs. One was hauled from his home and beaten, forced to kiss and American flag while others were beaten and their homed destroyed. More detail in McDaniel, Howard Zinn and Lois Mottonen Fistfight in the Equality State, 81
11. "Historians label unequal treatment of women as Wyoming's top story of the 20th century," *Wyoming History News*, Published by Members of the Wyoming State Historical Society, Vol. 47, No. 1 (February 2000)
12. Larson, *History of Wyoming*, 2nd Edition, 141
13. Guenther, *List of Good Negroes*, 26, 4, 12
14. Id., 24, 27
15. Berlet and Lyons, 6
16. Larson, *History of Wyoming*, 2nd Edition, 443
17. *House Journal of the Special Session of the Twenty-second Legislature*, Laramie Printing Co. (1933), 10-11
18. *Wyoming Eagle*, June 23, 1933, 12.
19. Diamond, *Roads to Dominion*, 9
20. Berlet and Lyons, 18
21. The Free Dictionary, https://www.thefreedictionary.com/McCarthyism#:~:text=Mc·Car·thy·ism%20%28mə-kär'thēïz'əm%29%20n.%201.%20The%20practice%20of%20publicizing,or%20accusatory%20methods%20in%20order%20to%20suppress%20opposition, accessed June 7, 2022
22. Plato, Phaedo, cited in After Jesus: Before Christianity, 83
23. "Memorial Services Held in the Senate and House of Representatives of the United States, Together with Remarks Presented in Eulogy of Lester Callaway Hunt: Late a Senator from Wyoming," 20
24. Id., 16
25. "Senator Hunt's Son Convicted on Morals Charge," *Washington Post*, October 7, 1953
26. Johnson, *The Lavender Scare*, 59
27. Congressional Record, July 24, 1950, reprint of the June 1947 letter to Marshall on page 10806
28. *Lavender Scare*, 22
29. Congressional Record, 81st Congress, 2nd Session, April 19, 1950, 96:5403

30　Neil Miller, *Out of the Past*, 259
31　Robert D. Dean, *Imperial Brotherhood: Gender and the Making of Cold War Foreign Policy*, University of Massachusetts Press (2001), 76, citing "Bridges Wants Manhunt for Master Spy" Washington Post, March 28, 1950
32　Rick Ewig, *McCarthy Era Politics: The Ordeal of Senator Lester Hunt*, Annals of Wyoming, Vol. 55, Number 1, Spring, 1983, see footnote 45 for a listing of those newspapers that carried the story and those that did not.
33　"Smears and Tears Plague the Senate" Column by Marquis Child, *Washington Post*, June 30, 1954
34　Eisenhower, Dwight D.: The Dwight D. Eisenhower Presidential Library and Museum Records as President, White House Central Files, Alphabetical File, "Hunt, Lester C."
35　Letter from Mike Manatos to Rick Ewig shared with author, April 30, 1980
36　Letter from Hunt to J.J. Hickey, June 4, 1954, Hunt papers, box 19, folder: "Hunt-Personal-1954" AHC
37　Notes from an interview T.A. Larson conducted with Leslie Miller on October 19, 1966, Larson papers, Box 18, AHC
38　Drew Pearson Diaries, 321
39　Ewig interview of Hunt, Jr. December 29, 1989, 7
40　The Political Dictionary, https://politicaldictionary.com/words/bircher/#:~:text=Most%20active%20in%20the%20aftermath%20of%20the%20McCarthy,wealth%20redistribution%2C%20unionization%2C%20communism%2C%20workers'%20rights%2C%20and%20socialism, accessed June 7, 2022
41　Mulloy, *The World of the John Birch Society*, 6
42　Id., 8
43　Id., 49.
44　"Cody's Birchers Smile, Right-to-Worker Avers" *Wyoming Eagle*, May 2, 1963, 4
45　Wooster, *Too Good to be True*, 3-4.
46　"Right wing Politics" *Look Magazine*, January 26, 1965, Vol. 29, No. 2, 21.
47　Morrissey interview, 38.
48　Strannigan interview, November 5, 1989, 10; "Interviews with Gale McGee/Oral History," McGee papers, box 958, AHC
49　Strannigan interview, November 5, 1989, 10; "Interviews with Gale McGee/Oral History," McGee papers, box 958, AHC
50　Strannigan interview, November 5, 1989, 44; "Interviews with Gale McGee/Oral History," McGee papers, box 958, AHC
51　"Memorandum for the President" Sen. Gale W. McGee to President Kennedy, August 16, 1963, 1.
52　"Memorandum for the President," Senator Gale W. McGee to President Kennedy, August 16, 1963, Papers of John F. Kennedy. Presidential Papers, President's Office Files, Subjects. Right-wing Movement, Digital Identifier: JFKPOF-106-013, http://www.jfklibrary.org/Asset-Viewer/Archives/JFKPOF-106-013.aspx, 3
53　"Simpson Asserts He's No Bircher," *Wyoming Eagle*, August 13, 1963, 4.
54　"McGee Indicts Detractors of American Government," *Wyoming Eagle*, January 11, 1964, 4.
55　Digest of Senate Journal, 1963, 171.

56 Larson, *History of Wyoming*, Second Edition Revised, 557.
57 Digest of House Journal, 1963, 505.
58 Digest of House Journal, 1963, 506-7.
59 Digest of House Journal, 1963, 501.
60 "Super Court Measure Approved," *Wyoming Eagle*, February 13, 1963, 4.
61 "McGee Charges State Legislators Voted to 'Destroy Our Democracy," Wyoming Eagle, January 14, 1964, 4.
62 " Wold Speaks Out Against Sen. McGee," *Wyoming Eagle*, August 2, 1963, 24.
63 "Phelan Says GOP Chairman Should Take 'Sanity Oath,'" *Wyoming Eagle*, August 3, 1963.
64 "Politics: The Outer Fringe," Edwin Newman, *NBC News*, June 12, 1966, NBC Learn Web 16 September 2017
65 Quotes from recorded speeches on Gale McGee.com, https://www.galemcgee.com/lectures.html, accessed July 16, 2022
66 Berlet and Lyons, *Right-Wing Populism*, 185
67 Urban Dictionary, https://www.dictionary.com/e/slang/trumpism/, accessed June 7, 2022
68 "Two books dig into the 1990s for the roots of the Trump-era Republican Party," *National Public Radio*, August 9, 2022, https://www.npr.org/2022/08/09/1116350743/two-books-dig-into-the-1990s-for-the-roots-of-the-trump-era-republican-party, accessed August 14, 2022
69 Id.
70 Layton McCartney, "Conservative group seeks to rid Wyoming of 'RINOs'" *WyoFile*, August 14, 2012, https://wyofile.com/conservative-group-seeks-to-rid-wyo-gop-of-rinos/ accessed June 20, 2022
71 "Sen. Case censured by his own party in Fremont County, May 10, 2022, https://www.newsbreak.com/news/2598747599063/sen-case-censured-by-his-own-party-in-fremont-county, accessed June 20, 2022; "Zwonitzer Calls Complaint About Residency A 'Political Hit Job'" *Cowboy State Daily*, January 28, 2022, https://cowboystatedaily.com/2022/01/28/zwonitzer-calls-complaint-about-residency-a-political-hit-job/, accessed June 20, 2022; "GOP chastises Harshman and Hicks for 'uncouth' actions," *Casper Star Tribune*, November 16, 2021, https://trib.com/news/state-and-regional/govt-and-politics/gop-chastises-harshman-and-hicks-for-uncouth-actions-decides-not-to-rebuke-bray/article_d15a4c6e-f35b-5529-bab1-33c8895b7bc3.html, accessed June 20, 2022
72 Supra., Urban Dictionary
73 Kerry Drake, "WyWatch leaves Wyoming without saying goodbye," *WyoFile*, October 18, 2016, https://wyofile.com/wywatch-leaves-wyoming-without-even-saying-goodbye/, accessed June 9, 2022
74 "Wyoming GOP chairman quietly assumed power as party fractured, *Gillette News Record*, May 23, 2022, https://www.gillettenewsrecord.com/news/wyoming/article_18c9dfc4-ede7-5d7c-8d65-038b41f623e7.html, accessed June 20, 2022
75 RINO: a disparaging acronym meaning "Republicans in Name Only"
76 "Oath Keepers leader, 10 others charged with 'seditious conspiracy' in Jan. 6 Capitol attack, *NBC*, January 13, 2022, https://www.nbcnews.com/politics/congress/oath-keeper-leader-10-others-charged-seditious-conspiracy-jan-6-n1287434, accessed

June 28, 2022
77 "Wyo GOP chairman quietly assumed power as party fractured,' *WyoFile*, May 20, 2022, https://wyofile.com/wyo-gop-chairman-quietly-assumed-power-as-party-fractured/
78 "Details emerge as former Wyoming GOP secretary reaches plea deal in assault case, *Casper Star Tribune*, March 30, 2018, https://trib.com/news/state-and-regional/govt-and-politics/details-emerge-as-former-wyoming-gop-secretary-reaches-plea-deal-in-assault-case/article_bf7a77d4-69f7-5bee-9f6b-d27ca06578a8.html, accessed June 21, 2022
79 "Two Wyoming GOP Chairmen Fight Over Weekend, One Gets Cited, June 29, 202, *Cowboy State Daily*, https://cowboystatedaily.com/2020/06/29/two-wyoming-gop-chairmen-fight-over-weekend-one-gets-cited/
80 "Park County Republican Sends Obscene Email to State Senator, September 21, 2021, *Big Horn Radio Network*, https://mybighornbasin.com/park-county-republican-sends-obscene-email-to-state-senator/
81 Ed Kilgore, "'RINO' Just Means 'Disloyal to Trump,'" *New York Magazine*, March 24, 2022, https://nymag.com/intelligencer/2022/03/rino-just-means-disloyal-to-trump-now.html?regwall-newsletter-signup=true#_=_, accessed June 20, 2022
82 http://www.thegreenpapers.com/P16/WY-R, accessed June 11, 2022
83 "Ted Cruz sweeps Wyoming Republican Convention, *CNN*, April 17, 2016, https://www.cnn.com/2016/04/16/politics/wyoming-republican-convention-election-results/index.html, accessed June 13, 2022
84 "How an Anti-Trump Plotter in 2016 Became His Champion Against Liz Cheney," *New York Times*, September 2, 2021, https://www.nytimes.com/2021/09/27/us/politics/harriet-hageman-liz-cheney-trump.html, accessed June 11, 2022
85 "Platform and Resolutions of the Wyoming Republican Party, 2016, "Done in Convention," April 16, 2016, https://d3n8a8pro7vhmx.cloudfront.net/ccwygop/pages/79/attachments/original/1496094440/2016.platform.and_.resolutions.pdf?1496094440, accessed June 13, 2022
86 "Liz Cheney Endorses Trump," *Newsmax*, August 12, 2016, https://www.newsmax.com/Politics/liz-cheney-endorse-trump-rips/2016/08/12/id/743406/, accessed June 11, 2022
87 "Report on the Investigation into Russian Interference in the 2016 Presidential Election Vol. I, 187
88 Id., 197
89 Id., Vol. II, 3
90 Liz Cheney's "Statement on Release of Mueller Report," April 18, 2019, https://cheney.house.gov/2019/04/18/statement-on-release-of-mueller-report/, accessed June 28, 2022
91 Mudde, Cas and Kaltwasser, Cristóbal Rovira, *Populism: A Very Short Introduction*, New York: Oxford University Press, 63
92 Leonnig and Rucker, *I Alone Can Fix This*, 491
93 "Wyoming delegation condemns Capitol riot after being evacuated," *Casper Star Tribune*, January 6, 2021, https://trib.com/news/state-and-regional/govt-and-politics/wyoming-delegation-condemns-capitol-riot-after-being-evacuated/article_414b768b-d701-5d2d-9f76-33d59efe3347.html, accessed June 20, 2022

94 "Wyoming Legislators, GOP Ask Gordon To Join Texas Election Lawsuit," *Cowboy State Daily*, December 10, 2020, https://cowboystatedaily.com/2020/12/10/wyoming-legislators-gop-ask-gordon-to-join-texas-election-lawsuit/, accessed June 24, 2022

95 "Wyoming officials face growing pressure to audit state elections," *Oil City News*, August 26, 2021, https://oilcity.news/general/2021/08/26/wyoming-officials-face-growing-pressure-to-audit-state-elections/

96 "Wyoming GOP at the crossroad," *Wyoming Tribune Eagle*, July 3, 2022, A2

97 "Not only was he a member of the 'mob,' said a resolution passed by Natrona County Republican Central Committee seeking Eathorne's resignation in June 2022, "he has done nothing to condemn the insurrection – an attempt to overthrow the election." *Casper Star Tribune*, June 21, 2022, https://trib.com/news/state-and-regional/govt-and-politics/natrona-county-gop-asks-wyoming-republican-chairman-eathorne-to-resign/article_0ac0a9e0-f1ac-11ec-995e-, accessed June 22, 2022

98 Hassan, *The Cult of Trump*, 64

99 "Trump's false or misleading claims total 30,573 over 4 years," *Washington Post*, January 24, 2021, https://www.washingtonpost.com/politics/2021/01/24/trumps-false-or-misleading-claims-total-30573-over-four-years/, accessed June 28, 2022

100 Steve Peoples and Mead Gruver, *Associated Press*, "Liz Cheney braces for primary loss as focus shifts to 2024," *Wyoming Tribune Eagle*, July 23, 2022, 1

101 "Liz Cheney offers a stark message to the GOP members who continue to support Trump," June 9, 2022, *National Public Radio*, https://www.npr.org/2022/06/09/1104083111/liz-cheney-stark-message-gop-trump-supporters, accessed June 24, 2022

102 "Liz Cheney given 10% chance of winning reelection," *Washington Examiner*, June 16, 2022, https://www.washingtonexaminer.com/news/liz-cheney-10-chance-winning-reelection-cnn, accessed June 22, 2022

103 "Poll results: Cheney reelection chances hurt by role on Jan. 6 panel," *Casper Star Tribune*, July 22, 2022, https://trib.com/news/state-and-regional/govt-and-politics/poll-results-cheneys-reelection-chances-hurt-by-role-on-jan-6-panel/article_5c220cc6-0849-11ed-a52d , accessed July 22, 2022

104 McCarthy, Andrew C., *Ball of Collusion: The Plot to Rig an Election and Destroy a Presidency*, Encounter Books (2019)

105 Andrew C. McCarthy, "Liz Cheney Is Winning the January 6 Committee," *National Review*, June 18, 2022, https://www.nationalreview.com/2022/06/liz-cheney-is-winning-the-january-6-committee/, accessed June 22, 2022

106 "2022 Profile in Courage Award," John F. Kennedy Presidential Library, https://www.jfklibrary.org/events-and-awards/profile-in-courage-award/award-recipients/defending-democracy-2022/liz-cheney, accessed June 24, 2022

107 Kennedy, *Profiles in Courage*, 21

BIBLIOGRAPHY

Periodicals

Guenther, Todd, "The List of Good Negroes: African American Lynchings in the Equality State," Annals of Wyoming 81, No. 2 (Spring 2009)

American Heritage Center (AHC) University of Wyoming

Bell, Tom, Papers, Collection No. 03755. Collection contains material about a WWII veteran, teacher, conservationist, and Founder of the Wyoming Outdoor Council and High Country News.

Gressley, Gene M., Collection No. 400051. Collection is composed of correspondence, research files, manuscripts, and journals that document the life and career of historian and archivist Gene Gressley.

Hebard, Grace Raymond, Collection No. 400008. Collection materials relating to Grace Raymond Hebard's career as University of Wyoming professor, librarian, and western historian with subject files containing correspondence, manuscripts, transcripts, and printed materials concerning places and events Hebard researched and participated in such as the women's suffrage movement, Wyoming history, and the University of Wyoming.

Hunt, Lester C., Collection No. 00270, Lester Calloway Hunt was the 19th governor of Wyoming from 1943 to 1949 and a United States senator from 1949-1954. Collection contains subject files and other materials related to his political and personal life.

Kennedy, T. Blake, Collection No. 00405. Collection contains a detailed two-volume memoir written by Kennedy in 1956; correspondence dealing with court cases and other legal matters (1924-1957); speeches and addresses (1950-1956); opinions of cases (1924-1955); and six scrapbooks.

Powder River Basin Resources Council, Collection No. 6836. Collection contains newsletters, annual reports, publications, maps, and presentations regarding the Powder River Basin Resource Council.

O'Mahoney, Joseph C., Collection No. 00275. Collection includes legislative files, campaign files, and personal materials of a five-term U.S. Senator from Wyoming.

Parsons, Barbara, Collection No. 12691. This collection contains manuscript material, copies of newspaper clippings, correspondence, publications, meeting minutes, and scrapbooks related to her time on the Wyoming Outdoor Council.

Roberts, John, Collection No. 00037. Collection includes numerous notes and drafts as well as printed versions of Robert's translations of church literature into the Arapaho and Shoshone languages. Other material includes history of the region and biographical information about Roberts and his family, friends and prominent citizens of the area including Sacagawea.

Roncalio, Teno. Collection No. 02160. Collection includes legislative records and press relations/media activities records, and scrapbooks of this Democratic congressman from Wyoming who served five terms in the U.S. House of Representatives.

Simpson, Milward, Collection No. 26. Collection includes file from his career as a lawyer, governor, and U.S. senator from Wyoming.

Trenholm, Virginia Cole, Collection No. 03597. Collection includes correspondence (1929-1979); subject files containing correspondence, research notes, etc. (1929-1974); newspaper clippings; and research notebooks which contain correspondence, contracts with publishers, etc.

University of Wyoming President's Office records, Collection No. 510000. Collection includes the official records of UW president Dr. William Carlson.

Wyoming Outdoor Council, Collection No. 08958. Collection contains photographs, newspaper clippings, printed materials, correspondence, and subject files, containing newspaper clippings, reports, research notes and reports regarding conservation, recreation, industrial development, and environmental protection in Wyoming.

Unpublished Works

Coombs, Frank Alan (1968) *Joseph Christopher O'Mahoney: The New Deal Years* [Unpublished Doctor of History Degree dissertation] University of Illinois

Harlow, Susan J. (1981) *High Country News: Survival and Change* [Unpublished Master of Arts Thesis] Department of Journalism and Communication, University of Wyoming

Published Works

Abbey, Edward, *Desert Solitaire: A Season in the Wilderness*, New York: Ballantine Books (1968)

Alter, Robert, *The Hebrew Bible: A Translation with Commentary*, New York and London: W.W. Norton & Company (2019)

Ambrose, Stephen E., *The Wild Blue: The Men and Boys Who Flew the B-24s Over Germany 1944-45*, Simon and Schuster (2001)

Anderson, Jeffrey D., *One Hundred Years of Old Man Sage: An Arapaho Life*, Lincoln and London, University of Nebraska Press (2003)

Berlet, Chip, and Matthew N. Lyons, *Right-Wing Populism in America: Too Close for Comfort*, New York and London: Guilford Press (2000)

Billington, Ray A., *America's Frontier Heritage*, Chicago-San Francisco: Holt, Rinehart, and Winston (1966)

Bohrer, John R., *The Revolution of Robert Kennedy: From Power to Protest After JFK*, Bloomsbury Press (2017)

Breslin, Jimmy, *How the Good Guys Finally Won: Notes from an Impeachment Summer*, The Viking Press (1975)

Brewster, Melvin G., *Numu Views of Numu Cultures and History: Cultural Stewardship Issues and a Punown View of Gosiute and Shoshone Archeology in the Northern Great Basin*. Ph. D. diss., University of Oregon (2003)

Brigham Young, *Journal of Discourses* (October 9, 1859)

Brodie, Fawn. M., *No Man Knows My History: The Life of Joseph Smith*, New York: Vintage Books (1945)

Brown, Dee, *Bury My Heart at Wounded Knee*, New York, Henry Holt and Company (1970)

Calloway, Collin G., *One Vast Winter Count: The Native American West Before Lewis and Clark*, Lincoln: University of Nebraska Press (2003)

Chernow, Ron, *Grant*, New York: Penguin Press (2017)

Clark, Ella, *Indian Legends from the Northern Rockies*, University of Oklahoma Press, Norman (1986)

Coburn, Broughton and Leila Bruno, *Ahead of Their Time: Wyoming Voices for the Wilderness*, Wyoming Wilderness Association (2004)

Connell, Evan S., *Son of the Morning Star: Custer and the Little Big Horn*, San Francisco: North Point Press (1984)

Cozzens, Peter, *The Earth is Weeping: The Epic Story of the Indian Wars for the American West*, Alfred A. Knopf (2016)

Crenshaw, Kimberle; Gotanda, Neil; Peller, Gary; Thomas, Kendall, editors, *Critical Race Theory: The Key Writings That Formed the Movement*, The New Press-New York (1995)

Davis, John W., *The Trial of Tom Horn*, Norman: University of Oklahoma Press (2016)

DeVotio, Bernard, ed., *The Journals of Lewis and Clark*, Mariner Books (1953)

Diamond, Sara, *Roads to Dominion, Right-Wing Movements, and Political Power in the United States*, New York: Guilford Press (1995)

Donahue, Debra L., *The Western Range Revisited: Removing Livestock from Public Lands to Conserve Native Biodiversity*, Norman: University of Oklahoma Press (1999)

Dunbar-Ortiz, *Indigenous Peoples' History of the United States*, Boston: Beacon Press (2014)

Ehrlich, Gretel, *Heart Mountain*, Penguin Books (1988)

Estes, Nick, Melanie K. Yazzie, Jennifer Nez Denetdale, and David Correia, *Red Nation Rising: From Bordertown Violence to Native Liberation*, PM Press (2021)

Fagan, Brian M., *Ancient North America: The Archology of a Continent*, 3rd ed. London: Thames and Hudson (2000)

Fowler, Loretta, *Arapahoe Politics 1851-1978*, Lincoln and London: University of Nebraska Press (1982)

Fowler, Loretta, *The Arapaho*, New York and Philadelphia: Chelsea House Publisher (1989)

Greenleaf, Robert K., *Servant Leadership: A journey Into the Nature of Legitimate Power and Greatness*, Paulist Press-New York/Mahwah, New Jersey (2002)

Hämäläinen, Pekka, *Indigenous Continent: The Epic Contest for North America*, Liveright Publishing Corporation, a Division of W.W. Norton & Company (2022)

Hannah-Jones, Nikole, *A New Origin Story: The 1619 Project*, New York: One World (2021)

Hardy, Deborah, *Wyoming University: The First 110 Years 1886-1986*, University of Wyoming (1986)

Hardy, Donald L., *Shooting from the Lip: The Life of Senator Al Simson*, University of Oklahoma Press: Norman (2011)

Hassan, Steven, *The Cult of Trump: A leading Cult Expert Explains How the President Uses Mind Control*, Free Press (2019)

Hebard, Grace Raymond, *Washakie: Chief of the Shoshones*, University of Nebraska Press (1930)

Higuchi, Shirley Ann, Setsuko's Secret: *Heart Mountain and the Legacy of the Japanese American Incarceration*, University of Wisconsin Press (2020)

Hosakawa, Bill, Nisei: *The Quiet Americans*, New York: William Morrow and Company (1969)

Isenberg, *The Destruction of the Buffalo*, Cambridge University Press (2000)

Johnson, David K., *The Lavender Scare: The Cold War Persecution of Gays and Lesbians in the Federal Government*, Chicago and London: The University of Chicago Press (2004)

Kimmerer, Robin Wall, *Braiding Sweetgrass: Indigenous Wisdom*, Scientific Knowledge, and the Teachings of Plants, Milkweed Editions (2013)

Larson, T.A., *History of Wyoming*, 2nd Ed, University of Nebraska Press (1978)

Leopold, Aldo, *A Sand County Almanac*, New York: Oxford University Press (1949)

Kashima, Tetsuden, forward by, *Personal Justice Denied: Report of the Commission on Wartime Relocation and Internment of Civilians*, Civil Liberties Public Education Fund and the University of Washington Press (1977)

Kennedy, John F., *Profiles in Courage – Memorial Edition*, New York, Evanston, and London, Harper and Row (1964)

Knight, Dennis H., Jones, George P., Reiners, William A., Romme, William H., *Mountains and Plains: The Ecology of Wyoming Landscapes*, Yale University Press (2014)

Knox, Kurt, *School of Hard Knox*, published by Cheyenne Newspapers, Inc. (2001)

Larson, T.A., *Wyoming's War Years 1941-1945*, Wyoming Historical Foundation (1993)

Leonnig, Carol, and Philip Rucker, *I Alone Can Fix It*, New York: Penguin Books (2021)

Lewis, Tom, *Divided Highways*, Penguin Putnam Publishing (1997)

Mackey, Mike, *Heart Mountain: Life in Wyoming's Concentration Camp*, Western Historical Publication (2000)

Mackey, Mike, *Meeting in Cheyenne: Wyoming's Constitutional Convention*, Western History Publication (2010)

McDaniel, Rodger, *The Man in the Arena; The Life and Times of U.S. Senator Gale W. McGee*, Potomac Books, an Imprint of the University of Nebraska Press (2018)

McDaniel, Rodger, *Dying for Joe McCarthy's Sins: The Suicide of Wyoming Senator Lester Hunt*, Cody, Wyoming, WordsWorth Publishing (2013)

"Memorial Services Held in the Senate and House of Representatives of the United States, Together with Remarks Presented in Eulogy of Lester Callaway Hunt: Late a Senator from Wyoming," United States Government Printing Office (1955)

McFee, John, *Rising from the Plains*, Farrar, Straus, and Giroux Publishers (1987)

McManus, John C., *The Dead and Those About to Die*, Dutton Caliber (2019)

Means, Russell, Where White Men Fear to Tread: The Autobiography of Russell Means, New York: St. Martin's Press (1995)

Miller, Neil, *Out of the Past: Gay and Lesbian History from 1869 to the Present*, Vintage Books (1995)

Miller, Robert J., *Native America Discovered and Conquered: Thomas Jefferson, Lewis and Clark, and Manifest Destiny*, Lincoln: University of Nebraska Press (2008)

Morgan, Dale L., *Shoshonean Peoples and the Overland Trails: Frontiers of the Utah Superintendency of Indian Affairs, 1849-1869*. Edited by Richard L. Saunders, Logan: Utah State University Press (2007)

Muller, Eric L., *Free to Die for Their Country: The Story of Japanese American Draft Resisters in World War II*, Chicago and London, The University of Chicago Press (2001)

Mulloy, D.J., T*he World of the John Birch Society: Conspiracy, Conservatism, and the Cold War*, Nashville: Vanderbilt University Press (2014)

Murphy, Warren, *On Sacred Ground: A Religious and Spiritual History of Wyoming*, Cody, Wyoming, WordsWorth Publishing (2011)

Mumford, Lewis, *Highway and the City*, Praeger Publishing (1981)

Nerburn, Kent, *Neither Wolf nor Dog: On Forgotten Roads with an Indian Elder*, Novato, California: New World Library (1994)

Newton, Jim, *Justice for All: Earl Warren and the Nation He Made*, New York: Riverhead Books, a member of Penguin Group (USA) (2006)

Nobokov, Peter, *Native American Testimony: A Chronicle of Indian-White Relations from Prophecy to the Present, 1492-2000*, New York: Penguin (1999)

O'Donnell, Kenneth P., *Johnny, We Hardly Knew Ye*, Little, Brown, and Company (1970)

O'Gara, Geoffrey, *What You Can See in Clear Water*, Vintage Books (2000)

O'Hashi, Alan, *Beyond Heart Mountain*, Winter Goose Publishing (2022)

Pearson, Bradford, *The Eagles of Heart Mountain: A True Story of Football, Incarceration, and Resistance in World War II America*, New York, London, Toronto, Sydney, New Delhi, Atria Books (2021)

Peyer, Bernd C., *The Tutor'd Mind: Indian Missionary Writers-Writers in Antebellum America*, Amherst: University of Massachusetts Press (1997)

Robinson, Kim Stanley, *Ministries for the Future*, Orbit Books (2020)

Reeves, Richard: *Infamy: The Shocking Story of the Japanese Internment in World War II*, New York: Henry Holt and Company (2015)

Ryan, Cornelius, *The Longest Day: The Classic Epic of D-Day*, Simon and Schuster (1959)

Schlesinger, Arthur M. Jr., *Robert Kennedy and His Times*, Houghton Mifflin Company (1978)

Shepard, Judy, *The Meaning of Matthew*, Penguin Group (2010)

Smith, Joseph Fielding, *The Way to Perfection*, Salt Lake City: Deseret Book (1950)

Sorensen, Theodore C., *Kennedy* (1965)

Stegner, Wallace, *The Sound of Mountain Water: The Changing American West*, New York: Doubleday (1969)

Stoll, Steven, *U.S. Environmentalism Since 1945: A Brief History with Documents*, Boston, New York: Bedford/St. Martin's (2007)

Stone, Irving, *Clarence Darrow: For the Defense*, Doubleday, Doran & Company (1941)

Takaki, Ronald, *A Different Mirror: A History of Multicultural America*, New York, Toronto, London: Little, Brown and Company (1993)

To Secure These Rights: The Report of President Harry S. Truman's Committee on Civil Rights, Boston, New York, Bedford/St. Martin's ((2004)

Trenholm, Virginia Cole, *The Arapahoes, Our People*, Norman and London, University of Oklahoma Press (1986)

Trenholm, Virginia Cole and Maureen Carley, The *Shoshonis: Sentinels of the Rockies*, Norman: University of Oklahoma Press (1964)

Treuer, David, *The Heartbeat of Wounded Knee: Native America from 1890 to the Present*, Riverhead Books (2019)

Twiss, Richard, *Rescuing the Gospel from the Cowboys: A Native American Experience of the Jesus Way*, IVP Books (2015)

University of Wyoming College of Law, *Land and Water Law Review*, Vol. XXVI, No. 1 (1991)

Vearncombe, Erin, Brandon Scott, and Hal Taussig, *After Jesus, Before Christianity*, New York: Harper Collins Publishers (2021)

Vizenor, Gerald, *Native Liberty: Natural Reason and Cultural Survivance*, Lincoln: University of Nebraska Press (2009)

Warren, Andrea A., *Enemy Child: The Story of Norman Mineta, a Boy Scout Imprisoned in a Japanese Internment Camp During World War II*, New Yok: Holiday House-Margaret Ferguson Books, (2019)

Weglyn, Micji, *Years of Infamy: The Untold Story of America's Concentration Camp*, New York: William Morrow and Company (1976)

White, Phil, *Wyoming in Mid-Century: Prejudice, Protest, and the Black 14*, Self-Published by the Author, 2021

Wiles, Sara, *The Arapaho Way: Continuity and Change on the Wind River Reservation*, Norman: University of Oklahoma Press (2019)

Williams, Robert A., *Like a Loaded Gun: The Rehnquist Court, Indian Rights, and the Legal History of Racism in Americas*, Minneapolis and London: University of Minnesota Press (2005)

Woodard, Colin, *American Nations: A History of the Eleven Rival Regional Cultures of North America*, Penguin Books (2011)

www.ingramcontent.com/pod-product-compliance
Lightning Source LLC
Chambersburg PA
CBHW040056200426
43193CB00060B/2932